D1400131

QUEBEC'S LANGUAGE POLICIES: BACKGROUND AND RESPONSE

Travaux du Centre international de recherche sur le bilinguisme
Publications of the International Center for Research on Bilingualism

A. — **Études / *Studies***

1. *Les Indices d'utilité du vocabulaire fondamental français,* Jean-Guy SAVARD & Jack RICHARDS (1969).
2. *Les Droits linguistiques des Franco-Américains aux États-Unis,* Heinz KLOSS (1970).
3. *Contribution à l'étude du statut des langues en Europe,* Jean FALCH (1972).
4. *Les Noms de lieux et le Contact des langues / Place Names and Language Contact,* Henri DORION, édit. (1972).
5. *La Sélection en didactique analytique,* Lorne LAFORGE (1972).
6. *L'Aménagement constitutionnel des États de peuplement composite,* Bernard TOURET (1972).
7. *Computation in Language Text Analysis,* Michael S. MEPHAM (1973).
8. *Conflit entre les Néo-Canadiens et les francophones de Montréal,* Paul CAPPON (1974).
9. *Les États multilingues: problèmes et solutions / Multilingual Political Systems: Problems and Solutions,* textes présentés par Jean-Guy SAVARD & Richard VIGNEAULT (1975).
10. *Atlas géographique des langues et ethnies de l'Inde et du Subcontinent: Bangladesh, Pakistan, Sri Lanka, Népal, Bhoutan, Sikkim,* Rolland J.-L. BRETON (1976).
11. *Identité culturelle et francophonie dans les Amériques (I).* Colloque tenu à l'Université d'Indiana, Bloomington, du 28 au 30 mars 1974, publié par Émile SNYDER et Albert VALDMAN (1976).
12. *Le français en contact avec l'anglais en Amérique du Nord,* Jean DARBELNET (1976).
13. *Quebec's Language policies: Background and Response,* Compiled and Edited by John R. MALLEA (1977).

E. — **Inventaires / Inventories**

Composition linguistique des nations du monde / Linguistic Composition of the Nations of the World, vol. 1: *L'Asie du Sud, secteurs central et occidental / Central and Western South Asia,* Heinz KLOSS & Grant D. MCCONNELL, édit. (1974).

F. — **Bibliographies**

1. *Bibliographie analytique des tests de langue / Analytical Bibliography of Language Tests,* Jean-Guy SAVARD (1969).
2. *Language Contact and Language Planning in China (1900-1967), A Selected Bibliography,* Rosaline Kwan-wai CHIU (1970).
3. *Bibliographie internationale sur le bilinguisme / International Bibliography on Bilingualism,* William MACKEY, dir. (1972).
4. *Bibliographie analytique du bilinguisme chez l'enfant et de son apprentissage d'une langue seconde / Child Bilingualism and Second Language Learning: A Descriptive Bibliography,* Evangelos AFENDRAS & Albertina PIANAROSA (1975).
5. *Contact des langues et bilinguisme en Europe orientale: bibliographie analytique / Language Contact and Bilingualism in Eastern Europe: Analytical Bibliography,* Daniel GUNAR (1977).

QUEBEC'S LANGUAGE POLICIES: BACKGROUND AND RESPONSE

Compiled and Edited
by John R. MALLEA

Queen's University

Travaux du Centre international de recherche sur le bilinguisme | ***Publications of the International Center for Research on Bilingualism***

A-13

LES PRESSES DE L'UNIVERSITÉ LAVAL

QUÉBEC, 1977

Dépôt légal (Québec), 2e trimestre 1977
I.S.B.N. 0-7746-6822-9

TABLE OF CONTENTS

Acknowledgments

The International Center for Research on Bilingualism gratefully acknowledges permission to reproduce those materials which first appeared under the auspices of the Canadian Ethnic Studies Association, Centre québécois des relations internationales, Information Canada, McClelland & Stewart, the Official Editor of Quebec and Peter Martin Associates.

Acknowledgements

I would like to express my sincere appreciation to the institutions and individuals who helped make the compilation and editing of this book possible. Queen's University generously agreed to a negotiated leave in order that I might work on these and other materials. The International Center for Research on Bilingualism, Laval University, provided a supportive environment in which to work and its members gave freely of their time and expertise to help the project along. Special thanks are due to the Director of the Center, Jean-Guy Savard, for his enthusiastic support, William F. Mackey for his encouragement and wise counsel, John Meisel, Andrew Orr and Gilles Grenier for their perceptive comments and Richard Vigneault for his able editorial and administrative assistance. Finally, I should like to thank Mme Dorothy Bolduc, Mme Danielle Cardinal and Mrs. Sharon Lillis for their skilful typing and unfailing cheerfulness during the preparation of the manuscript.

April 1976

John R. Mallea

Preface

In the 1960s there came a sudden realization among the French of Quebec that they had been swept into the very life against which their leaders had always preached, and that they themselves had been condemning the modern economic world while working hard to advance in it. The resolution of these conflicts came about in a fundamental shift in the goals, conduct and style of Quebec society which became known as the Quiet Revolution. By 1970 there was hardly an institution left in Quebec which had not undergone a fundamental change — politics, government, education and the Church.

One of the main components of this Quiet Revolution was the secularisation of French Canada and the consequent rise in the importance of temporal power above ecclesiastical authority. Concentration of activity in regions over which this new temporal power had political control resulted in a shift for French Canada from a continental to a regional destiny. One indicator of this regionalisation of French Canada can be seen in the fact that the 24th of June was no longer to French Canadians what the 17th of March had been to the ethnic Irish. It became much more. During the Quiet Revolution it had evolved from an ethnic revival to a national holiday, from a religious feast to a symbolic rite.

Quebec's French-speaking majority had now learned how, through the concentration of political power, it could control its own fate. It accepted and often insisted on government intervention, even in the control of language usage. As the French population assumed the posture of a majority, the formerly dominant English-speaking population took on the protective behavior of a minority, defending rights which had never before been questioned. They also saw the need to adapt to the new distribution of language power, as French-dominated political forces of society took precedent over the English-dominated economic forces.

Once political forces intervene in matters of language, over and above the right to use one's mother tongue in interpersonal relations, the emphasis shifts from the individual to that system of arbitrary symbols, itself an indicator of ethnicity, which any language essentially is. This change of emphasis is analogous to shifting from the tolerance of all religions to the promotion of some of them. Once the state becomes committed to the survival of a language, it is difficult for it not to get involved in the modification and control of individual human behavior, in the belief that it can thus increase the probability of language survival.

Language use is a reflection of power and status. The economic dominance of English in Quebec in a traditional society not dominated by economics had a limited effect on the survival of French in rural areas. As soon as economics became a dominant factor in what had become an urban French culture, the Quebecers asked their government to control some of these economic forces in their favor.

The difficulty, however, was that urban Quebecers had become more bilingual, making the problem different and much more complex than it would have been in a unilingual polity. The difference is between choice and necessity. Once the possibility of language choice enters the linguistic equation, the choice is either free or it is imposed. If it is free, the stronger language will dominate; if it is imposed, the state must eventually regulate individual language behavior. This has happened in Quebec. It is something which Anglo-Canadians have been slow to understand and reluctant to accept. For the politics of cultural accommodation are new to the Canadian scene.

It is not surprising that the idea of cultural autonomy as distinct from political independence was not understood by Anglo-Canadians, since it was foreign to anything they had ever experienced. When Quebec declared a policy of cultural autonomy and enacted a corresponding language policy, therefore, it was not accepted by Anglo-Canadians.

Few scholars have taken the trouble to explain to them what it all meant. It is to the credit of John Mallea that he has not only recognized this national need, but that he has also decided to do something about it. On the occasion of his year as visiting scholar at the International Center for Research on Bilingualism, Dr. Mallea compiled and edited an enlightened volume which will not fail to supply answers to the perennial question: What does Quebec want?

William F. Mackey
International Center for Research
on Bilingualism

April 1976

INTRODUCTION

The most succinct analysis of the status of the French language in Canada available in English is Richard Joy's *Languages in Conflict* written in the mid-sixties. Here Joy documented the extent to which assimilation is affecting younger French Canadians outside Québec and concluded that the historical evidence indicated that "two languages of unequal strength cannot co-exist in intimate contact and that the weaker of the two must, inevitably, disappear".[1] He predicted that although the relative strengths of the two major language groups might remain unchanged, a much more pronounced linguistic separation would take place. French would be spoken within Québec and English elsewhere. Nor did he believe that legislation could reverse this trend. Indeed, if French were to survive in Québec, the full force of the National Assembly would have to be exerted to make French the preferred language.[2]

Joy's conclusions now form part of the Canadian debate over languages. In Québec, meanwhile, the controversy surrounding the province's language policies has increased considerably since the publication of *Languages in Conflict.* Almost any discussion of the future of Québec revolves, at least in part, and often centrally, around the security of the French language. At the federal level we have seen the promulgation of an official policy of bilingualism supported by all the major political parties. In Québec, on the other hand, the formulation of language policies has played an increasingly important role in partisan politics. Since 1968, three highly volatile language bills have been introduced. The most recent of the three was introduced into law as the Official Language Act in July, 1974. Among other things, the Act was clearly an attempt by the provincial Liberals to offset recent gains achieved by the *Parti Québécois.* Supporters of political independence, for their part, seized on the language issue to fuel their opposition to the federalist policies of the incumbent Bourassa government. One result has been to polarize the Francophone and Anglophone communities of Québec. Confusion abounds. The former often perceive Anglophones with a mixture of fear and aggression; the latter view Francophone aspirations with alarm and suspicion.

The aim of the present book is a modest one. It presents to an Anglophone audience selected materials which are basic to an informed understanding of Québec's language policies. Most of the contributions first appeared in French, and this by itself is significant. Scholarly work on the subject in English is of relatively recent origin,[3] a fact that stands in marked contrast to the intense interest in the subject displayed by French-Canadian scholars.[4]

The text is divided into five sections. The first centres on the politics of culture and deals with the societal coordinates of the language issue. A discussion of demographic trends follows, underlining the crucial role they play in matters of cultural sovereignty and contemporary politics. Section three provides commentary on questions of cultural diversity and the language of instruction. Section four examines the status of French as the language of work. The final part of the book includes two articles which discuss the Francophone and Anglophone response to recent language legislation.[5] The legislation itself, with accompanying regulations, is reproduced in the appendices.

The political culture

A valuable introduction to the broad political implications of language is provided by the distinguished political scientist Léon Dion. In "French as an Adopted Language" he argues persuasively that the socio-political ramifications of the language issue in Québec are multi-faceted and complex. The article begins by exploring basic premises, reviews notions of collective and acquired rights, and examines the formidable task faced by Québec in adapting traditional values to the needs of the modern world. It then turns to a consideration of the official status of French and English, the language of instruction in schools, the language of work, and the integrative capacity of the Francophone community vis-à-vis immigrants.

Occasionally Professor Dion is more than a guide. In discussing the language of instruction, for example, he states that he is unaware of any inalienable right of parents to choose the language in which their children will be educated. He also contends that this "right" was initiated without sufficient study or caution by the *Union Nationale* Government in 1969 (Bill 63), and it was therefore hardly surprising that the Anglophone community responded angrily when it was withdrawn in 1974 by the passage of the Official Language Act. Dion believes that language legislation is a necessary but not a *sufficient* condition for the survival of the French language in Québec. In his opinion, this can only be guaranteed if French becomes the primary language of economic activity. And this in turn can only come about if French-Canadians extend their control of private enterprise. The implementation of language safeguards, moreover, will appear less odious and be far more effective if they are accompanied by broad economic, social, and cultural efforts aimed at increased use of French.

While he believes that Francophones have not always taken full advantage of the possibilities inherent in Canada's political framework, Dion thinks it remains to be demonstrated that the Québec community could achieve full development within the limits of a Canadian confederation. Meanwhile, the Québec government must assume the major responsibility for the promotion of French, and to be successful it will need the enthusiastic support of all the major social institutions. A compact must be formed among government industry, labour and the universities, for the task facing Francophone Québécers is neither simple nor short term. It will, he concludes, involve nothing less than the fashioning of a new Québec spirit and soul.

Demographic trends

Jacques Henripin argues convincingly that a knowledge of demographic trends is essential to a full understanding of Québec politics. Recent demographic trends, he contends, indicate that French Canadian society "is losing ground, not only compared with Canada as a whole, but even within the Province of Québec itself". This trend is particularly serious in Montréal where French Canadians make up only two-thirds of the population. And the proportion may well fall to between 53 and 60 per cent by the year 2 000 if immigrants continue to integrate into the English-speaking community at the present rate.

Professor Henripin and his colleagues carried out two hypothetical projections to determine how serious such a threat might be to the French presence in Montréal. On the basis of their findings (and they show themselves to be more aware than most of the difficulties of demographic forecasting), they concluded that "if recent migration trends continue, and if immigrants continue to opt predominantly for the English language, the French-speaking community of Québec is bound to see its majority seriously reduced, particularly in Montréal". According to Henripin, this should result in the loss of the only power the Francophone community possesses: the power of making laws and electing governments. He therefore advocates the introduction of policies inducing immigrants to associate themselves with the French community and culture. Sensitive to the problems involved — but convinced that they must be overcome if French is to survive — Henripin ends by stating that the necessary conditions for this survival will not only require the leadership of an energetic government, but an unusual measure of good will and wisdom on the part of the English-speaking population.

Professor Caldwell's study examines language transfers; that is, the extent to which individuals are either transferring themselves or being transferred by their parents from one language to another. According to Caldwell, the evidence of the past thirty years unequivocally supports the conclusion that "French has lost its place as the major beneficiary of language transfers in Québec". In recent years the trend has apparently become even more pronounced. In 1972, the percentage of language transfers from "other" languages to English in the Montréal Catholic School Board reached 89 per cent. Of even greater significance, perhaps, is the fact that the French presence in English schools is also on the increase. Citing data for the years 1969-1974, Caldwell notes that the children of French-Canadian parents accounted for 12 per cent of all pupils enrolled in English schools. Combining these figures for the school year 1973-74, French-speaking students and "others" accounted for 35 per cent of the total English school population.

Like Professor Henripin, Caldwell believes that steps must be taken to facilitate the integration of immigrants into the French-speaking milieu. He believes that French is in the process of becoming the working language of Québec, but considers Anglophones born in Québec to be less able to adapt to a changed linguistic and social context than the immigrants. Thus, while he is optimistic that the present generation of English-speaking Québécers attending elementary school will be bilingual, he is much less confident that the adult generation of Anglophones will easily adapt to their changed circumstances in contemporary Québec.

The language of instruction

In 1961 a Royal Commission of Inquiry was established to study the organization and financing of education in Québec.[6] Five years later the Commission's fourth and final report concluded that the role of the State was of crucial importance in the development of policies to ensure the future of the French language. The French-speaking community and its culture, the report continued, would not elicit the respect of others until the community itself had achieved sufficient self-respect to insist upon and use everywhere a language of which it could truly be proud. The task of the state, moveover, was to protect the language, to regulate its official use, to encourage its improvement and to ensure the fullest possible development of the culture it expressed. To this end the Commission advocated governmental protection of the French language in the work force (particularly at the managerial level) and throughout all levels of Québec society. Nor was government intervention and protection enough to achieve these declared goals. It demanded a fundamental re-ordering of attitudes, and a social solidarity that superseded all other claims and royalties.

The Commission recognized the right of the state to introduce enforcing legislation regarding the language of instruction. It did not, however, recommend that the state exercise this right. Rather the Commission called for the establishment of closer ties between the Francophone and Anglophone educational systems, assuming of course, that English would continue to be the language of instruction in the Anglophone public schools. On the other hand, it believed that to use languages other than French or English (as the language of instruction) would weaken the public school system.

More importantly, the Commission recognized the tendency for immigrants to prefer English schools, and took the position that to force them to enter French schools would place Québec in the questionable position of other provinces vis-à-vis their treatment of French-Canadian minorities. Rather optimistically (or so it seems in the light of later developments) the Commission concluded that all would be well as soon as French-language schools offered education of unquestionable quality in all the various disciplines and subject matters.

In 1963 the Royal Commission on Bilingualism and Biculturalism was established by the Federal government,[7] and, in 1967, the Commission published the first volume of its report. Like the "Parent" Commission,[8] the "B and B Commission", as it became popularly known, considered the school to be the basic agency for maintaining language and culture. Drawing attention to what it described as "grave inequalities in the opportunities for the French-speaking minorities (as compared to Anglophone minorities) to have an education in their mother tongue", the Commission argued that the basic reason for these inequalities was the unwillingness of the English-speaking majority in Canada to recognize the right of Francophones to educate their children in French. The reverse was true in Québec, however. Here English-speaking residents had long enjoyed the opportunity to educate their children in English. In the opinion of the Commission the situation in Québec was a model worthy of emulation. Subsequently, the Commission also recommended that the right of Canadian parents to educate their children in the official language of their choice be recognized throughout Canada.

The federally appointed "B and B Commission" was continuing its work when, in December 1968, the provincial *Union Nationale* government established a Commission of Inquiry on the Position of the French Language Rights in Québec. The Commission's terms of reference were to investigate and report on the position of French as the language of usage in Québec, and to recommend measures designed to guarantee:

a) the linguistic rights of the majority as well as the protection of the rights of the minority;
b) the full expansion and diffusion of the French language in Québec in all fields of activity and also at the educational, cultural, social and economic levels.[9]

The stance taken by the "Gendron" Commission[10] differed from the two previous Commissions in that it did not assume that schooling was the key factor in language retention or transfer. It also queried whether the school was the principal means for integrating the immigrant into the French-speaking community. What the Commission did observe was that before 1934 the French school system had attracted more children of immigrants than had the English system; that from 1935 on a gradual change had occurred; and that since 1961 this trend had not only become more noticeable but was in the process of reaching "alarming proportions". Nevertheless, the Commissioners concluded that "the school situation does not involve the degree of urgency or primacy which is sometimes attributed to it". Other factors were presumably of greater importance. The Commission therefore decided to adopt a wait and see attitude regarding the effects of An Act to Promote the French Language in Québec (1969).[11]

The most important conclusion reached by the "Gendron" Commission was that the language of work, *not* the language of instruction was the crucial variable for the maintenance and promotion of the French language in Québec. For example, the Commission argued that the proclivity of immigrants to integrate with the Anglophone community stemmed from causes "quite beyond the mere fact" that their children attended English-speaking schools. Economic motivations were far more important. Thus, "if French were used as language of communications at work and became increasingly useful and necessary in this area, English-language schools would no longer enjoy that degree of success they know today". In short, the Commission considered that the trend for immigrants to place their children in English language schools was not irreversible.

When the Commission finally published its report (in December 1972) it quickly became a focus of controversy.[12] Critics accused it of being ambiguous and indecisive (but in a sense the Commission's report helped draw the lines more clearly than before). Some — especially the nationalists — considered its recommendations to be far too cautious and moderate. For their part, the non-Francophone minorities mostly accepted the report. On one point all were agreed, however. The political struggle over language would continue. But before we turn to look at the next stage of its development, it is important to examine the significance of the language of work.

The language of work

In the mid 1960's the "B and B Commission" commissioned several research studies designed to determine the use of the French language in industry. Not surprisingly, perhaps, their results confirmed earlier impressions that Francophones were proportionately underrepresented in higher salary levels across Canada; that English was the language of business communication in the middle and higher levels of the Québec manufacturing industry; and that "in terms of concentration in the command posts of Canadian manufacturing industry, the Anglophone presence was overwhelming, even in the regions where they were very much in the minority".

As the Commission took pains to observe, the studies it had commissioned utilized data for the years 1941-1961 whereas fairly significant changes had taken place in the ensuing decade. Nevertheless, it still believed that the data had underestimated the gravity of the situation. This situation it considered to be not only highly unjust but one which had far-reaching implications for work performance, career advancement and the retention of linguistic and cultural identity. Improvements notwithstanding, the Commission declared, the inequality of partnership between the English and French remained a disquieting reality.

Research carried out on behalf of the "Gendron" Commission generally confirmed the results of these studies. It found, for example, that the structure of primary and secondary industry in Québec was dominated by English speakers at the top and French speakers at the bottom. In addition, there appeared to be a direct relationship between the low level of use of French in functional communications in any given sector and the overrepresentation of English-speaking people — especially in administrative and professional positions. What existed was a situation whereby business and other work organizations had developed "language policies which reflect much more their own interests rather than a respect for the individuals who make up the majority of Québec's workers and whose mother tongue is French". Such a marked degree of under-representation was a clear aberration in a province where Francophones formed the majority. The French-speaking people of Québec, the Commission declared, possessed an undeniable right to expect the use of their language throughout all sectors and all levels of economic activity in the province.

The Commission used some of its strongest language in criticizing government for having shown neither enterprise nor initiative in legislating language use. The unfortunate result was the "abundantly evident" divorce of the worker's mother tongue from the language in which he had to work. This was one of the major reasons for the present wave of language discontent in Québec. What was urgently needed was government intervention. French must become a necessity for all who worked in the province of Québec, and all Québécers must recognize it as a common language they both knew and could use.

Legislation and Response

The "Gendron" Commissioners were correct to point out that before 1968 legislation had never been introduced to ensure the primacy of the French language in Québec. Nor was the introduction of the ill-fated Bill 85 a result of government initiative.[13] It was introduced by the *Union Nationale* government in an effort to defuse what came to be known as *L'Affaire Saint-Léonard.*

In November 1967, in the north-east section of Montréal, controversy broke out over a proposal to phase out a bilingual program in the Saint-Léonard School Commission whose schools enrolled the children of large numbers of Italian immigrants. The dispute continued (with opposing groups organizing their resources) until June 1968. Following hotly contested school elections, the school commission, now controlled by members committed to a unilingual French program, passed a resolution to phase out bilingual classes beginning that September. The response of the immigrant and English-speaking communities was angry and bitter. They felt themselves betrayed and immediately renewed their efforts to obtain adequate instruction in English for their children.[14]

The *Union Nationale* government attempted to keep the affair at arms length by claiming that it was a local matter and therefore should be resolved at the school board level. Their efforts, however, proved unsuccessful. And as positions hardened the demand for government intervention grew. Bowing to pressure, Premier Bertrand announced that he would introduce legislation to protect minority rights and in December, 1968, Bill 85 was introduced.

From the beginning, as Dr. MacDonald points out, Francophone reaction was overwhelmingly negative. The nationalists voiced vigorous objection to the principle of parental choice of the language of instruction. Its implementation, they declared, would further reduce the status of French in Québec. Anglophones, on the other hand, expressed apprehension about the power given to the government in terms of implementing the Bill. The government's decision to send the Bill to Committee (rather than allowing it to proceed to second hearing) provided Francophone pressure groups with the opportunity they desired. Group after group denounced the Bill. The intensity of the public debate that surrounded it grew. And only four months after its introduction the Bill was withdrawn. It was, Premier Bertrand declared, "*un bébé que personne ne veut*".

The crisis in St-Léonard remained unresolved, and demands for the government to act continued. In October 1969, it introduced Bill 63 (An Act to Promote the French Language), which confirmed the parents' option to choose either French or English as the language in which courses would be given to their children. Like its predecessor, Bill 85, it was immediately and vigorously attacked. The opposition outside the National Assembly was led by René Lévesque who charged that the legislation placed the survival of the French language in jeopardy. According to Lévesque, English as the language of instruction should be restricted to Anglophones, and all immigrants should be made to send their children to French Schools.

The Francophone groups once again girded themselves for battle. The government, however, was determined to enact the Bill, and quickly. On November 28, 1969, despite lively and vocal opposition, Bill 63 was enacted. For the first time in the history of Québec, English language schools, and a parent's right to choose the language of instruction of his children, had a basis in law.

In the spring of 1970 the *Union Nationale* government was defeated by the Liberals. Understandably cautious, and determined to avoid the mistakes of their predecessors, the Liberals promised to consider changes in Bill 63 only after receiving the recommendations of the "Gendron" Commission. In December 1972, the long-awaited report of the "Gendron" Commission was handed to the government. Among its major recommendations was one advising the government to wait three to five years in order to measure the effects of Bill 63 before considering its repeal. The government responded by promising to study the report and undertook not to introduce legislation on the language issue until after the next provincial election.

In the October, 1973 election, the Liberals won 102 of 110 seats in the National Assembly. Despite this apparently overwhelming mandate, however, Professor Stein tells us that the party was still apprehensive about introducing legislation on language. In fact, it waited six months and then, at the end of May 1974, introduced the Official Language Act, or Bill 22 as it became widely known.

Section I of the Bill declared French to be the official language of Québec and included among the major specific features of the Bill were the following stipulations:

1) the requirement that French would be the official language of the public service and no one would be admitted to an administrative office in this service unless his knowledge of that language was appropriate to the employment sought;
2) all contracts with the government and para-governmental bodies would have to be written in French and another language if contracted elsewhere;

3) governmental contracts would be awarded under a preferential system to companies favoring the use of French;
4) the government would provide grants and teaching assistance to businesses wishing to comply with its guidelines on the use of French;
5) tests would be administered by school boards to determine whether a child is to be placed in the English-language or French-language schools.

Once again the new legislation appears to have pleased very few groups. In Professor Stein's judgement it fell between two poles of public opinion representing two conflicting principles. "The Anglophones and non-Francophone immigrants were committed for the most part to the principle of bilingualism and to the absolute right of parents to choose the language of instruction of their children. The Francophones were devoted to what they regarded as their collective right to exist as a nation and to making French at least the priority language and therefore primary vehicle of integration of immigrants."

In brief, Francophone unilingualists argued the Bill did not go far enough. Anglophones complained angrily that rights guaranteed by Bill 63 had been removed, and the ethnic groups spoke bitterly of discrimination. The English language press roundly criticized the legislation on the grounds that it downgraded English, and the provisions of the Bill left it wide open to administrative abuse. The Francophone press demanded more radical provisions for the integration of non-Francophone immigrants, to ensure that French would become the primary language of activity at all levels in Québec. On one point, however, all were agreed: the legislation and its procedures for implementation were vague and confusing.

On July 13, 1974 public hearings on Bill 22 were abruptly terminated when the Liberals employed their guillotine and brought the legislation back from committee to the floor of the Assembly for second reading. Several important amendments had been introduced by this point, however. They included a guarantee for the continuance of English-language schools (but with limits on their expansion); an assurance that the Minister of Education would take the necessary measures to ensure instruction in English as a second language to pupils whose language of instruction was French; and compulsory francization certificates for firms wishing to be eligible for provincial grants and loans. There was never any doubt about the outcome of the vote and the Bill was returned to committee. Here the *Parti Québécois* launched a filibuster which prevented discussion moving beyond the principles of the legislation. Opposition outside the Assembly mounted and Premier Bourassa finally invoked closure. On July 30, 1974 the Bill was passed 92 votes to 10 and became law.

No sooner had the law been passed then its severest critics threatened to launch legal challenges to its constitutionality. Three cases have been brought. One sought a judgement on the interpretation of section 45 which deals with notices in newspapers. The second challenged an interpretation of the educational regulations governing the implementation of the law. In fall 1975, the issue again occupied the front pages when a highly publicized and vigorous campaign was waged against Bill 22's educational clauses by the Anglophone community of Montréal. The third, and most important challenge, resulted in April 1976 in a decision by Judge Deschênes Chief Justice of the Province of Québec, confirming the constitutionality of the clauses in Bill 22 dealing with the language of instruction.[15]

Language, then, continues to be the symbol of both hope and bitter disappointment. In the present context, Francophone and non-Francophone groups alike are deeply concerned over questions of economic status and cultural survival. The Anglophone community, however, appears pessimistic over its chances to retrieve a situation which many consider places it in an unfair and adverse position. Unilingualists and nationalist groups meanwhile seek to strengthen the laws ensuring the use of French. That the language question will continue to be a political issue of some consequence seems likely. And as the debate sharpens, so will the larger debate over separatism or federalism, independence or confederation. In this sense, language is an important barometer of French-Canadian politics and provides a guide not only to the future of Québec but to the future of the Canadian nation itself.

Québec
April, 1976

J.R.M.

Note:

On November 15th, 1976, the *Parti Québécois* won a stunning victory over the Liberals and prepared to make good on their promise to repeal Bill 22. New legislation is expected to be introduced in the next session of the National Assembly beginning March 8th, 1977.

Québec
February, 1977

J.R.M.

NOTES

[1] Richard J. Joy, *Languages in Conflict*, Toronto: McClelland and Stewart Limited, 1972, p. 135.

[2] *Ibid*, p. 133.

[3] I refer here to studies dealing specifically with the development of Quebec's language policies.

[4] See, for example, F. Albert Angers, *Les droits du français au Québec*, Montreal: Editions du Jour, 1971; Richard Arès, *Nos grandes options politiques et constitutionnelles*, Montreal: Les Editions Bellarmin, 1972; Guy Bouthiller et Jean Meynaud, *Le Choc des langues au Québec, 1760-1970*, Montreal: Les Presses de l'Université du Québec, 1972; et Alain Prujiner et Gilles Grenier, *Les droits linguistiques au Québec*, Québec: Les Presses de l'Université Laval, 1976 (In process).

[5] Additional sources dealing specifically with the educational aspects of the legislation include: Heather Lysons, "The Language Question and Quebec Education", In T. Morrison and A. Burton, Eds., *Options: Reforms and Alternatives for Canadian Education*, Toronto: Holt, Rinehart and Winston of Canada, Ltd., 1973, pp. 317-339. Roger Magnuson, "Education and Society in Quebec in the 1970's", *Journal of Educational Thought*, Vol. 7, No. 2, August 1973, pp. 94-104; and, Robert J. MacDonald, "Education, Language Rights and Cultural Survival in Quebec, A Review Essay", *Journal of Educational Thought*, Vol. 9, No. 1, April 1975, pp. 49-64.

[6] *Report of the Royal Commission of Inquiry in the Province of Quebec on Education*, 4 Vols., Quebec: Government of the Province of Quebec, 1966.

[7] See the *Report of the Royal Commission on Bilingualism and Biculturalism*, 4 vols., Ottawa: Information Canada, 1967-1970.

[8] So-called after the Chairman of the Royal Commission of Inquiry on Education in the Province of Quebec, the Rev. Alphonse-Marie Parent, former rector of Laval University.

[9] *Report of the Commission of Inquiry on the Position of the French Language and on Language Rights in Québec*, 3 vols., Québec: Official Editor of Québec, 1972.

[10] Named after Jean-Denis Gendron, formerly associate dean of the Faculty of Letters, Laval University, Chairman of the Commission of Inquiry on the Position of the French Language and on Language Rights in Quebec.

[11] See Appendix I.

[12] On its appointment in December, 1968, the Commission was expected to present its report in twelve months.

[13]See Appendix I. Bill 85: An Act to Amend the Education Department Act, the Superior Council of Education Act and the Education Act (First Reading).

[14]Two theses have been written in English on the controversy. See John E. Parisella "Pressure Group Politics: Case Study of the St-Léonard Schools Crisis", Unpublished M.A. Thesis, McGill University, 1971; and, Robert Issenman, "Contemporary French Canadian Nationalism and the M.I.S.", Unpublished B.A. Thesis, Harvard University, 1968.

[15]Albina Dagenais v. Pierre Courcelles, 1974, Cour Supérieure Québec 403; Gignac v. Commission Scolaire de Ste-Foy, C.S. 200-15-001816, 26 November, 1975; and *The Protestant School Board of Greater Montréal* v. *Minister of Education of the province of Québec*, C.S. 500-05-015374-752, Montréal, 6 avril 1976 (Juge Jules Deschênes).

SECTION ONE

The Socio-Political Background

FRENCH AS AN ADOPTED LANGUAGE IN QUEBEC*

Léon Dion

The language question in Quebec is a thorny one. To raise it is to set sail in dangerous waters and undertake, at the risk of foundering, to define a variety of coordinates of demographic, economic, socio-psychological, cultural, juridical and political bearing. Great are the risks of misunderstanding along the way. The problems to be resolved are more than likely to beget violent disputes, since they are visceral in quality and invite irrational reactions.

Canadians are rapidly becoming aware of the seriousness of this language question in Quebec itself. Two important commissions of enquiry have looked, or are looking, into it. The Commission on Bilingualism and Biculturalism largely concerned itself with the situation in Canada as a whole and, except in the third volume of its report, has made few recommendations relating directly to the francophone population of Quebec. However, its list of proposals constitute in the aggregate the framework of a possible action program applying to Quebec. The Commission of enquiry into the French language in Quebec (Gendron Commission) is concerned with matters relating to the quality of the language, its teaching, the use of second languages, and diverse aspects of the coexistence of two languages in the same environment.

Whatever benefits may ensue from these labours, the situation is such as to require immediate action. The passing of Bill 63 "to promote the French language in Quebec", and the need to pursue consideration of Bill 62" concerning school organization on the Island of Montreal", are most urgent reasons in that regard.

On the other hand, it would be wrong to consider the matter exclusively in the light of problems resulting from these two laws. This is not the time for polemics. Although the situation prompts us to action, it also suggests broadening the range of our concerns in such a way as to cover the numerous aspects of this language problem. This first step should lead to the formulation of a balanced program likely to find concrete expression in projects both coherent in themselves and in relation to one another.

---

*The English version of this article refers to Paul M. Migus, Ed., *Sounds Canadian: Languages and Cultures in Multi-Ethnic Society*, Toronto: Peter Martin Associates Limited, 1975, p. 42-58. (This article first appeared in French in *Le français langue de travail*, Québec, Les Presses de l'Université Laval, 1971, p. 45-74).

If the integration of immigrants and non-francophone ethnic groups has recently moved to the centre of discussions on the future of the French language in Quebec, this is perhaps chiefly due to the demographic situation. With the abrupt decline in the Quebec birth rate since 1965, the "revenge of the cradles" era has come to a close. In order to maintain their ratio of about 80% of the province's whole population, or even continue to exist as a separate language group, Quebec's francophones have only one recourse: to proceed as quickly as possible with the integration of non-francophones, especially those of non-British stock. Since their assimilative capacity with Quebec is weaker than ever at present, can the latter expect to improve it rapidly and, if so, how?

Besides, the problem of integrating the non-francophones cannot be considered separately from other aspects of the language question. Any careful analysis of this subject must take into account the constraints perculiar to this environment, as well as the means of modifying it. Consideration must, therefore, be given to such factors as the flow of immigrants, education levels, the professional aspirations of individuals, and the relative weights of French and English in the economic field both nationally and internationally.

I have no intention here of dealing with every aspect of this problem of integrating the non-francophone ethnic groups in Quebec. I shall merely attempt to clarify it somewhat and suggest some elements of a possible solution. My aim is rather to stimulate reflection, a process which will be long and difficult, I know. These questions are in fact complex and do not easily lend themselves to dogmatic or even satisfactory responses. My remarks will more often assume the conditional mood, occasionally the indicative, and seldom the imperative. After setting out certain premises basic to a study of the subject, I shall briefly outline the language situation in Quebec and suggest the goals that Quebec's language policy should pursue.

The Basic Premises

Let us begin with a painful but necessary confession. The human sciences on which we rightly depend to guide man in his uncertain attempts to gain more knowledge of himself and the world, have devoted very little effort to perfecting multi-disciplinary tools for examining the conditions of a bilingual environment and its influence on individual languages, persons, institutions, groups and the community as a whole. Certain general observations more or less substantiated have been advanced, for example that in order for a language to survive in a bilingual environment there must exist unilingual nuclei, that is, sufficiently numerous groups of persons who find it very inconvenient to use the other language. We now possess, thanks to the patient labours of the Commission on Bilingualism and Biculturalism, a great deal of information on the most diverse aspects of the language situation in Quebec. However, this information hardly goes beyond factual description. It might on occasion inspire caution, but it is not of much use for the development of working methods likely to produce more useful guides to action than those of instinct, goodwill, stubbornness, and suicidal or vindictive impulses. Is it possible in the present state of our disciplines to develop processes capable of achieving results of relatively uncontested worth? To answer such a question will require far more extensive research work than has been conducted until now.

Failing the aid of science, many look to natural law for guidance and justification. Nothing could be more hazardous. Is it not said of principles that if you lean on them long enough, they always give way? True, there are certain inalienable rights to life and the integrity of the person which cannot be legitimately infringed upon for any reason. But their guarantee is far from assured in practice. Moreover, the tests employed to determine their modes of application are often uncertain; and they are based on Christian and humanist concepts which are not always as clear as one would wish. Furthermore, the exercise of such rights is often governed by special conditions, as a result of which both individuals and groups remain subject to many external constraints in the most varied aspects of their lives.

Those who feel that there exists an inalienable right to education calling for positive action on the part of the state (building schools, staffing them with teachers, etc.) can point to an almost universal consensus on this subject in contemporary societies. But does there exist as obvious a right regarding the language of instruction? In unilingual countries, the problem does not arise. But the diversity of school systems found in bilingual countries, as well as the often deep antagonisms dividing these countries, suggest that the parents' right to have children educated in the language of their choice is everywhere relative at best, and often subject to severe restrictions rooted in history and in particular sociological conditions.

The same comment applies to collective rights. Group rights often result from the outcome of historic struggles. They usually benefit the victorious side to the detriment of the vanquished, which casts some doubt on their essential merit. Even undisputed, the exercise of a collective right involves limits of time and place imposed either by equity or the play of opposing forces.

Lastly, there is the question of acquired rights. Whatever its origin, an individual or collective right is so considered when a presumption of legitimacy is established in its favour, and it may be exercised with impunity under certain conditions. While an acquired right is not as soundly based as one considered inalienable, the conditions of its use are often much more precise. It is generally difficult to abolish an acquired right, even when the possibility to do so exists and circumstances require it: equity or decency stand in the way. There are thus some previleges it seems best not to grant for fear that the consequences might be such as to require their cancellation.

In the field of language, the law of might was applied implacably everywhere in Canada except Quebec. With a wealth of laws voted by democratic majorities,

French was banished from schools and denied conditions of use likely to preserve its vitality. Subsequently, a disingenuous notion of justice was invoked for a long time in order to oppose bringing legislative remedy to a situation resulting from legislative action, which condemned French to a slow death: one had to be especially careful not to mix politics with language and culture!

The federal Government's current efforts to promote the use of French in all fields of activity under its jurisdiction and the creation of bilingual districts coordinated with the programs of some provincial governments, appear as tardy reparations for an ancient wrong. One should forgive the repentant sinner, and hope it may still be possible for him to repair the damage done. More importantly, one must avoid falling into the same error.

The francophones for their part have had plenty of time to realize that "between the mighty and the weak, it is liberty that oppresses and the law which liberates". Who could reasonably be offended by the desire of Quebec's francophone majority to rely on the government they control more immediately to remedy the necessary insufficiency of federal laws in the linguistic field, by adopting measures designed to ensure the supremacy of French in all fields of activity within Quebec, with due regard to circumstances and the legitimate rights of the anglophone minority? Any attempts to inhibit the francophone people of Quebec in their desire to establish a coherent language program for themselves are bound to fail. In my view, however, their action should not be based principally on a "collective right", since such a justification would only generate opposition in the name of "individual rights" and lead into a conflict of abstract ideas.

The decision to legislate in the language field, like any other group decision, is first of all a political question. It is up to the government and people of Quebec to decide on the merit of putting paid to an old policy of inaction in that respect. With equity safeguarded, any law concerning languages should then only be judged on its merits and foreseeable effects. The sole justification of a legislative measure on languages in Quebec is the individual and collective distress it echoes, and should aim to alleviate.

Like all other laws passed by the National Assembly of Quebec, this language legislation will be examined in relation to the country's constitutional framework. It will undoubtedly open a new dimension in federal-provincial relations and be an additional source of possible conflict. However, it is at this time of constitutional review that the main lines of a language program should be laid down in order to formulate in advance, in case they are required, the necessary constitutional provisions.

The demands addressed by the people to their political representatives on the question of language rights are without doubt contradictory; we do not yet know to what extent the political system may be able to entertain them, any more than we can foretell the effects of a language bill.

But we have no other option than to act. And in this obligatory search for an appropriate strategy, the government cannot go it alone: it must have the support of the entire community. Our common task consists, therefore, in developing under the government's auspices a coherent program of action embracing the main aspects of the language situation. We must conceive and put into effect measures designed to correct tendencies prejudicial to the French language, without interfering with the free circulation of goods, ideas and persons.

The Situation

Between the francophone and anglophone people of Quebec, there has developed a kind of division of labour: the anglophones dominated the economy while the francophones dominated politics. Now the latter are no longer content with that state of affairs, having finally realized that the economy is the determining force behing policy. It is hardly surprising that the economic organization of Quebec should not favour the interests of the majority, since it is not subject to any real political control. This "surrender" of economic control to the anglophones is not, of course, the only reason for the inferiority of francophones. The effects of an obsolete educational system, of a religion promising all too easy compensation for the hardships of this world, the paternalism of leaders — all these are inter-related factors which have contributed in one way or another to the prevailing status of inferiority in which the francophones find themselves.

In the third volume of its report, the Royal Commission on Bilingualism and Biculturalism undertook to review the facts. The situation it described is bad in many respects, almost desperate. In the matter of earnings, education and control of business, the francophones are far behind the anglophones and hardly better off than the Italians who have for the most part lived less than twenty-five years in Quebec. This largely explains, the wretched position of French as a working language, and it is clear that the necessary corrective steps go well beyond measures directly related only to languages. Also involved are problems of education, career options, industrial investment and control of business affairs.

There is one aspect of the problem, as it emerges in Quebec, that the commission of enquiry did not come to grips with. And that is the demographic situation. Yet this question is one which raises the most serious doubts about the future of French in Quebec.

It is a fact that despite the predictions of alarmists, the percentage of francophones in Canada has been remarkably stable since 1881 (30% in 1881 and 30.4% in 1961, as regards ethnic origin). The proportion of francophones in Montreal today is higher than it was at the time of Confederation.

Fears are entertained, however, about the growing influence of urbanization and technology. The preservation of a traditional social framework has long served as a protective shield against contamination from the outside. But now that Quebec has taken up the challenge of modernity, concern is felt about the possible survival of five million francophones on a continent peopled by 215 million anglophones, which is at the threshold, moreover, of the post-industrial era. Given a more favourable environment French would stand an excellent chance here, since the inferiority of the francophones is especially apparent by contrast with the superiority of their neighbours. On the world scene they rank among the best, but the absolute and solid superiority of the Anglo-Americans sets them down. Having been in contact, long before France, with the increasingly exciting progress of an English-speaking world, Quebec's francophones are condemned, in order to avert assimilation, to be the eternal translators of a foreign mentality and vocabulary undergoing constant and incredibly rapid transformations. Hence the vital significance of the dictionary for the francophone Quebecer. He might well serve himself as a live dictionary for the entire francophone world. Dictionaries are, in a manner of speaking, the cemetery of language. . .

This accession then to the modern world is taking place at an awkward turn of the francophone demographic cycle. The birth rate, which had regularly been about thirty per thousand of population during the two previous decades, suddenly began to decline in 1965-66, dropping in 1968 to 16.3, one of the lowest indexes in North America. Furthermore, as a result of poor economic conditions, the net migration balance which had been favourable since 1954 began to swing downward, and it has been unfavourable for the past two years.

Demographic experts tend to be cautious about long-term predictions. Thus, in an article published in the November 4, 1969 issue of *Le Devoir* which was the subject of much comment during the debate on Bill 63, Charbonneau, Henripin and Légaré formulated two sets of hypotheses, one favourable and the other unfavourable. According to the first, the percentage of francophones in the year 2000 would be virtually unchanged, whereas the second foresaw a considerable decline in the percentage of francophones in the province from 82.3% to 71.6%, and a drastic reduction of their numbers in Montreal from 66.4% to 52.7% which would at that time contain more than half the total population of Quebec.

How can one explain the anxiety felt in certain quarters about the demographic future of the francophone element in Quebec? It owes less to the actual situation or even to foreseeable trends than to the realization that the birth rate can no longer be counted on to safeguard the francophone position. Given the progressive aging of the population in the coming years, the natural growth of the francophone element will decline substantially unless the birth rate rises, and might even drop to nothing.

Thus the only long-term hope for the francophones lies in immigration. But even in Quebec the bulk of immigrants are integrated with the anglophones and, as a result of alterations in the employment structure as well as changes in the socio-economic character of immigrants, this trend has become stronger in recent years. The assimilating power of the francophones is so slight that the number of those among them who become anglicized in Quebec is greater than that of anglophones who adopt French (68,339 as against 53,383 according to the census of 1961, representing, however, only 1.6% of the total francophone population, as opposed to 9.4% of the anglophone population). To the extent that the demographic growth of francophone Quebecers depends on immigration, the future thus appears gloomy. Hence the pressure increasingly brought to bear upon governments for the adoption of measures designed to reverse current trends.

Apart from the problem of population, concern is also expressed about the quality of oral and written French. Some fear its "galloping bastardization"; others say that the language is improving thanks to the influence of better teaching and the electronic media; while yet others feel that the linguistic gap between the élite and the mass of the people is widening dramatically. Only scientific studies will enable us to establish these evolutionary trends, and the Gendron Commission is expected to shed light on this vitally important question.

It is admissible not to share these fears about the future of French in Quebec, yet it is impossible to prove that they are groundless. Demography, although a relatively exact science, helps to generate both alarmist and optimistic views. The truth is that we do not know if there exists a critical level below which a language cannot survive. Languages spoken by large numbers of people have nevertheless disappeared, while in other cases a few thousand individuals have managed to ensure the survival of some tongues. Besides, in the case of minor languages at least, the transition from a traditional to a modern society is always a period of crisis. There are important languages in Africa which industrialization and urbanization are threatening with extinction.

Now it is precisely at this critical moment of evolution that the fate of the French language in North America is being settled. A community long held back by its traditions is at last embracing modern ways — in an exceptionally favourable environment for all its plans. Yet a doubt persists: in the post-industrial society of tomorrow, are there any guarantees for the survival of French in Quebec? The answer to this question will require a collective decision, and it is up to the government to assume the burden as spokesman for the community.

The solution of the language problem in Quebec should be sought in final analysis at the economic and cultural levels. The prestige of a language is closely tied to the image of those who speak it, and in our own context that prestige is assessed according to economic criteria. Like the dollar, science and machines — it is said — speak English in North America. Insistence on the use of French by the business community in Quebec would, according to some, isolate it from the rest of a continent which does not know French, and ensure its debility. In replying to this criticism, one must distinguish between the knowledge of English and the use of it as a working language. Like it or not, the current international scientific and technological context favours the use of English. At a time when young Frenchmen, Germans, Italians and Japanese are learning English in order to improve their career prospects not only in the international field but in their respective countries as well, only an ignoramus or a fanatic would advise young

Quebec francophones not to learn English. What seems abnormal, in my opinion, is that they should be told at the same time that they will have to earn their living in English in Quebec itself. While admitting the supremacy of English in the international business world and maintaining essential connections with this wide-ranging network of affairs, we should aim at establishing in the Quebec labour field a sufficiently broad francophone base so that French may be used as a language of work at every level. Francophone Quebecers may desire in addition to learn English in order to increase their mobility and pursue a more diversified career. This is a legitimate ambition which must be differentiated nevertheless from the obligation of working in English in order to live a normal life in Quebec.

As long as Quebec's francophone element think of themselves as "beggars", they will have a beggar's mentality. And while one may take pity on beggars, few will extend sympathy to the point of becoming beggars themselves. One is not moved to integrate with a community or a people by a feeling of mercy, adopting its language as well as its style of thought and action. Nor can this be brought about by force. One has to be impelled by the conviction that this is a valid option materially and spiritually; that one is giving up one's nationality for an equal if not better way of life.

An investigation would no doubt substantiate in some measure the accuracy of impressions gained by observing the reaction towards "foreigners" and the "English": suspicion, aggressiveness, envy, feelings of inferiority, etc. But if this is true, what is the cause of such rather unflattering traits? Here we have to refer to history. Quebec's francophones must in one way or another settle their accounts with history. They must stop considering themselves a conquered people. There may be pity for the conquered party, but very few membership applications.

Quebec's francophones now accept the challenge of modern living but they cannot do so successfully by merely jettisoning the undisputed traditional values long associated with them. They must undertake the formidable task of transforming these characteristics, now outmoded and cumbersome, into new values better adapted to the times. They must fashion themselves a new soul. Should they reject this "conversion", they will become mere by-products of the fallout of American civilization, that is, human refuse. One may pity human scrap, but one is hardly inclined to join up with it.

The "denominational" character of public schools forms part of the traditional values that must be reassessed inthe light of this orientation toward modern living. This question involves not only francophone Quebecers but also the children of immigrants who have to attend French public schools, and whose historical background contains quite different convictions about religious freedom and the schools question.

However, it would be a pity to waste time and energy on a new conflict over denominationalism. Efforts must be devoted instead to constructive tasks: improving the quality of teaching, creating a more meaningful popular culture and a liking for business, developing higher studies and the progress of scientific research in all fields. Folk cultures may be entertaining, but few are tempted to make them their own.

Nothing is more characteristic of the low prestige of French in Quebec than the eagerness of francophones to speak English at every opportunity. Persons of other tongues who want to speak French are almost unable to do so in Quebec unless they already know it well. Efforts designed to raise the value of French as a language of work will meet with apathy or, in some cases, with opposition from many francophones who are among the first to hold that the dollar "speaks" English in North America, and that this is quite all right. Those who suffer from cultural alienation may deserve sympathy, but they attract few imitators.

This long list of handicaps under which francophone Quebecers apparently labour may seem cruel, yet it corresponds sadly to reality. And it is not complete. We have here a community organized for its own "protection" and "preservation", but not for its "development". Having been trained to live curled up on itself, is it surprising that it should now be frightened by strange new developments? Or to be wondered at that it lacks absorptive capacity? An immigrant landing in Quebec or anywhere in America is first of all looking for security and freedom. He hopes to find here a promising future, a materially and spiritually enriching environment. He will inevitably gravitate toward those who best conform to the image he has of a free and prosperous people.

Objectives and Conditions

A coherent language program for Quebec has to comprise an option concerning the official status of languages, and calls for measures leading to the attainment of objectives having to do with the teaching language, the working language and the assimilative capacity of French.

1. *Official bilingualism*

The first question to settle is the choice between official bilingualism or French unilingualism within Quebec borders. One way or the other, this is apt to generate many acrimonious debates. This is certainly an important question because of the symbolic character it assumes, and of the moving force symbols of this nature are likely to engender.

It must be agreed, however, that whatever option is chosen the difference in practice might be very slight. Indeed, a declaration making French the only official language would have to be balanced with clauses defining English language rights, whereas the maintenance of bilingualism presupposes the adoption of measures aimed at making French the dominant language in Quebec. Whatever their own choice, if people are reasonable they will have to accept the constraints imposed by actual social conditions, which cannot be rejected with impunity.

The fact that Quebec is a part of Canada and that this country is increasingly strengthening its position as an officially bilingual entity not only at the federal level but in the two provinces containing the next largest numbers of francophones, New Brunswick and Ontario, should encourage Quebec to remain officially bilingual.

There is also a strategic aspect to this question. The official proclamation of French unilingualism is likely to create extreme concern among the anglophones, which would then have to be appeased by means of practical concessions that would not have to be offered if Quebec stayed officially bilingual.

2. *The language of instruction*

a) French should be the language of instruction for the children of all francophone parents. I am not aware that Quebec parents can invoke an inalienable right to the free choice of the language in which their children are educated. There are many bilingual countries where such freedom of choice does not exist, or else is subject to various restrictions. It does not appear, moreover, that any pressing demands have been made by the francophones to obtain a right not previously granted to them. This right was initiated, without sufficient study or caution, by Bill 63. Until then freedom of choice had been withheld on religious grounds which served also to safeguard the French language, since all francophone children were considered Catholic by law and in fact required to attend French schools.

To grant freedom of choice is to create an acquired right that could not subsequently be abolished, even if it had the most troublesome consequences, without grave prejudice to those who were accustomed to exercising it. If francophone parents are given the right to decide in which language their children will be educated, no one can foresee what choice the parents will finally make or what the situation will be five, ten or twenty years from now: the future of the French language on this continent is already too uncertain. It would be extremely dangerous to strike such a spark today and risk starting a blaze that could not later be controlled.

It may be objected that in the second volume of its report, the Commission on Bilingualism and Biculturalism recommended (Recommendation No. 9) "that parents have the right to choose for their children either the school of the majority or the school of the official language minority, if both exist in the locality".

The purpose of this principle is to promote bilingualism, not to create major problems for either one of the two official languages. It does not, in my view, take into account the true situation of the majority language in Quebec, particularly in Montreal. It seems to me, therefore, that it should not apply unilaterally in the case of the two official majorities. It should be judged legitimate and acceptable that, through laws enacted by the provincial assemblies and carrying the approval of a large majority of the public, this principle be balanced by restrictive clauses (New Brunswick might eventually have to do this as regards English) or even declared inoperative should the linguistic situation of the majority reasonably require it.

There are many restrictions of all kinds which citizens must accept for the good of all. The obligation for francophone parents to send their children to French schools should be looked upon as a constraint of that nature.

b) English should be the language of instruction for the children of all anglophone parents who so desire. The anglophones in Quebec have an acquired right to their own schools, which could not be abolished without serious injustice toward them and without exposing the entire community to a violent backlash. Furthermore, they have an excellent school system to the financing of which, given their high income, they contribute adequately. Following a recommendation of the Commission on Bilingualism and Biculturalism, the federal Government may grant a financial and technical compensation to the provinces to help them defray the additional costs of school systems for official minorities. Its educational autonomy being guaranteed, Quebec might take advantage of this aid.

There is also the fact that, since the English language is deeply anchored in North America and French is the language of the majority in Quebec, the children of anglophone parents should be given access to French schools.

Lastly, while the principle of English instruction for the children of anglophone parents seems to me indisputable, the organization of an appropriate school system for that purpose has sociological implications and raises problems of administrative efficiency.

c) An attempt should be made to ensure attendance at French schools by the greatest possible number of children from immigrant families whose mother tongue is not English. Various means of persuasion and dissuasion should be used to encourage the immigrants to opt for a French education. Perhaps a special tax might be levied on parents whose children attend English schools. Although our experience with bilingual schools in Canada has not been encouraging, such schools might be established and would probably be attended by the children of immigrants from countries where bilingualism is currently the rule. Should it turn out despite every effort to be impossible to attract a substantial number of these children to French schools, more radical measures of coercion would have to be resorted to. As a matter of principle, such attendance might be made obligatory, but this would be a hard rule to apply, at least while there are still English schools. Moreover, the existence of such a measure might well dissuade immigrants from settling in Quebec. A study of immigrant motivation should doubtless be conducted in order to assess the possible results of such a measure and, should the need arise, to facilitate the choice of means likely to prevent the undesirable effects foreseen.

d) The children of all anglophones and immigrants should acquire a working knowledge of French, and steps should be taken to bring this about. French could be taught in English schools from the earliest grades; summer camps could be established for the practical use of French, etc. Various penalties might also be imposed on those who have not acquired adequate knowledge of French after five years or more of residence in Quebec. They might, for example, be ineligible for graduation diplomas, in which case the impartiality of the tests and of the persons giving them would have to be guaranteed.

Once the knowledge of their mother tongue is assured, young francophones should be given every opportunity to learn English, since it will in all probability remain the principal working language of the continent on which the francophones will spend their lives. Its knowledge will, therefore, be required for the full and free exercise of most professions. Furthermore, as the language of technology and to a great extent of science and politics, English has become the foremost *lingua franca* in the world.

3. *The language of work*

Let us first set out the objectives which should guide our steps in this field. Bill No. 63 "for the promotion of the French language in Quebec" provides that "the French Language Board should under the direction of the Minister. . . *b)* advise the government on any legislative or administrative measure that might be adopted in order to make French the language of work in all public and private enterprises in Quebec; *c)* develop, in consultation with these enterprises, programs designed to ensure that French is the language of work, and to impart to their managers and employees a practical knowledge of that language; . . . *d)* establish a language research centre and coordinate throughout Quebec all research activity in this field." Also worthy of note is Recommendation No. 42 in volume III of the report of the Commission on Bilingualism and Biculturalism, regarding *The Work World*, which reads as follows:

> We recommend that in the private sector in Quebec, governments and industry adopt the objective that French become the principal language of work at all levels, and that in pursuit of this objective the following principles be accepted: *a)* that French be the principal language of work in the major institutions of the province; *b)* that, consequently, the majority of work units in such firms that until now have used English as the principal language of work in the middle and upper levels become French-language units; and that such firms designate all management and senior positions as posts that require bilingual incumbents; *c)* that the majority of smaller or specialized firms should use French as their language of work, but that there should be a place for firms where the language of work is English, as there should be a place anywhere in Canada for such firms where the language of work is French; and *d)* that the main language of work in activities related to operations outside the province remain the choice of the enterprise.

For its part, the counter-draft to the defunct "Bill 85", submitted by the Parti Québécois, stipulated that "French is the principal language of economic activity" (Section 1, sub-section 1).

Although the phrasing varies, these three recommendations all have the same purpose: promoting French as the language of work in Quebec in order to make it, in the words of Bill 63, the "language of current use" in any enterprise, or according to the more cautious wording of the Commission on Bilingualism and Biculturalism "the principal language of work at all levels", or again according to the Parti Québécois "the principal language of economic activity". There may be better ways of defining this objective, but this one has the merit of clarity. The aim is to ensure that French really becomes the language of work in Quebec.

The essential concern, therefore, bears on the means of establishing and developing this francophone work base in Quebec. This is a very complex question requiring for its solution an accurate knowledge that we do not yet possess of all the practical problems involved. We should, therefore, tackle it without delay, since 75% of Quebec's francophones are unilingual, and those who are bilingual find it seriously inconvenient for the most part to use English. This represents, of course, a guarantee for the survival of French in the province. When two languages are thus spoken in close contact, only the existence of substantial unilingual groups can ensure that neither one disappears. The advent of integral bilingualism in Quebec would mark the end of French in North America.

One must distinguish clearly, first of all, between the many possible fashions and levels of familiarity with a language, and then differentiate language requirements according to the types of enterprises and activities involved. The ultimate aim of this process of discrimination is to facilitate the adoption of French in firms that have heretofore operated in English. It also aims at discovering the circumstances required so that a firm may adopt French as its principal language of work, and what is meant by the expressions "language of work" and "predominantly francophone enterprise".

The degree of mastery one must have of a second language in order to use it as a language of work is often greatly exaggerated. The misconceptions held by anglophones on this subject, often as a result of views expressed by francophones, must be dispelled. To require that an anglophone have an advanced knowledge of French in order to be able to work in that language would be to invite failure for any program of reform. It is hardly by such radical means that the anglophones on this continent succeeded in converting to the use of English tens of thousands of persons of other languages and cultures. True, the social and economic context favoured the use of English, whereas it is prejudicial to French. That is the reason why, as regards the development of French, one cannot trust to the normal course of events. One must endeavour in some way to reproduce systematically in various enterprises conditions favouring the use of French, similar to those that the balance of affairs has so long maintained in favour of English.

That is why it should be easier to implant the use of French in business by opting for institutional rather than individual bilingualism. A firm could thus operate in French without all of its members being obliged to know French, or even to know it perfectly in order to use it as a language of work. The choice of institutional bilingualism would permit an optimal utilization of all degrees of linguistic ability. Between persons who understand and read the second language (passive bilingualism) and those who speak and write it easily (active bilingualism), or again between those who have a partial knowledge of the second language restricted to their work requirements (functional bilingualism) and others who know it perfectly (total bilingualism), there is a broad and fruitful range of language abilities which, properly employed, should facilitate the language conversion of any firm and reduce the stress on individuals. The institutional bilingualism option requires a definition of the linguistic capacity demanded for each job, and the assurance that all employees have the necessary language qualification to do their work satisfactorily: the elevator operator, the foreman, the engineer, the personnel director, the sales manager and the president of the firm are all concerned with different types of oral and written communication. Each of these functions carries special language requirements and a correlative vocabulary.

Besides, language conditions vary enormously according to the different firms. There are firms that have been in operation since the establishment of an anglophone community in Quebec, and must be regarded in a special light: such are, for example, enterprises of a cultural character (newspapers, radio or television) and the anglophone educational establishments, or again small firms of all kinds located in an anglophone environment, whose staff and customers are anglophone. Head offices of firms offer another case in point, and because of their importance to the enterprise as a whole, require special consideration. Here a distinction should be made between headquarters' operations directed abroad, often the more numerous and significant, and, in the case of firms that have branches in Quebec, operations relating directly to their environment. Furthermore, language requirements may differ considerably according to whether these are manufacturing, financial, professional or service organizations. One must also take into consideration the geographical location of the firm and distinguish between different types of activities, since language demands vary substantially according to whether plant, office, management or collective agreement operations are involved. Finally, one must take into account the orientation of communications, internal or external, vertical or horizontal, addressed to special clients or the general public, and so on.

This question of the language of work is clearly a very complex one. Discrimination of the different possible categories, and the placement of firms and activities within these categories, is an operation requiring time and expert knowledge. Unless one proceeds with caution, there is the risk of becoming locked in sterile discussions, and of generating antagonisms that would prevent reaching any valid solution. Such a task is beyond the normal capacity of individual firms as it is of the regular public service. It is unsound to divide responsibility for the promotion of French between three different branches of the public service, as is presently the case in Quebec. Nor is it appropriate for the Prime Minister either to engage in personal dialogue with individual firms about the use of French, as he did last autumn, or to announce along the way technical details concerning the implementation of French programs by a particular firm. There is no need for special legislation with respect to language of work requirements, the present law for the promotion of French in Quebec being at least adequate in that regard. It would be enough to amend the labour code in such a way as to require that French be used in the collective bargaining process, as the Quebec management council itself recommended in a recent statement. However, in order to ensure the wider use of French throughout the labour field a broad, systematic and concerted effort will be required.

That is why, as the Commission on Bilingualism and Biculturalism has recommended, there must be appointed a special action group responsible for defining the scope of the objective according to circumstances prevailing in each category of enterprise; for providing appropriate information and technical assistance needed to reach the objective; for counselling advertising and publicity services about the use of French terms; for locating experts whom the firms might need to attain the objective, etc. This action group will also exercise such control as seems proper in order to ensure that the necessary measures are carried out efficiently and on time.

The action group will comprise representatives of business, unions, the universities and the government. It will be established by the government with the status of an independent and permanent board. It will submit an annual report to the National Assembly on the exercise of its mandate. Its members will be appointed for a period of five or seven years, and may not be dismissed except on evidence of incompetence or prejudice.

As an independent board, the action group will enjoy State support without interference by the government of the day, and will be protected from the hazards of political life. Moreover, it will have a freer hand by not being subject to the delays and hesitations of administrative services. It will have a higher degree of credibility among private firms. Lastly, it will be more exposed to public scrutiny and subject to control by public opinion.

The practical measures to be adopted will of course vary according to the different categories of firms and operations. The following seem to be among the more promising: the organization of special mobile teams charged with assisting and advising firms in the implementation of their French language programs, notably as regards the establishment of francophone units and the identification of strategic jobs from the linguistic standpoint; the preparation by experts employed by the language board, in consultation with the firms, of special French textbooks and vocabularies for management training programs; the listing of key words for different classes of employment, for publicity, labelling, posters, collective agreements, etc.

The federal Government itself has a special responsibility concerning the language of work in Quebec. It must ensure that French is the principal language used in federal undertakings and offices in Quebec; that the francophone population is served in French; and project a French image in Quebec as well as in francophone countries. Moreover, the federal Government might act as spokesman for Quebec with private enterprise in Ontario and abroad, especially the United States, drawing to their attention the fact that French is the basic language of economic activity in Quebec.

These and similar measures taken by business firms with the continuing assistance of the language board will reduce the psychological tension experienced by francophones who have to use English as a language of work, and enhance their career opportunities. However, were this reform movement to be limited to the linguistic field, it would accomplish only half the task required for a complete revaluation of French. Beyond language, there is in fact the problem of culture, and the dominant culture of any organization is that of its executives. This raises with particular emphasis the problem of big business control in Quebec. It is essential, through the increase of public and private investments and the improvement of management ability, to extend the control by French-Canadians of private enterprise.

Efforts by Quebecers to make French the principal language of work in business enterprises comes into conflict with the interests, prejudices and fears of anglophone and even francophone businessmen. Avoiding needless provocation, it would be wiser to try to convince these persons of the legitimacy and realistic character of these efforts. The reforms to be accomplished will require both money and time. On the technical plane at least, the State will be called upon through its language board to assist firms for a certain length of time. These firms, of course, have well-defined responsibilities to the community in which they are established and prospering. And in the final analysis, it is the firms that will be the first to benefit from the improved status of French as the language of work. Enabled at last to contribute to the common undertaking in their mother tongue, the francophone employees will indeed be off to a quicker and better start in their careers, and will give a more efficient performance throughout their life.

4. *The assimilative capacity*

All efforts to promote French as the language of instruction and work would be more or less useless if one were to overlook a third point directly concerned with French as a language of adoption. It is probably in dealing with this third aspect that the root of the trouble may be uncovered and acted upon.

The diagnosis is as follows: francophone Quebecers have no assimilative capacity. One is surprised to note how superficial are the reasons advanced until now to explain this phenomenon, and how inefficient the steps proposed to remedy the situation. There is need to consider this question without delay.

At first sight, the situation of the francophone Quebecers is paradoxical: here is a community which has an overwhelming popular majority in the province, yet must be protected in order to ensure, if not its survival, at least its normal development. This dual phenomenon of an "overwhelming majority" and of "a community in need of protection" gives weight to the theories of "foreign occupation" of the territory, as of Anglo-American "colonialism". In every situation of this kind, whether the case be that of Eastern Europe under the iron rule of Germany and Russia, of "colonial" Africa or of "exploited" South America, politics provide the solution. I share the opinion of those who feel that Quebec has not known how to use to best advantage all the possibilities inherent in Canada's political framework, either at the federal or the provincial level. It nevertheless remains to be demonstrated that the Quebec community could achieve full development within the limits of a Canadian confederation. A functional approach to politics is probably the best that might be conceived in the present circumstances. Yet it is essential to state the problems accurately, to clearly define the objectives, and to take courageous action.

The root causes of the trouble must be dealt with first, if the promotion of French is to succeed and these are of a political, economic and cultural character. Now the primary source of any corrective action — one is tempted to say redemptive — is the State. But the State alone would be powerless: it needs the support of all the major social institutions — especially industry, the labour unions, and the universities. It is not the worth of the individual Quebecer that is in question: he has demonstrated in the past that he is endowed with surprising physical and spiritual qualities. The shadow of doubt lies on the social cadres: groups, institutions and leaders in all fields.

The promotion of French in Quebec is thus indestructibly linked with the progress of society itself. When French becomes socially useful, non-francophones will need no urging to learn the language. A language policy must, of course, be formulated and applied, but the legislative safeguards will seem less odious and be more effective — some may even become superfluous — if their implementation is accompanied by a broad economic, social and cultural move toward the use of French.

Quebec would run a dangerous risk if the two main aspects of the problem — the linguistic and the socio-political — were to be dissociated. Legislation on languages alone, even applied with perseverence and courage, will not produce the anticipated results. Uncontrollable waves of mounting frustration will then appear. It is the failure of politics that is the true cause of direct action and violence. The challenge is a formidable one, but it must be met.

SECTION TWO

Demographic Trends

QUEBEC AND THE DEMOGRAPHIC DILEMMA OF FRENCH CANADIAN SOCIETY*

Jacques Henripin

The political situation of the Province of Quebec cannot be fully understood unless the demographic situation of French Canadians is taken into consideration. The French Canadian community and the Province of Quebec are not synonomous, but one of the basic realities underlying Quebec's political problems is the fact that 76 percent of Canadians of French origin, and 82 percent of those whose mother tongue is French, live in the province, and, numbering about five million, constitute four-fifths of its total population. A community of such a size, with all the political powers of a Canadian province, cannot be easily swept away. Yet recent demographic trends indicate that the French Canadian society is losing ground, not only compared with Canada as a whole, but even within the Province of Quebec itself. This situation merits close examination.

The Demographic Erosion of French Canadian Society

In Canada, no other important ethnic or linguistic group is concentrated to the same extent in a single province. French Canadians have migrated from the St. Lawrence valley to other parts of Canada (as well as to the United States), but Canadian studies leave no doubt about what has happened to them when they have settled too far from "home": they or their children have gradually adopted English as their mother tongue. Consequently, in 1961, while 23.6 percent of Canadians of French origin were living outside Quebec, only 17.8 percent still claimed French as their mother tongue. Exceptions to this general situation are to be found in a few areas such as northern New Brunswick, the Ottawa River valley, and north-eastern Ontario, where French Canadians are relatively concentrated; but even in these regions, the number of Canadians of French origin who have

*This article first appeared in Dale C. Thomson, Ed., *Quebec Society and Politics: Views from the Inside*, Toronto: McClelland and Stewart Limited, 1973, pp. 155-166.

adopted English as their mother tongue is far from negligible.

As a matter of fact, in all provinces except Quebec, this trend has been accelerating since 1921 in practically a geometric progression. Table 1 shows the results of this process.

TABLE 1

Percentage of Canadians of French Origin Who Have Adopted English as Their Mother Tongue, by Province, 1961

Province	Percentage of English Mother Tongue	Province	Percentage of English Mother Tongue
Newfoundland	85.0	Ontario	38.0
Prince Edward Is.	55.0	Manitoba	30.0
Nova Scotia	57.0	Saskatchewan	43.0
New Brunswick	12.0	Alberta	50.0
Quebec	1.6	British Columbia	65.0
		Total Canada	9.9

Source: Statistics Canada, *1961 Census of Canada,* Bulletin 1.3-5, Tables 95 and 96.

By projecting this trend until 1981, we can estimate that six provinces will have an assimilation rate above 75 percent and two others will have a rate between 50 and 60 percent. These percentages only refer to Canadians of French origin who claim English as their mother tongue. According to the definition used by Statistics Canada, the mother tongue is the first language learned during infancy, provided it is still understood. However, many persons living outside Quebec whose mother tongue is French use English predominantly in their daily lives. In other words, the level of assimilation to English is still higher than is indicated when the mother tongue is used as the basis of measurement.

According to one estimate, both the proportion of French-speaking persons, and their absolute numbers, will decline in almost all provinces in the immediate future.[1] A study of these trends leads to the conclusion that, if there is any hope of a French-speaking community's [sic] surviving in North America, this can only be in the Province of Quebec. They lend credence to the growing opinion that the five million French-speaking persons living in Quebec must consider themselves the only viable group capable of maintaining the French Canadian culture. Most are strongly identified with that culture; they want it to survive and continue to develop; and they insist on having the political and economic power necessary to ensure that it does. These facts and opinions do not prove the absolute necessity

for political independence, but they [illegible]
political option. To a large proporti[illegible]
real danger of the French-speaking [illegible]
Anglo-Saxon majority of the North Ame[illegible]

This threat is not new; French C[illegible] threatened by their neighbours and their [illegible] somewhat new is that this threat is becomi[illegible] that is, within the Province of Quebec. De[illegible] Quebec is far from homogeneous. The metropo[illegible] about 40 percent of the total population, and will [illegible] the year 2000. And it is precisely in Montreal [illegible] the non-French population: nearly 80 percent of them li[illegible] [illegible]mographic concentration has great political significance; Montr[illegible] economic and intellectual centre of the whole Province (although [illegible]ebec City remains important too). And yet French Canadians make up only two-thirds of the city's population and may well fall to between 53 and 60 percent by the year 2000. This trend is largely due to the fact that most immigrants to Quebec settle in Montreal, and choose to integrate into the English community.

Throughout their history, French Canadians have had to face the constant and very significant threat of being over-run, if not completely eliminated, by the English-speaking population and English culture of North America. In earlier years, French Canadians resorted to an exceptionally high birth rate in order to counterbalance the inflow of immigrants, who were either English-speaking or generally adopted the English language. While this strategy was successful for some time, it has faltered since World War II. It also had draw-backs: there is a high cost associated with an excessive fertility rate — for instance, in terms of standards of education, health, and economic well-being. French Canadian society still faces the same dilemma: it can maintain its relative demographic position within Canada, or at least within Quebec, by continuing to bear the economic costs of a higher fertility rate; or it can allow its birth rate to drop, in which case the cost may well be its very survival as a distinct, organized society.

The Demographic Challenge and Response in Retrospect

Present-day French Canadian society, made up of about five million persons in the Province of Quebec, half a million just outside it, and another half million scattered throughout the rest of Canada, has had a rather unique demographic history. After the founding of the colony in 1608 with a mere 70 settlers, the St. Lawrence valley remained for a century and a half an exclusively French-speaking community (except for the Indians).* The threat to their survival was present

*Another French settlement was founded in Acadia, on the Atlantic coast, at about the same time. It was ceded to England and its population was deported to Louisiana. Some escaped into the woods, and others returned; today their descendants make up most of the French-speaking population of the Maritime Provinces, about 260,000 persons in 1961.

[illegible]g the first winter, two settlers died, one was sentenced to [illegible] were sent back to France as prisoners. During the second winter, [illegible] deaths. The first married couple arrived in 1616, but both spouses [illegible]ng the same year. The first marriage was celebrated in 1618, and resulted [illegible]e first of an almost fabulous series of births; but both mother and child died almost immediately. Twenty years after the foundation of Quebec, there were still only 30 inhabitants in New France, and only one farm.

The first census, taken in 1666, reported a population of 3200. France wanted to populate the colony, but was most reluctant to send emigrants from France. During the whole French Regime (1608-1760), emigration to Canada amounted to not more than 10,000 persons, or an average of about 65 per year. In 1760, when Canada was ceded to England, there were some 70,000 inhabitants in New France, compared to one million and a half in New England, a ratio of one to twenty. This comparison illustrates the potentially significant political consequences of demographic phenomena. France and England were engaged in a demographic and political struggle during the 17th and early 18th centuries. France had a population twice the size of England's; it had almost the entire North American continent, from the Appalachian to the Rocky Mountains, at its disposal, since it controlled the entrances to the St. Lawrence and Mississippi Rivers. But it failed to occupy that territory. As Alfred Sauvy has put it dramatically: "At the very moment when French was becoming the predominant language in Europe, thanks to its demographic underpinnings, it was losing in the long run on the global plane, because a few more shiploads of illiterate individuals were leaving little England each year."[2]

From 1760 to 1960, the French Canadian population grew at an exceptional rate. The world's population multiplied during these two centuries by three, the population of European origin by five, and the French Canadian population by about 80, notwithstanding a net emigration — mostly to the United States — of about 800,000. But even this remarkable performance was not sufficient to counteract the inflow of immigrants into the territory which is now Canada. After American Independence, a new demographic race began within British North America. United Empire Loyalists from New England and immigrants from the British Isles flowed into the area. By 1806, the English-speaking and French-speaking populations were about equal; by 1871, as indicated in Table 2, a state of equilibrium had been reached both in Canada as a whole, and in the Province of Quebec. Since that time, the proportion of persons of French origin has been approximately 30 percent throughout Canada, 80 percent in Quebec.

TABLE 2

Percentage of French Origin in Total Population, Canada and Quebec, 1760 to 1961

Year	Canada	Quebec
1760	—	100.0**
1806	50.0	—
1827	40.0	75.0**
1850	—	77.0**
1871	31.0	78.0
1901	30.7	80.1
1921	27.9 (26.6)*	80.0 (79.2)*
1951	30.8 (29.0)*	82.0 (82.5)*
1961	30.4 (28.1)*	80.6 (81.1)*

*Percentage of French Mother Tongue, according to Canadian census statistics.
**Rough unpublished estimates, made by H. Charbonneau. Calculations exclude natives.

This remarkable stability over the last century, reflected in Table 2, is largely the result of two counter-balancing factors: migration flows which favoured the English-language community, and a differential fertility which favoured the French-language community.

Another important factor favouring the English-language community is the tendency, even in the Province of Quebec, for the majority of immigrants whose origin is neither French nor English to adopt English for themselves and their children. The ratio is approximately three to one in favour of English (throughout Canada, it is roughly nine to one). There are indications that this trend is increasing. For instance, until recently, one immigrant group at least — the Italians — had been more favourable to French, but they now send three-quarters of their children to English schools in Montreal, where most of them are concentrated. The figures in Table 3 reflect this situation. Comparing British and French origins, and the corresponding mother tongue, we note that the French group did not gain many adherents from other groups, while the English group gained 130,000 persons, an increment of nearly 25 percent.

TABLE 3

Population Distribution of the Province of Quebec, by Ethnic Origin and Mother Tongue, 1961 (by thousands)

Ethnic Origin	Population	Mother Tongue	Population
French	4,241	French	4,269
British	567	English	697
Italian	109	Italian	90
Jewish	75	Yiddish	35
German	39	German	32
Others	228	Others	136
Total	5,259	Total	5,259

Source: Statistics Canada, *1961 Census of Canada*, Bulletin 1.2-5, Table 36, and Bulletin 1.2-9, Table 64.

The impact of the factor of fertility, which favoured the French Canadians on the other hand, is reflected in Table 4.

It will be noted that the excess fertility of French-speaking ever-married women is greater in the Province of Quebec than in Canada as a whole; in Quebec, it is twice as great for women of 50 years and over. These women were born before 1911 and had most of their children before 1950. After that date, the excess fertility ratio decreases progressively. We can conclude that, before that date, the price that French Canadians had to pay to counterbalance the English-oriented immigration was to have about twice as many children as English-language families. That price has been reduced since World War II; in 1961 the excess fertility was about 50 percent for Quebec women aged 35-39 years, and it is probably still less for younger families. That means that the challenge of English immigration is no longer being met, and that the French-speaking proportion of the population will decline even in the Province of Quebec, and more particularly in Montreal.

TABLE 4

Ratio of French to English Mother Tongue Fertility,* by Five-Year Age Group, Canada and Province of Quebec, 1961

Age Group in 1961	Canada	Province of Quebec
30-34 years	1.18	1.26
35-39 years	1.35	1.47
40-44 years	1.51	1.64
45-49 years	1.62	1.81
50-54 years	1.78	1.99
55-59 years	1.88	2.13
60-64 years	1.92	2.14
65 years+	1.98	2.05

*Number of children born per ever-married woman.
Source: Statistics Canada, *1961 Census of Canada,* Bulletin 4.1-8. Table H-9.

Some commentators have predicted that there will soon be an English-language majority in Montreal. This seems quite improbable in the near future, but such statements are sometimes accepted at face value. Consequently there is a widespread feeling that the survival of the French Canadian community is threatened, even in Quebec, and that something has to be done. Suggested counter-measures include political independence, with a panoply of miracles flowing therefrom; the elimination of English-language schools; compulsory French-language education for immigrant children; and the imposition of French as the working language at all levels in private firms.

Is the threat serious? Is there a real possibility that the French-speaking population will lose their demographic majority status in Montreal, or even in the whole province? Two colleagues and I have tried to project an answer for the next 30 years.[3] We have not tried to make predictions, but rather hypothetical projections, which are as realistic as possible. The task has been difficult because of the absence of relevant information about linguistic groups, mortality and fertility rates, and migration flows between Montreal and the rest of the Province, and between Quebec and the other provinces and other countries.

We have made the assumption that the excess natality of French Canadians throughout Quebec will continue to decrease, and will disappear by 1985. For the Montreal metropolitan area, there was already no natality differential in 1956-61, and we have assumed that this situation will persist. Possible mortality differentials have also been disregarded. As for migrations, we have used two sets of hypotheses: one favourable to the English-Canadians, and estimating a net annual immigration of 30,000, with only 15 percent French-speaking; the other as favourable to the French-speaking group as seemed plausible, with a net annual immigration of 13,000, 30 percent of it French-speaking. The results appear in Table 5. With both sets of hypotheses, the percentage of French-speaking persons continues to decrease. In Montreal, neither set of hypotheses leads to a reversal of the majority-minority linguistic relationship, but the first, the most unfavourable to French Canadians, predicts a situation not far from it in the year 2000.

These projections have not taken into account all possible future developments; in fact, any radical changes in demographic trends have been deliberately excluded. For instance, we rejected the possibility of a substantial excess fertility within the French-speaking population on the grounds that it is unlikely to recur. But other radical changes might intervene, such as policies that would lead immigrants to adopt the French instead of the English language. Or conditions might arise that would induce non-French-speaking Quebecers to leave the Province. While we do not suggest this as a solution, it is a possible outcome. And it may even have become manifest in the last two or three years. During the period 1960-66, the average annual net immigration in Quebec was 14,000. It was 14,000 again in 1967. But in the following three years, there was an increasing net *emigration* of 5,000 in 1968, 13,000 in 1969, and 34,000 in 1970. And according to a rough estimate, about three-quarters of the emigrants in 1970 were English-speaking.

TABLE 5

Percentage of French Mother Tongue in the Province of Quebec and in Montreal Metropolitan Area, 1961 to 2000, According to Two Sets of Hypotheses

	Province of Quebec		Montreal	
Year	A	B	A	B
1961	82.3	82.3	66.4	66.4
1971	80.7	81.8	64.9	66.0
1981	77.6	80.8	60.5	64.3
2000	71.6	79.2	52.7	60.0

Whatever the outcome of present political uneasiness in Quebec, the old demographic equilibrium has been upset. French Canadian families have ceased to rely on excess fertility to balance English-oriented immigration. And if nothing else changes, they are bound to see their demographic strength decrease, even in the Province of Quebec.

The Cost of the "Revanche des Berceaux"*

While there is widespread opinion in favour of increasing the French Canadian birth-rate again, it seems to us of little real advantage. Any move in that direction would have to affect French Canadian families more than the others and it is difficlut to imagine any policy which could ensure this result. To indicate the economic costs of such a step, we shall compare the Provinces of Quebec and Ontario. Although Ontario has achieved a higher level of economic development, both Provinces began to industrialize at about the same time, and had comparable population increases. From the demographic point of view, the main difference was that the population of Ontario increased through a relatively moderate birth rate and an appreciable net immigration, whereas Quebec relied only on its birth rate and experienced a net emigration. Tables 6 and 7 illustrate these phenomena. The differences they reveal imply economic effects and an appreciable inequality of opportunity in economic terms. In this respect, the Province of Quebec was certainly handicapped in comparison to the Province of Ontario.

TABLE 6

Crude Birth Rate* for the Provinces of Ontario and Quebec, 1846 to 1966

Period	Ontario	Quebec
1846-56	47.5	45.0
1856-66	46.8	43.0
1866-76	44.8	43.2
1876-86	37.2	42.0
1886-96	31.3	39.3
1896-1906	28.8	38.3
1906-16	29.1	38.0
1916-26	26.3	36.3

*A popular expression referring to reaction to the British conquest of New France, which can be translated as "the revenge of the cradle."

Period	Ontario	Quebec
1926-30	21.0	30.5
1931-35	18.5	26.6
1936-40	17.5	24.7
1941-45	19.9	28.4
1946-50	24.6	30.4
1951-55	26.1	30.0
1956-60	26.4	28.6
1961-65	23.5	24.0

*Annual number of births per 1000 population.
Sources: 1846-1956 — J. Henripin, *Trends of Factors of Fertility in Canada*, Ottawa, Statistics Canada, 1972, p. 366.
1926-1966 — Statistics Canada *Vital Statistics*, annual reports.

Three of the many aspects of this problem are examined here:

1. Between 1891 and 1946, a critical period of industrialization for both Provinces, Ontario's population multiplied by 1.94, Quebec's by 2.44. The annual rates of increase were 1.21 and 1.63 percent respectively. But there is an economic cost to population increase: new capital has to be created so that national income increases at least as fast as the population. This new capital is called demographic investments. Only when demographic investments are satisfied can supplementary investments result in an increase in living standards. And the greater the rate of population increase, the greater the demographic investments, and the more difficult it is to devote supplementary investments to improving living standards. To put it more simply, let us assume that both Provinces had been able to increase their total production by 3 percent a year during that period. Population increases would have absorbed 1.21 percent in Ontario and 1.63 percent in Quebec, leaving Ontario with 1.79 percent to increase the living standard, compared to 1.37 percent for Quebec. That is a relative difference of 30 percent, using the Quebec percentage as a base. The reality was not that simple, but our calculation indicates the kind of economic burden that is attached to a rate of population increase such as existed in Quebec in this period.

TABLE 7

Net Migration* for Ontario and Quebec 1881 to 1966 (by thousands)

Period	Ontario	Quebec
1881-91	- 84	- 132
1891-1901	- 144	- 121
1901-11	+ 74	- 29
1911-21	+ 46	- 99
1921-31	+129	- 10
1931-41	+ 75	- 32
1941-51	+304	- 13
1951-56	+377	+ 96
1956-61	+308	+109
1961-66	+237	+ 64

*For the period 1881-1941, estimates relate to population 10 years and over only.
Sources: 1881 to 1941 — Nathan Keyfitz, "The Growth of Canadian Population", in *Population Studies*, June, 1950, p. 53-54.
1941 to 1951 — Statistics Canada, *1951 Census of Canada*, Vol. X, Table 3.
1951 to 1961 — Statistics Canada, *1961 Census of Canada*, Bulletin 7.1-1, Table 2.

1961 to 1966 — Statistics Canada, *1966 Census of Canada*, Bulletin S-401, Table 2.

2. In addition to having a higher rate of population growth between 1891 and 1946, and thus having to devote a large share of its production to demographic investments, Quebec also had a smaller proportion of its population in the labour force. The following table indicates the number of persons in the labour force in Quebec and Ontario per 1000 inhabitants for some census years:[4]

	Ontario	Quebec	Difference	Percentage Difference
1911	394	331	63	16.0%
1931	392	357	35	8.9%
1951	411	364	47	11.4%
1961	384	336	48	12.5%

Three factors explain these differences:

(a) The rates of participation are lower in Quebec than in Ontario. For instance, of the 11.4 percent difference in 1951, 3.5 percent is due to that factor.

(b) A high level of fertility reduces the proportion of adults, and consequently of the labour force. This is another cost to be borne by a population with a high fertility rate.

(c) Net immigration usually increases the proportion of adults. From this point of view, Ontario was definitely in a better situation. According to Nathan Keyfitz, Ontario's net gain from migrations was 324,000 between 1901 and 1941, whereas Quebec had a net loss of 170,000. Keyfitz adds that, of all the provinces of Canada, Quebec has supplied the largest number of persons to other provinces and to the United States.

3. It must be obvious that the most direct economic effect of an excess level of fertility is on the living standard of individual families. Quebec ever-married women born between 1880 to 1911 bore from 58 to 73 percent more children than did Ontario women of the same age group. It can be roughly estimated that this excess burden represented approximately 12 percent of an average family budget, and 10 percent of the total economic production. This burden was bound to have serious effects on living standards, on savings and capital formation, and on the general welfare of the Quebec population. And it is reflected in social indicators for that period, which show that Quebec was consistently behind Ontario with regard to rates of mortality — especially infant mortality rates — levels of schooling, the quality of the labour force and labour productivity, hospital facilities and number of physicians per capital, and the quality of housing. These deficiencies certainly cannot all be attributed only to the demographic characteristics of the Quebec population. But they are partly related to the economic cost of a very high fertility rate and the raising of children — many of whom later left for other regions.

Such was the price paid by French Canadians for maintaining their relative demographic strength in Canada, and the Province of Quebec. There does not seem to be the slightest hope of such a goal being successfully pursued with regard to the whole of Canada. In the Province of Quebec, the situation is less clear. In all probability the "*revanche des berceaux*" approach has been well and truly abandoned. Accordingly, if recent migration trends continue, and if immigrants continue to opt predominantly for the English language, the French-speaking community of Quebec is bound to see its majority seriously reduced, particularly in Montreal. This would mean losing their only power: that of making laws and electing governments.

There are two possible developments: adoption of policies to induce immigrants to associate themselves with the French community and culture; or, if that democratic process fails, a turbulent minority could succeed in creating a situation which would force the non-French-speaking population to leave the Province. It must be hoped that the first solution will prevail. But for that to happen, two things are required: an energetic Government, and an unusual measure of good will and wisdom on the part of the English-speaking population.

NOTES

[1] Robert Maheu, *Les Francophones au Canada, 1941-1991*, Montreal: Editions Parti Pris, 1970, pp. 57-59.

[2] Preface to Marcel Reinhard, *Histoire de la population mondiale de 1700 à 1948*. Paris: Domat-Montchrestien, 1949, p. 12.

[3] H. Charbonneau, J. Henripin and J. Légaré, "L'avenir démographique des francophones au Québec et à Montréal en l'absence de politiques adéquates," in Revue de géographie de Montréal, Vol. XXIV, No. 2, 1970, 199-202.

[4] Jacques Henripin, "Population et main d'oeuvre", in André Raynauld, *Croissance et structure économiques de la province de Québec*. Ministère de l'industrie et du commerce de la province de Québec, 1961, p. 258.

ASSIMILATION AND THE DEMOGRAPHIC FUTURE OF QUEBEC*

Gary G. Caldwell

Assimilation

Although assimilation is the usual outcome, what we intend to discuss here is, strictly speaking, "language transfers". To what extent have and are individuals either transferring themselves, or being transferred by their parents,[1] from one language to another. For the purposes of this discussion, language transfers will be considered a direct and valid indicator of assimilation. Discussions of language transfers in Quebec have, unfortunately, often been limited to a discussion of those transferring to English or French from Other languages: transfers between the two principal language groups being largely ignored until recently.[2] Consequently, I would like to order the discussion in terms of two distinct types of transfers: transfers from Other languages to one or other of the official languages, English or French; and transfers between French and English, beginning with the first type.

That those Quebecers of Other mother tongues transfer — or if they don't, their children do — is of little doubt. The central question in Quebec is whether they transfer to English or French. In this respect, the evidence seems quite unequivocal: *in the past thirty years, French has lost its place as the major beneficiary of language transfers in Quebec.* French has quite rapidly been displaced by English. Why the decline in the attractiveness of French should have occurred so suddenly, and so recently, is a very intriguing question — a question sociologists concerned with the consequences of the industrialization and urbanization of Quebec have been exploring for some time.[3] Moreover, the

---

*This chapter first appeared in Gary G. Caldwell, *A Demographic Profile of the English-Speaking Population of Quebec 1921-1971*, Quebec: International Centre for Research on Bilingualism, 1974, pp. 51-60, 95-112. Only the locations of certain tables have been changed.

"renaissance" associated with the Quiet Revolution has not, as of yet, been effective in checking, let alone reversing this erosion of the attractiveness of French in the eyes of those in the process of being integrated into North American society.

TABLE 1

Percentage distribution of language transfers to English and French by those of Other ethnic origin, 1931-1971

YEAR	% transferred to the English-speaking sector	% transferred to the French-speaking sector
1931	48	52
1941	64	36
1951	70	30
1961	70	30
1971	62	38

Sources : Calculated from data in Government of Canada, *Census of Canada 1931*, vol. IV, Table 61; *Census of Canada 1941*, vol. IV, Table 14; *Census of Canada 1951*, vol. II, Table 49; *Census of Canada 1961*, vol. I.3, cat. 92-561, Table 121; *Census of Canada 1971*, vol. I.4, cat. 92-736, Table 23.

The evidence upon which this assessment is based is of two sorts. Census cross-classifications of ethnic origin and maternal language (or since 1971, maternal language and language spoken at home) provides an indication of which language group, English or French, is gaining and which is losing, relative to the other.[4] The second type of data central to the discussion of "assimilation" in Quebec is the information made public by the Montreal Catholic School Board as to the ethnic origin of the children in their French and English sectors. This information, although incomplete in that it pertains only to the jurisdiction of the Montreal Catholic School Board, has the advantage of being available on a yearly basis. Relevant instances of both types of data are presented in Tables 1 and 2. Of the two types of data, that derived from the census trends is not very responsive to recent developments,[5] because recent language transfers are submerged in the accumulated body of all past living transfers; the school data, however, reflects the situation at precisely the moment at which the language choice is being confirmed by the all important educational decision.

Although the figures in Table 2 are limited to the Montreal City area, a sizeable proportion of new Canadians in Quebec live in Montreal. It should be

TABLE 2

Language transfers of Others as reflected by the language of instruction in the English and French schools of the Montreal Catholic School Board, 1931-1972

1) The percentage distribution of new-Canadian students by language of school.[a]

Academic Year	Percentage in English Schools	Percentage in French Schools
1931-32	48	52
1938-39	57	43
1947-48	66	34
1955-56	69	31
1962-63	75	25

2) The distribution of pupils whose mother tongue* is neither English nor French, by language of instruction, 1967, 1971, 1972.[b]

Language of Instruction

Year	English		French		Total	
	N	%	N	%	N	%
1967-68	24,404	87.7	3,422	12.3	27,826	100.0
1971-72	26,435	89.2	3,198	10.8	29,633	100.0
1972-73	22,978	89.0	2,844	11.0	25,822	100.0

*Statistics on the mother tongue of CECM students are not available for 1967 or 1971; language spoken in the home has been used as an indicator of mother tongue for 1967, 1971 and 1972.

[a]Derived from tables in Émile Bouvier, "L'assimilation rampante est-elle irréversible? " in *Le Campus Libre* (Sherbrooke), vol. 1, no. 1, 1969.

[b]La Commission des Ecoles Catholiques de Montréal, Service de l'Informatique/Bureau de la Statistique: *Langue Parlée à la Maison*, September 30, 1967; *Langue Parlée*, September 30, 1971; Relevés, May 31, 1972.

recalled, however, that we are here speaking of Catholic schools only. Those immigrants who were not Catholic — Greek Orthodox for instance — and who opted for English are not reflected in Table 2. Which would suggest — the French Protestant sector being extremely small[6] — that the percentage of those

FIGURE 1

Percentage distribution of children enrolled in English-language schools in Quebec by religion, 1960-61 to 1970-71

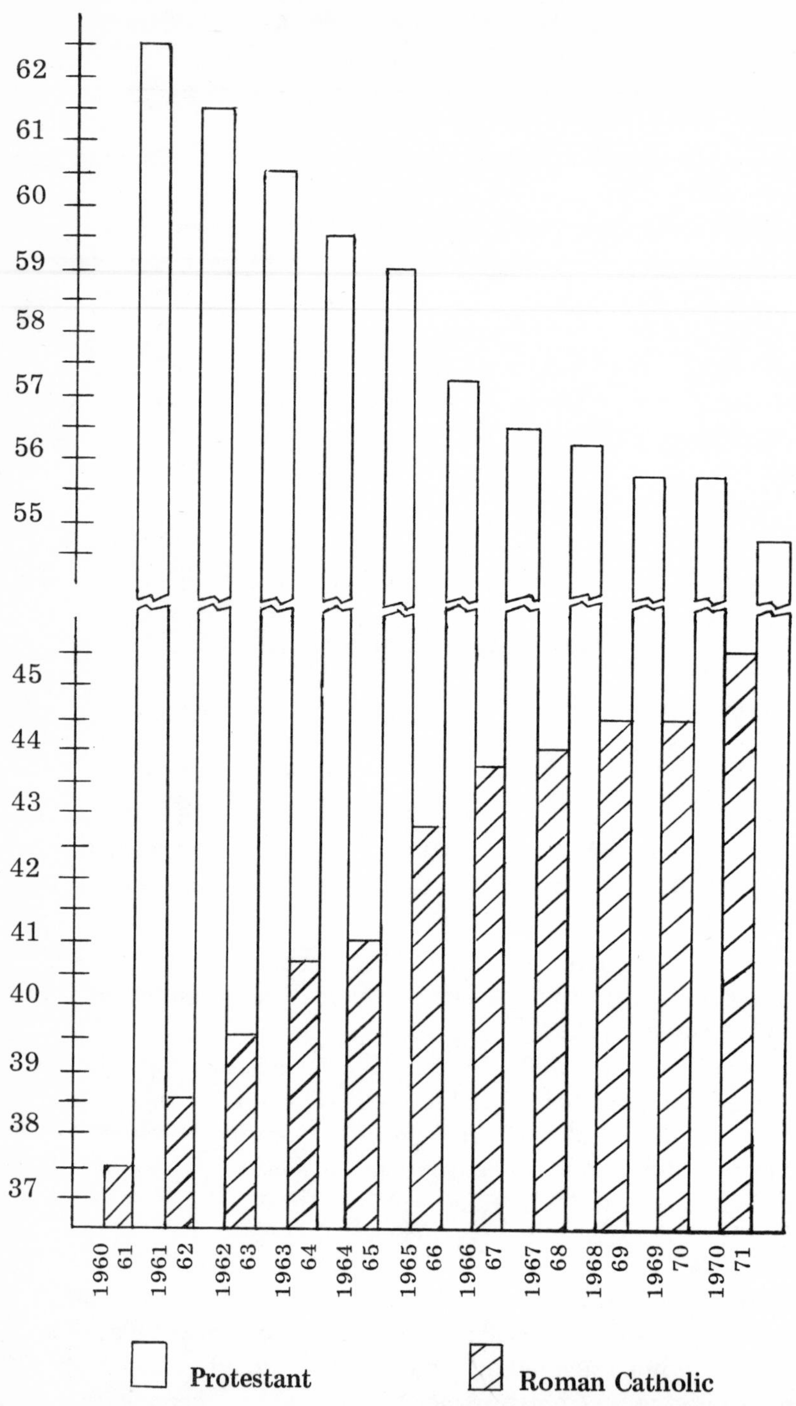

Protestant **Roman Catholic**

Source: *Report of the Steering Committee English Language Post-Secondary Institutions to the Heads of Institutions on Enrollment Projections to 1979-80, revised as of December, 1971, unpublished.*

transferring to English is greater than Table 2 would suggest (89% in 1972), Protestants and non-Catholics being more likely to assimilate to an English milieu. Nonetheless, the fact remains that the majority of non-English speaking immigrants to Quebec have been, since the war, Catholic. In fact, at the time of the 1961 census, 41% of all post-war immigrants to Canada were Catholic.[7]

In passing, it is worth mentioning that as a result of this Catholic immigration to Quebec and subsequent transfers to the English language, the religious composition of English schools in Quebec has changed dramatically (Figure 1). *Catholic students are now very close to constituting a majority of all students in the English language schools of Quebec* — a far cry from the day when English and Protestant were considered to be coterminous.

On the basis of the data presented in Tables 1 and 2 and subsequent qualifications, we have arrived at *an assimilation factor for Others, expressed in terms of the percentage transferring to English: 75% in 1961 and 90% in 1971.* Had we allowed fully for the fact that Protestants probably transfer to English even more massively than Catholics, we would have fixed the assimilation factors at an even higher level; on the other hand, our estimates rely heavily on what is happening in Montreal and census data evidence, comparable to that presented in Table 1, suggests that French fares better outside of Montreal than it does in the metropole.

We move on now to the second type of language transfer, transfers between English and French. Surprisingly enough, a substantial portion of Quebecers who declare themselves to be of British ethnic origin give French as their mother tongue — in fact, almost one in ten (9.4%) in 1961 and one in six (16.5%) in 1971. This percentage, as Table 3 indicates, has been growing steadily.[8] Although language transfers are obviously at the origin of this phenomenon, selective out-migration (the French-speaking British ethnics being, perhaps, less inclined to leave Quebec) and differential fertility (the former higher fertility of the French-speaking population) possibly account for a substantial portion of the growth in the percentage of British ethnics who are French speaking. To the extent that such is the case, these percentages over estimate assimilation from English to French.[9]

The second section of Table 3 attempts, on the other hand, to get at the extent of transfers from French to English. In this case, we have a small, but also growing, percentage of Quebecers who declare French ethnic origin and whose mother tongue is English, almost 2% in 1971. Again, to the extent that the considerations cited above apply (differential out-migration and fertility) these percentages probably under-estimate assimilation from French to English. *Nonetheless, relative to the size of the English-speaking population itself, those who are English-speaking and of French ethnic origin constitute a considerable proportion: 11% of the English-speaking population and 52% of those who are English-speaking but not of British ethnic origin.*

TABLE 3

Transfers between the English and French-speaking populations, 1931-1971

1) The percentage of the population of British and French ethnic origins that has French/English as its mother tongue, 1931-1971

Year	Population of British ethnic origin with French mother tongue		Population of British ethnic origin	Population of French ethnic origin with English mother tongue		Population of French ethnic origin
	N	%	N	N	%	N
1931	24,465	5.7	432,726	12,653	0.6	2,270,059
1941	33,351	7.4	452,887	25,723	1.0	2,695,032
1951	41,291	8.4	491,818	45,710	1.4	3,327,128
1961	53,383	9.4	567,057	68,339	1.6	4,241,354
1971	105,660	16.5	640,045	88,255	1.9	4,759,360

Sources : *Census of Canada 1931*, vol. IV, Table 61; *Census of Canada 1941*, vol. IV, Table 14; *Census of Canada 1951*, vol. II, Table 49; *Census of Canada 1961*, vol. I.3, cat. 92-561, Table 121; *Census of Canada 1971*, vol. I.4, cat. 92-736, Table 23.

As alluded to in note 4 (see page 73) a much more refined analysis of English-French assimilation in Quebec is now becoming available in the work of Charles Castonguay. Using transfers from maternal language to language most often used at home, broken down by age groups, he has been able to purify assimilation figures of transfers which did not take place in the lifetime of present members of the population; as well as being able to examine the progression of assimilation by five year intervals...a very considerable advance in the analysis of assimilation in Quebec.

We have just considered French to English transfers in terms of the total numbers of accumulated transfers in the population. However, as was the case for Others, there exist school statistics which allow us to delimit the phenomenon in terms of the most recent generation. The Quebec Department of Education now has available mother tongue and language of instruction data for the four school years 1969-70, 70-71, 72-73 and 73-74.[10]

During the four academic years covered by the data the French-speaking students in English schools rose from 1.6% to 1.8%, an increase of 13% in four years. The same students, looked at in terms of their presence in English schools, constituted 8.4%, 9.3%, 10,0% and 12.4% respectively of all students in English schools in the same four academic years.[11] Thus the most recently available figures indicate — on a Quebec-wide basis — a French-speaking presence in English schools of 12%. From region to region this percentage can and does vary considerably: in the 1973-74 academic year the percentage in the Eastern Townships (Region 5) was 19%; whereas it was 11% in the Montreal region.[12] In fact, outside of Montreal it is not rare to find English schools where from 30 to 50 per cent of the students are French-speaking.

The presence of French-speaking and, as we saw earlier in this chapter, of Others in English schools is growing. More precisely, in the school year 1971-72 some 31% of all students in English schools were French-speaking or Others. By 1973-74 this non-English presence had risen to 35%;[13] although, admittedly, most of the Others who constitute two-thirds of this presence are thoroughly assimilated, linguistically, by the time they finish the elementary level.

Mention of such a development inevitably leads to the issue of Bill 63[14] and its impact on assimilation and the direction of assimilation. Although the evidence presented here is not sufficient upon which to evaluate the impact of Bill 63, I would suggest that, in the Montreal area at least Bill 63 institutionalized a process already at work.[15] Yet the process now having been institutionalized, the fierce opposition of the English school systems (and all whose livelihood depends on them) to its de-institutionalization (Bill 22)[16] is quite comprehensible...they face a potential loss of one-third of their clientele. This is one of those lucky instances where defense of a principle (freedom of choice) coincides with the defense of organizational interest. Unfortunately, in such instances it is difficult for an observer to determine if it is indeed a principle or rather a rationalization of organizational interest which is being advanced.

Probing Quebec's Demographic Future

Any attempt to make predictions concerning Quebec's demographic future is extremely hazardous. Recent developments, both in terms of fertility and migration, have vitiated all contemporary predictions. In Table 4 we have presented three recent predictions of net migration made by Henripin and Martin, Robert Maheu and the Government of Quebec, respectively. All three were wide of the mark. Even the very recent government prediction in which the precaution of advancing five projections based on five different hypotheses failed — despite a range of 50,000 between the lowest and the highest forecast — to come close to the actual net migration three years later. Failure to anticipate the decline in net migration and the extent of the decline in natural increase resulted in pre-census estimates of the 1971 population that were all, to the best of my knowledge, too high.

Understandably, not being a demographer, I am hesitant about making predictions of any kind. What I will hazard is simply a number of comments concerning the short-term future of the immediate demographic determinants of population growth (natural increase, migration and assimilation). Although, it is not our purpose in this study to concern ourselves with the total Quebec population; nonetheless, any comment on the future of the English-speaking population of Quebec requires some discussion of the future of the overall demographic context of which it is a part.

Three years ago it was forcibly argued by one of Quebec's leading professional demographers, Jacques Henripin, that the then (1971) low crude birth rate was, to a very great extent (50 to 75%) a reflection of a change in the child-bearing calendar. The very low "momentary" crude birth rates reflected the introduction of a fashion whereby children are postponed. He went on to argue that these postponed children will eventually be born, and when they are, there will be a "momentary" high in the birth rate owing to the accumulation of these births, and those of the following generation, who, having been socialized to give birth "late" will be having their undelayed "late births at the same time".[17]

Since this thesis was argued in the 1972 Quebec Yearbook the expected upward correction in the crude or momentary birth rate (13.8 in 1972) has failed to give any indication of its imminent appearance. More recently Professor Henripin and the University of Montreal demography department have directed their attentions to the study of family size intentions. Combining previous technical extrapolations and family-size intention data Henripin, in a 1973 A.C.F.A.S.[18] communication, arrived at the conclusion that the cohort of Quebec females born in 1951 (23 years old in 1974) was unlikely to reproduce itself.[19]

To put the low Quebec crude birth rate in further perspective, it should be added that the fertility of married women in Quebec was, as late as 1969, as high as that experienced in Ontario.[20] In other words families were, in 1969 at least,

TABLE 4

A comparison of net migration projections for Quebec and the observed net migration, 1961-1971

Year	Observed net migration[a]	Net migration projections: Henripin & Martin[b]	Maheu[c]	Provincial government[d]				
				I	II	III	IV	V
1961	11,870	25,135	30,857					
1962	15,142							
1963	8,577							
1964	9,707							
1965	13,927							
1966	14,802			nil	20,000	24,000	30,000	36,000
1967	13,194			nil				
1968	1,915			nil				
1969	-14,507			nil				
1970	-36,365			nil		24,000	30,000	36,000
1971	-21,440	25,135	30,857	nil	20,000	32,000	41,000	50,000

[a] The observed net migration is the difference between population increase and natural increase for the relevant year.

[b] In *La Population du Québec et de ses Régions, 1961-1981* (Les Presses de l'Université Laval, Québec, 1964), Jacques Henripin and Yves Martin projected a total net migration of 502,700 for Quebec between the years 1961 and 1981, an average of 25,135 per year.

[c] Robert Maheu *Les Francophones du Canada 1941-1991* (Editions Partis Pris, Ottawa, 1970) estimated that net migration in Quebec for each five year period between 1961 and 1991 would approximate 154,285, an average of 30,857 per year.

[d] Estimations of the migratory balance in Quebec for the years 1966 to 1996 were formulated in the light of five different hypothesis: hypothesis I — no migration; hypothesis II — a steady migration of 100,000 per five year period; hypothesis III — a slowly increasing migration; hypothesis IV — an average growth migration; hypothesis V — a rapidly increasing migration (Government of Quebec, *Quebec Yearbook 1968-69*).

no smaller in Quebec than in Ontario. That this could have been the case despite the fact that Quebec has experienced lower total fertility (births over all fertile women) since 1960 (Table 6) is due to a persisting lower marriage rate and later marriage in Quebec. Nonetheless, despite the similarity of legitimate fertility rates in 1969, the trend in the two provinces (Table 5) would suggest that Quebec's rate (having experienced substantial declines in 1967 and 1968) has probably

TABLE 5

Age-specific legitimate fertility rates, Quebec and Ontario, 1931-1969

Year	Fertility rates per 1,000 married women by age groups							Legitimate fertility rate
	15-19	20-24	25-29	30-34	35-39	40-44	45-49	
Quebec								
1931	511.6	438.1	343.7	258.0	193.8	90.0	11.6	225.3
1941	496.3	430.7	323.0	222.3	151.7	66.1	8.5	201.1
1951	517.8	406.0	298.1	212.1	140.0	55.7	6.2	192.9
1956	544.7	417.1	301.8	202.4	134.4	51.1	5.4	187.5
1961	510.4	394.8	274.6	183.0	112.4	44.3	4.5	167.3
1962	504.2	381.0	264.0	177.9	106.0	41.2	3.8	160.8
1963	512.9	381.6	256.4	169.3	100.3	37.8	3.7	156.0
1964	493.2	370.3	247.5	163.1	93.2	36.0	3.6	149.7
1965	472.8	341.3	223.4	139.6	83.9	30.9	3.3	134.8
1966	451.7	308.2	198.1	120.9	70.5	25.6	2.8	119.4
1967	369.6	286.4	177.7	103.2	59.7	20.8	2.5	106.7
1968	322.5	264.4	170.7	95.8	51.0	17.4	2.1	98.9
1969	299.2	250.4	170.2	92.5	47.7	14.8	1.5	95.5
Ontario								
1931	510.3	322.1	214.4	144.2	90.0	34.8	3.7	129.9
1941	446.5	293.7	194.9	122.0	68.7	23.5	2.0	118.0
1951	488.0	312.2	219.0	143.7	78.4	24.5	2.0	137.8
1956	549.6	349.7	239.2	150.4	81.6	25.9	1.8	145.7
1961	543.0	354.4	240.1	147.4	76.4	24.6	1.8	141.6
1962	509.1	352.3	238.2	145.9	71.9	24.4	1.6	138.4
1963	485.3	342.7	235.1	144.8	72.5	23.5	1.5	135.8
1964	467.4	325.4	228.9	139.5	70.6	22.6	1.8	130.8
1965	478.6	289.1	204.3	123.9	64.6	19.7	1.7	118.2
1966	466.3	263.7	180.8	107.0	57.2	17.8	1.5	106.5
1967	410.2	256.3	169.2	95.7	49.5	14.6	1.1	99.2
1968	363.7	248.4	165.6	89.7	44.1	12.5	1.1	95.0
1969	346.3	244.9	169.9	89.0	40.9	11.5	0.9	95.2

Source : Dominion Bureau of Statistics, *Vital Statistics 1969*, cat. 84-202, February 1972, p. 75.

continued to decline; meaning not only fewer and later marriages in Quebec, but smaller families.

For reasons to be argued elsewhere[21] I strongly suspect that fertility in Quebec's predominately French-speaking population will remain below the level of self-perpetuation (total fertility of 2.2) for sometime to come. In passing, these reasons have to do with the consequences, in the specific social context of Quebec society, of a residual family male-female role segregation, a still very present but physically threatened extended kin structure and most important of all, the extensive and rapid penetration of North American life style values which are so instrumental in determining "needs" in the "needs-resources-costs" fertility model advanced by Hawthorne.[22]

However, the birth rate is only one of two components determining natural increase; future trends in the other component, the death rate, must also be considered. Quebec's population is aging; and as the major gains in life expectancy to be realized from improved medical service and public health facilities are close to being maximized,[23] the death rate will probably begin to rise in Quebec in the next decade. Such a rise will be a small but certain further drag on the rate of natural increase. In this respect at least, Quebec will not be at a disadvantage with Ontario.

We now come to migration, the most important factor in the balance. I can see nothing in the present structural arrangement of the North American economy to suggest that Quebec will experience anything but negative net inter-provincial migration in the seventies, with perhaps momentary reversals such as that experienced in 1961-1962. Whether Quebec will be able, as she has in the past, to offset this by international immigration is a mute point. Quebec has had, for several years now a ministry of immigration; and in terms of an increase in the number of immigrants entering Quebec, it has had very little impact.

An area in which Quebec might conceivably be successful in counteracting the present demographic drift would be in the retention of immigrants. To accomplish this, the integration of immigrants into Quebec society — (which means, in the present context, into the French-speaking community) — must be facilitated. Quebec's record in this respect is very bad, and getting worse, as was noted in the discussion on assimilation. Admittedly, the attraction exerted by English-speaking North American culture on the immigrant living in Quebec is very great, and increasingly pervasive.

Although I would be the first to argue that the language in which the best employment opportunities are available is the decisive factor in facilitating the integration of immigrants into one or the other of the linguistic communities, the attitude of the host population is certainly of consequence; and xenophobia has been a problem in French-speaking Quebec.

To-day, the major newly-arrived foreign ethnic group is the Catholic Italians. Whatever the reasons may be, a greater and greater proportion of them are being attracted to English schools: 52% of Italian children under the jurisdiction of the Montreal Catholic School Board were in French schools in 1943, by 1972 this

TABLE 6

Age-specific fertility rates, Quebec and Ontario, 1941-1972

Year	Fertility rates per 1,000 total women by age groups 15-19	20-24	25-29	30-34	35-39	40-44	45-49	Total fertility rate	General fertility rate
QUEBEC									
1941	21.5	137.7	189.9	157.4	114.3	50.6	6.5	3,389	102.0
1951	29.2	176.0	217.3	170.3	113.3	44.2	4.7	3,775	117.2
1956	32.4	193.6	227.6	168.5	112.7	41.7	4.2	3,904	119.5
1957	34.8	201.5	234.8	169.9	112.9	42.5	3.9	4,001	121.6
1958	34.0	201.2	233.4	167.2	108.2	39.6	4.1	3,938	118.7
1959	33.9	203.8	233.4	165.3	106.9	38.5	3.8	3,928	117.3
1960	33.3	199.6	220.5	158.2	100.3	37.3	3.7	3,764	111.4
1961	31.5	198.6	216.8	155.9	96.3	37.3	3.6	3,700	108.6
1962	29.9	195.2	208.9	151.9	91.7	34.9	3.1	3,518	104.4
1963	29.6	193.5	203.2	145.6	87.3	32.2	3.1	3,473	101.0
1964	27.7	185.0	197.5	141.0	81.5	30.9	2.9	3,333	96.7
1965	26.4	168.4	179.6	121.5	73.8	26.7	2.7	2,996	87.1
1966	25.4	150.2	161.2	105.6	62.3	22.2	2.4	2,646	77.4
1967	23.3	139.3	144.3	90.6	53.3	18.3	2.1	2,357	69.7
1968	22.3	128.2	137.5	84.5	46.1	15.4	1.8	2,179	65.0
1969	21.9	120.8	136.2	81.6	43.5	13.2	1.3	2,093	63.1
1970	20.7	113.9	131.0	77.4	39.0	11.8	1.0	1,974	60.2
1971	19.8	107.2	127.6	75.1	34.6	10.5	0.8	1,878	57.8
1972	17.9	94.1	124.7	69.9	29.6	8.4	0.7	1,726	53.3
ONTARIO									
1941	36.8	133.3	137.3	96.3	55.9	19.1	1.7	2,403	73.1
1951	60.1	186.4	181.8	125.2	68.1	21.0	1.9	3,222	99.8
1956	66.9	225.8	205.7	135.6	73.2	22.6	1.6	3,657	110.1
1957	73.0	228.7	209.0	133.3	74.2	22.6	1.9	3,714	111.5
1958	70.6	228.8	208.3	133.0	72.8	20.9	1.7	3,680	109.8
1959	71.7	239.5	214.7	133.3	73.0	20.8	1.7	3,773	111.2
1960	70.9	241.2	217.1	134.7	71.7	21.6	1.5	3,793	110.8
1961	69.5	239.8	211.6	134.2	69.8	21.9	1.6	3,742	108.3
1962	64.5	239.9	210.5	133.9	65.6	21.9	1.4	3,689	105.6
1963	60.3	233.7	208.1	133.1	66.2	21.1	1.2	3,618	102.9
1964	57.8	219.7	202.4	128.6	64.6	20.4	1.6	3,475	98.6
1965	58.3	192.9	180.6	114.5	59.3	17.8	1.5	3,125	89.0
1966	57.4	171.3	160.2	98.8	52.8	16.2	1.3	2,790	80.3
1967	53.4	162.0	149.2	88.6	45.9	13.4	1.0	2,567	74.8
1968	50.1	155.1	145.0	83.0	41.1	11.5	1.0	2,434	71.7
1969	49.5	152.5	148.4	82.3	38.3	10.7	0.8	2,412	72.0
1970	49.4	148.5	152.2	83.3	36.4	9.8	0.6	2,401	72.8
1971	44,2	137.2	145.9	77.4	31.2	7.8	0.4	2,220	68.4
1972	42.7	122.2	138.6	72.8	27.2	6.4	0.3	2,051	64.1

Source : Statistics Canada DBS, *Vital Statistics 1969*, cat. 84-202, February 1972, p. 72; *Vital Statistics 1972*, cat. 84-201.

percentage had fallen to 9%.[24] One obstacle, which is an indication of the kind of exclusivity an immigrant encounters in certain aspects of French-speaking life in Montreal, is the remarkable ethnic homogeneity of the personnel of French schools of the Montreal Catholic School Board as late as 1971. Of all the teachers at the elementary level in the French sector, slightly over 2% were Others (mother tongue other than English or French); as opposed to 23% in the English sector.[25]

The attraction and retention of immigrants will, I suspect, become a matter of urgent national concern for Quebec. The implication of this may well be that all "outsiders" may expect a warmer welcome in the future, at least in terms of government aid and official policy. Perhaps the reluctance of the French-speaking population to "accept" immigrants will be overcome, as Quebecers come to realize that if they wish to enjoy the freedom our consumer society accords the small family, and at the same time enjoy the benefits of a demographically stable society, then immigrants are indispensable. In point of fact, in 1970 immigration saved Quebec from an absolute population decline.

Reflections on the Demographic Future of the English-Speaking Population of Quebec

It should be noted that what is to follow is not an extrapolation of the statistical profile which has been the burden of this report. No projections have been attempted: we have, statistically, concerned ourselves with describing what has happened. The highlights of this demographic profile of the English-speaking population of Quebec are reviewed in the concluding "Summary". What follows immediately is simply a number of reflections and insights which arose in the process of preparing the report. They constitute comments — hopefully informed comments — on a number of considerations which may be of relevance to the demographic future of the English-speaking population of Quebec. No attempt has been made to assess the relative weight of the factors touched on; nor are they systematized in the sense that the relationships between them have been explored. Rather, they are presented as discrete and not necessarily connected points: points upon which the readers' commentary would be most welcome.

The first comment has to do with the Quebec born, or indigenous, element of the Quebec English-speaking population. They appear to be less able to adapt to a changed linguistic and social context than the non-natives. A long tradition of avoidance mechanisms and attitudes puts them at a serious disadvantage in the process of re-adaptation now necessary. This re-adaptation, in starkest terms, means that excepting the case of a select few occupations, a young English-speaking Quebecer must be able to function socially in the French-speaking milieu in order to find a job. The same culturally instilled resistance of adaptation does not seem to be as common among English-speaking international, or inter-provincial, migrants.

This leads us directly to the most basic migration consideration. It has only recently become apparent to young English-speaking Quebecers of job-market age that you must speak French in Quebec to find a job; consequently, an increasing number have, in recent years, decided to move to Ontario. The gradual displacement of English in the public and commercial arena is not something which has happened overnight, nor will French become the working language overnight. French is simply "becoming" the working language (at least given the continuation of recent social developments in Quebec), whether English-speaking people like it or not. Thus, the 27% of the five hundred person sample in the CBC sponsored Adcom Research survey[26] (the results of which were incorporated in the documentary "Les Anglais: A Look at the English in Quebec") who said they would leave Quebec the day French became the working language may never see themselves confronted with that "day". Rather, they will find themselves confronting, individually, and by degree, the penetration of French into their work milieu.

Concurrent with this process will be an increasing degree of bilingualism among the English-speaking population. Many young parents and youths themselves are ready to accept the need for a command of French; those who are not, are either old or will not be able to find satisfactory jobs in Quebec, and will voluntarily leave. The generation of English-speaking Quebecers now in elementary school, will, I suspect, be largely bilingual. In fact, in terms of the competition for jobs in Quebec, these young bilingual Quebecers may find themselves in a very advantageous position, particularly if what appears to be a decline in bilingualism in the French-speaking population continues.

Admittedly there is considerable resistance in some school boards to teaching French; to a large extent this is a reflection of the insecurity generated amongst English-speaking teachers and administrators by the present linguistic context. The spectre of a declining English-speaking population threatens their jobs; but an even greater threat is the potential acceptance by school boards of the arrangement whereby a part of the regular curriculum is taught in French in English schools. Such teaching could not, except in rare instances, be done by themselves. However, parental pressure (at least from those who intend to stay in Quebec) will, I suspect, bring most English school boards to take advantage of the legislative provisions which make possible the teaching of part of the curriculum in French.

In terms of the influence of the English educational system on the demographic future of English-speaking Quebec, the CEGEPs[27] present some rather interesting dimensions. The existence of the CEGEPs has provided access to educational opportunities which were never available to certain segments of the English-speaking population of Quebec. Demographers tell us that people with higher educational qualifications and transportable skills tend to migrate more often and further. It may well turn out that the CEGEPs are, and will, play an important role in accelerating out-migration among unilingual English-speaking Quebecers. And if this is the case, the continuing high enrollment and remarkably high transition rate from the secondary level to CEGEPs, may be, in part, explained by the fact that they are perceived as spring-boards out of Quebec.

A very particular structural facet of the post-secondary educational system in Quebec has also had a certain influence on migration. A Quebec secondary V (Grade 12) graduate can go to Ontario and, after one further year of high school, go on to university. Or, if he has completed the first year of CEGEP (C1), he can move directly into the first year of university in Ontario or the Maritimes; whereas in Quebec the law requires him to have graduated from a CEGEP before he can enter university. It is also true, however, that once in a Quebec university he could complete the equivalent of an Ontario four-year honour degree in three years. This arrangement has resulted in a substantial drain of English-speaking youths out of Quebec into post-secondary institutions in Ontario and the Maritimes.

Despite this, enrollment, as mentioned earlier, is holding up very well in the English CEGEPs, largely because of a high and improving transition rate from secondary V. The rate was 53% in 1969 and 62% in 1972.[28] Yet there is another factor at work contributing to the strong English-speaking CEGEP enrollments. At present somewhere between 10 and 15% of the students in several of the English CEGEPs are French-speaking.[29] Although the transfer of French-speaking students to the English-speaking system is not a new or sudden phenomenon,[30] Bill 63 which explicitly recognized the right to do so, has institutionalized a process which shows no sigh of relenting. Consequently one of the objects of a resolution passed at the convention of the Liberal Party of Quebec in the fall of 1972, a 1972 private member's bill in the National Assembly sponsored by the Parti Québécois and Bill 22 is to stop this "leakage" from the French-speaking educational system.

All of what has just been said must, I suggest, be tempered by a very important qualification. The English-speaking population of Quebec, in many respects (level of bilingualism, percentage of French-speaking students in English schools) consists of two distinct realities: the Montreal area or "metropolitan" English-speaking population, and the outside of the Montreal area, or "non-metropolitan" English-speaking population. When, for instance, we suggested that most young English-speaking Quebecers are aware of the necessity of learning French if one wishes to work in Quebec, some might want to argue that, if this is true, it applies only to the non-metropolitan English-speaking population.

Let me turn now to the question of the reception accorded by Quebecers to immigrants and English-speaking Quebecers wishing to participate more fully in the wider Quebec society. I suspect that English-speaking Quebecers who are prepared to work in French will be increasingly well-received. The reason for this belief is that articulated earlier:[31] the realization on the part of the French-speaking community of the absolute necessity of integrating marginal elements into the mainstream of Quebec society. Among these marginal elements will be, I suspect, a growing community of recent American immigrants.[32]

Finally, at one point in the work on this study it occurred to me that, given a number of economic and demographic "if's": a continued French-speaking out-migration at the present rate; continued English-speaking immigration at its present rate; a decline in English-speaking out-migration when the panic-stricken and the unilinguals are gone; a further drop in the rate of natural increase in the French-speaking population; a growing number of French-speaking Quebecers in English schools; continued assimilation of Others towards the English-speaking milieu; and a continuing integration of Quebec into the continental economy...it is not entirely preposterous that Quebec may — in a long-term perspective — become anglicized,[33] despite the current French cultural renaissance.

Summary

Despite the events of the sixties, the English-speaking (mother tongue) population of Quebec is holding its own. In fact in the last decade the English-speaking share of the total population declined less that it has in any decade of this century, with the one exception of the decade (1921-31). However, this new staying power is not a result of an improved rate of growth; on the contrary, the growth rate of the English-speaking population declined sharply in the last decade. What has happened is that the growth rate of the rest of Quebec's population has skidded down so far that, in relative terms, the very slow growing English-speaking population is holding its own — even if the turnover (movements in and out) within this population is considerable.

There is, nonetheless, a component of the English-speaking population that is not holding its own: those of British ethnic origin. The English-speaking population of Quebec now represents 13% of the total Quebec population, and only two-thirds of these are of British ethnic origin (1971). In terms of the total non-French-speaking population of Quebec — 20% of the total — English-speaking British ethnics represent less than one-half. Moreover, the rate of natural increase of the English-speaking population of British ethnic origin is now so low that it is no longer perpetuating itself. Among the reasons for this is the "old" age structure of this population. In fact, the entire English-speaking population is, relative to the French-speaking population (itself aging) old. However, the 1971 census revealed that in the decade of the sixties the age structures of the English and French-speaking populations began to converge; a process which has had and will have the result of improving the relative fertility of the English-speaking population.

If the age-structures of the two populations are now converging, one of the causes is the infusion of young blood into the English-speaking population which is made available by the assimilation of the children of those whose mother tongue is neither French nor English (Others). The relentless force of the attraction of the English milieu on those who speak neither French nor English has been much commented on. The superior attractiveness of English — a reversal of the pre-war situation — has intensified to the point where 90% of the children of Others are raised in the English milieu. The infusion of new young members that the English-speaking population receives from this source is so considerable that, according to our estimates, close to half of the internal increase in the English-speaking population can be attributed to language transfers.

But what of the "exodus" of English-speaking people from Quebec. First of all, it must be appreciated that all language constituents of the Quebec population — English, French and Other — experienced heavy outflows of population in the sixties. Heavy outflows in the sense that the numbers leaving were considerable and, in the case of the French-speaking population, more left than entered. The relevant demographic concept is net migration balance. We have estimated a net migration balance, for the sixties, of -116,000 for the French-speaking and +5,000 for the English-speaking population. With respect to the resident English-speaking Quebec population this unanticipated positive balance is deceptive. In fact the English-speaking out-migration from Quebec was considerable, at the very least 78,000 and more probably 100,000. English-speaking out-migration was, relative to French-speaking out-migration, at least two and a half times as intensive. How then does the English-speaking population end up with a positive net migration balance, given the extent of out-migration? The answer lies in the steady and substantial stream of English-speaking immigrants to Quebec. Were this factor — a disproportionate English-speaking immigration into Quebec — to cease to apply, the English-speaking population would be experiencing consistent migration deficits. If in addition, the English-speaking population were to attract only its proportionate share of those assimilated, the two major props of this population would be gone and it would — given the present rates of out-migration and natural increase among the native population — decline very rapidly.

One relatively unknown yet potentially crucial variable in this complex and dynamic demographic equation is the assimilation of French-speaking Quebecers to the English-speaking milieu. At the moment, the student population of English-speaking schools is 12% French-speaking. The reasons why these students are there, and the consequences in terms of their eventual cultural and linguistic affiliation are relatively unexplored.

The demography of the English-speaking population of Quebec, besides being of interest and concern to the English-speaking community itself, is, given the precarious demographic situation of Quebec, of considerable consequence to Quebec society generally. Quebec now has a very low growth rate; in 1972 growth was 0.5%, and there was even a month in 1970 during which the numerical size of the population declined. Out-migration, dwindling immigration and a still-falling birth rate have created a situation in which Quebec — at least if she continues to participate in an economy premised on growth — desperately needs bodies. She can no longer afford to exclude or neglect marginal ethnic or language groups living on her territory. More than likely Quebec will be constrained to adopt a more aggressive and constructive stance towards the integration of such citizens.

Integration into a mainstream culture strong enough to assure the social and economic conditions necessary for the retention of its members presupposes the survival and integrity of that mainstream culture. However, the survival and integrity of the mainstream culture in Quebec is by no means assured. In fact, a linear projection of the present rate of French-speaking out-migration, and natural increase, the linguistic composition of immigration and the direction of assimilation could very possibly lead to a demographic erosion of the French-speaking community. The necessary obverse of this situation is a long term anglicization of Quebec...a distinct possibility.

NOTES

[1] As a result of their parents' decision to send them to an English or French school.

[2] *Cf.*, note 4 below.

[3] Richard Joy (1972) in his discussion of the rate of assimilation of French-Canadian minorities in rural Canada and urban New England makes some pretty compelling remarks in this respect.

[4] In this regard there have been two notable studies, apart from Joy's more general work. One, Robert Maheu, *Les francophones du Canada: 1941-1991*, Ottawa: Editions Parti Pris, 1970, was done without the benefit of the language spoken at home data, and in the other Charles Castonguay and Jacques Marion, "L'anglicisation du Canada", in *Le Bulletin de l'Association des Démographes du Québec*, vol. 3, no. 1, March 1974, pp. 19-40, makes use of this newly available type of data.

[5] This qualification ceases to apply where the ethnic origin and the language cross-classifications are available by age group. Charles Castonguay, communication presented in the demography section of the Association Canadienne Française pour l'Avancement des Sciences conference, Laval University, Quebec City, May 9, 1974, using maternal language and language spoken at home, has begun to examine the data by age group.

[6] In 1972, 1,064 pupils, *cf.*, Claude Ryan "La proportion des francophones n'a guère changé depuis cinq ans dans les écoles de l'île de Montréal" in *Le Devoir*, jeudi, 11 janvier 1972.

[7] W.E. Kalbach, *The Impact of Immigration on Canada's Population: 1961 Census Monograph* (Ottawa: D.B.S., 1970) p. 162.

[8] Given the inordinate jump between 1961 and 1971 in the numbers of British ethnics whose mother tongue is French (52,383 to 105,660) the remarks on page 43 concerning the reliability of ethnic origin statistics almost certainly apply here; particularly in light of the fact that only 49,065 British ethnics gave French as the language most often used at home.

[9] Incidentally, the same considerations (differential out-migration and fertility) apply in the case of Others, which would suggest that the percentages of transfers to English and French found in Table 2 may, because of the cumulative nature of the Census data used, under-estimate the extent of transfers to English.

[10] Sources: "Données préliminaires statistiques de l'enseignement", nos 22-G-70-71-1, 22-G-72-73-1, "Statistiques de l'enseignement 73/74", 22-G-73, 74-1, *SIMEQ, Department of Education, Quebec* and Duchesne, Louis "La situation des langues dans les écoles du Québec et ses régions administratives

(1969-70 à 1972-73)" in *Bulletin de l'Association des Démographes du Québec*, vol. 3 no. 1 (March 1974) pp. 3 to 18. All of these sources include, in the tables we have drawn from, public and private pre-elementary, secondary and collegial level students, but not CEGEP and university students.

[11] *Ibid.*, percentages calculated from figures in Table 3 of Duchesne's article, p. 9 and 73 of "Statistiques de l'enseignement 73/74".

[12] *Ibid.*, Statistiques de l'enseignement 73/74", p. 73.

[13] *Cf.*, note 10 above.

[14] Bill 63, which came into force on July 1, 1970, permits parents to send children to the school of their choice, irrespective of language.

[15] This statement is based on an examination of the CECM document *Elèves du secteur français qui demandent de recevoir leurs cours en anglais* for the years 1970, 1971 and 1972 prepared by the Service de l'Informatique, Bureau de la Statistique.

[16] Bill 22, deposited for first reading in the National Assembly in May 1974 abrogates Bill 63.

[17] Jacques Henripin and Yves Péron, "Evolution démographique récente du Québec" in the *Quebec Yearbook 1972*, pp. 202 to 215.

[18] Association Canadienne-Française pour l'Avancement des Sciences.

[19] Henripin, Jacques "Fécondité récente et prochaine de la province de Québec", *Comptes Rendus du 41e Congrès A.C.F.A.S., 1973*, Vol. 40.

[20] *Cf.*, Table 5.

[21] A paper presented at the 1974 A.C.F.A.S. meeting, Demography Section, and now being revised.

[22] Hawthorne, Geoffrey *The Sociology of Fertility* (London: Collier-Macmillan, 1970).

[23] Quebec has recently achieved an infant mortality rate which is lower than that of the United States of America.

[24] Source: documents available from the Montreal Catholic Board, *cf.*, Table 2, footnote b.

[25] Source: Service de l'Informatique/Bureau de la Statistique, Commission des Ecoles Catholiques de Montréal, *Caractéristiques générales du personnel enseignant, en september 1971.*

[26] As reported in *Québec-Presse*, November 24, 1972.

[27] C.E.G.E.P. is the French abbreviation of "Collège d'éducation générale et professionnelle".

[28] Jan Morgan, "The English-speaking Québécois: A Statistical Analysis of Some Educational Problems", paper delivered at the 1972 Bishop's University Symposium on *The English-speaking Québécois: The Past and the Future*, November 22, 1972.

[29] *Cf.*, Caldwell, chapter 10, page 105.

[30] An examination of documents produced by the Service de l'Informatique/Bureau de la Statistique of the Montreal Catholic School Board

concerning transfers in their system for the years 1970, 1971 and 1972 (Bill 63 took effect on July 2, 1971) showed no appreciable acceleration in this, admittedly, short time span. Approximately 0.7% of the students in the French sector transferred in each of the three years to the English sector. However, more recent data for Quebec as a whole indicates an annual increase in the percentage of French-speaking students in English schools. *Cf.*, p.

[31] *Cf.*, Table 5, Gary G. Caldwell, *A Demographic Profile of the English-Speaking Population of Quebec 1921-1972*, Quebec: International Centre for Research on Bilingualism, 1974, p. 44.

[32] The number of American immigrants coming into Quebec increased steadily from 1,463 in 1951 to a level of little over twenty-seven hundred in 1970. In 1971 2,737 American immigrants represented 14% of all immigrants to Quebec and the most important national grouping in terms of country of origin. *Cf.*, Mireille Baillargeon "L'Atelier Immigration" (*Bulletin de l'Association des Démographes du Québec, vol. 3, no.1*).

[33] J.R. Mallory in his article "English-speaking Quebecers in a Separate Quebec" in R.M. Burns (ed) *One Country or Two* (Montreal: McGraw-Hill, Queens University Press, 1971) raises just this possibility, p. 133.

SECTION THREE

French as the Language of Instruction

CULTURAL DIVERSITY IN THE FIELD OF EDUCATION AND THE FUTURE OF QUEBEC*†

Introduction

In addition to its religious diversity and pluralism, the Quebec school system must face the problem of linguistic diversity and cultural pluralism. Quebec presents unique characteristics among the Canadian provinces. It is the only bilingual province, with both French and English acknowledged as the official languages in the Legislature and the courts of justice; French and English are also in current use, whether in advertising, in mass communications media or in the educational system. At the same time, Quebec is the only Canadian province with a French majority. Historically it was the centre of the French possessions in America; it remains the recognized centre of the French fact on this continent, and its French-speaking population — regardless of origin — constitutes a very large majority. Finally, in addition to the Indians and Eskimos, with whom we shall deal in the next chapter, Quebec also includes an increasing minority of groups of diverse ethnic origin whose members have immigrated more or less recently and who generally adopt Canadian nationality. The image of a Quebec at once bilingual, predominantly French and comprising a minority of ethnic groups of mixed origin is neither simple nor without ambiguity. And the complexity of this situation has repercussions on the educational system, involving its structures, its programmes, its philosophy and the demands that are made of it. It is now appropriate to study this major problem, of vital importance for the cultural future of Quebec. It is closely linked to changes in the demographic and socio-economic aspects of the Quebec environment — though these questions are not explicitly a part of our Commission's mandate — nor can it be discussed without taking into account the new awareness that has become manifest on this subject, especially during the last decade, as much throughout Canada as in Quebec.

---

*Chapter III, Report of the Royal Commission of Inquiry on Education in the Province of Quebec, Part III, *Educational Administration,* Quebec: Government of the Province of Quebec, 1966, pp. 89-115.

†Paragraph numbers and marginal headings have been omitted.

I. French and English Schools in the Quebec Educational System

The Quebec educational system consists of schools where instruction is given in French and schools where instruction is given in English. The French schools are almost all in the Roman Catholic sector, with only a handful in the Protestant; the majority of the English schools are in the Protestant sector, although a large group of English-language schools, particularly in Montreal, are in the Roman Catholic sector. The section of the population that is neither of French nor of British origin is divided almost equally between Roman Catholics and non-Roman-Catholics, but tends to place its children, as we shall see, in English-language schools, whether Roman Catholic or Protestant.

It has been pointed out that ever since the beginning of the English regime, there have been in the cities a few English-language private schools sometimes attended by French-speaking students.[1] In 1787, and then in 1801, the government sought to open public schools throughout the province. The French-speaking population generally did not welcome this overture, seeing in it a threat of assimilation, whereas centres with Protestant majorities turned it to greater advantage. The "fabrique schools", authorized in 1824, witnessed only a very limited development. The 1829 Act gave public schools their first start by creating trustee schools, of which there were 1,372 in 1835, but this beginning came to nothing following the withdrawal of grants. The English-speaking population, as a consequence of the interest it showed in public schools and because of the enterprise it demonstrated in this field, succeeded, despite all the difficulties that attended the beginnings of the school system, in maintaining and developing with a certain degree of continuity a system of English-language public schools. This is sometimes accomplished only by assessing itself to meet financial burdens which the French population often resisted, whether because of its poverty, or because it saw less clearly the advantages of a good education, or because it was unaccustomed to democratic institutions.

The school system that grew up in Quebec after 1841 was not established in terms of a division of the population between French-speaking and English-speaking Canadians. As we have seen, since this division corresponded, by and large, with the division between Roman Catholics and Protestants, legislation based the distinction between schools on their confessional rather than on their linguistic character. So also, the British North America Act assured religious groups protection for educational rights already established under law; but it accorded no protection to the French or English schools of the French or English-speaking groups which might find themselves in a minority in any one of the provinces. It is a matter of record that the French minorities outside Quebec have constantly encountered great difficulties in this connection. In Quebec, the school system gradually split into two substantially independent sectors, under the respective authority of the Roman Catholic and the Protestant Committees of the Council of Education, which at the outset had been conceived as a unified body. In this way the Protestant sector of public education was able to develop a system of English-language schools which have known none of the difficulties that have confronted the French minorities in the other provinces; and gradually a large number of English schools were opened in the Roman Catholic sector, with its French majority, the earliest of these intended to serve Irish and English immigrants of the Roman Catholic faith.

This educational dualism corresponded, during the last century, to the dualism of ethnic origin, French and British, which then existed. But toward the end of the nineteenth century, and especially since the beginning of the twentieth century and as a consequence of the two world wars, numerous immigrant groups of various other ethnic origins have come to settle in Canada and Quebec. As the following table shows, these new citizens today constitute in Quebec a portion of the population almost as large as that represented by people of British origin.

TABLE I

Distribution of the population of Quebec according to ethnic origin in 1961

Ethnic Origin	Number	Percentage
French origin	4,241,354	80.6%
British origin	567,057	10.8%
Other ethnic origins	450,800	8.6%

Source: The 1961 Census of Canada.

Over two-fifths of the population of Quebec is today concentrated in Montreal and its metropolitan area, the exact statistics being 2,190,509 of the 5,259,211 inhabitants. This is the area which has profited most from the process of urbanization and industrialization in Quebec. Being one of the principal ports of entry for Canada, and even for maritime traffic toward the United States, and lying close to the American border, Montreal is the head-quarters for a great number of industrial, commercial and financial activities which extended not only throughout Quebec but often over the whole of Canada. Thus problems of every sort that affect Montreal cannot fail to have vast repercussions on Quebec as a whole. The provincial capital, Quebec City, principally a governmental, administrative and political centre, the other smaller cities, the regions of low population density flanking the St. Lawrence River and the vast vacant stretches of northern Quebec find it difficult to counterbalance the massive population and economic power of the metropolis.

The proportion of Canadians of French origin is much smaller in the region of metropolitan Montreal than in the province as a whole; indeed it is only 64 per cent in the Montreal region, while it is 80 per cent in Quebec. On the other hand, the great majority of Canadians of other than French origin are concentrated in the metropolis, 66.6 per cent of those of British origin and almost all the Jews and Italians, as the following table shows:

TABLE II

Concentration in Montreal of the population other than French in origin

	In Quebec	In Montreal	Percentage in Montreal
Population of British origin	567,057	377,625	66.6%
Jews	104,727	101,460	98 %
Italians	108,550	102,724	93.5%
Other ethnic groups	237,523	169,240	71.2%

From the educational point of view, the French-speaking and English-speaking people of Quebec are not equally apportioned at the different levels of education. The disparity between the two groups is especially apparent at the pre-school and secondary levels. The English-language Protestant population has long had the advantage of a far greater proportional number of kindergarten classes than the French. However, as a result of a major effort by school commissions during the last three years, the gap is narrowing, as the following table shows:

TABLE III

Enrolments in Roman Catholic and Protestant public kindergartens

	Roman Catholics	Protestants
1958-1959	925	5,597
1959-1960	1,121	5,559
1961-1962	2,496	5,333
1964-1965	17,846	6,691

Source: Reports of the Superintendent of Education and, for 1964-1965, Hebdo-Education, Vol. I, No. 37, Feb. 5th, 1965.

This table has been drawn up in terms of religion rather than language, because of the lack of adequate information on the division between French-speaking and English-speaking pupils. The Roman Catholic school population, however, is 92 per cent French-speaking, and the Protestant school population is almost entirely English-speaking.

Yet the most serious disparity between the French and the English groups is found at the secondary level; the gap, however, has been rapidly narrowing during the last few years. To give an idea of this change and of the present situation, we must again turn to the apportionment of students as between Roman Catholics and Protestants. Of course, in considering Table IV, allowance must be made for the fact that a considerable number of French students in the Roman Catholic sector attend private secondary institutions; they are not included in the table. As a matter of fact, the percentage of secondary enrolments is slightly higher on the Roman Catholic side than the table shows. Even if this correction is made, it still remains true that the Roman Catholic population, in great majority French-speaking, is still backward in school attendance as compared to the Anglo-Protestant population; fortunately this backwardness is now in the process of being corrected. On the Protestant side, secondary enrolments will soon represent a third of the total elementary and secondary school population; the rapid increase of secondary enrolments in the Roman Catholic sector, to which must be added enrolments in private institutions, makes it possible to hope that here the same proportion will soon be reached.

TABLE IV

Enrolments in Roman Catholic and Protestant elementary and secondary schools in the public sector, from 1950-1951 to 1964-1965 (in thousands of pupils)

Roman Catholic Schools

	1950-51		1954-55		1960-61		1964-65	
	No.	%	No.	%	No.	%	No.	%
Elementary	518	91.2	647	90.4	797	82	890	75.9
Secondary	50	8.8	69	9.6	175	18.0	283	24.1
Total	586	100.0	716	100.0	972	100.0	1,173	100.0

Table IV continued. . .

Protestant Schools

	1950-51		1954-55		1960-61		1964-65	
	No.	%	No.	%	No.	%	No.	%
Elementary	51	72.9	75	81.7	82	73.1	87	69.1
Secondary	19	27.1	18	19.3	30	26.9	39	30.9
Total	70	100.0	93	100.0	112	100.0	126	100.0

Without pretending to deal with all the factors explaining this disparity, a certain number of them may be mentioned. Some of these are tied to history or the conditions of life in Quebec. The English-language Protestant schools often preceded the Roman Catholic schools of the French majority in the evolution of the public education system. Since the beginning of the nineteenth century, the English-speaking Protestants were thus the first to make use of state subsidies, particularly within the framework of the Royal Institution, against which the French-Canadian clergy was opposed for fear of assimilation. Only after more than twenty years did the French-speaking Canadians begin to make use of scholastic institutions dependent for their support on local responsibility. Ever since, this tradition has been developed with a certain continuity on the English side, whereas among French Canadians, particularly during certain periods, it encountered popular resistance against school taxes. It must be noted that English-speaking Canadians — generally better trained in business arrived here after the conquest with the intention of organizing commerce and industry, and influenced both by the tradition of British liberalism and by the example of American democracy and its educational institutions — were without doubt better prepared than the French-speaking Canadians to take into their own hands responsibility for the local organization of education.

With the pragmatism of shrewd administrators, the English-speaking Protestants adjusted themselves to a school system based on a division into two distinct sectors in such a way as to guarantee administrative and instructional autonomy and to make it possible for them to develop whatever schools they saw fit. Above all they wanted to develop a broad public sector intended to prepare a middle-class bourgeoisie of considerable size, adapted to the requirements of modern society. In order to accommodate the majority of English-speaking students, they agreed to levy upon themselves school taxes higher than those paid by the Roman Catholics for their public schools. In 1961, the Protestants had 18 elementary and a score of secondary private schools, which accommodated only 7,500 pupils, in contrast to the 115,000 enrolled in their public schools leading directly to university studies. The principle of centralization and amalgamation was adopted by the Protestant educational authorities as early as 1925, when, for financial reasons, a central Protestant commission in Montreal and, later on, nine others in various regions of the province were created. Because the confessional character of the Protestant schools was much less marked than that of the Roman Catholic, and because their secondary education was more complete, the Protestants were able to accept in the schools under their jurisdiction Jewish immigrants from a variety of countries — these now make up 20 per cent of their school enrolment — as well as other New Canadians from all over the world.

We have often called attention to the fact that, prior to certain recent proposals for coordination, educational structures on the French side had led to preferential treatment for a small group of students, who were expected to attend the university, and neglected the great majority of young people in the same age group, who, after their public school studies, were confronted with a blind alley. The educational structure of the English-language school system — at once more unified, more simple, more flexible and more democratic than that which has hitherto characterized the French-language system — has for a long time encouraged a more rapid passage from the secondary course to the university and has certainly played its part in producing a relatively higher rate of school attendance by English-speaking students at this level.

Nothing in the British North America Act expressly obliges a province to provide public schools for its French or English minorities. In Quebec, the English-language schools have made secure for themselves a right to exist, which no one today, as far as we know, would think of contesting. Because of its inclination toward confessionality, our school legislation has for more than a century favoured the development of these schools. They satisfy needs which the English-speaking minority can rightly consider legitimate. They have even established within the school system of the province a noteworthy educational tradition and have made valuable cultural contributions to the society of Quebec as a whole. Therefore we believe that the English-language public schools should not only continue to exist, but that they must also progress in their own fashion. We envisage this progress, however, within the framework of the reforms that we propose and in close association with the progress of the entire system of education. For this reason we consider it of the highest importance that the English-language schools become as completely integrated as possible within the rest of the system.

However, we think that if the existence or even the admissibility of languages of instruction other than French and English — the only two official languages of Canada and especially of Quebec — were recognized, the result would be a weakening of the public school system. Elective courses at the secondary level will permit the teaching of Italian, German and other modern languages; moreover, in the next section of this chapter, we shall advocate certain measures to help young pupils in elementary school whose families have recently arrived from abroad to adapt themselves to their new country, without thereby sanctioning other linguistic sectors in public education.

As is the case with the division based on religious belief, the division of schools based on language lies at the level of teaching and of the individual school and not at the administrative level. A clear distinction must be made separating financial and administrative from educational organization and management. We have proposed that wherever there are Roman Catholic, Protestant and non-confessional schools, there should be a director of education for each of these groups. Each of these educational directorates based on confessionality or non-confessionality will be duplicated whenever there exist French and English schools for one or more of the three types in question. It would seem desirable to us that these directors of education for French schools organize themselves into a French schools committee to study whatever problems they may have in common; the same thing would apply to the directors of education for English schools. This association based on the linguistic aspect of the schools, over and above religious differences, would stimulate coordination of studies, healthy rivalry and the general advancement of education. Regular joint meetings should likewise take place bringing together the French and English directorates in a given region, so as to permit the exchange of points of view and of the results of experiments which might be of value to all concerned.

The disparities to which we have already referred, truly regrettable for the French majority in Quebec, should not overshadow the potential contributions and the stimulus of friendly competition implicit, for the school system as a whole, in the present high level of development which has been achieved by education on the English side. It is a great asset for Quebec to have within its boundaries what is certainly the best known English university in Canada, two of the most celebrated university hospitals in North America and an English-speaking population with the highest school attendance record in the country. This English-language education of excellent quality in Quebec can only contribute to the progress of the province and its development, particularly in the academic field, once better coordination is established for all education. The existence in Quebec of an English-language education coordinated with French-language education can only encourage, throughout America, understanding of the type of education provided in the French schools of Quebec. The accreditation extended all over North America to students of Quebec's English-language schools should normally, in a well-coordinated structure, also be extended to students in French schools at the same level. It is therefore in our interest to retain this asset and to let it develop and progress. For its part, English-language education can greatly profit from close association with French-language education, were it only to benefit from educational experiments in other French countries and, at the level of higher education, from more frequent contacts with French-speaking university teachers and research workers. Even in the universities, the language barrier too often constitutes an obstacle to communication between those engaged in research. Cultural diversity therefore represents an important source of enrichment that can make the only Canadian province with a French-speaking majority also the most interesting and richest from the cultural point of view. Reform should not be directed toward curbing English-language education in Quebec, but rather toward encouraging French-language education to achieve as quickly as possible a comparable level in its quality and its services.

II. The Extent and Urgency of the Problems of French-language Public Education in Quebec

Canada's French-language culture is centred in the Province of Quebec. In the first place, Quebec is a French province by virtue of the majority of its inhabitants. In a total population of close to 20 million Canadians, approximately 6 millions have French as their mother tongue; 4,500,000 of these French-speaking Canadians live in Quebec, where they make up 80 per cent of the population. Because almost all of this French population traces its ancestry to colonists and soldiers who came to Canada under the French regime before 1760, it is proud of its origins and of the vast adventure of settlement and colonization which marked the beginnings of its history. Canadians of French origin were the first Europeans to settle in this country, to explore it and clear its forests, to found towns and villages, to establish institutions, to implant ways of life, handicrafts and a folklore still living today. In spite of their isolated position in North America, surrounded by more than two hundred million English-speaking people, they have developed a definite French culture, distinct from that of any other French-speaking group. Psychological and sociological traits, ways of thinking, and artistic cultural responses, collective attitudes have emerged and are developing, and they characterize and distinguish the kind of man who is a French-speaking Canadian. Though chiefly concentrated in Quebec, the French Canadians are also widely scattered throughout the other provinces, especially in New Brunswick, where the Acadians make up half the population, as well as in Ontario and other provinces. This French-speaking community has preserved its language and many of its customs despite the expanding pressure exerted on its culture by the presence in North America of millions of English-speaking people, despite the economic power of the United States, despite the fact that in their own country, French-speaking Canadians live among the English-speaking majority of Canada and despite the leading role played by the English community in the economic and business life of Quebec.

The cultural and socio-economic future of Quebec, that is to say, its desire not only to survive but to expand and to realize the aspirations that it now cherishes, rests largely on the system of education it will adopt. French Canadians must more than ever before understand that only by unifying their efforts in this direction can they make themselves capable of occupying the place in Quebec which should be theirs and to which they aspire. All the reforms that we have proposed throughout the preceding volumes and chapters are intended to improve the educational system as a whole; but because of the present inequalities and disparities between French and English education, and because backwardness in the French sector has been considerable and cumulative, greater efforts must urgently be devoted to it.

Among the principal aims to be pursued in order to improve the education of the French-Canadian community in Quebec, stress must first be placed on the urgent need to offer secondary education to the whole of this population. At this level in 1961-1962, the proportion of the age-group between 13 and 16 years enrolled in all types of secondary schools were as follows:

Roman Catholic boys	67%	Protestant boys	103%
Roman Catholic girls	68%	Protestant girls	104%

Since Protestant students are almost wholly English-speaking, and since the English-speaking group is rather small on the Roman Catholic side, it is easy to appreciate the effort that remains to be made by French-speaking Canadians. This means that necessary space must be provided and school facilities must be expanded, that teachers must be recruited and trained, that administrative personnel must be found, and that secondary education must be organized in the pattern comprehensive in order to accommodate more young people and keep them in school.

Moreover, a comprehensive education at the secondary level will better prepare the individual student for life, work and the responsibilities of the citizen. This it does by offering job preparation courses to those who need them — approximately 25 per cent of the school population — and by giving everyone some acquaintance with the techniques and the arts, as well as basic training in the sciences, the humanities, and the rudiments of the social sciences, particularly economics. Education at the Institute level will tend to be more specialized and will prepare more directly for employment in commerce, industry, the various branches of technology, office and secretarial work, etc. Thus everyone will be able to enter the labour market well enough equipped to earn his living and play a useful role in society. And everyone will have had an opportunity to develop his native aptitudes and will have been given a chance to prove his capacities and talents. In 1961-1962, in order to reach optimum school attendance at this level — which means keeping in school through at least the thirteenth grade some fifty per cent of young people 17 and 18 years old — it would have been necessary for the Roman Catholic French-speaking majority to double its enrolment of boys and to increase sixfold its enrolment of girls. Despite progress achieved since that time, there still remains much to be done, especially on behalf of girls.

It is urgent as soon as possible to open the doors of the French universities to all who are qualified to enter them. If the proportion of young men and women in the 20 to 24 year-age group who have the abilities needed for higher education is set at 17 per cent, then the goal must be to double the enrolment of French-speaking young men at the university level, while the present enrolment of French-speaking young women must be multiplied at least by 15. In addition, it must also be remembered that because of the population explosion, future generations will be numerically larger. Therefore tremendous efforts must be made in the French-language universities and in higher education. The structural reforms that we have proposed will result in easier access to pre-university studies for a greater number of young people.

The expansion of the universities must therefore be undertaken as soon as possible, bearing in mind the quarters and space that will be required, and giving immediate thought to recruiting the best students now working at this level so that they may serve as the professors of the future. University education will require increasingly higher qualifications, and a proportionally greater number of professors, even assuming that full care is taken to use them only in the most rational and economic and at the same time in the most fruitful manner in the field of research. Just as the number of undergraduates will obviously increase, so, the number of those doing research work at the various graduate levels will grow like a pyramid. It is therefore not only for the sake of its intrinsic utility that the scope of research must be broadened in the universities, but also because it is an integral part of university education, and because it is the natural consequence, of, and the necessary sequel to, undergraduate studies.

We have seen[2] that for schools that are mainly French and Roman Catholic, 3,880 new teachers must be trained annually between 1966 and 1972, and for the Protestant schools, 300 annually; these figures apply to secondary education, including technical instruction at this level. At the pre-university and vocational level, a total of approximately 500 new teachers annually will be needed during the same period, presumably divided in a similar proportion between the French-speaking Roman Catholics and the Protestants.[3] We have recommended that teacher training take place in the universities and in university centres. The creation of university centres and of at least one new French-language university will help apportion in more realistic fashion this burden and responsibility; therefore it is of urgent necessity to launch these institutions immediately. The "Ecole normale supérieure technique", established last year, is already training teachers for technical subjects and disciplines of all sorts at the secondary and Institute levels.

Evening, summer and weekend courses, primarily designed for adults, in 1961 included approximately 9,416 students in the French universities and 12,205 in the English. In 1965 the numbers involved were far greater because since 1961 a number of additional courses for adults have been instituted, both at the secondary level and in higher education. In a previous volume[4], we have indicated the increasing importance of this type of education in contemporary societies. By all available means, and by the use of audio-visual techniques, television, radio and other methods of mass teaching, it is essential to encourage retraining, advanced studies and a return to school by people of many types — technicians and professionals, men teachers, women who wish to return to work or find a job, persons desiring to make use of their leisure time, to seek a better understanding of the world in which they live, or to add to their own knowledge.

At all levels of education, it is necessary to develop, not only knowledge of economics and business practice as well as a spirit of initiative in economic and social life, but also a sense of civic responsibility in general. It would seem that education has often been particularly deficient with regard to the inculcation of a sense of social responsibility, a feeling for the common good. Reverence for the privileges associated with a given profession, a given social group, a given type of education can act as a serious impediment to the development of the French-Canadian community. Among French-speaking Canadians, those in established positions often lose sight of the urban and rural masses which still suffer from ignorance and poverty; but the culture of a community cannot be maintained or developed without concern for the condition of the masses and without seeking to better it. The essence of French-Canadian culture is first of all to attempt this in the field of education and economics. The school has the duty of awakening children to these realities so that they may play their proper part both in Quebec and elsewhere; it is important to give them a feeling of belonging to the community, which they themselves must help to improve.

Before giving thought to the protection and development of the French-speaking cultural community, it must first be asked to what extent it really is French-speaking and truly desires to be so. During the past few years, several organizations and important public figures have become aware that the French language has problems in the Quebec environment. There have been many demands for the state to enforce improvement of the quality of the language. Language is the means of establishing contact between citizens, between the state and the people, and it is the primary tool of education and of culture. It is the task of the state to protect it, to regulate its official use, to encourage its improvement and the fullest possible development of the culture it expresses. The government of Quebec has already initiated a basic effort in this direction by creating an "office de la langue française" and by establishing cultural relations with other French-speaking countries. The sociological and psychological role of the language used by the people is of essential importance. Any education truly reflecting national aspirations must above all depend on language. A community whose language is defective is a community whose intelligence is shackled, whose entire psychological outlook is impaired, whose distinctive character is threatened and diminished. In the chapter on the teaching of the mother tongue[5], we stressed the importance of the socio-economic context, of the working environment, of all managerial activities and of bill-board advertising as being included within the protection which the state must extend to the language used by the majority of the people of Quebec. In spite of the efforts of the schools, the French used in Quebec will continue to deteriorate in lamentable fashion if energetic and dynamic measures are not rapidly adopted to safeguard it and to improve its quality. The French-speaking community and its culture in Canada will not elicit the respect of others until they themselves have achieved sufficient self-respect to insist upon and use everywhere a language of which they can be truly proud. This is a fundamental ingredient in personal and collective dignity.

Education, from kindergarten to university, will not command the respect of those who receive it unless it is transmitted in acceptable language. All the areas of knowledge — mathematical, scientific and technical as much as literary or philosophic — can be taught in a truly formative way only when they are based on clear, correct and precise expression, indicating an exacting mind and a sensibility able freely to externalize itself. In many cases, even university teaching is subject to criticism on this score. At all levels, reform, awareness and personal dedication are necessary.

In the preceding section of this chapter, we proposed that the director of education for French Roman Catholic schools, the director of education for French Protestant schools and the director of education for non-confessional French schools constitute, in each regional commission, a French schools committee; the directors of education for the English-language schools will form a concomitant committee. We believe that this French schools committee in each regional commission must be invested with full responsibility for the protection, the progress and the quality of the French used in the schools. This responsibility must include some control over the choice of teachers, and over regulations, instructions and publications circulating in the schools, over posters, and over the language used in the corridors and during recreation. Methods can be found which, without indulging in petty or officious meddling, or encouraging preciosity, will arouse among teachers and students a taste for succinct, clear, correct and accurate speech. This French schools committee should also, and even more, be concerned, with the various reforms already listed through which the education imparted in the French schools of Quebec may be able to make up for lost time — full school attendance, preparation for life and for work, opportunities for admission to higher education for all those having the necessary qualifications, development of research, adult education, development of a civic sense, development of research and knowledge in economics.

In our opinion, the cultivation of a national feeling among French Canadians should above all rest upon the cultivation of a feeling of social solidarity. Only to the extent that each individual becomes capable of grasping the problems of Quebec — and especially those connected with education, envisaged as governing the future of the entire community — can that which is called French-Canadian culture cease to be something more or less theoretical, entrusted to the care of a few small groups of intellectuals. By basing their policies on the active participation of parents in every sector of society, and on public opinion in general, those in charge of the school system will eventually place the problems of education in their true context and orient them truly toward the common good. Over and above local loyalties of all sorts, over and above its ingrained attitudes, the French-speaking Canadian community should rediscover the solidarity it needs in a determination to make the education offered to all the principal means of its survival and fulfilment. It should be willing to make the financial sacrifices involved in the progress of education at all levels. It should be willing to act in unison so as to attain its essential common objectives. There must be a general awareness that the renewal required in public education involves the responsibility of the French-Canadian community as a whole, as well as of all those concerned with education. This quickening and this renaissance will require the concrete cooperation of everyone, the sacrifice of various selfish interests and local loyalties, an accurate understanding of the challenge which the French-language public school must meet. At all levels and in all their day-to-day activities, every director of studies, every school principal, every French-speaking teacher must be aware of the stakes at issue.

III. The Problems of English-Language Education

The English-speaking community of Quebec also faces a challenge, but one that is quite different in its terms. The first elements in their community came from Great Britain and the American colonies shortly after the conquest of 1763. Initially, they took up residence in the cities of Quebec and Montreal; somewhat later, during the American Revolution, the Loyalists settled areas bordering New England and New York; and prosperous fur merchants bought a number of seigniories at about the same time. During the early part of the nineteenth century, a small but steady stream of immigrants from England, Scotland and Ireland brought new English-speaking people to farms and cities; this flow of immigrants has never ceased. But during the last century, two important changes have taken place. First, the "colonization" movement among French Canadians led a large number of them into the Eastern Townships, where they bought the land of English-speaking farmers who, in turn, moved to the cities, especially Montreal. The second change resulted from the heavy immigration of new citizens of non-British origin, most of whom also settled in the region of Montreal. As a result, of more than one million English-speaking people, almost half are not of British origin. A little less than two-fifths of the people of British origin are Roman Catholic, whereas those of non-British origin are divided almost equally between Roman Catholics and non-Roman Catholics. Two groups that are both almost entirely concentrated in Montreal require special mention. The first of these — the Jews — number more than 100,000, and some families among them settled in Quebec during the nineteenth century; the second — the Italians — slightly larger than the Jewish group, has grown very rapidly since the end of the last war. Obviously, in so diverse a population it is not easy to find any common denominator for the organization of education.

For a century, the Protestant and Roman Catholic educational systems have developed along different lines. The Protestant system was conceived for the training of an active and enterprising middle-class bourgeoisie. Inspired by the example of New England and Scotland, where the principles of Calvinist education were rigorously applied, the Protestants here offered an education centred on the mother tongue, the sciences and business, and its curricula prepared not only for the liberal professions but, perhaps principally, for business, commerce and engineering. Protestant schools and universities were quite readily able to accept non-Protestant students. It is also interesting to note that, in response to pressure by a few daring pioneers, Protestant institutions began to receive young women before the end of the nineteenth century. High schools for girls were founded in Quebec and Montreal shortly after Confederation; Royal Victoria College was founded at McGill University in 1884. During some thirty years thereafter, a number of young women were able to enrol in the professional faculties; one of the most remarkable of these was Dr. Maude Abbott, who became an eminent professor of medicine at McGill University and gained an international reputation as a specialist in heart diseases. It is in the light of such instances that one can somewhat better understand the deep attachment of the English-speaking population for the educational institutions it built up over the years.

But certain problems that require special attention confront English-language education. What was said in the preceding section on the need to protect the purity of the French language and culture also applies on the English side. Though it is true that the English population of Quebec has close cultural ties with the 200 million English-speaking people of North America, this in no way constitutes a guarantee of its security. The voice of this small community is subject, with little that can act in its defense, to the pressure of American mass communications media and is utterly submerged within the vast chorus of which it forms a part in Canada, and even more in the United States. When the English-speaking people of Quebec seek to protect the purity of the language in their schools, they must take into consideration that more than half of those who speak English here have no real cultural and literary attachment to this language, and that it is for them merely the simplest and quickest means of identifying themselves with American civilization. A constant battle must therefore be fought against the tendency to reduce teaching to utilitarian programmes, without depth or richness, and giving more attention and importance to the spoken than to the written language. The English schools must not yield to these pressures and lose all interest in English culture.

As we have already said in the preceding volumes, English educational institutions must raise the quality of their education. To accomplish this, educational methods must be improved, libraries must be developed, and a better use must be made of audio-visual techniques. The student will be required to devote more time to the study of French, which is the language of the majority in this province, and also to that of other modern languages, to acquire a deeper knowledge of the natural and social sciences, and to develop more completely his manual and artistic capacities. The time devoted to the teaching of the English language cannot be increased, but it can be used more effectively, and all programmes of study at all levels should be revised with this in view.

The general pattern of English-language education, both Roman Catholic and

Protestant, obviously will conform with the pattern of the school system of the province as a whole. Even though a large proportion of English-speaking children complete the secondary course and go to university, the number of those who seek technical education and government employment remains far below what might be expected. Taking advantage of English predominance in economic life and of less advanced school attendance on the part of the French-speaking population, English-speaking youth in Quebec generally has found it quite easy to obtain employment in business and industry after finishing high school, even without necessarily having technical or vocational training. This situation is in process of changing rapidly. The need for specialized technicians in increasing, but at the same time the level of required qualifications is also rising, and the number of French Canadians qualified to fill these jobs is greatly increasing. Consequently English educational institutions at all levels will find themselves obliged to intensify their efforts to make their curricula and educational methods conform more closely with these new demands. English-language education should above all exert itself to establish Institutes offering a two-year composite course before young people enter the labour market or the university. This runs counter to the habits and traditions of the English-speaking people of Quebec, who until now have given too exclusive a preference to the preparation of young people for college, without sufficient concern for the considerable number of students who need practical training for life.

Adult education has until now been made available by a variety of institutions, but this vast educational area calls for better coordination. For some years government services supplemented by various voluntary associations, have offered a programme of education in the English language to New Canadians. McGill University has over 10,000 students enrolled in its courses for adults, most of which are given in the evening and do not lead to any official diploma. At Sir George Williams University, almost the same number of part time students is enrolled in courses leading to a high school diploma or to university degrees. Certainly these services constitute an auspicious beginning, but they are inadequate at a time when the demands and the mobility of the labour market and the needs resulting from increased leisure require a far more extensive effort. Additional language courses will have to be organized for students wishing to learn English or French; in this sphere, collaboration between several institutions will doubtless be necessary. Provision must likewise be made to meet the growing demand on the part of adults for specialized courses preparing for various branches of technology, and appropriate courses in the Institutes and the universities must be provided. But it should always be remembered that educational problems in the field of continuing education are far different from those of regular education. It will therefore be necessary to train groups of teacher specialists for this type of education. These teachers should also be thoroughly versed in the special problems of Quebec and the cultural heritage of French-speaking and English-speaking Canadians.

This same knowledge of Quebec will be required of all teachers. We have several times expressed regret over the unhappy consequences of the division of Quebec's school system into isolated sectors between which there exist no means of communication or of consultation. In the last analysis each sector considers itself autonomous, and those who direct its destinies are in danger of overlooking the broader aspects of the school system as a whole. There is no doubt that in the past the English-language and French-language groups lived and evolved independently of each other, having only rare and often superficial contacts. Each of the two English sectors of education, Protestant and Roman Catholic, believed that it could develop alone, without relation to the other. This was as true of higher education as of the elementary and secondary schools. The members of this Commission realize that they learned many things about each of the two sectors, and they believe that the two linguistic and cultural groups have much to learn from one another. We therefore believe that in the academic field means of regular communication must be developed and maintained between the two communities, so that the aspirations and attitudes of both can be better interpreted and better understood.

IV. The Minority Ethnic Groups in the School System

Alongside the French Canadians and the Canadians of British origin who have dwelt together in Quebec since 1763, immigrants of various other ethnic origins have arrived since the end of the nineteenth century to settle in Canada or in Quebec. Almost 400,000 of these immigrants have established themselves in the Province of Quebec. These varied groups of new citizens, the great majority of whom take up residence in the Montreal region, generally turn toward English-speaking rather than French-speaking Canadian culture; this preference is especially noticeable with regard to schooling. Here is a situation which must force the French-Canadian majority in Quebec to wonder about the reasons for this choice, about its own attitudes and about the part the school should play in this connection.

The problem of choice between French and English-language culture on the part of New Canadians first became manifest at the turn of the century. Even though at that time there were a number of Jewish children in the French or English Roman Catholic schools, most of them even then attended the English Protestant schools in Montreal. The same tendency has continued to apply to the most recent waves of immigrants. Today even French-speaking Jews recently come from North Africa are likewise sending a large number of their children to the English Protestant rather than to the French Roman Catholic schools. The English Protestant schools also take care of Catholic children of German, Ukrainian, Scandinavian and other origins. Except for those belonging to the Jewish community, the Protestant School Board of Greater Montreal has no statistics regarding the ethnic origins of its students. It is a matter of record that of the 63,194 students of the Protestant School Board of Greater Montreal, 17,725 are Jewish, as are 20 per cent of the teachers in these schools. Moreover, the five French schools under the Protestant Board in Montreal accommodate a certain number of French-speaking children of Canadian, European or other origin.

In the Roman Catholic sector, it is still toward the English schools, originally intended in the main for the education of Irish youth or for Roman Catholics of British origin, that New Canadians turn, as is shown by the figures given in Table V for Montreal. Even the majority of those for whom French would normally be the most natural language to adopt — if this choice were based on linguistic similarities alone — prefer English schools. In general, immigrants in Montreal who choose the Roman Catholic public schools have a much greater tendency to place their children in the English Roman Catholic schools under the jurisdiction of the Montreal Catholic School Commission than to place them in French schools. Consequently in the English-language Roman Catholic schools in Montreal there are today far more children of various other than of British ethnic origin.

TABLE V

Distribution of students according to ethnic origin in the French and English schools of the Montreal Catholic School Commission 1962-1963

Ethnic origin	French schools		English schools		Total
	Number	%	Number	%	100%
English and Scottish	1,028	11.0	7,262	89.0	8,290
French	149,814	96.9	4,832	3.1	154,646
German	137	17.2	658	82.8	795
Hungarian	127	19.9	513	80.1	640
Irish	578	17.7	2,689	82.3	3,267
Italian	4,175	25.2	12,381	74.8	16,556
Polish	261	12.2	1,976	87.8	2,137
Portuguese	89	16.4	454	83.6	543
Spanish	63	23.1	210	76.9	273
Ukrainian	124	8.2	1,378	91.8	1,502
Others	1,070	37.0	1,821	63.0	2,891

Source: Bureau of Statistics of the Montreal Catholic School Commission.

Various reasons, some of which are sociological, political and psychological, and of which others derive from the schools themselves, explain this preference of the majority of New Canadians for English-language schools. First of all, the immigrant who comes to Quebec often lands with the idea that he is immigrating, not specifically to Quebec, but to Canada, or even to North America, and that, if he does not find in Quebec what he is looking for or what he expected, he will go elsewhere, to another Canadian province or to the United States. Under these conditions, it is easy to understand that he will naturally prefer the English language, which assures him the mobility he desires. In addition, many European immigrants may already have had an opportunity in their homeland to learn English, a second language more widespread than French in many countries, especially since the last war. But another factor, whose influence cannot easily be measured, certainly plays its part. This is the fact that in Quebec itself, economic power belongs to the English-speaking minority. After all his sacrifices of expatriation and breaking established bonds, the immigrant naturally counts on bettering his lot. He has no interest in identifying himself with that part of the population which is limited mainly to subordinate positions, which has little share in the management of industry, and whose income is unquestionably lower than that of a powerful minority.

That many immigrants are little aware, when they decide to settle in Quebec, that they are coming to a province with a French majority may also depend on the fact that the federal immigration services, in Canada and abroad are basically concerned with the whole of Canada rather than with any particular province. Indeed, this is why several of the provinces play an active part in immigration and entrust responsibility for this important problem to a provincial department, something which Quebec has not yet done. The field of immigration is wide open for provincial action, and here joint federal and provincial efforts can be very fruitful, particularly for a French province in its dealings with countries of Latin culture such as Italy, France, Spain, Portugal, Switzerland, Belgium, Lebanon, the countries of North Africa, etc.

Finally, the long continued isolation of French Canadians, the defence reflexes arising from their minority situation in Canada as a whole and their economic inferiority in Quebec have without doubt poorly prepared them to extend a generous welcome to new citizens whose ways of life and whose mentality differ from their own. Organizations of French-Canadian volunteers, subsidized if necessary by the provincial government, could have played a great role in attracting New Canadians to the French side of Canadian life by means of services designed to welcome, give assistance and supply information about the political institutions of the country, about the rights of citizens, about the advantages of social security. Such organizations should play an equally important part with relation to the people as a whole, in order to accustom it to an attitude of understanding, sympathy and generous assistance toward these new citizens and to accustom it to see in them essential constituent elements in the population of Quebec, as full fledged citizens who must fully participate in its social and political life, today as much as tomorrow. It should not be forgotten that often an immigrant has been attracted to Canada, where certain of his relations and friends had already been living for several years, because of a personal interchange of information and opinion. The more welcome New Canadians feel in Quebec, especially among French-speaking citizens, the more will they make this known in their native lands, and the better will they prepare prospective immigrants to consider the possibility of casting their lot with the French-speaking majority, as, in the natural course of events, a considerable number should be expected to do.

In the preceding section of this chapter, we have indicated how urgent is the need to institute reform on all fronts so that French-language public education may reach a level comparable to that of public education in the English Protestant schools. It is not surprising that, when they see such differences in services and in quality, New Canadians should have been inclined to choose the better equipped schools, in which the teachers are ordinarily better prepared. For a certain number of New Canadians, the problem of choice between a French or an English school will be settled the moment French-language public education is of unquestionable quality and gives access to all university faculties. Only then is it reasonable to think that they are truly free to make a choice between French and English public schools of comparable merit.

In addition, the Roman Catholic character of all the schools provided for French Canadians may have made these schools practically unacceptable for French-speaking non-Catholics. By contrast, the Protestants, already accustomed within Protestantism itself to the pluralism of its constituent sects, tend toward an education broadly Christian in character, but able to accommodate without too much difficulty not only Christians of the various Protestant denominations but also, and notably, children of the Jewish faith or children for whom their parents normally would have sought non-confessional schools. The creation of non-confessional schools, as recommended in the preceding chapter, will offer, as much on the French side as on the English, a choice of education to suit all general objectives and all specific tastes.

The problems connected with the adherence of New Canadian citizens of neither French nor English origin to either the French-speaking or the English-speaking cultural group are far from being simple, as we have seen. Most of the questions which arise lie outside the explicit mandate of our Commission, but the specifically scholastic aspects of the matter cannot be passed over in silence. Apart from the educational and structural reforms that we have just discussed, other steps helpful in working out a solution merit mention. When it is feasible, and as the administrators of the English Roman Catholic sector are at present doing, children of the same ethnic origin might be brought together in a single school within the French sector. For instance, since the Italians in Montreal are often concentrated in certain sections of the city, it would be possible to gather them together in French schools, with teachers who know their language. Instruction in English would have to be excellent in these schools, and during the elementary years, it might even be possible to teach religion in the mother tongue, the elective system at the secondary level later permitting these children to continue more advanced studies of their mother tongue. So also, at the level of adult education, the Institutes and the universities should make every effort necessary to attract new citizens who now mainly attend the courses for adults offered by English-language institutions. It will be easier to attract the immigrants of the future to French culture than it is to attract those already established here, of whom a considerable number have already chosen to link themselves with the English-speaking group; yet a major effort will still be required, since what must be done is to reverse tendencies and habits already of a good many year's standing among these ethnic groups.

Even when French public education has the requisite quality, even when French-speaking Canadians from all levels of society themselves acknowledge this quality and are satisfied with it for their children — as is the case with the English-speaking Protestants with regard to their public schools —, even when there are French public schools able to meet all the varied inclinations and aspirations of parents, even when all French public schools practise, in their attitude toward New Canadians, a policy of generous welcome, especially in great centres like Montreal where the immigrants prefer to settle — when all these conditions are met, there will still remain practical problems to be solved in encouraging New Canadians to adopt the French manifestation of Canadian culture at the educational level. The first problem is that of instruction in the second language. One of the reasons which induce immigrants to place their children in the English-language schools is that there they will learn the language spoken throughout most of North America. It is likely that if the teaching of English in the French schools were promptly improved, especially at the level of studies where this teaching could not enter into conflict with a thorough knowledge of the mother tongue of French-speaking students, there would be fewer parents, not originally English-speaking, who would be inclined to enrol their children in English-language schools. In a preceding volume[6], we have pointed out some of the problems raised by this aspect of education in a bilingual country and taking into account the special position occupied by the French language in Quebec. If it is useful for a citizen of Quebec to know English well in the midst of an America with 200 million English-speaking people, it should in turn be equally natural for a Quebec Canadian who is English in culture to know French well and to speak it fluently. In some English Protestant schools on the Island of Montreal, in addition to regular instruction in French, certain courses — geography for example — are taught in French, so as to make certain that students obtain a better knowledge of this language; such experiments and practices could find wider application. French-language courses should also be offered to English-speaking adults, especially those engaged in the public services.

Just as the Protestants receive Jewish students and teachers in their schools, or as English-speaking Roman Catholics have observed a policy of very warm welcome with regard to New Canadians, particularly Italians, so should the doors of the French public schools be opened wide to immigrants of every origin. To effect this, many French Canadians will have to make a real effort to break a traditional inclination to keep to themselves, to be suspicious of newcomers. In a country like Canada, which must rely on immigration if it is to grow and develop fully, it will henceforth be necessary to accept willingly and eagerly the contribution that these new citizens can make to Quebec.

Culture and the French fact in Quebec will have to lean more and more on those immigrants who choose to become a part of the French-speaking cultural group. And it should occasion no surprise to find a French-speaking citizen of Quebec with a name that is neither French nor English in origin. Situations of this kind — often encountered in European countries with very ancient civilizations— will become commonplace in a country like Quebec, which must count on heavy immigration if it is to reach full development. Like that of the United States, a culture can enrich itself from many varied ethnic sources and through contributions by people of every origin. Moreover, it is to be hoped that English-speaking Canadians in Quebec, just like the New Canadians, will be able to participate in the development and flowering of a French culture, without thereby losing their own ethnic and cultural character. The more substance the French personality of Quebec acquires, the more these situations can multiply. French-Canadian culture cannot be based solely on the descendants of Canadians who lived here under the French regime; immigration will continue to be one of the means by which our province is populated, bringing it not only the manpower needed for its development, but also a notable renewal of its cultural strength.

In the same manner that the structures we propose are designed to respect religious freedom while safeguarding the unity of the school system, so likewise we believe that within the school system itself the cultural diversity inherent in the traditions of Canada and of Quebec can be respected, and collaboration between the French and the English schools can be encouraged under a unified administration. Even though the state has the right to enact regulatory measures concerning language, it would seem only just that no one be forced to place his children in a French or an English school; to behave in any other way would be to act somewhat in the same fashion as that for which criticism has been leveled at the other Canadian provinces because of their treatment of French Canadians. The school census which we have proposed in the preceding chapter should record the preference of parents for a French or an English education, just as it will record their preference for Roman Catholic, Protestant or non-confessional education. It would be possible to ask on the census form which language is usually spoken at home and, if a French family chooses education in English, to make inquiry as to why they did so, but without exercising any constraint. Knowledge of the reasons for such a choice could serve to improve certain specific situations in the school, such, for instance, as poor teaching of the second language.

The whole problem of the adherence of New Canadians to French-language culture on the educational level could, in each region, be placed within the competence of the French schools committee, whose creation we propose in a preceding section of this chapter. Aside from the functions enumerated above regarding the general renewal of French schools, this committee should also concern itself with the scholastic problems of New Canadians. It should also study and ascertain, when necessary in collaboration with the departments and social groups concerned, the best means of leading immigrants who settle here to link themselves with the French form of Canadian culture. The directorates of education for the French schools of each of the school commissions in the Montreal region, where the problem of the New Canadians is more acute, should also hold joint meetings to consider these questions, see to it that the necessary surveys are made, adopt useful measures, and propose over-all solutions to the provincial government. The English schools committee could, in collaboration with the French schools committee and with university specialists, arrange for research projects dealing with the problems of teaching the second language and with the problems in linguistics and in teaching techniques which arise in a bi-cultural country. Quebec could make a notable contribution in these fields.

V. Conclusion and Recommendations

The problems raised in this chapter are of altogether vital importance for the future of French-language Canadian culture in Quebec. We are convinced, moreover, that enlightened citizens with an English cultural background accept the attitudes expressed in this chapter, aware that such attitudes are a part of the rich contribution which its dual culture can make to this country, and equally aware that the current resurgence of vitality on the part of French-speaking Canadians tends irreversibly in this direction. The thoughts which we have felt it necessary to express regarding these matters have led us to make the following recommendations.

We recommend that the unified school system which we propose for Quebec be made up, by law, of both French and English schools.

We recommend that, in each regional school commission which includes education in the French language of more than one type, the directors in charge of each type constitute a committee with the status required to ensure the coordination and improvement of education dispensed in the French language, and that, in each regional school commission which includes education in the English language of more than one type, the directors in charge of each act correspondingly.

We recommend that a serious and systematic effort be made by all state services and by educational institutions at all levels to improve the quality of spoken and written French in Quebec.

We recommend that the Department of Education and all public bodies responsible for education give their attention to maintaining close contact between education dispensed in French

and education dispensed in English, so as to encourage the mutual enrichment which can ensue.

We recommend that French-language educational institutions at all levels, especially in the region of greater Montreal, adopt a more effective policy in welcoming those New Canadians who desire a French education for themselves or their children.

NOTES

[1] *Report of the Royal Commission of Inquiry on Education*, Volume I, para. 9 et seq.

[2] *Report of the Royal Commission of Inquiry on Education*, Volume II, page 301.

[3] Ibid, page 303. Table IV makes no division between Roman Catholic and Protestant or between French and English-speaking teachers.

[4] Idem, Chapter IX.

[5] *Report of the Royal Commission of Inquiry on Education*, Volume III, Chapter XII, para. 620 et seq.

[6] Volume II, Chapter XII and Chapter XIII, para. 679 et seq.

EDUCATION*

In this first Book we are concerned with a comparison of the status and use of Canada's two official languages as evinced by their protection through laws, statutes, and customs. This is a first step towards examining the possibility of a more equal partnership between those who speak the two languages. A similar examination of the institutions of the two communities will be the subject of succeeding Books. However, the opportunities to use a language are of little significance unless there exist at the same time opportunities to learn it and retain it — opportunities for an adequate education in the language. We therefore believe it is imperative, when we are suggesting the language régimes appropriate at various levels in Canada, to indicate some of the changes required in the educational systems within each level. At this point our comments will be very general, but a full discussion of the implications of new language régimes for education will follow in the Book on education.

The failure of the B.N.A. Act to protect English and French as languages of instruction in Canada has resulted in a great disparity in the use of these languages in our school systems and grave inequalities in the opportunities for the French-speaking minorities to have an education in their mother tongue. In Quebec, both languages were placed on an equal footing, and the principle establishing the right of both English-speaking and French-speaking children to be taught in their mother tongue was enshrined in the educational system of the province, in spite of the fact that it was not required by law. Because this linguistic equality was not firmly guaranteed for the country as a whole, however, the French-speaking minorities have been largely deprived of the right to an education in their mother tongue.

This inequality and its consequences were the subject of many briefs presented to the Commission by Canadians of both language groups. The school is the basic agency for maintaining language and culture, and without this essential resource neither can remain strong. Of course the situation varies from province

---

*Chapter VI, Royal Commission on Bilingualism and Biculturalism, Book I, *The Official Languages*, Ottawa: Queen's Printer, 1967, pp. 121-131

to province, but the fact remains that many Francophones outside Quebec have been steadily losing their language.

Where the French Canadian population is scattered, it is obviously not easy to provide a suitable programme of education in French. But the real stumbling block has been not so much this as the unwillingness of the English-speaking majority to recognize the right of French-speaking parents to educate their children in French. In Quebec, where the right to equal access to an education in either official language has been respected, even remote and numerically insignificant English-speaking communities have been provided with reasonable opportunities for schooling in English. In most of the other provinces, until very recently, such teaching in French as was permitted was intended simply as a means of transition to the English language. Parents who wanted their children educated in their language and their culture had to bear the costs of a private education while still having to contribute to the English-language public school system.

Even in the provinces where they constitute a sizable minority — for example, 425,000 in Ontario and 35 per cent of the population in New Brunswick — the situation of French-speaking Canadians has suffered seriously by comparison with that of the English mother-tongue minority of 13 per cent in Quebec. Almost without exception, it has been impossible for a French-speaking student outside Quebec to complete his education in French through the elementary and secondary public schools. But in Quebec, Anglophones have access to a complete education in English through the public schools of the province — elementary, secondary, and university. Even English-speaking Roman Catholics have enjoyed a large measure of autonomy within the Catholic system. As a result, their language has never been in danger and they have been able to concentrate on improving curriculum and administration.

In most of the English-speaking provinces there has recently been evidence of modifications in the restrictions against French as a language of instruction. In some cases these changes represent little more than slight improvements on the *status quo*; in other provinces a real attempt is being made to redesign the French-language programme to be more nearly comparable to the English-language programme. It is fair to say that, in general, French-language education outside Quebec has suffered principally from two weaknesses. First, it has been largely achieved through the struggles of French-speaking Canadians despite the resistance of the English-speaking majority. The toll in efficiency and vitality is readily appreciated. Second, it has not constituted a "system." There have been serious gaps and dislocations in the sequence from one educational level to another; essentials such as teacher-training, guidance, and so on, have left a great deal to be desired; a technical or scientific education has been largely unavailable. As a consequence, even where conditions have been most favourable, French-speaking children have been seriously handicapped in their education, with the result that often they were deficient in both languages. Not only has there been injustice in human terms, but these Canadian citizens have not been able to make their potential contribution to society. Therefore, any serious reforms will need to deal realistically with these two situations.

We believe that equal partnership in a bilingual Canada implies the fullest development and expression of both official languages compatible with regional circumstances. We interpret this to mean that it must be accepted as normal that children of both linguistic groups will have access to schools in which their own language is the language of instruction. Therefore, *we recommend that the right of Canadian parents to have their children educated in the official language of their choice be recognized in the educational systems, the degree of implementation to depend on the concentration of the minority population.* This is our only recommendation in this volume in respect to education. More specific recommendations and more detailed information will be forthcoming in the Book on education. We believe this recommendation is basic to any future changes. In practical terms, it will mean extending French-speaking Canadians' opportunities for schooling in the French language, since the English-speaking residents of Quebec already have the opportunities we are recommending.

We shall now indicate, again in general terms, how we consider the schools will be affected by this principle in the bilingual provinces, the bilingual districts, and in large urban centres which have a substantial official-language minority.

A. In Bilingual Provinces

The principle of equal partnership implies comparable educational régimes for the minorities in the three officially bilingual provinces. This will make it possible for many Francophones to live more completely in their own language. In New Brunswick and Ontario, the desirability of classroom instruction in the child's maternal language is already recognized and the right of parents to have their children educated in either French or English has been conceded in principle.[1] There is considerable disparity, however, in the ways this principle is applied in the three provinces. As we have seen, in Quebec instruction at all levels is available to the English-speaking minority in its own language. The situation of French-speaking Canadians in the other two provinces varies from that standard. We suggest that it would be advantageous for the three officially bilingual provinces to agree jointly upon the norms to be established for minority education. In Ontario and New Brunswick it is a matter of officially recognizing what is now unofficial practice, of extending this recognition to all levels, of adopting standard procedures for establishing these schools throughout the province. Equivalent educational facilities and academic standards must be ensured and maintained, whether the language of instruction is English or French; the appropriate administrative framework must be established and the necessary officials appointed. Compulsory education already obliges the provincial government to provide schools for all children. This will be extended to include the provision of French-language schools wherever there are enough French-speaking children to populate them. The provincial government of Quebec already fulfils the obligation to provide English-language schools wherever there are sufficient numbers of English-speaking children. In the officially bilingual provinces, then, there will be complete and parallel systems of education in French and English, from the elementary schools through the institutions of higher learning.

B. In Bilingual Districts

Educational facilities represent a vital part of the régime for the language minority in the bilingual districts. (We must note once again that we are considering now the French-speaking minorities, since Anglophones in Quebec already have these facilities.) It is in the bilingual districts that we can expect to find enough French-speaking children to populate schools in which the language of instruction is French. A local school, however, cannot exist in isolation; it must be seen as only a part of a complex educational system. Teachers must be trained, curricula must be planned, textbooks and teachers' guides must be developed, and inspection and guidance must be provided to maintain uniform academic standards. The minority schools will be no exception. They too must be part of an educational system which provides these essential services. What then will be the organization and administration of schools for the minority in bilingual districts?

C. Administration of Minority Schools — Role of Federal and Provincial Governments

Among the suggestions considered by the Commission was a proposal that the federal government should accept responsibility for minority schools. A federal system would have the advantage of ensuring a uniform curriculum and uniform standards for minority French-language schools. However — apart from the fact that, in the present Canadian Constitution, education is a provincial responsibility — there are considerations which count against this solution. Local schools must be adapted to the needs of the community they serve — technical and commercial programmes, for example, should complement the regional economy — and the advantage of a uniform curriculum from coast to coast would have to be sacrificed to some extent to the need for regional adaptation. Therefore we do not suggest a transfer of educational responsibility for minorities from provincial to federal jurisdiction, although we foresee a role for the federal government in helping to meet certain additional provincial costs. This is an example of what should become a new dimension in the role of the federal government as the only political institution shared by all Canadians.

Provincial administrations have a special knowledge of the educational needs of their provinces. It is obviously easier for an existing department of education to draw on its knowledge and experience and adapt its programme to the needs of the provincial minority than it would be to duplicate this administrative competence in a federal department. The argument is even more convincing because the language of instruction has no bearing on so many administrative decisions, and existing provincial regulations on school construction, school equipment, transportation, and health services will be equally applicable to minority-language schools.

Through provincial administration, uniform academic standards can be maintained for all the children in the province. Schools providing instruction in the language of the minority without maintaining high academic standards would be a handicap rather than a privilege. In every province teacher-training programmes and elaborate certification procedures have been developed to ensure a competent teaching staff. Textbooks, equipment, examinations, and departmental supervision have all been integrated into an educational system designed to achieve the highest possible standards. Only by establishing an equivalent system adapted to their own needs can there be any assurance that students attending the minority-language schools will receive an education equivalent to that provided for other children in the province.

The adaptation of the existing provincial school systems to bilingual education will require careful planning. Teachers will have to be specially qualified. Not only must they have the qualifications required for teaching in the provincial schools but they must also be able to teach in the language of the minority. There are many French-speaking teachers now, especially in Ontario and New Brunswick, but more will be needed. Adequate supervisory services must be provided. It is obvious that these various measures will increase the costs of education. We accept as a principle the responsibility of the federal government to contribute to the additional costs involved. The way in which this principle can be applied without interfering with provincial autonomy in education, and other aspects of the administration of minority-language schools, will be discussed in a subsequent study.

As we have seen in the preceding chapters, bilingual districts may be created in all provinces, whether officially bilingual or not. The basic assumption is that there is a public responsibility for education in French as in English. The extent of the services offered will be governed only by considerations of educational and economic practicality. In the provinces other than Ontario, Quebec, and New Brunswick, however, to establish French-language schools where they have not hitherto been provided will create a new situation and certain attendant problems. In the three officially bilingual provinces, for instance, the minority population is large enough that we can expect necessary administrative measures and services to be provided within the province. In other provinces, where there will be few minority-language schools, it will not be feasible for each provincial department to undertake the necessary curriculum development and teacher training for these schools, and interprovincial co-operation will be necessary. However, such inter-provincial planning in education is already beginning. For the designated bilingual districts outside Ontario, Quebec, and New Brunswick, therefore, the same principle applies as for the designated regions within those three provinces. Parents will have the right to have their children educated in the official language of their choice.

D. Outside the Bilingual Districts

The plan of developing services in both official languages in areas where there are appropriate numbers of French-speaking or English-speaking Canadians is intended to guarantee certain basic rights to these minorities. But members of such linguistic groups living outside these areas should not be excluded from similar opportunities to be served in their maternal language. Programmes for such minorities must range from a minimum to a maximum service according to population concentration, but will still proceed from the acknowledged right of parents to have their children educated in the official language of their choice.

For most English-speaking citizens of Quebec and for most French-speaking citizens in the other provinces, this right will be established through the bilingual districts. But whether these districts are located in an officially bilingual province or not, there are settlements of provincial minorities outside these designated regions, and their need for teaching in their mother tongue is at least as important. Indeed, in view of their linguistic isolation, their need is probably much greater. Here, however, the right to an education in the minority language needs to be qualified by other considerations. In practice a school can only provide the normal options or maintain the required academic standards if the student body is large enough to warrant the necessary specialist teachers and equipment. The minority-language group is large enough in some communities outside these designated areas for a minority-language school, but in other communities it will be too small. The problem is to establish the right to an education in the minority language when it is feasible, without imposing an obligation on the provincial governments when it is impracticable.

The fact that minority-language schools already exist shows that such schools are feasible. However, controversy has arisen in the past when a request by the minority for a French-language school was rejected by the local school board. A formal procedure is required, by which the minority can assert its right to such a school. Provincial departments of education can decide from their experience the minimum number of students for either an elementary or a secondary school. It is proposed, therefore, that the departments of education formally state the requirements and the procedures by which a minority group outside the designated areas can establish its right to a minority-language school at either the elementary or the secondary level. Further, the basis upon which minority-language schools are made available should be such as to provide the maximum opportunity, rather than merely improving on the present situation. Hence, minority-language schools will not be restricted to bilingual districts but will be provided wherever the minority group in a community is large enough, in the judgement of the provincial authorities, to warrant a school.

Isolated families and scattered groups will not qualify for minority-language schools by the above terms. In some cases it will be possible to provide an elementary but not a secondary school; in other cases not even an elementary school would be feasible. For these children a variety of solutions is possible. Within the school, separate classes might be provided with the mother tongue used as the language of instruction in some subjects, although for other subjects the student would have to study in the language of the majority. For parents who want their children to follow a complete minority-language programme, other possibilities exist, such as boarding schools or television teaching. Departmental regulations or at least departmental guidelines would help clarify the rights of the minority in these special situations.

E. In Large Urban Centres

One of the objectives which led to the Commission's recommendations on bilingual regions was the creation or consolidation of a network of bilingual areas across Canada, to provide services to Francophones in those regions and to give the actual image of the dual nature of Canadian society. In this plan, as we noted above, the large urban centres have a major role to play, as poles of attraction for all Canadians. For reasons of mobility if for no other, it is essential that educational opportunities in the French language be provided in these centres for Francophones who, without assurance that they can preserve their children's language, may rightly be reluctant to leave Quebec. In major urban centres where the number of French-speaking residents will not automatically ensure the existence of French-language schools, we propose basically the same arrangements as for bilingual districts, with certain additional administrative arrangements, such as transportation facilities. Students will have the opportunity to be educated in French, although they will often have to accept the inconvenience of travelling farther to school than English-speaking children. In this way, there will be — depending on local circumstances — separate French-language education in separate classrooms or in a separate school.

Moreover, the school might be considered as part of a French-language cultural complex. For the urban area as a whole, the cost of special administrative arrangements will be compensated for by the provision of facilities which will help to attract and retain French-speaking citizens who might otherwise never come. Such facilities will also be a stimulus and encouragement to the Anglophones of those areas who are interested in the French language and culture. The interest which many Anglophones have recently shown in learning French[2] and in having their children learn French, has been frequently frustrated by the lack of opportunity in many areas of the country to practise the language or to be adequately taught. Apart from the importance of fostering communication and understanding between the two language groups, the need for bilingual Canadians will increase as activities involving both groups become more common, and as the trend towards larger administrative structures in business, government, and social organization increases the contacts between Francophones and Anglophones. The Commission was expressly charged in its terms of reference with the responsibility of recommending procedures which will enable Canadians to become more bilingual. We intend to discuss fully the important question of second-language learning in our Book on education. Here we wish simply to point out that, because Canada will need more bilingual citizens in the future than it has in the past, a minimum objective must be for all students to receive a basic introduction to both official languages so that they may become bilingual if the need or the opportunity should arise. Indirectly, of course, the designation of the necessary services within bilingual districts will have the effect of stimulating greater individual bilingualism.[3]

F. Characteristics of French-language Schools

French-speaking children may be educated in a variety of situations, including schools where the instruction is entirely in the minority language and others where its teaching is limited to a few hours. Without attempting to lay down a fixed pattern for such schools, there are certain general characteristics to bear in mind.

Since the principal objective is to enable French-speaking children to expand their knowledge and enjoyment of their native language and culture, the quality of the teaching is tremendously important. The precise, sensitive command of one's own language is the essential and inestimable foundation of thought and communication. Lacking an adequate command of his language the child suffers the handicap of confused thinking and limited means of expression. Top priority therefore must be given to the teaching of the mother tongue, and the need for specially trained teachers and high quality texts cannot be over-emphasized. This is true of any language in any situation, but where the mother tongue is under the constant influence of a second language, much greater care has to be exercised to make the native language secure.

At the same time, students in the minority-language schools need to acquire an adequate command of the language of the majority. In the English-speaking provinces a knowledge of English is seen as an economic and social necessity. We were often told that "this is an English-speaking province," or even that "this is an English-speaking continent," and that a citizen was seriously handicapped in his career or his life in the community unless he knew the language. The English-speaking minority in the province of Quebec has not in the past been as conscious of the importance of learning the language of the majority, and has consequently lived rather apart from the French-speaking community. French-speaking residents of Quebec, while recognizing that a knowledge of English was an asset, would frequently say that "this is a French-speaking province," and the implication was that a resident of Quebec who did not know French was not fulfilling his responsibilities toward his community. In both cases, it is obvious that the minority is expected to learn the language of the majority. Again, the school is usually seen as the institution where this language should be learned.

Fortunately, learning the language of the majority presents few problems in these circumstances. Students can learn to speak two languages and, for children who belong to a linguistic minority, the learning situation is ready-made. The key factors in language learning are the desire and the opportunity to practise. Given motivation and opportunity, there is no reason to fear that the minority will not learn the language of the majority. Nonetheless, special curricula must be developed for language instruction in the minority-language schools. It is not enough to teach English to French-speaking students from textbooks and course outlines designed for English-speaking children, although this is the pattern today in most English-speaking provinces. Special programmes are required to meet the special needs of the minority.

But language, important as it is, is not the only distinguishing feature of minority schools. The courses of study for English and French will obviously be different and the language of instruction for other subjects will vary. We shall later consider to what extent the programme and content of studies should also be different because they must reflect the cultural character of the minority.

For French-speaking minorities especially, cultural identity has in the past been intimately linked with the confessional character of the schools. However, there appears to be an increasing tendency within French Canadian communities across Canada to separate the question of language from religious objectives. Although we plan to come back to this complex question in a later Book, we wish to state here that what we consider essential under our terms of reference is to promote the establishment of French-language schools for the French-speaking minorities independently of religious considerations.

G. Conclusion

In the foregoing pages we have insisted on the right of parents to have their children educated in the official language of their choice, but at the same time we have suggested considerable flexibility as to how this right is exercised. We are convinced that it is important for Canada to maintain strong and vigorous links in the chain of French language and culture across the whole country. We believe furthermore that “equal partnership” for Francophones necessitates a change of policy, from offering the minimum of education in their mother tongue to offering the maximum.

NOTES

[1] The Premier of Ontario, the Honourable John Robarts, in an address to the Association canadienne des éducateurs de langue française on August 24, 1967, said, "It is a fundamental necessity of 1967 that the Franco-Ontarians be enabled to experience the full benefits of our educational system. Encompassed in this recognition of necessity is the proposal to extend what now is being done to provide, within the public school system of Ontario, secondary schools in which the language of instruction is French. . . .It is only practical that such French-language secondary schools and classes can be established wherever the numbers of French-speaking students are great enough to warrant instruction in French. As far as possible, they should provide for French-speaking Ontarians the counterpart of the existing English-language educational programme. . . .In doing so, we would be meeting the needs of our French-speaking Ontarians for equal eduction opportunities at all levels of education, elementary, secondary and university. . . ."

[2] Canadians seem to favour individual bilingualism in principle. The Social Research Group asked the following general question in a survey made for the Commission: "Do you think that it would be a good thing if everyone in Canada spoke both French and English? " Of the people interviewed, 77 per cent said "Yes," while 15 per cent said "No." This opinion favouring individual bilingualism is not equally shared by persons of different ethnic origins. Of those of British origin, 71 per cent answered "Yes," compared with 96 per cent of those of French origin. Opinions also varied between regions; 80 per cent of those of British origin in Quebec and the Atlantic Provinces were favourable to individual bilingualism, 72 per cent in Ontario, and 58 per cent in the four western provinces.

[3] In reply to the question: "Do you think that in Canada, English-speaking children should learn French in primary school? ", 79 per cent of all the people interviewed across Canada in the Social Research Group survey said "Yes," 15 per cent said "No," and 6 per cent either qualified their answer ("It depends") or had no opinion. Although the proportions varied between regions and between different ethnic groups, the great majority of people supported the proposition. For example, among English Canadians three-quarters were in favour, less than a fifth against, and 5 per cent were uncertain; among French Canadians there was hardly any division, with almost 95 per cent in favour; among Canadians of ethnic origins other than English or French, more than two-thirds also supported the idea. It is interesting to note that in the Prairies Provinces and British Columbia, two-thirds said "Yes" and slightly less than 30 per cent voted "No." On the related question: "Do you think that in Canada, French-speaking children should

learn English in primary school? " the degree of support on the average was even higher. Ninety-two per cent of all Canadians said they were in favour of the idea and only 5 per cent were opposed. English Canadians and other ethnic groups across the country replied "Yes" 90 per cent, "No" 6 per cent; French Canadians themselves supported the idea that their children should learn English in primary school to almost exactly the same extent (95 per cent) as they supported the idea that English-speaking children should learn French in elementary school; only 4 per cent were opposed.

EDUCATION FOR IMMIGRANTS*

This chapter deals with the role which has been or could be played by education for immigrants, or the importance of the school with regard to the position, the enhancement and development of the French language in Québec. In other words, as far as Québec is concerned, is the school the principal means for integrating the immigrant into the French-speaking community?

Working on the assumption that the position of the French language is threatened, can we expect to rectify the situation through measures to provide special education for immigrants? What sort of measures should be taken? Should we proceed by coercive or persuasive means? To which groups should the measures apply? The facts and figures will provide our answer.

1. Academic integration and language concerns

Only recently has a language threat become apparent in the school sector. It coincides with French-Canadians' awareness of their position as a distinct majority in Québec. At the same time, figures given in the Parent Report reveal a trend on the part of ethnic groups towards English Catholic schools. The figures show, for instance, that in 1962-63, 25.2% of the children of Italian immigrants went to French-language schools while 74.8% went to the English Catholic schools of the MCSC.[1] This situation was considered alarming as compared to that prevailing in 1930-31 when 52.2% enrolled in French schools and 46.8% in English schools. There was never an in-depth study, however, to discover the causes of this situation and whether it was simply the choice made by the parents of non-French and non-British children which led to the 1971-72 situation in which only 10.7% of the children were enrolled in French classes and 89.3% in English classes.

---

*Extract from Chapter II, "Forms of Integration and Contributions". Report of the Commission of Inquiry on the Position of the French Language and on Language Rights in Québec, Volume III, *The Ethnic Groups*, Québec: The Official Editor of Québec, 1972, pp. 193, 201-236, 262-279.

No one questioned sufficiently the causes of this situation; no one asked why enrollment in French-language schools fell from 52% to 34.3% and increased from 46.8% to 65.7 in English-language schools between 1930-31 and 1950-51 at which time there was no immigration because of the economic crisis. Yet it was during the economic crisis and continental isolationism that the great migration towards English schools took place.

Historian Michel Brunet urges a study of the causes of this situation in order to achieve a better understanding of the present state and so be in a position to take the appropriate steps to combat deficiencies in the future. To this end he reminds us that impatience solves no problems. Only an objective knowledge of the past can suggest more efficient means of facing the problems of the present and the challenges of the future.[2]

In his opinion, the major cause is the anti-state attitude preached in the name of religion by the leaders of the community to protect the status quo:

> They opposed compulsory education, the standardization of school textbooks, the creation of the École des hautes études commerciales, the centralization of schools in cities, the abolition of rural schools, the creation of specialized schools directed by the state, the improved organization of the teaching profession, the reform of the Department of Public Instruction, and so forth. To recall these exhausting and sterile debates is to underline the recent causes for delayed progress in education in French Canada. These were added to those of the last century. It is difficult to evaluate the disastrous consequences. One even wonders whether the French Canadian community will ever manage to catch up in the field of education. That there be some doubt is understandable.[3]

Since the tragic lack of a large well-trained teaching body is considered to be one of the disastrous consequences of the opting out of the state, the author concludes that

> the entire educational system of the French Canadian community is two generations behind and this is an optimistic evaluation.[4]

The report of April 11, 1957

A report prepared in 1965 by René Gauthier mentions a secret report submitted to the superintendent of Roman Catholic Schools on April 11, 1957 by a seven-member subcommittee responsible for an in-depth study of the school problem of New Canadians. This report reveals that around the year 1930, ethnic groups welcomed English-speaking American priests to serve in their parishes. These priests invited non-British and non-French parents to send their children to English Catholic schools. More serious yet, the report in question reveals that the French Catholic schools commissioners were in the habit of sending all non-French, non-British children to English-language schools.[5]

At this point, mention should be made of the confessional character of

Québec schools and it should be stressed that, since the beginning of the century, Jews had by law been assimilated into the Protestant group and were naturally sent to English-language schools. Later, Orthodox and non-Catholic children were usually sent to Protestant schools. Since the school boards in question had never been asked to set up a French Protestant section, all the above-mentioned children were educated in English.

Between 1950 and 1960, however, the Catholic Church made praiseworthy efforts as regards the reception and entertainment of ethnic groups but this was done primarily through Christian charity and in order to preserve Catholicism. The contribution these ethnic groups might make was never taken into consideration, and the language problem was first mentioned by the Académie canadienne-française only in December 1954.

The Gauthier Report,[6] dated January 27, 1967, noted that adult classes were organized by the MCSC between 1948 and 1964, without emphasizing the immigrant himself or his problems. The goal was to have immigrants learn French and to give this language priority in the curriculum. However, Montréal, which had a real language problem, spent $100,000 a year on adult education while Toronto allocated $1,723,000 for this purpose!

The same report recommended that a non-confessional French-language system be set up as well as special bilingual schools for New Canadians only.[7]

The allogenes, who wanted bilingual schools, influenced the thinking of school authorities, who proposed, in 1957, that such institutions be set up for the children coming from ethnic groups. The issue was dodged until May 17, 1961, and, when the Roman Catholic Committee of the Council of Education decided, in May 1962, to proceed with the project, English-speaking people opposed it; the French-language press and French-speaking Québecers remained silent. Yet, 165 parents had already enrolled their children in the bilingual classes which were to begin in eastern Montréal. Minister René Lévesque was the only one to defend bilingual schools before the Québec Legislature.[8]

A bilingual school was opened by the St. Léonard School Board after 1963. However, as we have already noted, the same teachers often taught French and English and, as many of them had not perfectly mastered their native language, the results were mediocre. These classes were abolished in 1968, an action which led to the St. Léonard crisis, then to Bill 63, adopted by the Legislative Assembly on November 28, 1969.

Turning back to the 1950's, we can observe another reason for the defection from French-language schools by the children of ethnic group members: confessional differences within groups of the same language. Thus the Germans, Ukrainians, Hungarians, Swiss, Dutch, and so forth, were sent to English- or French-language schools depending on whether they were Protestant, Orthodox or Catholic.

Even if the language choice had worked to the advantage of French-language schools, the academic structure of the time would have exerted little attraction.

To this must be added the fact that sponsored immigrants were reunited with members of their families who already attended English-language schools. They would naturally do likewise. This group represented approximately 30% of the immigrants.

The Parent Report

The Parent Report mentioned other causes leading to the precarious situation of education in the French-language schools. The Commission which drew up this report was itself the result of a sudden awareness of the weaknesses of the French Catholic school system.

The structures of French-language public schools, as we now know them, are recent, and obligatory school attendance only dates back to 1943.[9]

The Parent Commission revealed the cultural pluralism created by the arrival of groups of immigrants after the war and by modern society.[10] Among other things, its Report revealed that French-language teachers in Québec had formed professional associations 75 years after their Protestant colleagues.[11] It pointed out the poor quality of textbooks.

> Elementary grade teachers and their pupils have suffered the consequences; many minds remain scarred by bad taste, by banality of expression, by empty religiosity, by dessicated and inadequate knowledge.[12]

The Report emphasized that in the French-language schools the teaching of English was:

> . . .a painful, boring obligation, drudgery for both teacher and pupils.[13]

It requested that parents be given a certain freedom of choice as regards the teaching of this subject[14] and proposed that optional courses be offered for the study of other living languages which might interest certain students.[15] The Report also emphasized that:

> One of the most pressing needs is the thorough screening of textbooks now in use, the short-comings of which contribute to the poor language habits of the pupils.[16]

The Report comments on the difficulties involved in confessional education and suggests that non-confessional courses be provided whenever a sufficient number of parents request it. It opts for the choice of schooling by the parents but requests an annual census to enable them to choose freely, after sufficient reflection, and thus provide the school board with an essential tool for rational planning.[17]

As regards New Canadians, the Report deplores the fact that the minority situation, the economic inferiority and attitude of French Canadians, the absence of an adequate reception system, and defense reflexes have discouraged the necessary rapprochement of the two:

> It should not be forgotten that often an immigrant has been attracted to Canada, where certain of his relations and friends had already been living for several years, because of a personal interchange of information and opinion. The more welcome New Canadians feel in Québec, especially among French-speaking citizens, the more will they make this known in their native lands, and the better will they prepare prospective immigrants to consider the possibility of casting their lot with the French-speaking majority, as, in the natural course of events, a considerable number should be expected to do.[18]

The same report added:

> In the preceding section of this chapter, we have indicated how urgent is the need to institute reform on all fronts so that French-language public education may reach a level comparable to that of public education in the English Protestant schools. It is not surprising that, when they see such differences in services and in quality, New Canadians should have been inclined to choose the better equipped schools, in which the teachers are ordinarily better prepared. For a certain number of New Canadians, the problem of choice between a French or an English school will be settled the moment French-language public education is of unquestionable quality and gives access to all university faculties. Only then is it reasonable to think that they are truly free to make a choice between French and English public schools of comparable merit.[19]

Lastly, the Report, while demanding a broader reception policy, particularly in Montréal, asks that a good quality of teaching of the second language be considered the primary means of attracting immigrants towards French-language studies.

> One of the reasons which induce immigrants to place their children in the English-language schools is that there they will learn the language spoken throughout most of North America. It is likely that if the teaching of English in the French schools were promptly improved, especially at the level of studies where this teaching could not enter into conflict with a thorough knowledge of the mother tongue of French-speaking students, there would be fewer parents, not originally English-speaking, who would be inclined to enrol (sic) their children in English language schools.[20]

Certain ethnic groups submitted briefs to the Parent Commission. All were unanimous in requesting bilingual schools for their children, including Jews from North Africa, who were of the French culture and who declared French was a moral necessity for them.[21] However, since no effect was given to the recommendations of the Parent Report with regard to the social and educational integration of immigrants, many were disappointed in their expectations.

It was not until 1971 that the Maisonneuve Regional School Board took the initiative of allowing Jewish students from the Laval area to attend its secondary schools, while offering them courses in the Hebrew language and culture.

Moreover, it was only at the end of November, 1972 that the Department of

Education accepted the request of the Sephardic and French-speaking Jews to open a private French-language school[22]: 20% of the cost is assumed by the parents.

Subsequent policies

The Québec Government's inactivity continued until 1968, when reception centers were set up following the St. Léonard crisis.[23] It created a Department of Immigration and appointed the Commission of Inquiry on the Position of the French Language and on Language rights in Québec in 1968, organized the immigrant orientation and training centers (COFI), was instrumental in having Bill 63 assented to in 1969, and obliged English-language schools to begin teaching French in the first year of elementary school. Bill 64, which was adopted in December, 1970, allowed many professional associations to accept candidates having a working knowledge of French, thus enabling them to practice the profession for which they were qualified, regardless of their citizenship, on condition that they request Canadian citizenship after having completed the legally required period of time in the country. For the past two years record of the language spoken at home has been kept in student files.

The setting up of introductory classes, the Private Education Act and the agreement of May 18, 1971 between the provincial Department of Immigration and the federal Department of Manpower and Immigration with a view to improving information are some of the means recently instituted to help immigrants. Moreover, these same means facilitate the application of a policy for enhancing and developing the French language in Québec.

Conclusion

Even though we can find only a distant analogy between the situations in various countries as regards immigration, an analogy still more distant where Québec is concerned, a certain constant emerges from general observations.

Indeed, whatever the degree of importance given to the school system in the immigrant's adaptation to any milieu, the results, for all practical purposes, depend on other factors which, while not directly related to the school system are equally determining.

For example, a certain precondition seems necessary to any consideration of the role of the school in the integration of one language group into another; this precondition is the objective of a country or a state as regards immigration, as well as the knowledge and understanding of the content of this objective.

Every study on education or the school as a means of integration assumes that the immigrant feels wanted or needed by the community of which he hopes to become a part. The problem of the integration of the immigrant largely surpasses the role of the school and becomes fundamentally a question of motivation, as various studies have revealed.

These include works done by Morrison[24], the United States Department of Health, Education and Welfare, Joti Bhatnagar, who carried out a masterly study[25] in England, in which he states that "The social acceptability of immigrant children appears to be reflecting the general state of race relations in the country.", and R.A. Taft in Australia.[26]

Three dimensions of motivation are involved here:

(a) that of the host country where motivation is the result of a consciousness of its immigration objectives (need, suitability, goal), which become tangible in the form of adequate recruiting, welcoming, supporting and orientation measures;

(b) that of the host population which is sufficiently informed of the reasons for and benefits of immigration to accept and integrate the new arrivals;

(c) that of the new arrivals who have sufficient prior knowledge of the social conditions of the country to understand and accept reactions.

Any concept of motivation presupposes that in Québec a knowledge of the French language is desired.

The question then becomes one of methodology. How can the objective, in this case acquiring the French language, be made attractive? How can its advantages be pointed out to those we wish to interest? How can the educational system assume a share of this role in Québec and how is this being done at the moment?

These considerations must seem fairly abstract, particularly since in practice the situation seemsto have been quite different. It is the immigration policy itself which must determine the measures to be taken but, in fact, we have generally been forced to take measures in the absence of any policy. Moreover, internal circumstances peculiar to each country determine policy. In short, only a thorough knowledge of the specific conditions of the country can inspire the proper measures to be taken.

It is vitally important for Québec to determine its particular circumstances vis-à-vis immigration.

2. Québec's demo-linguistics situation in a historical context

If the problem of immigrant assimilation is considered on the provincial level, it can be seen that the immigrant population in Québec has increased in large part because of the numbers of English-speaking people who began to arrive as far back as the Seven Years War.

Even though official statistics are not available before 1851, it appears that large groups of English-speaking people were concentrated in Montréal, the Eastern Townships and the Outaouais Valley region.

During this same period, according the historian Jean Hamelin[27], Montréal had an English-speaking majority of 54.9%. English-speaking people made up 41.7% of the population of Québec City[28] and 83.7% of that of Sherbrooke.

It is evident that prior to 1760[29], the settlement of New France, at least in the beginning was accomplished only through immigration. Whether it be judged as "directed" or not, this immigration involved mostly French Catholics, thus conforming to the commitments of the companies which controlled it. The relatively small group of other immigrants that were noted included fugitive and Protestant Englishmen, French Huguenots, some black slaves, and a few citizens of Hamburg, all of whom the Québec population assimilated well. The social and language picture at the time of the conquest was thus entirely French.

Immediately after the English take-over, immigration began from two sources, the Loyalists fleeing the American Revolution who were obviously English-speaking, and people from the British Isles. Toward 1830 Ireland provided more English-speaking immigrants.

Haldiman estimated the number of British settled in the colony to be 2,000 in 1780, or 1.6% of the population.[30]

In 1784 there were 25,000 inhabitants of Anglo-Saxon origin in Québec resulting from Loyalist immigration, which was itself surpassed by immigration from the British Isles, according to the same author.

Between 1815 and 1823 the total of arrivals in Québec City from English-language countries represented 21% of the population of Lower Canada. However, French Canadians maintained their numerical superiority by reason of their birthrate and their concentration in the province of Québec, and because of a circumstantial diversion of immigration from Britain to the United States.

After 1848 the arrivals primarily increased the number of English-speaking people.[31] The figures regarding immigrants entering Québec according to their last country of residence up to 1961, and to ethnic origin after 1961, bear witness to this.

3. Language pattern of groups arriving in Québec

It seems that generally speaking, from 1948 on, a large proportion of the immigrants who arrived were, because of their geographic or ethnic origins, English-speaking. In addition, some immigrants may have been attracted to the English-speaking group because they already had a knowledge of English as second language. In the Appendix we reproduce a table establishing the number of immigrants arriving from 1948 to 1971 in accordance with their last country of residence.[32] This table does not show any English-language, French-language or other-language grouping. Such a distribution would only be hypothetical at any rate since statistical yearbooks record immigrants by last country of residence without specifying the language spoken, mother tongue or the first language learned as a second language.

Professor Jacques Brossard[33], writing on the Canadian situation emphasizes that

> as a whole, immigration has scarcely served the interests of French Canada. A very small proportion of the immigrants when they arrive are assimilated more easily by the French-speaking than by the English-speaking population. From 1945 to 1964, a third of the immigrants were actually of British origin, and about a quarter belonged to other related ethnic groups, such as the German, Dutch and Scandinavian; an even greater proportion of new citizens during this period were of Anglo-Saxon origin.

And, adds the same author:

> Even in Québec, about 65% of the British, Germans, Dutch, Scandinavians, Poles and Jews, as well as 60% of the Russians and Ukrainians know only English.[34]

If other indices are consulted, such as those provided by the statistical studies on the census of immigrant households in Québec, according to the ethnic origin of the head of the household before 1946 and from 1946 to 1961, the predominance of the English-speaking immigrant group compared with the French-speaking immigrants appears even more marked.

In fact, 41,692 families in which the head of the household was of English origin had immigrated to Québec before 1946 and from 1946 to 1961, that is 28,806 before 1946 and 12,886 from 1946 to 1961.

By contrast, of the 20,329 families in which the head of the household was of French origin, 13,129 immigrated to Québec before 1946 and 7,200 from 1946 to 1961.

The same statistical tables show figures on the number of ethnic households other than French and British which immigrated to Québec during the same period and already spoke English as their second language, or were more naturally inclined to join the English-speaking group.

Thus, 28,093 households, in theory English-speaking, as well as 41,692 that are actually British, that is an overall total of 69,785 households using the English language, entered Québec prior to 1961. This does not include the 47,176 households uncertain of their language allegiance, which proved to be mainly English-speaking, with the exception of the Italians. Such figures indicate a marked trend toward the English-speaking group.

Lastly, the figures quoted by Joy[35], show that before 1946, 141,000 immigrants entered Québec, and from 1946 to 1961, 248,000, of whom 55% spoke only English before 1946 and 46% after 1946.

On the other hand, the calculations of the provincial Immigration Office concerning the numbers of immigrants coming to Québec from French-language and English-language countries, as compared with the overall immigration numbers, indicate that immigrants coming from English-language countries predominated over these arriving from French-language countries between 1964 and 1971.

The following numbers of immigrants arrived in Québec from French-language countries:

in 1964, 5,851, or 22.5% of the total immigrant population;
in 1965, 6,424, or 21.2% " " " " "
in 1966, 8,883, or 22.7% " " " " "
in 1967, 11,729, or 25.7% " " " " "
in 1968, 9,821, or 27.7% " " " " "
in 1969, 5,859, or 20.8% " " " " "
in 1970, 4,595, or 19.9% " " " " "

The last countries of residence considered as being French-language are Algeria, Morocco, Tunisia, St-Pierre and Miquelon, Belgium, Luxembourg, Switzerland, France and Lebanon.

The following numbers of immigrants arrived from English-language countries:

in 1964, 6,362, or 24.5% of the total immigrant population;
in 1965, 8,188, or 27% " " " " "
in 1966, 11,142, or 28.4% " " " " "
in 1967, 12,067, or 26.4% " " " " "
in 1968, 8,692, or 24.5% " " " " "
in 1969, 9,457, or 33.5% " " " " "
in 1970, 7,940, or 34.1% " " " " "

Countries considered as English-speaking are Great Britain, Ireland, the United States, British Guiana, Jamaica, Trinidad and Tobago, Bermudas, Barbados, the rest of the British West Indies, Australia, New Zealand, India, Pakistan, Kenya, the Republic of South Africa and Ceylon.

The Immigration Office does not take into consideration the immigrants coming from other countries such as Scandinavia, Germany, Greece, Russia, Poland, the Ukraine, etc., among whom defection from their mother tongue to the advantage of English or French was shown to favor the English-speaking group in proportions ranging from 56.9% to 21.3% respectively as at the 1961 Census.[36].

A report from the Immigration Branch to the Department of Cultural Affairs, prepared for a Québec immigration policy, states that

> twice as many British as French arrive, even though their numbers account for only 10% of the total Québec population. Moreover, if we consider that, theoretically, certain ethnic groups, such as the Germans, Austrians, Dutch and a great many of the immigrants coming from the United States, almost naturally integrate with the English-speaking group, the inevitable conclusion is that at least 50% of the immigrants electing Québec residence are already familiar with the English-language and culture.[37]

The report also adds:

> By language and cultural affinities, the English population of Québec can count on "natural allies" such as the Germans, Dutch, Scandinavians, etc.[38]

It is indisputable — and perhaps this is one of the major reasons for the fact that immigrants enter the English-language sector — that this population already established has, by force of circumstances, exercised and continues to exercise a power of attraction over immigrants, who are neither British nor French by origin, to an extent which is difficult to assess.

There is nothing particularly surprising in this predominantly English-speaking population's selecting the English-language sector of the educational system in force, offered them [sic] for the education of their children.

What is the extent of the school age population represented by this demographic increase?

Where is it?

Which educational system did it enter?

Because of the very definition of "mother tongue" as the "language spoken in childhood and still understood", statistics on persons less than twenty years of age have a greater validity. To the extent that mother tongue may be defined as the language generally used in the home, the children's mother tongue becomes a better indication of the parents' language preference. Therefore, we shall describe this immigrant population under twenty as compared with the whole population, the under-twenty population of Québec, as well as the whole immigrant population. It is self-evident that such data does not take deaths, departures or returns to the country of origin into account. However, they are indicative of the proportion of the under-twenty newcomers to Québec and the advantage they represent for the group to which they have chosen to belong.[39]

4. The demo-linguistic educational situation

When the question is more closely examined, we discover that the newly arrived under-twenty population constitutes only a very small proportion of the total population of the Province of Québec, that is, for the census period 1951 to 1961, it accounted for 1.15% of the total population. It also represents a very small portion of the under-twenty group, that is, for the same period, 2.28% of the population under-twenty. For the 1961-1971 census period, it represented 1.46% of the total population of the Province of Québec and 3.34% of the under-twenty population.[40]

According to the 1961 census, the total population of Québec was 5,259,211, of whom 2,330,821 were under twenty and 60,320 were immigrants under twenty.

According to the 1971 census, the total population of Québec was 6,027,765, of whom 2,406,827 were under twenty and 81,645 were immigrants under twenty.[41]

The number of children of immigrants in the under-twenty age group who arrived in Québec in 1971 was 5,034, about half of them of school age. Most of them were English-speaking.

If we refer to the data given by the provincial Department of Immigration in Montréal, the proportion of the under-twenty immigrant group for each of the years 1958 to 1970 inclusive, compared with the total population under twenty in Québec, is somewhere between 0.2% and 0.5%.[42]

However, since the vast majority of Québecers of other ethnic origins settle with their children in the Montréal area and its suburbs, the presence of these children in the school system becomes a legitimate question of concern.

It is quite obvious that the city of Montréal is the preferred place of residence for most of the people arriving in Québec; therefore, the figures, to the extent that they seem similar in the various reports, remain quite a conclusive indication of the newcomers' school option.

Québec City is in seventh place as regards the number of children of immigrants enrolled in school. Integration of children of immigrants into the school situation takes place naturally; the few English-speaking families who settle here generally enroll their children in the English-language schools, in particular at St. Patrick's and Holland Schools. The same is true for French-speaking persons who wish to take advantage of the opportunity to learn a second language.

Statistics on the choice of New Canadian parents of a school for their children's education are complicated and incomplete.

The only available statistics concerning the distribution of the children of immigrants among French and English classes in the Montréal Catholic School Commission show that before 1934, the French section attracted more Canadians of other ethnic origins than the English section. After 1935, the roles were reversed; although the change was slow, it was steady. Since 1961, this trend has become more noticeable and is reaching alarming proportions.

We have attempted to complete the statistics supplied to the Commission by the Montréal Catholic School Commission with figures subsequently supplied by the Montréal Catholic School Commission and the Department of Education.[43]

However, considering the limitations of these statistics, the most that can be gained from them are general indications. Under these circumstances, it is almost impossible to describe the demo-linguistic school situation either in general or in detail.

The best that can be suggested is that uniform accurate statistics be kept and compiled over a sufficient length of time so as to obtain a clear idea of the position. As long as such statistics are lacking, there is a serious risk that in legislating for the minorities either the majority or the minorities will be discriminated against.

The number of New Canadian children in the French section of the MCSC has been steadily decreasing; the number of non-British, non-French children in the English schools of the MCSC has been steadily increasing. In 1955-56 the non-British, non-French children already equaled the number of children of British origin in the English Catholic School section in Montréal.[44] This is demonstrated in the following figures:

pupils of British origin: 8,992 or 40.9%;
pupils of other ethnic origins: 8,866 or 40.4%;
pupils of French origin: 4,112 or 18.7%.

Immigrants alone are not responsible for the increase in the number of pupils in the English-language schools because according to R. Joy[45] the number of English-speaking children in the province of Québec have themselves increased in number. From 1931 to 1961, there was an increase in the size of the English-speaking family. The English-speaking school-age population has more than doubled since 1931, while the number of children from French-speaking families has only increased by 80%.

It seems that in the MCSC English classes alone, the children multiplied three-fold between 1931 and 1963. Italians, Spanish and Portuguese are generally considered, because of their cultural affinity, to gravitate towards the French language, but they enroll their children to a great extent in the English sector of the MCSC.

It would be vain to close our eyes to the implications of the data set forth below:

1. the general tendency of New Canadians to choose for their children the English-language educational system, although in the Catholic sector;
2. the statement of quite a number of pupils, in the elementary and secondary levels of the English system, that French is the language usually spoken at home;
3. the marked trend during the past few years of the Italian group to enroll in the English language schools of the Catholic sector;
4. the heavy concentration of pupils of Italian origin in B region of the English sector of the MCSC, where they constitute the majority in 16 elementary and 3 secondary schools.

Here we must stress the difficulty in finding comparable statistics on school enrollment according to ethnic origin and language. For the future, as already mentioned, a permanent inventory according to uniform variables of these enrollments is essential if we wish to obtain an adequate view of the situation.

For example, there does not exist, or it was impossible to obtain from the Protestant schools of Montréal, statistics on the distribution of school enrollments according to ethnic origin comparable or even similar to those supplied by the MCSC for the years prior to 1970.

The Protestant School Board of Greater Montréal and that of Greater Québec have not taken such variables into consideration.

Other statistics emanating from the Department of Education confirm the state of affairs for 1970. They describe the school population of the Montréal administrative region according to language spoken at home, and according to religion in the French and English Catholic public schools, in the French and English Protestant public schools and in the private Catholic and Protestant schools.[46]

The only variables considered are: the language spoken at home, English, French or other languages; religion, Catholic, Protestant or others.

The Catholic public sector

In 1970, the pupil enrollment in the MCSC schools of the Montréal region, (which totalled 222,964) was divided according to the language spoken at home in the following manner:

In the French schools, out of a total enrollment of 179,663,

- 175,535 pupils state they speak French at home, that is 97.7%;
- 1,282 pupils state they speak English at home, that is 0.72%;
- 2,846 pupils state they speak a language other than French or English, that is 1.58% of the total.

In English schools, out of a total enrollment of 42,810,

- 3,675 pupils state they speak French at home, that is 8.58%;
- 15,566 pupils state they speak English at home, that is 36.3%;
- 23,569 pupis state they speak a language other than French or English, that is 55.02% of the total.

In bilingual schools, out of 491 pupils,

- 475 state they speak French at home;
- 16 state they speak English;
- none state they speak a different language.

In the MCSC schools, the pupils who state they speak a language other then French or English at home account for 11.8% of the total enrollment of 222,964.

However, the percentage of pupils who state that they speak a language other than French or English at home, compared with the enrollment in the English Catholic schools, is 55%.

The Protestant public sector

In 1970, the pupil population in the public Protestant sector of the Montréal region were divided according to the language spoken at home in the following manner:

In the French schools, out of a total enrollment of 327 pupils all speak French at home.

In English schools, out of a total of 60,698 pupils,

- 2,654 state they speak French at home, that is 4.37%;
- 46,889 state they speak English at home, that is 77.24%;
- 11,155 speak a language other than French or English at home, that is 18.38% of the total enrollment.

In bilingual schools, out of a total of 2,682 pupils,

- 991 state they speak French at home, that is 37.3%;

— 1,108 state they speak English at home, that is 41.3%;
— 583 state that they speak a language other than French or English at home, that is 21.4% of the total.

This means that, out of a total enrollment of 63,707 students in the public Protestant sector of the Montréal region, 21.4% speak a language other than English or French at home.

The Private Catholic sector

As shown in the table of the pupil enrollment in the private Catholic sector of the Montréal region for 1970, out of a total of 40,133 pupils in the French schools of the private Catholic sector:

— 38,973 give French as the language spoken at home;
— 696 give English as the language spoken at home;
— 464 give a language other than French or English as the language spoken at home, that is, 464/40,133 = 1.15%.

In the English schools, out of a total of 4,139 pupils:

— 839 give French as the language spoken at home;
— 2,870 give English as the language spoken at home;
— 430 give a language other than French or English as the language spoken at home, that is 10.4% or 430 out of 4,139.

The Private Protestant sector

As indicated in the table of the pupil enrollment of the private Protestant sector in the Montréal region, for 1970, out of a total of 15 enrolled in a French school registered as part of the private Protestant sector:

— 2 give French as the language spoken at home;
— 10 give English as the language spoken at home;
— 3 give a language other than French or English as the language spoken at home, that is 3 out of 15 or 20%.[47]

In the English schools, out of a total of 3,954 pupils:

— 148 give French as the language spoken at home;
— 3,661 give English as the language spoken at home;
— 145 give a language other than French or English as the language spoken at home, that is 145 out of 3,954 or 3.7%.

In the bilingual schools, out of the total of 1,999 pupils:

— 1,317 give French as the language spoken at home;
— 577 give English as the language spoken at home;
— 105 give a language other than English or French as the language spoken at home, that is 105 out of 1,999 = 5.02%.

"Other" schools

In the "other" French schools, out of a total of 305 pupils enrolled, 305 speak French at home.[48]

In the "other" English schools, out of a total of 4,326 pupils enrolled:

- 360 give French as the language spoken at home;
- 2,012 give English as the language spoken at home;
- 1,954 give languages other than English or French as the language spoken at home, that is 1,954 out of 4,326, or 45.2%.

It is not possible to sort out Québecers of other ethnic origins from among the persons included in these data; however, we can easily consider as such those who say they speak a language other than English or French at home, that is 2,634 compared with the total enrollment in the private sector, which is 54,871, constituting 4.83%.

Conclusion

Once again, these figures, although fairly precise, do not enable us to define accurately, or comparatively, the actual number or geographic location of children of the third group in the schools of the Montréal Catholic School Commission, the Protestant School Board of Greater Montréal and the private education sector.

The enrollments do not cover the same areas, they are not differentiated as regards ethnic origin or even the true status of the immigrant. If we study them as they are presented however, restricting ourselves to those who say they speak a language other than French or English at home and are obviously of other ethnic origins, recent or distant, we see that only the English schools of the public Catholic sector have an appreciable proportion of New Canadian pupils: (55.02%).

5. Into which educational system in Québec will the immigrant integrate?

Obviously, the immigrant who comes to a bilingual country and settles in a province with a French majority faces a different situation from that he would encounter in a province with a large English-speaking majority.

Generally, no one disputes the fact that school legislation in the Province of Québec has accepted this duality which recognizes that differences exist, that the ethnic and religious personality of the two founding peoples must develop normally and that each cultural heritage must be set off to advantage.

In any case, the school system developed gradually and legislative text followed upon legislative text until the 1941 office consolidation of school laws and the Education Department Act of 1964 came into being.

It seems worthwhile to recall certain historical highlights which might have had some effect on the instruction given immigrants of all races and religions.

a) Historical landmarks

The 1801 proclamation of the Royal Institution establishing a system of free non-confessional English schools, the only ones to be subsidized, gave rise to opposition and the creation of a Catholic school system.

The first act pertaining to schools, voted in 1801, was entitled "An Act for the Establishment of Free Schools and the Advancement of Learning in this Province". This Act contained the seed of a non-confessional system. It naturally had many opponents among the Québec clergy but was passed at the third reading, thanks to the support of certain French-Canadian members.

In 1824, an act known as the Fabrique Schools Act was passed to make the parish the basis of the school organization.

In 1829, an "Act for the Encouragement of Elementary Education" was passed to reinforce and make more effective the first two.

An act repealing the above-mentioned laws was passed in 1841 to create and maintain public schools in the Province. It established the principle of confessional schools. According to some documents, the Protestant groups were in the main responsible for requesting that the separation of Catholics and Protestants in the school system be written into the 1841 act.[49]

At last, in 1856, the basic school system, Bill 9, Victoria, ch. XXVII, created the Council of Public Instruction and finally resulted in the confessional school duality of today which still remains a controversial subject:

1 — a Protestant public sector and a Catholic public sector divided yet again into English, French, bilingual and "other" schools;

2 — a Catholic private sector including both English and French schools, a Protestant private sector with English, French and bilingual schools and other schools belonging to no denomination in particular but with either French or English as the language of instruction.

The distinction between English and French schools in Catholic School Commissions is a response to the force of numbers but it is also an answer to the need to give English-speaking pupils in the Catholic system an English cultural education.

Separation by religion was confirmed at Confederation by Section 93 of the British North America Act which guaranteed the education rights of religious minorities.

Although not stated in so many words, the protection of the pupils' mother tongue was in a certain manner ensured since Catholics were considered as being French-speaking and Protestants English-speaking. Protection was therefore "de facto" rather than "de jure".

This lack of precision as regards language majorities and minorities has always been maintained and has led to situations in which language sometimes gave way to religion and religion sometimes gave way to language, but misunderstandings and latent conflicts have always been entangled with the question of religion.

Between 1900 and 1960, the two religions each had their own complete education system financed by elementary and secondary school taxes[50] under the auspices of a Council of Education which heads two all-powerfull committees, the Roman Catholic Committee and the Protestant Committee.

The Parent Commission recommended that all educational services be united within the framework of one department. This was acted upon only in 1964 and at present the principle of Protestant and Catholic confessional schools, both French and English, public and private is maintained. Only very recently, that is since 1969, has it become possible, at least in theory, to cross religious and language lines in the school system.

> From now on, Department legislation and regulations, standards and procedures apply equally to Catholics and Protestants, to English-speaking and French-speaking citizens, that is, to the entire student population of Québec.[51]

The Québec education system has thus been developed in terms of a liberal, secular respect for the rights of the English-speaking minority.

It is into such a system that the immigrant has been required to integrate, at least since 1867.

It is not surprising that the majority of immigrants, largely English-speaking, have been drawn toward the English schools with the majority ending up in the English Catholic or Protestant sector of the Québec education system, especially since, through negligence, indifference, inertia, ignorance of the situation and perhaps even powerlessness, the French-speaking group does not seem to have done anything until two years ago to encourage immigrants to send their children to French schools.

b) Bill 63

The "Act to promote the French language in Québec" (Bill 63), assented to on November 28, 1969, confirms the exclusive right of French-speaking and English-speaking parents to choose their children's schools.

This provision frees certain non-Catholic ethnic groups from the obligation to register their children in English-language Protestant schools.

c) Effects

It is hardly possible to evaluate the effect of Bill 63 on the behavior of immigrants as regards schools because of the lack of perspective and of comparable information, the great cultural and language diversity of the subjects, the unreliability of available statistics and so forth.

Moreover, it is impossible to say with any precision, how many children of immigrants took advantage of Bill 63 to go over to the English-language system, since in all probability such transfers were being carried out even before the bill was passed and, more particularly, since there is no way of telling how many of the 1,075 children who went over to the English-language system between 1969 and 1970 were Canadian-born French-speaking children and how many were really immigrants.

Student records for 1970 mention on one form the child's language of instruction for the year 1969 and 1970 and, by this very fact, deal with the same group of students. All preceding statistics when there are any, deal with a different group of students, and consequently population variations cannot be interpreted comparatively. Moreover, the language of instruction given in earlier records is sometimes the language of the school and sometimes the language of the child. Finally, these statistics are not available in all School Boards.

The only valid figures on the transfer of children from one language of instruction to another, in this case from French to English, also have their limitations since the records were useful for only 72% of the enrolled pupil population. It should also be specified that the records make use of factors which clearly distinguish the pupils whose language is neither English nor French and who can thus be considered as immigrants; but they do not distinguish immigrants within the English-speaking or the French-speaking groups.

Once these limits have been defined, the fact remains that, considering only the distribution of Québec pupils whose mother tongue is neither French nor English in kindergarten, in elementary and secondary schools or in schools for exceptional children, in the private and public sectors, it will be noted that:

- between 1969 and 1970 the French education sector lost 414 students from all levels combined, or 0.69% of its "other" student population;
- the "other" education sector[52] during the same period, experienced a drop of 661 students, or 1.10% of the "other" student population at the same levels.

These two sectors lost 1,075 "other language" pupils to the English-language education sector, or 1.79% of the "other" student population estimated to be 60,111 students at the levels in question.[53]

According to a survey carried out for the Department of Education by Sorecom Inc. on April 1, 1971,[54] 1,920 of the pupils who transferred (70.7%) chose English schools, while 796 (29.3%) chose French schools. A total of 2,716 pupils were involved, a tiny fraction of the 2,406,827 pupils in Québec in 1971.

Mrs. V. Neal, chairman of the French Committee of the Québec Federation of Home and School Associations believes that the Sorecom survey failed to take into consideration the French immersion programs set up by the Protestant schools in which 5,253 pupils are enrolled at present.[55]

Bill 63's effect was the removal of religion as an obstacle which had limited the choice of parents as regards language. It was to be hoped that this would result in a more pronounced preference for French-language schools, but this was not the case. It is not difficult to attribute their hesitation to the economic and social insecurity, the threat of possible coercion, the quality of instruction or any other cause.

As already mentioned, it would be premature and practically impossible to assess the effects of Bill 63 on the behavior of immigrants as regards schools and to make value judgements. At the most, the statistics provided give a few general indications which suggest that extreme caution be used in the methods chosen to deal with the situation. There is no doubt that extended observation and a very careful interpretation of the results of such observation would be required to avoid adopting measures which would shift the emphasis with regard to the problem without solving it.

The problems undoubtedly lie in the causes, not in the symptoms, and involve the immigrant at the moment of exposure to the causes, that is to say, long before he faces the school problem, and above and beyond this problem, which is but one episode in his integration. The welcome received and the importance of English in professional activities and for social mobility are two of the causes and these exert major pressures which affect the choice of school.

Finally, it must be remembered that Bill 63 also requires the Department of Immigration, in conjunction with the Department of Education, to take the necessary steps enabling immigrant applicants to acquire a knowledge of the French language before they even arrive in Québec; no action has as yet been taken in this direction.

These same departments should take measures to have immigrants learn French and to have their children taught in schools where classes are given in French. The recently created introductory classes fulfill the hopes placed in them since the great majority of the 500 pupils received annually continue their studies in French.[56]

It must now be considered whether everything possible has been done to encourage immigrants and their children to learn French. Some steps taken to facilitate the integration of immigrant children into the French-speaking sector and to help the adults learn French will be described in the following paragraphs. One conclusion can be drawn even before the quality and quantity of these measures is presented, a conclusion identical to that concerning school transfers: it is too soon to judge objectively the extent of favorable results or to make reliable appraisals.

6. Various barriers to choosing French-language schools

The demo-linguistic situation in schools shows that English is the mother tongue or second language of most of the children of immigrants in Québec. This is a major obstacle to the choice of French-language schools. Other obstacles also affect this choice, be they economic, religious, or purely academic such as the quality of instruction or the qualifications and attitudes of the teachers and pupils.

a) Economic imperatives

The post-1929 economic crisis brought immigration into Canada and Québec to an abrupt halt. The restrictive American immigràtion laws and the very negative effects of the depression throughout the North American continent prevented a new population "drain". During the forties, however, the decision was made to begin teaching English in French schools only in Grade six (the equivalent of Grade five today) instead of the Grade in (the equivalent of Grade three today) as had previously been the case. These changes were very badly timed. Surprising as it may seem, a major landslide towards English-language schools took place during the depression between the two world wars. This move coincided, moreover, with the decline of French as the world's first international language.

The depression which began in 1929 thus had deplorable effects on the school situation. This is a factor which is too often forgotten when the enhancement and development of the French language are studied.

The effects of school transfers between the two world wars extended beyond that period, for after 1946, immigrant parents who were neither French nor British and who were able to choose schools followed the established pattern and sent their children to English-language schools. Moreover, the economic, political and language influence of the United States was such that it was difficult to ignore the absolute necessity to know English, the new international language. This need was also felt by the French Canadians who set the example in Montréal and made extensive use of English as the language of communication at work.

b) The confessional system

The distinction between Protestant and Catholic schools systems prevented many parents from making a free choice. European immigrants in particular considered the system an anachronism since they were accustomed to non-confessional schools. Restrictions resulted from official regulations as well as from current practice. Jewish children, for example, were directed towards the Protestant and consequently the English-speaking sector as a result of the 1903 act, 3 Ed VII, ch. 16, sec. 6. Also, as already seen,[57] local Catholic school authorities, directors and even teachers refused to admit non-Catholic pupils, or those professing no religion, and the French-speaking sector thus lost a number of Orthodox Christian, French-speaking Jewish and other non-Catholic immigrants, usually because of religious zeal or a desire to avoid complications. This isolationist trend did not favor close relations between the ethnic groups and the Québec majority group.

c) The quality of education

In the past, the Government of Québec showed little interest in public education. The education budget in 1946, for instance, was about $9 million. It increased to $107 million in 1960 and to $701 million in 1969, to climb to over a billion dollars in 1972.

As already mentioned, public education became compulsory only in 1943 and was considered lacking on many points as compared to that provided by the English schools.

The ethnic groups have always called for non-confessional bilingual schools or French-language schools where a satisfactory amount of English would be taught. They requested that, where the number of pupils and the interest warranted it, other languages be taught for a few hours each week.

The failure of efforts to create such classes has been pointed out in another section. The Parent Report recommendations on this point and similar recommendations by the Interdepartmental Committee in 1967 remained dead letters.[58]

More recently, in the briefs submitted to the Commission by various ethnic groups and during seminars organized by the Commission, adequate English instruction was again requested as a prerequisite to the choice of French-language schools.

It was not only the representatives of the ethnic groups who called for an improvement in the teaching of English. The MCSC, in a brief submitted to the Commission in September, 1969, deplored the poor quality of second-language instruction. Surveys and inquiries among both French-speaking and English-speaking parents brought the same concerns to light.

1) The opinion of the MCSC

In its brief, the MCSC described as follows the situation which already existed in 1958:

> English is taught in our schools from the fifth to the twelfth grade inclusively, to over 100,000 children. The timetable allows for four half-hour classes, or two hours each week in grades 5, 6 and 7 and in secondary school, five 45 minute periods. This would be sufficient under ideal teaching conditions but, as shall be shown further on, the real situation is quite different.[59]

The brief goes on to say that

> in spite of the efforts made, particularly in elementary classes, results remain debatable. The lack of competent teachers is the main reason for this partial failure. This is also the opinion of the Association for the teaching of English in Québec which stated in a report on teacher training: "There are very few experts in TESL in the Province and practically no resources for training the people who now teach ESL."
>
> ......

The following are additional observations which account for the relative failure of the steps taken:

— the time provided for in the timetable is not always respected;
— English is sometimes actually omitted from the timetable and the allotted time granted to other subjects;
— pupils are less motivated since English is not included in the general average on report cards;
— some teachers attribute little importance to this subject.[60]

2) Studies and surveys

In March 1971, the Public Relations Department of the MCSC carried out a survey among the members of the MCSC's Consultative Committee on the teaching of second languages in French-language and English-language schools. At the time of the survey, English schools began teaching French in Grade three. Of the French-speaking parents, 63.38% asked that English schools begin teaching French at an earlier period and 75.2% of the English-speaking parents were in agreement. The survey was also carried out in French-language schools where English courses are at present begun in Grade 5. Of the French-speaking parents, 78.4% asked that English courses be introduced in a lower grade and the majority of English-speaking parents (91.6%) made the same request.[61]

Another inquiry resulted in a general statement by the parents of their desire to see increased French instruction in the elementary schools of the PSBGM. Thirty-six per cent of the 25,830 replies received (representing 59% of the population consulted) would like to see the time devoted to French doubled, 7% want their children to receive half their instruction in French, 6% call for a completely French curriculum, 17% suggest that the amount of French be increased without any change in the present curriculum and 33% are satisfied with the present arrangement.[62]

d) Technical documentation

In view of the influence and scientific importance English is expected to have throughout the world during the next ten or fifteen years, insufficient instruction in English in the French-language schools is prejudicial to the children's education. Research carried out by the Commission supports this statement.[63]

In a typical year it is estimated that about two million documents and articles, 26,000 journals and 30,000 books on scientific and technical topics are published in a wide range of languages. A study of the contents of six major English-language abstracting publications results in the table of scientific literature by language of publication on the opposite page.[64]

TABLE 39

Breakdown by language of publication of literature indexed in SIX MAJOR English-language abstracting and indexing publications

Journals

Language	Chemical Abstracts	Biological Abstracts	Physics Abstracts	Engineering Index	Index Medicus	Mathematical Review
	%	%	%	%	%	%
English	50.3	75	73	82.3	51.2	54.8
Russian	23.4	10	17	3.9	5.6	21.4
German	6.4	3	4	8.6	17.2	8.7
French	7.3	3	4	2.4	8.6	7.8
Japanese	3.6	1	0.5	0.1	0.9	0.7
Chinese	0.5	1	0.1	0	0.4	0.2
Other	8.5	7	14	2.7	16.1	5.4

Source: Science Council of Canada, Report No. 6, September 1969.

e) Teaching second languages

Second language instruction must be improved: French, because it is the language of the majority and is bound to become the common language of use in Québec; English, because of its world-wide importance in the scientific field and because it is a prerequisite for the educational development of the child and an important factor in the choice of French-language schools by the children of non-French and non-British parents.

Immigrants who wanted to improve the employment prospects of their children by having them acquire a knowledge of English experienced difficulty in finding French schools offering English instruction corresponding to their expectations. As we have already seen, the teaching of English started in the second grade (today's 3rd grade) during the first third of the century but since the beginning of the 1940's it has started with the 6th grade (the present 5th grade), averaging two hours' instruction per week at most, and the teachers often being French-speaking.

Hence, at present, in most French schools, the teaching of English begins with the fifth grade in the public sector and in the third grade in schools in the private sector. The Commission's Research Service made a survey of the qualifications of teachers of English as a second language in the Catholic public sector of the Montréal administrative region (where most of the immigrant population is concentrated), and found that only one teacher has a Master's degree in English. In the private sector, the highest qualifications of teachers of English do not exceed a general master's degree in Education, held by only six of the teachers in this category.

Some immigrants turned to the so-called bilingual schools. These schools were rather few; however, in 1970, three teachers of English holding a Doctorate in English were teaching in these schools in the No. 6 administrative region of Montréal. Therefore, as regards the teaching of the second language both in schools of the Catholic School Commissions as well as in those of the PSBGM, the considerable efforts made to train teachers and improve methods proved unequal to the task.

Conclusion

Considering the ethnic origin of the newcomers to Québec since the country was surrendered to England, the immigrating population's adhesion to the English-speaking group was a foregone conclusion.

Over all those years, Québec's population was not particularly alarmed at this. For a long time, language considerations were put aside and demographic factors were the only ones taken into account, as Canada was in an initial stage of its development.

Demographic and economic factors apart, little attention was devoted to education or teaching as a means of integrating the immigrant.

It is true that there was no need to be alarmed. One has only to consider the school-age group of children attending Québec's schools whose language is neither French nor English to realize that the size of this group is small in comparison with that of the total under-20 age group in Québec's population.[65]

Even in Montréal where that particular group is concentrated and sometimes even exceeds the minority of British origin and the English-speaking majority in certain sectors, it would still be proportionately small if it had been distributed throughout the entire school-age population of the Montréal administrative region.

Consequently, it is quite clear that the problem of the integration of immigrants stems from causes quite beyond the mere fact that immigrants' children attend English-speaking schools. It is much more closely linked to the attitudes of the majority group, economic and denominational pressures, or the quality of the education dispensed, all of which are causes that have been and still constitute obstacles to the harmonious integration of immigrants' children into the schools.

OBSERVATIONS AND RECOMMENDATIONS*

Hindrances to School Integration — Possible Solutions

In the past, French-language schools have attracted little more than 50% of immigrant children and, since 1930, the preference of these children for English schools has been maintained. French Canada's intellectual leaders did not, however, fasten upon this situation until very late, at a time when it had become critical.

Before attempting to suggest solutions, the Commission probed beyond the symptoms to get at the root causes.

Several major factors hindering the free choice of schools emerge from the section dealing with the teaching of immigrant children and adults:

(a) the lack of interest shown until recently by French Canadians and the Québec government in the language problem and the attitude of non-acceptance and discouragement of the parents of immigrant children with regard to the enrolling of their children in French Catholic schools, manifested by the leaders of certain school commissions;

(b) since English was the mother-tongue or the second language of the majority of immigrants coming to Québec, their children naturally inclined toward the English school system;

(c) the definition along denominational lines which, until recent years, divided the school system in two, between Catholic schools (both French- and English-language) and Protestant schools (English). This division was

*Pages 237-261 of the original chapter have not been reproduced here. They deal with Quebecs' institutional responses to the education of immigrants.

detrimental to the French-language schools, especially since Jews were classed by law among Protestants and those of Orthodox and other non-Catholic persuasions were urged to send their children to English-language schools;

(d) another unfavorable element for the French-language schools was the quality of the teaching of English and the lack of sufficient teaching of that language. It was these shortcomings in teaching at French-language schools which led to the setting up of the Parent Commission and to its findings. Québec had to wait until 1964 to have an education department.

(e) finally — and of major importance, — is the econqmic factor. The goal of immigrants in coming to Québec was to improve their material lot and ensure a better future of their children. To earn a living, they had to work in English, following the example of French Canadians. They also noticed that, in Montréal at least, some French Canadian parents who had the means, sent their children to English-language or private schools. They therefore followed suit. Bilingualism seemed absolutely essential to them and they have never ceased calling for neutral bilingual schools in order to ensure the best possible education for their children.

The need for bilingualism

Again very recently, the need to be bilingual was accepted as a basically important factor by the three groups: French-speaking, English-speaking and "others". School is considered one of the various means through which a language can be learned. But there is a very direct link between initiation into a language and its future use at work. For it is not enough just to learn a language. The imposition of a language depends on economic imperatives, and the process of learning, development and use derives above all, from the work milieu. In Québec's present economic position, the knowledge of English and French:

> is perceived as the biggest asset which a student, newly arrived in the labor market, can offer to obtain the job of his choice.[66]

These observations, made by Québec pupils of different origins and accompanied by their parents' opinions, are revealed in a survey by Sorecom, which adds:

> language does not necessarily constitute a very basic value. . .and the 'primum vivere' remains the most important realistic factor where language choice is concerned. Persuading French-speaking people, English-speaking people, or Italians to opt for French for the simple reason that it is the language of the majority or an element of culture, would be something else again.[67]

Choice of a school system does not necessarily imply option for transfer of language. As we have seen,[68] Mr. Maheu has made it very clear that choice of school does not prevent Italians from making the language switch in favor of French-speaking people. It should be emphasized again that immigrants do not come to Québec concerned with language problems, but motivated by the economic benefits and the democratic freedom found here.

They realize[69] — and this is confirmed by the Commission's research — that technology is destined to influence the use of the English language and that English will remain the "lingua franca" for the foreseeable future. They are quick to recognize the importance of English as the language of work and the shortcomings in its teaching found in the French-language schools.

The vital importance of the work communication language

It will be difficult to persuade them to send their children to French-language schools as long as French has not become the language of communication at work, or unless it can be demonstrated to them that French-language schools teach English sufficiently well to ensure the professional and geographic mobility of their children.

The French-speaking group is affected by this situation in the same way. The following are the conclusions reached by Professors Jacques Brazeau and Serge Carlos in a survey they carried out at the Commission's request:

> Generally speaking, the salient point of this section is without doubt the importance of the work milieu as the context of initiation into the second language. For this very reason, the role of the school is diminished. This suggests that to depend on the school for spreading French would involve teaching-quality reforms very much more than the simple extension of the requirement to learn French at school. If, however, changes are not made at the level of work-world pressures, efforts directed in the school system may well be wasted. In view of the predominance of English and the importance of this same context concerning initiation into the second language, it might well be asked if the future of "French bilingualism" does not require the smashing of this vicious circle of the work world.[70]

There is no question that, if French were used as language of communications at work and became increasingly useful and necessary in this area, English-language schools would no longer enjoy that degree of success they know today. In order to retain their students, they would make every effort to offer excellent teaching of French. Why can the French-language schools not make a start by providing excellent instruction of both languages?

But, as far as the teaching of English is concerned:

> Teachers are the first to want to see English courses become optional. This is a border-area where students say they would not take English courses if these were optional and where teachers are aware that these students do not want to learn English.
>
> Almost 80% of students consider their English courses unnecessary.

Other causes of hesitation

Besides the socio-economic pressures which require the teaching of both languages, briefs from the ethnic groups frequently refer to two other reasons why immigrant parents are reluctant to send their children to French-language schools: unsatisfactory quality of the teaching of French and a hostile attitude toward non-French-speaking children.

Doubts have been expressed as to the equivalence of French school system diplomas with those in the rest of Canada. It is suggested this could be a hindrance to opting for the French-language system.

The Commission had no opportunity to examine the foundation for such fears. It simply passes them on to the Education Department with the request that the situation be explored and appropriate action taken.

A — GENERAL RECOMMENDATIONS

Given that in certain cases today school commission still refuse to accept either a) individual application for enrollment because of insufficient knowledge of the French language or adherance to another faith; or b) group request, for the reason that the introduction of another group would hamper the normal progress of a class, the Commission recommends:

> **that the Education Department pay constant attention to ensuring that French-language schools admit the children of immigrants or of those who have become citizens, regardless of language or religion;**
>
> **that the school commissions see to it that children who wish to attend French-language schools but have an insufficient knowledge of that language and the vocabulary of science and mathematics, are directed towards introductory or "immersion" classes; and that such children be subsequently integrated into regular classes as soon as their language abilities allow;**
>
> **that French language school commissions be required to set up introductory or "immersion" classes should the need become apparent or should they be requested by a sufficient number of parents.**

Given that the social context and the attitude of the host country contribute to the effectiveness of action in the education field, the Commission recommends:

> **that in the education milieus, teachers and pupils become aware of the immigrants' potential contribution to the Province and welcome them cordially.**

The Commission feels that every child, of whatever ethnic origin, has the right to the benefits of a sound education to ensure his professional and cultural development. Parental concern in this respect is justified. Moreover, this concept is repeatedly referred to in the preambles to the Education Department and Superior Council of Education Acts.

The Commission feels:

(a) that at the present time, French-language schools do not provide their pupils with sufficient teaching of French and English to ensure the full development of their personality and to equip them to become future leaders in various activity sectors, more especially in the economic area;

(b) that these educational shortcomings amount to a social injustice, in that those children whose parents have scant financial means are obliged to take these courses, whereas parents enjoying better financial circumstances can send their children to private or English-language schools.

(c) that not only does this situation work to the detriment of French-speaking children whose parents are poor, but it is also a major obstacle to the attraction of children of parents belonging to the other ethnic groups; in this way, it is detrimental to the development and enhancement of French among their numbers.

B — RECOMMENDATIONS REGARDING FRENCH-LANGUAGE AND ENGLISH-LANGUAGE SCHOOLS

Given the importance of language initiation in the schools, the Commission recommends:

> that adequate teaching of French and English be provided for pupils who attend French-language schools and that the Education Department supervise the organization of such teaching at the primary and secondary levels throughout the province;

And, to ensure that pupils acquire the best possible knowledge of French and English, the Commission recommends:

> that, wherever possible, English courses be taught by English-speaking teachers in French-language schools and French by French-speaking teachers in English-language schools.

Given the acute shortage of English teachers and the urgent need to train sufficient numbers of these, the Commission recommends:

> that the Government make available scholarships to speed up the training and specialization of second language teachers;

Consideration could be given to the teaching of a third or a fourth language to such secondary-level pupils as so desire. But option for one of these languages ought never to take the place of teaching English in French-language schools or French in Enlgish-language schools.

For this reason, the Commission recommends:

> that the teaching of French or English as a second language be compulsory and take priority over the teaching of any other language in schools at both the primary and the secondary levels.

The teaching of other languages than French and English would enrich Québec's culture and induce third-group parents to opt for French-language schools. For this reason, the Commission recommends:

> that following the example of English-language schools which at present offer certain courses in languages other than French and English, French-language schools adopt a similar policy if so requested by a sufficient number of parents, and that the appropriate credits be awarded.

Following the example of their French-speaking counterparts in Ontario, Québec's English-speaking pupils ought, in the future, to have a working knowledge of French, which would bring them the following benefits:

(a) the ability to communicate with their French-speaking compatriots;

(b) the ability to face competition from French-speaking workers in the same areas of activity;

(c) a chance to play a part in the political, civic and social life of Québec society;

(d) an understanding of the values and civilization of their French-speaking counterparts.

To achieve knowledge and understanding of the culture of the majority in Québec, the Commission recommends:

> that English-language schools provide courses in French-Canadian civilization, in a manner to be determined by the Education Department.

C — RECOMMENDATIONS REGARDING VARIOUS WAYS OF ENCOURAGING MUTUAL UNDERSTANDING BETWEEN PUPILS FROM QUÉBEC'S DIFFERENT COMMUNITIES

The Commission deplores and considers harmful the present isolation and lack of contact between French-speaking and English-speaking pupils. For this reason, it suggests that the school commissions and the Education Department take all possible steps to encourage a bringing-together of French and English-speaking pupils in mutual understanding contacts. Among these steps, it recommends:

that as often as is desirable and possible, joint French and English conversation courses be organized for French- and English-speaking pupils by the Protestant and Catholic school Commissions;

that in a spirit free of ethnocentric considerations, the English- and French-language and Protestant and Catholic School Commissions organize meetings of a cultural or sporting nature;

that exchange programs be set up and further developed throughout the Province between young French- and English-speaking Québecers and those of other origins;

that any other programs designed to foster mutual knowledge, understanding and acceptance be encouraged, with a view to promoting the unity of Québec groups in the respect of the specific contribution of each to the development of the Province.

D — RECOMMENDATIONS REGARDING STEPS DESIGNED TO ENSURE THE WIDER USE OF FRENCH

a) Integration not irreversible

The Commission considered steps designed to speed up the use of French among children whose parents belong to other ethnic groups. Selection of the best way of going about this was found to be delicate, since the other ethnic groups are made up of both members already settled in Québec and future immigrants. Finally, the Commission reached the conclusion that today's trend toward integration of immigrant children into the English-language schools is not irreversible. Its duty, it feels, is to find a solution which will ensure that the children already in Québec and those of future immigrants are attracted to French schools. And, it is in this spirit that it recommended at the outset the improvement of the French-language school system.

b) Restricted numbers of immigrant children and coercion

On the other hand, even if the Commission had reached the conclusion that the past and the present are irreversible and it should concern itself solely with the children of future immigrants, a preliminary question has still to be answered; would the number and probable origin of children of future immigrants justify coercive measures and what are likely to be the results?

We have seen that, for the 1961-1971 census period, the population of immigrants under 20 years of age amounted to only 3.34% of the population of the province in the same age-group and that the percentage of new immigrants under twenty years of age of each year between 1958 and 1971 never exceeded 0.5. In 1971, the number of immigrants within this age bracket was 5,034 out of a corresponding provincial population of 2,406,827, representing 0.2% of the total provincial population under twenty years of age. What makes the situation even more delicate is the fact that English is the mother tongue or the second language of the majority of these children. Considering that about three-fifths of the immigrants under 20 years old are of school age, some 3,000 immigrant children would be affected by a decision for the year 1971, and more than half of these would have English as their mother tongue or their second language. In view of the success of the introductory classes, decisions of a coercive nature would affect a few hundred children of immigrants annually.

The Commissioners felt that this sort of decision, affecting such a small number of children, would be premature and out of proportion with the anticipated results. In comparison, beneficial results as regards the integration of children of immigrants or already-installed citizens of other ethnic origins could be expected from a more understanding attitude.

c) Migration and coercion

The Commission also took into account the negative demographic aspects that such a decision could have as regards the future arrival of other immigrants; it took into consideration Québec's precarious demographic position compared with that of the other provinces. In effect, the drop in immigration to Québec has become so pronounced in recent years that its immigrant strength for 1972 is lower than that of British Columbia.

The Commission also felt that it would be unfair to force only the children of some immigrants to attend French-language schools, while at the same time allowing the majority who are already English-speaking to continue to swell the English-language school population. Such a decision would in no way have helped bring about a reversal in the proportion of these children attending French-language schools.

d) Example of the majority's freedom of choice

A still more difficult problem faced the Commission. Could it recommend coercive measures to apply to a certain category of immigrants' children while the French-speaking majority continued to enjoy freedom of choice as to schools? Throughout the world, the order applying to immigrants is dictated by the behavior of the majority. Would these children then be obliged to attend French-language schools as long as their parents had not become citizens? And what would become of immigrants' children born in Québec, that is, Canadians by birth?

In a study prepared for the Commission, the Belgian Professor W.J. Ganshoff van der Meersch rejects coercive measures until all inducements in the educational field have been exhausted.[73]

For his part, Professor Léon Dion does not believe in results achieved through constraint. He suggests measures of inducement:

> In principle, compulsory attendance at French-language schools could be imposed on the children of immigrant parents. But this measure would be very difficult to enforce, at least as long as the English-language school system continued to exist. In addition, the existence of such a measure could discourage immigrants from settling in Québec. An immigrant motivation study should certainly be conducted to determine the possible consequences of such a measure and, where necessary, to help establish the best method of offsetting the predictable negative effects.[74]

Professor Dion believes that, in an emergency situation, the children of immigrants could be forced to attend French-language schools only if the same obligation were to be imposed on all French-speaking children. But are we in a position of imminent danger? And is the restricted number of immigrants' children sufficient justification for imposing on Québec's majority the obligation to attend French-language schools, when its attendance at such schools is already overwhelming, even if the lack of adequate English teaching is often deplored? The French-speaking majority has always enjoyed freedom of choice in the education field.

The Commission reached the conclusion that, generally speaking, the school situation does not involve the degree of urgency or primacy which is sometimes attributed to it. It firmly believes that no distinction should be drawn between the children of future immigrants, be they English-speaking, French-speaking or other.

The Commission feels that the maintenance on a language basis of the past divisions created on a religious basis would be harmful.

e) If envisaged, coercive measures in the field of education should apply to all pupils at primary levels without exception

It is further convinced that all possible future coercive measures in the education field should apply in a uniform way to the French-speaking majority, the English-speaking minority, the third group and all future immigrants.

If, however, after the time periods recommended by the Commission in Book II dealing with "Language Rights in Québec", the situation in the education field required coercive legislation, the government should act at the primary level, since French should be learned at an early age because it is a more difficult language than English. Following this, at the end of the primary stage, parents would once again enjoy freedom of choice.

The reason why the Commission did not feel it advisable to recommend coercive measures in the education field at this time is that it considers that the use of French at work provides immigrant parents with the best inducement to send their children to French-language schools, provided, of course, that adequate teaching of English is also available.

f) Prerequisite attitude changes

The Commission also considers that all coercive measures are premature until there is a change in the reciprocal attitudes and motivations of French Canadians and the ethnic groups A repetition of the St. Léonard crisis must at all costs be avoided. In some situations, the positive solution lies in refraining from action rather than the alternative of precipitate interference.

Finally, the Commission feels that before moving on to coercive measures, there should be a waiting period to take stock of the results of the inducement measures which have been given added impetus with the new structures set up after 1969, such as the COFI, the introductory classes, the nurseries, the summer camps project and the general stepping up of the Immigration Department's various programs.

COFI*

Given that French is the principal language of work in certain areas, that in addition it constitutes a condition for the practice of a profession under Bill 64 and that several immigrants affected by these activities attend the COFI, the Commission recommends:

> that the Québec Immigration Department be authorized by the Federal Government to provide forty weeks of French teaching through COFI, instead of twenty weeks of English and twenty of French, for immigrants especially interested in learning the French language.

Given the acute scarcity of COFI-qualified teachers, the Commission recommends:

> that for the teaching of immigrants through COFI, the Immigration Department seek out qualified teachers specializing in teaching immigrants and that these be retained as career teachers; and that, if possible, these teachers should speak several languages;
>
> that training periods be provided by the Immigration Department for its civil servants and for COFI teachers, dealing with the psychological implications of the act of immigration, the various stages of the immigration process, and the needs and benefits of immigration, in order that immigrants be better understood.

In relation to areas of residence, the existing COFI centres are located in remote spots. Immigrants lose a great deal of time getting there. Travelling entails unnecessary expense. For these reasons, the Commission recommends:

> that the Immigration Department reorganize the COFI, improve their

**Centres d'orientation et de formation des immigrants.*

performance and take appropriate steps to ensure that, in the future, COFI courses be offered at locations which are easily accessible to immigrants.

Courses on initiation into Canadian and Québec life

Given the recognized popularity of voluntary courses on initiation into Canadian and Québec life, the Commission recommends:

> that the number of courses on initiation into Canadian and Québec life be increased and that they be offered in areas where ethnic groups are concentrated and in the language of the group concerned, at times suitable to mothers of children where possible; that the course content be revised to express Québec's French fact and other special characteristics of the Province.

Mothers of children

Given the special and difficult circumstances of mothers of children and in order to ensure that they may enjoy the same language advantages as other immigrants, the Commission recommends:

> that part-time language courses be established at times and in locations suited to the needs of mothers of children.

Statistics and inventory

Given that statistics on immigrants are incomplete and insufficient, and that consequently a genuine assessment of the situation is impossible, the Commission recommends:

> that an annual meeting be called by the Québec Immigration Department, in cooperation with any other provincial department concerned and with the Federal Manpower and Immigration Department in order to pool statistics of all kinds on all immigrants settled in Québec, according to ethnic group, last place of residence, mother tongue, language spoken in the home, second language learned, schooling, and so forth, and that to this end a survey be taken in public and private schools at all levels.

These statistics should cover: (a) the different ethnic and language characteristics of all the immigrants who have elected to settle in Québec; (b) those who register with the federal manpower and immigration services; (c) those who find work immediately; (d) those who have been brought into contact with the COFI language courses; (e) those who have been oriented towards the English and French job-training sectors.

In order to provide a clear and accurate picture of the situation, uniform and precise statistics should be compiled and analysed over a suitable period of time. This implies, that in order to keep abreast with the geographic, demographic and language paths of immigrants, the provincial authorities must become involved in the gathering and exchange of information between the federal Manpower department and the Québec Immigration Department.

French immersions courses

Given the obligation of the provincial government and of private enterprise to teach French to immigrants who find work immediately, the Commission recommends:

> that joint and concrete efforts be made by the Québec government and private enterprise, and that immigrants be provided with the material and technical means to make it casier for them to attend French-language immersion courses.

Introductory classes

Given that the classes — though a comparatively recent experiment — already have produced considerable results as to the respect of parents' right to choice of school and that, as already noted,[75] up to November, 1972, 542 pupils (of whom 63 were English-speaking) had attended these courses, the Commission recommend:

> that the introductory classes experiment be broadened and kept under constant observation for at least five years; that all possible steps be taken, including the allocation of adequate financial resources, to make this arrangement as attractive as possible to the immigrant at the time of his arrival and during his first weeks of residence; that information on introductory classes reach immigrants already installed, as well as all other citizens.

Ethnic schools

Given that the core of Québec's immigration problem lies in the Montréal metropolitan area and considering the difficulty of legislating for special cases, and given also the satisfactory results achieved by the recent setting up of private schools with French-teaching priorities, notably the Greek Socrates and St. George's Cathedral Schools, the Commission recommends:

> that the government offer technical and material assistance to private or associated ethnic schools which undertake to provide the major part of their teaching in French and that these schools agree to make use for their French courses of French-speaking teachers appointed by the Education Department.

Nursery schools

The acute shortage of nursery schools was stressed in several recommendations of the Royal Commission on the Status of Women in Canada.

The problem is even more acute for immigrants who, during their initial residence period, have to meet a host of responsibilities. Integration of immigrants' children into the French-speaking milieu should be encouraged at the earliest age, as the most reliable guarantee that the education process will continue in that language; in addition, the influence on the family surroundings will be beneficial.

Given the results of the recent nursery schools experiment and the need to set up other nursery schools where immigrant children can come in contact with French-speaking pre-schoolers, the Commission recommends:

> that the Québec Immigration Department, in cooperation with the Social Affairs Department, develop the nursery school system in Montréal; that these schools be easy of access and available to both the pre-school age children of immigrants and the French-speaking children of Canadian parents; and that the French language be used in these schools along with the vernacular tongue where necessary.

Summer Camps

Given the results achieved by the Françoise Cabrini summer camp and the need to establish summer camps where immigrant children can meet children of French-speaking Québecers for two or three-month periods, during which French could be taught or learned through contacts and friendships developing between immigrant children and children of French-speaking Québecers, the Commission recommends:

> that the Québec government, in cooperation with private voluntary associations, establish summer camps lasting for two or three months, in order to facilitate contacts between the children of immigrants and children of French-speaking Québecers and thereby speed up the initiation of the former into the French-language.

Bilingual schools

Given the unreserved attachment which the ethnic groups have shown for bilingual neutral schools and the beneficial effects these schools could have on both immigrant children and the children of English- and French-speaking people wishing to attend them, not only as regards language initiation but also for the creation of a spirit of Québec unity; given that these bilingual schools could and should give priority to the teaching of French; given that these schools constitute very useful experiments, the Commission recommends:

> that, considering their success, the existing bilingual pilot-schools attended by both the children of immigrants and those of French- and English-speaking people, be maintained on an experimental basis and that the creation of other bilingual schools be encouraged in accordance with demand, in order to provide a basis for assessment of their effectiveness as regards second-language teaching methods.

Discrimination and the Ombudsman

Given the possibility of discrimination against immigrant children during their integration into French-language schools and given that a harmonious relationship between children of various ethnic groups represents the essential condition for the greater attraction of other immigrant children to such schools, the Commission recommends:

> that the immigrants' "Ombudsman" be entrusted with every grievance concerning the admission of immigrant children into French-language schools, actions and attitudes prejudicial to immigrant children after admission to French-language schools, and any attempt at discrimination against persons of various ethnic origins; and that the said "Ombudsman" undertake appropriate investigation and endeavor to eliminate such prejudice.[76]

NOTES

[1] Parent Report, Part Three, ch. III, sec. IV, par. 186.

[2] Michel Brunet, *Québec Canada anglais*, p. 17.

[3] Brunet, *op. cit.*, pp. 87-88.

[4] *Idem*, p. 97.

[5] René Gauthier, "Intégration éducationnelle et scolaire de l'immigrant au Québec," p. 24.

[6] Gauthier, "Rapport. . .", *op. cit.*, p. 15. For more details on the language courses taught to adults on a part-time basis, see below, Part Two, Chap. II, A. 9, "Part-time language courses", *The Ethnic Groups.*

[7] *Ibid*, p. 43.

[8] R. Gauthier, "Intégration éducationelle et scolaire de l'immigrant au Québec," 1965, p. 33.

[9] Parent Report, *op. cit.*, Part I, chap. I, sec. V, para. 35.

[10] *Ibid.*, Part II, chap. I, para. 3 and chap. I, sec. I, para. 9.

[11] *Ibid.*, Part II, chap. IV, sec. I, para. 155.

[12] *Ibid.*, Part II, chap. IV, sec. I, para. 161.

[13] *Ibid.*, Part II, chap. XIII, sec. III, para. 686.

[14] Parent Report, Part II, chap. XI, sec. III, para. 700.

[15] *Ibid.*, Part II, chap. XIII, sec. V, para. 214.

[16] *Ibid.*, Part II, chap. XII, sec. II, para. 616. See also Chalvin, Solange and Michel, *Comment on abrutit nos enfants*, "La bêtise en 23 manuels scolaires" (How we Degrade our children, the Nonsense found in 23 Textbooks). Les Éditions du Jour, Ottawa, 1962.

[17] *Ibid.*, Part III, chap. II, sec. III, para. 189.

[18] *Ibid.*, Part III, chap. III, sec. IV, para. 190.

[19] *Ibid.*, Part III, chap. III, sec. IV, para. 190.

[20] *Ibid.*, Part III, chap. III, sec. IV, para. 193.

[21] Gauthier, "Intégration. . .", *op. cit.*, pp. 26-27.

[22] L'école Mainmonide (see *La Presse*, December 4, 1972, p. 8). This school had been requested for the past ten years in briefs to both the Parent Commission and to the Québec Government.

[23] See above, Part One, *The Ethnic Groups*

[24] Morrison, J.C., *Puerto Rican Study*, New York Board of Education 1953-1957.

[25] Bhatnagar, Joti, *Immigrants at School*, Cornmarket Press, London, p. 156.

[26] Taft, R.A., *Opinion Convergence in the Assimilation of Immigrants*, 1962.

[27] Hamelin, Jean, "La dimension historique du problème linguistique," (Historical Dimensions of the Language Problem), p. 27. Study prepared at the Commission's request.

[28] R. Maheu states that in 1851 English-speaking people made up 35% of the population. Cf. Maheu, *op. cit.*, doc. 416, p. 2.

[29] Guay, G.D. "Immigration sous le régime français", (Immigration during the French Regime), doc. 270/E, p. 1.

[30] Taken from Ouellet, Fernand, *Histoire économique et sociale du Québec 1760-1780, Structures et conjonctures, (Economic and Social History of Quebec from 1760 to 1780: Structures and Circumstances)*, Montréal, 1968, p. 143.

[31] From 1843 to 1847, of an annual immigration rate of 37,911, 33% came from England, 57% from Ireland, and 7% from Scotland. From 1848 to 1852, of an annual immigration rate of 37.795, 24% came from England, 53% from Ireland, and 13% from Scotland. Cf. Ouellet "Histoire économique. . .", *op. cit.*, p. 472.

[32] See Appendix II, Table A-11. *The Ethnic Groups*, Material compiled by the Research Service of the Commission in Quebec City, in accordance with the statistics for the corresponding years from the Canada Immigration Division, Department of Manpower and Immigration.

[33] Jacques Brossard, *L'immigration*, Les Presses de l'université de Montréal, 1967, pp. 17-19.

[34] *Idem*, p. 19.

[35] Richard Joy, *Languages in Conflict.* The Canadian Experience, pp. 62 and 58.

[36] See Appendix II, Table A-12, *The Ethnic Groups.*

[37] Report of January 30, 1967, p. 27 and ff.

[38] Report of January 30, 1967.

[39] See Appendix II, Table A-13, *The Ethnic Groups.*

[40] See Appendix II, Tables A-14 and A-15, *The Ethnic Groups.*

[41] Provincial Immigration office, Population of Québec, censuses of 1961 and 1971.

[42] See Appendix II, Table A-15, *The Ethnic Groups.*

[43] See Appendix II, Table A-16, *The Ethnic Groups.*

[44] See Appendix II, Table A-17, *The Ethnic Groups.*

[45] Joy, *op. cit.*, p. 41

[46] The following data were compiled by the Research Service of the Commission, according to the Statistics of the Data-processing Service of the Department of Education of Québec (SIMEQ).

[47] It is obvious that the data from the Québec Bureau of Statistics on this matter are incomplete. The School in question is called "Cours privé L. Farmer", of Montréal.

[48] "Other" designates certain schools which operate on a non-confessional basis.

[49] Lionel Groulx, *Histoire du Canada français*, vol. IV, Montréal, 1952, p. 63.

[50]Pierre de Grandpré, "Bilinguisme et système d'éducation au Québec face au rapport sur le bilinguisme et le biculturalisme" (Bilingualism and the Education System in Québec in view of the Report on Bilingualism and biculturalism). Conference held on December 13, 1970, p. 3.

[51]Except from an address given by Mrs. Thérèse Baron, Deputy Minister of Education, during a seminar on Québec culture and society ("Culture et société québécoise"), organized by the *Centre québécois des relations internationales* in Québec City on October 3, 1972.

[52]Ethnic schools.

[53]Information provided by the Department of Education (Commission doc. 1650 CXL).

[54]Étude de l'orientation linguistique de quelques groupes dans la région de Montréal.

[55]Quebec Bill 63 Statistics Misleading — H&S. *The Gazette*, October 24, 1972, p. 3.

[56]See *infra*, ch. II, A, 11, Introductory classes.

[57]See *supra*, Part Two, ch. II, A. 1, d. 1.

[58]Interdepartmental Committee, *op. cit.*, p. 44, See also *supra*, Part Two, ch. II, A, 1, d, 2, "Parent Report".

[59]Resolution XXV, Regular session of May 6, 1958, p. 27 of the brief.

[60]*Ibid.*, p. 29.

[61]The results of the survey were submitted to the Parliamentary Committee on Education in November, 1971.

[62]Québec Federation of Home and School Associations, "Report re French Instruction in Elementary Schools of the PBBGM", March, 1970.

[63]"Évolution des exigences linguistiques des familles de fonctions dans les entreprises québécoises pour les quinze prochaines années", (Development of Linguistic Requirements of Job Categories in Québec Enterprises for the next Fifteen Years), Ducharme, Déom et Associés, Ins., August 30, 1971.

[64]"A Policy for Scientific and Technical Information Dissemination", Science Council of Canada, Report No. 6, September, 1969.

[65]Cf. Appendix II, Tables A-14 and A-15, *The Ethnic Groups.*

[66]Sorecom Inc., "Survey. . .", *op. cit.*, p. 42.

[67]Idem, p. 47.

[68]R. Maheu, "*Groupes ethniques et linguistiques*" (Ethnic and Language Groups) Doc. 415 (c) pages 13-14.

[69]Ducharme, Déom et Associés Inc., "Evolution des exigences linguistiques des familles de fonctions dans les entreprises québécoises pour les 15 prochaines années" (Development of Language Requirements in Classified Tasks in Quebec Business over the Next 15 Years), August 30, 1971, p. 337.

[70]"Utilisation du français dans le monde du travail", (The Use of French in the Quebec Work World), *op. cit.*, p. 113.

[71] Mareschal-Boudon-Lapierre: "Étude sur les motivations des enseignants et des étudiants face à la situation linguistique au Québec" (Study of the Motivation of Teachers and Students in the Light of the Québec Language Situation), 1972, p. 26.

[72] For the texts of these preambles see *infra* Third Part, Chap. III, B, 2, a.

[73] W.J. Ganshoff van der Meersch, "*Rapport sur les principes juridiques, idéologiques et historiques relatifs aux droits linguistiques et culturels des minorités linguistiques*" (Report on Legal, Ideological and Historical Principles Concerning Language and Cultural Rights of Language Minorities) p. 32 and ss.

[74] Léon Dion: "*Le français, langue d'adoption au Québec*" (French, Adoptive Language in Quebec) in *Le français langue de travail* (French, the Language of Work) Presses de l'Université Laval, 1971, p. 63.

[75] See *supra*, Part Two, Chap. II, A, 11, *The Ethnic Groups*

[76] For the powers and responsibilities of the immigrants' Ombudsman, see *infra*, Part Three, Recommendation No. 68.

SECTION FOUR

French as the Language of Work

PARTICIPATION AND LANGUAGE USE IN THE PRIVATE SECTOR*†

Our research on the private sector was focussed on the larger corporate enterprises because they are playing an increasingly important role in the work world. They employ large numbers of people and, consciously or unconsciously, they have developed a corporate language policy. For these reasons their influence on language patterns extends well beyond their immediate sphere. Furthermore, many of the most skilled managers and scientific and technological experts — that is, those who have access to major sources of power in contemporary society — are employed by these same large corporations. It is important to discover the extent to which Francophones and Anglophones are found at the decision-making levels of these corporations, especially in Quebec.

As we have seen in Part 1 of this Book, the ownership of Canadian industry by Francophones is almost completely restricted to Quebec, and within that province it is very unevenly distributed among the different branches of industry. Francophones are owners and proprietors in large proportions in agriculture and to a lesser degree in the service fields and retail trade. In wholesale trade they play a still smaller role, while in finance and manufacturing they account for about one-fourth of the total. Moreover, within manufacturing itself, the pattern of ownership is also uneven. In small-scale manufacturing, such as the production of wood products, Francophones predominate; but in fields requiring large capital investment and highly advanced technology, such as the manufacture of chemicals and petroleum products, they play virtually no role in ownership or control.

Francophone participation in high-level occupations reflects a similar pattern. The proportion of Canadians of French origin in the higher occupational groups (that is, managers, professionals, and technicians) is considerably less than their proportion in the total work force, while the proportion in lower-level occupations is correspondingly higher. Between 1941 and 1961, in the country as a whole they consistently lost ground. The disadvantaged occupational position of

*Chapter XII, Report of the Royal Commission on Bilingualism and Biculturalism, Book III, *The Work World*, Ottawa: Queen's Printer, 1969, pp. 447-469

†Paragraph numbers and marginal headings have been omitted.

Canadians of French origin has its parallels in the areas of income and schooling.

While the data on occupations and incomes are consistent with facts about ownership and control of industry, they need to be supplemented by more detailed information. It is important to know whether the Francophones in the high-level occupations are to be found chiefly in small or large corporations and, to the extent that they are employed in large firms, whether they appear at all levels in the organizations or are clustered in particular levels or occupations. Such knowledge would let us see to what degree Francophones are in a position of real influence in the work world and to what extent the French language is used as the language of work.

To obtain such information we turned to the corporations themselves, particularly to those operating in Quebec. The focus of study is restricted to the manufacturing sector, the largest sector of industry in Quebec. In 1961 it employed almost 500,000 workers. It includes a substantial number of large firms and is a segment of industry where managerial competence and technical and scientific expertise are at a high level. Although the larger manufacturing firms may not be entirely representative of the rest of the work world, it is nonetheless likely that they reflect the way the rest of industry is moving.[1]

A. Participation

1. The general pattern

The following data are based on a sample survey of large manufacturing corporations which have operations of significant size in Quebec or in adjacent areas where Francophones form a substantial part of the population.[2] Many of the firms in the sample have operations elsewhere in Canada, and they were asked to report on these facilities as well. We were thus able to obtain both an accurate general picture of participation and language use within Quebec and an idea of the main characteristics of the situation in other provinces. However, the data drawn from our geographically biased sample cannot provide an accurate picture of the Canadian industrial scene as a whole.[3]

The findings of the survey confirmed the widely held impression that Francophone participation in large Canadian industrial firms is much weaker than that of Anglophones. In the sample, Francophones comprised approximately 45 per cent of the employees earning less than $5,000 a year and only 31 per cent of the personnel earning more than $5,000; Anglophones formed 55 per cent of the former category and 69 per cent of the latter. This comparison does not bring out the major difference between the Francophone and Anglophone positions, which appears only when the variations by salary level are examined.

The proportion of Francophones declined as the salary level rose in the large manufacturing corporations (Table 64).† Francophone personnel were always an absolute minority at the higher salary levels; they constituted about 36 per cent

†The table numbers in the original reference have been retained for purposes of cross-reference and clarity

of the total at the levels just above $5,000, and only about 15 per cent at the top levels. The *total* work force of the large corporations in the sample was approximately 43 per cent Francophone. Thus, participation by Francophones was not only somewhat below average in the group earning from $5,000 to $6,499 but very low at the higher salary levels, particularly among those earning $12,000 or more per year.

Table 64. Language Group of Salaried Personnel Earning $5,000 and Over

Percentage distribution within salary levels of salaried personnel in 36 large manufacturing firms, by language group[1] — Canada, 1964

Salary level	Number	Language group		
		Francophones	Anglophones	Total
$ 5,000 — 6,499	7,862	36	64	100
6,500 — 7,999	5,344	35	65	100
8,000 — 9,999	3,448	25	75	100
10,000 — 11,999	1,368	19	81	100
12,000 — 14,999	994	15	85	100
15,000 and over	872	15	85	100
All salary levels	19,888	31	69	100

Source: Morrison, "Large Manufacturing Firms."

[1] The language group was determined on the basis of mother tongue, or the official language of greatest fluency if the mother tongue was neither French nor English.

The 36 corporations surveyed can be divided into five groups according to the nationality and language of the owners (Table 65). Only 17 per cent were owned by Canadian Francophones. This low proportion parallels the pattern of ownership reported in Chapter IV.

There is also a noteworthy difference in the size of the firms owned by the two language groups. The nine Francophone-owned corporations employed an average of about 91 employees earning salaries of $5,000 or more a year. By contrast, the Anglophone-owned firms averaged 706 salaried employees at this level. The firms owned by Canadian or foreign Francophones were much smaller than the other firms in the sample.

Table 65. Ownership and Location of Manufacturing Firms

Numerical distribution of 36 large manufacturing firms, by nationality and language group of their owners, and by the location of head office — Canada, 1964

Language group and nationality	Location of head office		
	Quebec	Elsewhere in Canada	Total
French			
Canadian	6	0	6
Foreign	3	0	3
English			
Canadian	12	4	16
United Kingdom	4	0	4
United States	5	2	7
Total	30	6	36

Source: Morrison, "Large Manufacturing Firms."

Firms with different types of ownership had very different proportions of Francophones among their staff earning salaries of $5,000 or more. In those firms with headquarters in Quebec and whose owners were Canadian Francophones, 78 per cent of the salaried personnel were Francophones. Next came the firms owned by foreign Francophone interests, 62 per cent of whose salaried personnel were Francophones. In the Anglophone-owned firms with headquarters in Quebec, both those owned by citizens of the United Kingdom and those owned by Canadians, 35 per cent of the salaried staff were Francophones, but in those owned by Americans, only 23 per cent were Francophones. The Anglophone-owned firms with headquarters outside Quebec and lower proportions of salaried Francophones: 22 per cent in the Canadian-owned firms, and 15 per cent in the American-owned firms were Francophones. However, in actual numbers, the Anglophone-owned firms employed more Francophones earning salaries of $5,000 or more than did the Francophone-owned firms.

Clearly, the Francophone-owned firms employed a very small segment of the total number of employees earning more than $5,000 — 815 out of 19,888, or 4 per cent. The Francophones they employed accounted for only 3 per cent of this total and for about 10 per cent of the 6,100 Francophones in the sample. These Francophone salaried personnel were working to an overwhelming degree in the corporations owned by Anglophones.

The nine Francophone-owned firms tended strongly to employ only Francophone salaried personnel at these levels. Anglophone personnel within them were few and were employed almost entirely in sales work. By contrast, the corporations owned by Anglophones tended to employ higher salaried personnel of both language backgrounds and to employ them in a greater variety of functions and activities. The Francophone-owned corporations thus had a much more homogeneous work force than the other firms.

The differences in the composition of the work force earning $5,000 or more in corporations owned by Francophones and Anglophones can be seen vividly if we limit our comparison to Canadian-owned firms with head offices in Quebec (Table 66). In firms owned by French-speaking Canadians, Francophones constituted an overwhelming majority (except in the group earning salaries of $10,000 to $11,999, who were almost all sales personnel). In the firms owned by Canadian Anglophones, Francophone salaried personnel were in the minority at all levels. In both types of firms — as indeed for all types in the sample — the participation of Francophone salaried personnel was less at the upper than at the lower end of the income ladder. In the sample as a whole, although there were anomalies in the distribution in the firms owned by Canadian Francophones, the low participation of Francophones at the middle and upper levels was clear, the proportion of Francophones among those earning from $10,000 to $11,999 being less than half that at the $5,000 to $6,499 level.

A second survey [4] of manufacturing, designed to supplement the findings on the large firms, sought somewhat less detailed information on the policies and practices of 358 firms with head offices in Quebec and Ontario and employing from 50 to 1,500 workers. These firms employed an average of 200 workers each, and there was little difference between the two provinces in this respect. In absolute terms, these 358 firms together employed roughly half as many as the 36 large firms combined; in language of ownership, and proportion of Francophone and Anglophone employees, the patterns in general resembled those of the large firms.

This brief overview of the situation in manufacturing firms yields the following conclusions. The presence of Canadian Francophones in the ownership and control of large manufacturing firms was extremely meagre. Within such firms, Francophones formed a minority of those earning salaries of more than $5,000[5] (Francophone-owned firms excepted). Most Francophone salaried personnel at these levels in large manufacturing enterprises worked in firms under the control of Anglophones. In all such manufacturing firms, the proportion of Francophones tended to decline as salary level increased.

Table 66. Francophone Salaried Personnel Earning $5,000 and Over

Percentage of Francophone salaried personnel in 18 large Canadian-owned manufacturing firms with head offices in Quebec, by salary level — 1964

	In 6 firms owned by Canadian Francophones		In 12 firms owned by Canadian Anglophones	
Salary level	Number	%	Number	%
$ 5,000 — 6,499	260	95	3,415	38
6,500 — 7,999	104	63	2,581	44
8,000 — 9,999	75	71	1,662	33
10,000 — 11,999	61	46	611	20
12,000 — 14,999	38	68	487	15
15,000 and over	35	80	451	12
Total	573	78	9,207	35

Source: Morrison, "Large Manufacturing Firms."

2. Regional variations

The patterns of deployment of the two language groups in Quebec manufacturing differed notably according to whether a firm's operations were carried on only within the province or in other parts of Canada as well. Also, the patterns in areas of Francophone concentration outside Quebec appeared to differ from those inside the province. Within Quebec there were again notable differences between Montreal and the rest of the province.

These three geographic areas — Canada outside Quebec, Quebec outside Montreal, and the Montreal metropolitan census area itself — are in one sense three distinctive language regions. In the part of Quebec lying outside Montreal, those of French mother tongue formed 92 per cent of the male labour force in 1961. In Canada outside Quebec, they made up 7 per cent. In the Atlantic provinces and Ontario, the proportion of those of French mother tongue was slightly higher — 13 per cent in the Atlantic provinces and 7 per cent in Ontario. In the Montreal metropolitan census area, the percentages were 62 for those of French mother tongue and 38 for those of English and other mother tongues.

a) Canada outside Quebec

The general pattern of Francophone disadvantage is now familiar: in income, occupation, schooling, and position in the large corporations, Francophones rank low. This is not simply a factor of minority status, for the disadvantages of Francophone workers outside Quebec stand in sharp contrast to the place of Anglophone workers in Quebec.

In the Atlantic provinces, where a small fragment of the work force in our sample was located, roughly 13 per cent of all employees in the large manufacturing firms surveyed were Francophones, and the proportion decreased as salary level increased: they formed 10 per cent at the lower salary levels, less among personnel at the middle salary levels, and were virtually absent at the highest income level. Slight as such participation was, in the medium-sized firms the proportion was still lower — 7 per cent.

In Ontario the proportion of all Francophones employed in the sample firms was lower again: about 5 per cent. Those earning from $5,000 to $6,499 made up about 4 per cent of the total at this salary level, while at the topmost levels Francophone participation was around 3 per cent.

In the western provinces, Francophones made up less than 1 per cent of all employees in the large manufacturing firms, although their share of the positions with salaries of over $5,000 a year — 2 per cent — was somewhat higher. Among the smaller firms, the percentage of Francophones at all levels was as low as in the large companies — about 1 per cent.

In all establishments located outside Quebec, then, the participation of Francophones was very slight. It was most substantial in those areas in New Brunswick and Ontario where Francophones form a sizable part of the population. In such areas, however, their proportion was noticeably higher in the group earning less than $5,000. In the mainly Anglophone areas, the few Francophone employees on staff were more evenly distributed throughout the different wage and salary levels.

b) Quebec outside Montreal

Of the total male labour force in Quebec outside the Montreal metropolitan census area, almost 92 per cent were of French mother tongue. In the large corporations surveyed in this region, 86 per cent of the employees earning less than $5,000 and 85 per cent of all salaried workers were Francophones. Among the smaller firms the numerical predominance of Francophones was even more marked: the percentages of Francophones among wage-earners and all employees were 95 and 93 respectively. Roughly 90 per cent of employees in our samples of manufacturing firms in Quebec outside Montreal were of French mother tongue. However, the small Anglophone group was highly concentrated at the opposite end of the salary spectrum from the Francophone minority in manufacturing plants outside Quebec.

The highly advantaged position of Anglophones in the large manufacturing firms in Quebec outside Montreal can be summarized briefly: although only 15 per cent of all employees were Anglophones, they comprised some 30 per cent of those earning more than $5,000. Moreover, they made up 61 per cent of those earning from $10,000 to $14,999, and 77 per cent of those in the highest income range (Table 67).

Table 67. Language Group of Salaried Personnel in Quebec outside Montreal

Percentage distribution within salary levels of salaried personnel in 31 large manufacturing firms, by language group[1] — Quebec (excluding Montreal), 1964

		Language group		
Salary level	Number	Francophones	Anglophones	Total
$ 5,000 — 6,499	1,704	82	18	100
6,500 — 7,999	1,309	76	24	100
8,000 — 9,999	773	61	39	100
10,000 — 11,999	266	42	58	100
12,000 — 14,999	158	35	67	100
15,000 and over	132	23	77	100
All salary levels	4,342	70	30	100

Source: Morrison, "Large Manufacturing Firms."

[1] The language group was determined on the basis of mother tongue, or the official language of greatest fluency if the mother tongue was neither French nor English.

The striking advantages of Anglophones were inversely reflected in the proportion of Francophone managers in the higher salary brackets, which was almost halved every time the salary level went up $5,000: Francophones constituted approximately 80 per cent of those earning $5,000 to $9,999, 40 per cent of those earning $10,000 to $14,999, and 20 per cent of those earning $15,000 and over.

As noted above, there was a sharp distinction in the employment of Francophones at the higher salaried level between the large manufacturing firms owned by Francophone interests and those owned by Anglophone groups. In the firms owned by Canadian and foreign Francophones, 97 per cent of those earning salaries of $5,000 or more were Francophones. However, as in the whole group of Francophone-owned firms, the number of personnel employed by these firms was only a small fraction of the total employment by sample firms in Quebec outside Montreal. As a result, Anglophones predominated in the positions of influence in the large Quebec manufacturing concerns outside Montreal, despite the offsetting situation in the Francophone-owned firms.

In the smaller firms, the Anglophone employees did not enjoy as great an advantage. This reflects the very high proportion of smaller firms in the region which were both owned by Francophones and staffed for the most part with Francophone managers at all levels of responsibility. Even so, in these firms, Anglophones were proportionally three times more numerous among salaried personnel than among wage-earners.

The true extent of the Anglophone advantage in Quebec industry outside Montreal is very clear when contrasted with the position of Francophones outside Quebec. Approximately 30 per cent of all personnel earning more than $5,000 in the sample of large manufacturing companies in Quebec outside Montreal were Anglophones, a proportion which was over four times that of Anglophones in the male labour force of the areas. By contrast, less than 4 per cent of the personnel at the same levels outside Quebec were Francophones — a little more than half the proportion of Francophones in the non-Quebec male labour force. Whereas the proportion of Anglophones at the higher salary levels in Quebec outside Montreal increased as the salary levels rose, the proportion of Francophones outside Quebec slightly declined at the higher salary levels. Thus, in terms of concentration in the command posts of Canadian manufacturing industry, the Anglophone presence was overwhelming, even in the regions where they were very much in the minority.

As these patterns of participation indicate, firms relied heavily on the local labour market for blue-collar employees but very little for higher managerial and professional staff. This situation reflects the circumstances at the founding of many big operations in Quebec.[6] Many of these firms brought with them their own skilled craftsmen as well as foremen, engineers, and managers. They relied on the local community only for blue-collar workers, some clerical help, and a few more highly paid people to perform roles as intermediaries between the plant management and the Francophone workers and community.

Some changes have occurred, but strong traces of the old pattern still remain. The fact that 79 per cent[7] of personnel at salary levels from $5,000 to $7,999 were Francophones suggests that there has been both a sizable movement of Francophone blue-collar workers into supervisory and lower managerial positions and an increasing reliance on Francophones in the "relations" functions. However, there appears to have been little increase in the Francophone proportion of administrative and professional employees.

c) Montreal metropolitan area

In 1961 there were some 337,000 men of French mother tongue in the labour force of the Montreal metropolitan census area. They represented 62 per cent of the male labour force in the Montreal metropolitan census area; the other 38 per cent was split between those of English mother tongue (23 per cent) and those of other mother tongues (15 per cent). Montreal is a great mixer of peoples and languages, but numerically the two charter groups and the two official languages still predominate. Table 68 shows the relative position of Francophones and Anglophones in the Montreal operations of 36 large manufacturing corporations.

Table 68. Language Group of Salaried Personnel in Montreal

Percentage distribution within salary levels of salaried personnel in 36 large manufacturing firms, by language group[1] — Montreal metropolitan census area, 1964

		Language group		
Salary level	Number	Francophones	Anglophones	Total
$ 5,000 — 6,499	2,655	49	51	100
6,500 — 7,999	1,946	41	59	100
8,000 — 9,999	1,337	27	73	100
10,000 — 11,999	593	23	77	100
12,000 — 14,999	557	17	83	100
15,000 and over	525	17	83	100
All salary levels	7,613	37	63	100

Source: Morrison, "Large Manufacturing Firms."

[1] The language group was determined on the basis of mother tongue, or the official language of greatest fluency if the mother tongue was neither French nor English.

Francophones accounted for 60 per cent of total employment in the sample, almost exactly their proportion in the Montreal male labour force as a whole. But only 37 per cent of the personnel earning $5,000 or more were Francophones. At the level just above $5,000 they constituted slightly less than half the total; at the highest level their participation shrank to 17 per cent.

Once again, the firms owned by Francophones followed a different pattern. In those owned by Canadian Francophones, Anglophones accounted for only 5 per cent of the personnel earning $5,000 or more, and were mainly spread through the middle management echelons. The firms owned by foreign Francophones interests, on the other hand, employed a larger proportion of Anglophones — about 29 per cent — whose greatest concentration occurred at the higher salary levels and who, for the most part, held jobs in marketing.

In the smaller firms, the greater extent of Francophone ownership and the almost exclusive employment of Francophones produced an overall distribution more favourable to French-speaking personnel. Francophones formed 73 per cent of the wage-earners and 51 per cent of the salaried personnel.

Compared with the rest of Quebec, Montreal has greater linguistic heterogeneity. In the large Montreal corporations, the proportions of Francophones earning less than $5,000 and more than $5,000 were lower by 20 and 34 points respectively. In other words, for employees of the large corporations, Montreal was a much more Anglophone milieu. The difference between Montreal and the rest of Quebec was most acute in the lower salary ranks. The proportion of Francophone employees at the $5,000 to $6,499 level dropped from 82 per cent outside Montreal to 49 per cent within the metropolitan area, while among those earning $15,000 and over it fell only from 23 to 17 per cent.

Despite this situation, Francophone participation in the Montreal manufacturing industry remained far above that in the rest of Canada. To this extent the pattern in the bilingual metropolis still strongly reflected the French character of Quebec.

Obviously, the participation of Francophones and Anglophones in the Canadian manufacturing industry was influenced by regional factors. Outside Quebec, few Francophones were present and they followed one of two participation patterns. In areas of Francophone concentration, there was a larger proportion of Francophone employees earning less than $5,000 than those earning more than that amount; in Anglophone areas, the extremely rare Francophone employees were spread throughout the different wage and salary levels. In Quebec outside Montreal, Francophones were an overwhelming majority of the salaried employees, and the few Anglophones were concentrated in the higher positions. Montreal was something of a half-way stage, the proportion of Francophone and Anglophone employees being more nearly equal. Yet here, as elsewhere in the country, Anglophone predominance at the upper levels was clear.

B. The Place of French

It is difficult to measure the actual use of languages in the day-to-day activities of firms. For the large firms we have data on the number and function of specific positions designated as requiring a bilingual incumbent, on the language of work within specific work units,[8] and on the language of memos and other documents. The less-detailed questionnaire for smaller firms solicited information on the proportion of Francophone and Anglophone employees with bilingual ability, on the use of spoken and written French in various fields of work within the firm, and on the relative importance of the ability to speak French or English in various levels and divisions within the enterprise.

1. The general pattern

The general situation is well illustrated in the large corporations by the distribution of Francophone and Anglophone personnel earning $5,000 or more between posts that call for bilingualism and those without such a requirement (Table 69). In general, bilingualism was demanded of most Francophones but not of most Anglophones. Throughout his career, the probability of an Anglophone finding himself in a bilingual post was roughly one in seven, while for a Francophone the probability was seven out of eight. There are regional variations in this pattern; obviously, a firm's language practices are affected by the languages spoken in the area where it is situated.

Table 69. Salaried Personnel in Bilingual Positions

Percentage of Francophone and Anglophone salaried personnel occupying positions requiring bilingual ability in 36 large manufacturing firms — Canada, 1964

	Francophones		Anglophones	
Salary level	**Number**	%	**Number**	%
$ 5,000 — 6,499	2,830	68	5,032	8
6,500 — 7,999	1,870	81	3,474	12
8,000 — 9,999	862	88	2,586	13
10,000 — 11,999	260	82	1,108	15
12,000 — 14,999	149	87	845	15
15,000 and over	131	88	741	15
All salary levels	6,102	76	13,786	11

Source: Morrison, "Large Manufacturing Firms."

2. Regional variations

a) Outside Quebec

Considering the small extent of participation by Francophones in business outside Quebec, it is not surprising that French had a very restricted use as a language of work. According to our survey of large corporations, some 97 per cent of work areas outside Quebec operated totally in English. The only places where French was used to any noticeable extent were those few areas where it is the language of the local population and therefore of the blue-collar workers.

Among the employees earning more than $5,000, the use of French was extremely limited. In the operations of the large corporations outside Quebec, fewer than 2 per cent of the Anglophone managers were required by their job specifications to speak French. In the smaller firms as well, only a very small proportion needed to be bilingual. Those Francophones in this group — 2 to 4 per cent of the total — were almost all bilingual. For them the opportunity to use French at work was the exception rather than the rule and in most respects, including language of work, they were interchangeable with their Anglophone counterparts.

b) Quebec outside Montreal

In 1961 those of French mother tongue constituted less than 7 per cent of the male labour force in Canada outside Quebec, but 77 per cent within the province. Thus, the position of French in that province might reasonably be expected to have been the exact opposite to the position of English in the rest of Canada. This, however, was far from the case, even in the areas outside Montreal, where the population was 92 per cent of French mother tongue.

However, French was widely used among the employees earning less than $5,000; most spoke only French at work, and relatively few were bilingual. Also, compared with the rest of Canada, a much higher proportion of employees in this region who earned $5,000 or more were Francophones. Twice the proportion of work areas operated in French at this level outside Montreal as in the Montreal area. More Anglophones earning $5,000 or more — 59 per cent of them — than in any other region were required to be able to speak French.

Yet English is still used extensively among those earning $5,000 or more. Except for the two lowest salary brackets in that range, well over 96 per cent of the Francophones occupied posts for which one requirement was a knowledge of English. Though the Anglophone salaried employees in this region were as a group the most bilingual of any in Canada, some 41 per cent of them were still not required to use French on the job.

Nonetheless, there was a high incidence of bilingualism in this region. It is not surprising to find that the proportion of Anglophones earning more than $5,000 who must function bilingually was between three and four times as high as anywhere else, even Montreal; but it was less expected that the same proportion of Francophones as in Montreal functioned bilingually. Finally, 70 per cent of the work units operated in both languages, compared with 54 per cent in the metropolis.

The practices of the Francophone firms provide an interesting perspective on the question of language use in Quebec outside Montreal. At the lowest salary level above $5,000, only 19 per cent of the posts held by Francophones carried a bilingual requirement. As the salary level rose, however, the ability to speak both languages rapidly became a prerequisite attached to the majority of posts. Over 90 per cent of the positions in the $8,000 to $9,999 range and 100 per cent of those carrying salaries of over $12,000 had a bilingual requirement. Even though their fellow employees were predominantly of French mother tongue, the Francophones at the middle and top levels in Québec outside Montréal had, almost to a man, to possess the ability to speak English.

The language predicament of a Francophone working outside Quebec thus bears little resemblance to the situation of his Anglophone counterpart working in Quebec outside Montreal. First, at all levels in the overall sample of firms, a Francophone employed outside Quebec had few colleagues of his own mother tongue, since less than 4 per cent of those earning more than $5,000 outside Quebec were Francophones. Second, almost none of the Anglophones were capable of speaking French, so a Francophone had little choice but to work in English. An Anglophone in Quebec outside Montreal faced no comparable hardship: depending on his salary level, from one to four out of five of his colleagues were Anglophones. Among his Francophone colleagues, 80 per cent were capable of speaking English, so the Anglophone could be sure of a comprehending audience when speaking his own language.

c) Montreal metropolitan area

High-salaried employees in the manufacturing industry in Montreal worked in English to a great extent. Over 60 per cent of all those earning $5,000 or more in our sample were Anglophones, and only 14 per cent of these people were required to speak French in their jobs. Among the Francophones, 78 per cent had to be able to speak English. Moreover, 36 per cent of the work units in Montreal functioned in English alone — more than three times the proportion in Quebec outside Montreal, and more than three times the percentage functioning in French alone in Montreal.

Although the proportion of work units operating in English alone seems large in relation to the situation outside Montreal, the majority — 55 per cent — of all work units were bilingual. Unfortunately, there is no way of determining from our data the relative use of the two languages within these "bilingual" units. It may vary from an equal use of both languages to a very infrequent use of one or the other. As in all other regions of Canada, the proportion of Francophones required to be bilingual increased at the higher salary levels.

As in Quebec outside Montreal, there was a high bilingual requirement for posts within firms owned by Francophones in the metropolitan area. At the $5,000 to $6,499 salary level, 67 per cent of the positions held by Francophones required ability in both languages. Above this level, 93 per cent of the jobs had such a specification. Thus, for all except the lowest salary levels, most higher-level Francophone employees had to be bilingual, regardless of whether they worked as a minority group within Anglophone-owned firms or as a homogeneous majority within the companies owned by Francophones.

The smaller businesses in our sample required the use of English almost, but not quite, as much as the giant corporations: 79 per cent of salaried Francophones had to be able to speak English, but only 23 per cent of their Anglophone counterparts held jobs requiring a knowledge of French.

These figures on Montreal and the rest of Quebec leave no doubt that English was the language of business communication in the middle and higher echelons of the Quebec manufacturing industry.

3. Internal and external communication

The extent to which each official language was used varied in different fields of work as well as according to the level in the hierarchy. The language of oral communication frequently was not that of written communication. Printed material circulated inside and outside the firm might be linguistically adapted in several ways.

a) Internal communication

Since clear and rapid communication is necessary for efficient operation, ways of communicating vital information have been devised in those firms with staff of both language groups. Most firms have found that special translation facilities are too costly and too slow to be practical in the daily exchange of orders and information. The solution adopted has been to place a formal or informal bilingual requirement on those positions where communication between Anglophones and Francophones is a major part of the duties.

This is demonstrated by the job requirements and the characteristics of personnel in the employee relations function. In the large manufacturing corporations, proportionately more employee relations officers were Francophones than in most other groups. Moreover, Anglophones holding these posts were more often required to be bilingual than Anglophones performing other functions. An illustration of this pattern is provided by the corporations owned by Canadian Anglophones and having their headquarters in Quebec. In their operations in Quebec outside Montreal, the vast majority (86 per cent) of employee relations officers were Francophones. Of the small group of Anglophones in this field, 92 per cent were required to be able to speak French. This group of firms has gone further than others in its adaptation, but the same tendencies were manifested to a lesser degree by most firms.

Nevertheless, for the sample as a whole, a large number of the employee relations personnel were unilingual Anglophones, especially in the more senior posts. This is of particular significance in such a sensitive field, where clear communication with the workers and their union representatives is of utmost importance.

If communication between language groups is important in the employee relations field, it is even more so in plant operations. Those engaged in production work formed the largest group of employees earning $5,000 or more in our sample. In Quebec, both within and outside Montreal, there were proportionately more Francophones in these positions than in other types of work. There was also a bilingual requirement on more production jobs held by Anglophones than in most other fields of work. The smaller firms as well as the large corporations followed these patterns.

As with the employee relations officers, there was a discrepancy between the extent of bilingualism expected of Anglophone and Francophone personnel in production positions. A majority of the Anglophones were not required to be bilingual, so the burden of language adaptation was on Francophone blue-collar workers.

Of all the fields of activity represented within the large firms, the field of engineering, research, and development was — with the exception of top management — the one where the Francophone presence and the use of French were most attenuated. In the entire sample, only 22 per cent of the personnel in this area of work were Francophones. Less than 10 per cent of the Anglophone engineers, scientists, and technicians occupied posts with a bilingual requirement. However, for Francophones as well as Anglophones, bilingual ability was not as important here as in other fields. Although the majority of Francophones were required to know English, a higher proportion than elsewhere were permitted to function only in French. The fact that they work with things and mathematical symbols rather than words allows them a greater latitude to work in their mother tongue.

b) Printed documents

We can obtain a measure of language adaptation in the area of internal communication by comparing the availability of documents in French with the proportion of Francophone employees in each region. In these terms, French was used more than might be expected throughout Canada in such printed material as application forms (20 per cent), booklets describing employee benefits (27 per cent), benefit certificates (37 per cent), and employee newspapers (20 per cent). Within Quebec, these items — as well as such documents as copies of union contracts, notices, safety and direction signs, and identification cards and badges — were provided either in French alone or in French and English by the large majority of companies.

Most of these documents can be printed and distributed in large quantities, and revisions are likely to be infrequent. Because they are usually short, it is a relatively easy matter to have them translated or prepared separately in French. The language adjustments on these documents have a considerable usefulness and probably an even greater symbolic importance.

However, the efforts towards language adaptation of other classes of printed and written materials are less impressive. Such documents as interoffice memoranda, shop drawings, and training and instruction manuals are undoubtedly of much greater importance in the day-to-day conduct of work. These items are usually reproduced in small quantities and are speedily circulated and revised. Moreover, because they are technical and managerial communications, they are likely to be drafted in English by Anglophones.

Outside Quebec, the use of English in such documents was almost universal: only two large firms in the entire sample, for instance, had bilingual instruction manuals for use across Canada. When the figures for Quebec were included the picture improved somewhat, but 17 per cent of the firms still reported the exclusive use of English in training manuals, 26 per cent in instruction manuals, 48 per cent in interoffice memoranda, and 72 per cent in ship drawings. That the Francophone labour force should be forced to rely on an English-language version of so many of these documents — the mastery of which is vital to the acquisition of skills and job competence — is a clear illustration of the disadvantaged position of Francophones in the work world.

Although our data on them are less detailed, we noted that the smaller firms in Quebec outside Montreal displayed a relatively high use of French in internal communications; the overall average is undoubtedly raised by the large number of Francophone-owned enterprises. Approximately four-fifths of the oral communications and three-quarters of the written communication were carried on in French. The greatest use of French occurred among the labour force, the next among office employees, and the least (by a slight degree) in the top ranks. As in the large corporations, French was used more frequently by those working in the personnel, industrial relations, and production fields than by those in other areas.

c) External communication

Another important aspect of the language of work in business, an aspect affected by a quite different set of forces, is external communication between companies and shareholders, suppliers, customers, the local community, the various levels of government, and other individuals and agencies. The external patterns of language use are influenced by the nature of the product manufactured, for this determines who are the suppliers and customers. In our sample, the patterns of language use in firms manufacturing consumer goods were quite different from those in firms manufacturing industrial supplies.

In purchasing, two main factors shape the patterns of language use. Many firms in Quebec reported that they made it a policy to buy locally and in such contacts to use French as much as possible. Yet the great majority of the suppliers of raw materials are firms owned by Anglophones, so English is still used more often. French was used in purchasing by only 17 per cent of the large firms in our sample. The dependence on English-speaking sources for industrial supplies is also demonstrated by the fact that all the Francophone-owned firms in the sample of large corporations — irrespective of the location of their purchasing offices — regarded purchasing as a function requiring an ability to speak English.

Only two of the Anglophone-owned firms with purchasing offices outside Quebec regarded French-language ability as either a necessity or a significant advantage for their purchasing staff. On printed forms relating to purchasing, only English was used by most corporations outside Quebec. The smaller firms followed a similar pattern.

Of the large corporations with purchasing offices in Quebec, 72 per cent of those outside Montreal — but only 50 per cent of those within the metropolitan area — saw a purchasing manager who speaks French as either a necessity or a significant advantage. Throughout the province, between 59 and 68 per cent of the firms used only English for order forms, conditions of purchase forms, and specifications.

The use of French in sales and marketing exceeded its use in purchasing. Within Quebec, 57 per cent of the sales personnel employed by the large corporations in the sample (90 per cent of the Francophones and 20 per cent of the Anglophones) were required to be bilingual. However, in marketing, the nature of the product is a decisive determinant of language use. Industrial goods are most frequently sold to Anglophone customers because they are often exported to firms outside the province and also because, within the province, most industrial concerns are owned by Anglophones. Consumer goods, on the other hand, sold much more frequently in French, largely because their markets are more highly concentrated within Quebec.

The companies owned by Francophones were concentrated most heavily in the consumer goods field, with their markets largely localized in Quebec. The tendency to use French in marketing, already strong because the staff is almost exclusively Francophone, was thus reinforced. However, there was considerable emphasis on bilingualism because of the need to communicate with the sizable English-speaking portion of the market.

Companies located outside Quebec but selling in Montreal or the rest of Quebec adapted their language to that of the buyer — usually French for consumer goods and English for industrial goods. In companies operating in markets outside Quebec, the dominant language was English. However, the existence of some sensitivity to the language of Francophone customers outside Quebec was indicated by the fact that 10 per cent of the salesmen of large firms in Ontario and the Atlantic provinces were bilingual.

Within Quebec, the split between manufacturers of consumer goods and manufacturers of industrial goods is reflected in their patterns of language use. The former hired many more Francophones for marketing functions. Among manufacturers of industrial goods, 27 per cent of the marketing units in Quebec operated completely in English, but only 9 per cent of those among manufacturers of consumer goods did so. Advertising procedures also reflected the split. Of the firms in the sample marketing consumer goods in Quebec, only 4 conceived their advertisements in English and translated them, 7 conceived them separately in each language, and 3 translated their French-language material into English. Sellers of industrial goods were much less likely to use French. The manufacturers of consumer goods spent more per customer for advertising on the French-language market than on the English-language one.

Purchasing, marketing, and sales are the fields in which the greatest volume of external communication takes place. However, there are other smaller but important fields of activity in which external relations are involved. Public relations is one such sensitive and strategic function. Here, the exigencies of maintaining good relations with a linguistically diverse public are strongly mirrored in the selection of employees. In the sample as a whole, Francophones enjoyed the highest concentration relative to Anglophones in this numerically small field: about 55 per cent of all specialists in public relations were Francophones. The majority of Anglophones in this field are unilingual, but the proportion who are bilingual is higher than the average for other functions. Fewer work units than in any other sphere of activities used English alone. In the image they seek to convey to the public, the firms in our sample are clearly aware of the need to adapt to a bilingual and bicultural community.

Like public relations, the matter of relations with shareholders perhaps reflects a greater concern with image than with the details of internal administration. Among the firms providing their shareholders with an annual report there were varying degrees of sensitivity to language differences. The annual report of 22 out of 35 firms was available either in separate French and English versions or in a combined, bilingual edition. Twelve firms published their annual report only in English and one Francophone-owned firm published its report only in French. The practice of publishing only in English was most prevalent among American-owned companies. French was considerably less likely to be used in annual meeting and on share certificates than in annual reports.

One recurrent theme in the study of large corporations is that firms in the sample actually showed a greater use of French in external communication than market factors alone would compel. This appears to indicate a general desire to present a more "French" image in Quebec. Social and political pressures do seem to have been effective in increasing the use of French in recent years. For example, firms dealing with the Quebec government cited a new insistence by its agencies as a persuasive influence in changing their language patterns. Greater care was now exercised to submit bids and conduct correspondence in French and to use Francophone personnel in their relations with the government.

C. Summary

The foregoing figures demonstrate vividly the extent to which Anglophones have been the active element and Francophones the passive in the founding of the manufacturing industry in Canada. The ventures of Francophones as entrepreneurs and managers of firms outside Quebec have been very rare in comparison with the inroads made by Anglophones in the exploitation and development of the resources in regions originally settled and inhabited by Francophones. Unfortunately, we have no more detailed data on the participation of Francophones and the use of the French language in industry outside Quebec. The materials that have been presented, however, do provide a generally accurate description of the situation. The picture they reveal is a dark one from the standpoint of equal partnership. Clearly Francophones in these regions did not enjoy anything close to an equal partnership in private work institutions in terms of being able to work in their own language and cultural milieu, or in terms of proportional representation at the higher levels.

Within Quebec the situation was much more complex. Contrary to some popular myths, Francophones did have a substantial numerical presence at the managerial level in large manufacturing corporations, although considerably below their proportion in the total population of the province. Yet these bald figures tell little about the real situation of Francophone participation and French-language use in the world of business in Quebec. Although Francophones constituted 55 per cent of all personnel earning salaries of $5,000 to $9,999, they formed only 23 per cent of those earning $10,000 or more. They enjoyed their highest proportional concentration in the fields of work that required bilingual ability in order to perform a liaison function between an Anglophone higher management and a Francophone work force and public.

By far the largest group of Francophones earning $5,000 or more was concentrated at the lower levels in the production or manufacturing divisions of the large corporations. This strongly suggests that most of them occupied supervisory posts in the manufacturing plants, having worked their way up from blue-collar jobs. The Francophone managers with university degrees in our sample were heavily concentrated in the "relations" functions, and the Anglophones were more likely to be in the administrative and technical divisions that offer better prospects for long-term advancement to the executive levels.

This description of the distribution of Francophones among the corporate jobs gives some notion of the inequality of partnership that presently prevails. But, by itself, it underestimates the gravity of the situation. In terms of the opportunity to express themselves, to learn and to develop within a setting where the linguistic and cultural idiom is accepted and understood, Francophones are seriously handicapped. Roughly 90 per cent of the Francophones earning $5,000 or more in our sample worked in companies owned or controlled by Anglophones. Within these companies, 86 per cent of those with salaries of

$10,000 or more were Anglophones. Of these, only 18 per cent were in positions that had a bilingual requirement. English was overwhelmingly the language of work at the top levels. The relatively few Francophones at this level must work within a predominantly English-speaking milieu but, more important, the many Francophones at the lower levels are also forced to use English as their language of work. The meetings, conferences, telephone conversations, and written reports and memoranda were predominantly in English.

No one would deny that the exigencies of operating in the North American world of business and technology exert strong pressures on companies to use English extensively in their external communications. But this does not mean that they need use it exclusively as the language of work. The fact that unilingual Anglophones predominate at the higher levels in the firms in our sample produces what could be termed "arbitrary" pressures to its use beyond those exerted by the business environment. There are many units in these firms where French could easily become the language of daily work, were it not for the necessity of communicating in English with officers and units that do not have a bilingual capacity.

In our view, the present situation is highly unjust. These arrangements constitute major difficulties for Francophone employees; they have far-reaching implications with respect to work performance, career advancement, and retention of linguistic and cultural identity.

NOTES

[1] The data we needed had never been collected, so the Commission launched a series of research studies which generated a large body of information bearing on the two central concerns of this chapter: the participation of Francophones and the use of the French language within manufacturing enterprises. From a substantial number of very large firms we were able to collect very detailed information; from a much larger number of smaller firms we collected a much narrower range of data. The rest of this chapter summarizes the results of our research. Ecole des hautes études commerciales and The Graduate School of Business of McGill University, "Corporate Policies and Practices with Respect to Bilingualism and Biculturalism/Politiques et pratiques du monde des affaires relativement au bilinguisme et au biculturalisme," a study prepared for the R.C.B.&B.

[2] The survey covered 41 large manufacturing firms of which 36 made available the necessary data on salaried personnel earning $5,000 or more. For the criteria employed in drawing up the sample, *see* R.N. Morrison, "Corporate Policies and Practices of Large Manufacturing Firms," in *ibid. See* also Appendix VII, Book III, *The Work World*, Ottawa: Queen's Printer, 1969, pp. 573-576.

[3] Most of the large firms in our sample had establishments in English-speaking regions of the country, which naturally reduces the proportion of Francophones among their total numbers of employees. This fact is clear when one observes that of the 19,888 employees earning salaries of $5,000 or more in the 36 firms in our sample, 7,933 — 40 per cent — were working in establishments outside Quebec. The distribution of employees was as follows:

	Number	%
Quebec outside Montreal	4,342	21.8
Montreal metropolitan census area	7,613	38.3
Ontario	5,413	27.2
Western provinces	1,966	9.9
Atlantic provinces	554	2.8
Total	19,888	100.0

[4] R.N. Morrisson, "Small Firms Employing between 50 and 1,500 People in Quebec and Ontario," in the study cited above.

[5] It must be remembered that these observations are based on a sample of enterprises containing several with establishments outside Quebec (*see* note 2 above).

[6] *See* E.C. Hughes, *French Canada in Transition* (Chicago, 1943).

[7] This percentage applies to the large corporations in Quebec outside Montreal; the corresponding figure for Quebec as a whole is 59 per cent.

[8] The term "work unit" refers to departments of divisions within each firm defined both on a regional and a functional basis. For instance, a firm that operates manufacturing plants and sales offices in both Montreal and Toronto would be classified as having four separate "work units." Clearly, work units may vary greatly in terms of size. *See* description of Morrison, "Large Manufacturing Firms," in Appendix VII, Book III, *The Work World*, Ottawa: Queen's Printer, 1969, pp. 573-576.

OBSTACLES TO THE FULL DEVELOPMENT OF FRENCH AND TO ITS SPREAD THROUGH ALL SECTORS OF ACTIVITY *†

Examination of the facts concerning the use of languages in work communications allows positive identification of two phenomena. On the one hand, both French- and English-speaking groups enjoy a considerable degree of autonomy regarding the use at work of their mother tongue. On the other hand, when the third group becomes involved, when functionally important acts of communication are analysed, when contact situations between French- and English-speaking persons are examined and when the requirements facing workers in the course of their careers are studied, the predominance of English is noted. In order to understand this peculiar situation, we must go back to the socio-economic structures underlying the use of languages at work, and situate this use within the judicial, economic and social framework within which Québecers work and live.

A. Socio-economic segregation and stratification in the Québec work world**

In the section dealing with work situations, we pointed out those encouraging and those discouraging the use of French. From this was formulated a socio-economic structure which, we maintained, conditioned language use. Our data enable us to throw some light on what is concealed by such a structure which leads to this apparently contradictory situation of autonomy and language predominance, which we have described at length.

---

*Chapter II, Report of the Commission of Inquiry on the Position of the French Language and on Language Rights in Québec, Book I, *The Language of Work*, Québec: The Government of Québec, 1972, pp. 109-143.

†In the section of the report dealing with language rights will be found a description of the constitutional framework within which are defined the Québec Government's powers of intervention to promote the development and diffusion of French in all sectors of activity.

**We refer especially in this section to the research report drawn up by Mr. Serge Carlos on the use of French in the Québec work world.

1. Language autonomy and segregation

According to our information, the overall percentage of the use of French is in direct proportion to the number of persons forming the conversation group in which the worker is involved (Graph I. 60). For all groups of workers, the use of French increases in proportion to the number of French-speaking persons in this conversation group. Thus, for a French-speaking Montréaler, the use of French increases by 6.5% with an increase of 10% in the degree of French-speaking representation within the group. For English-speaking people, the corresponding increase in the use of French is 4.7%. Since Montréal's French-speaking people deal with others of their own language 75% of the time and those outside the urban areas do so 93% of the time, the high rate of use of French is understandable. The reason for this is simple. At work, spoken contacts made by French-speaking people are very largely made with members of their own language group. It should be noted that although French-speaking Montréalers make up 64% of that city's labor force, 75% of their communications are done with other French-speaking persons. The structures of the work world are such that more often than not French-speaking people find themselves concentrated in work groups where they are relatively greater in number than in the overall work force of the region.

This phenomenon of language segregation, however, is much more pronounced for English-speaking people. Although they constitute only 22% of the Montréal work force, 62% of their spoken contacts are with others of their own language group. Herein lies one of the reasons for the under-use of French by English-speaking people. Although in a distinct minority, they are enabled by the structures of the work world, which tend to bring them together in groups, to make widespread use of their own language in the same way as French-speaking people. It is evident that the concentration of individuals in natural "work units" tends to encourage a greater use of the mother tongue in certain types of communication.

This separation of language groups in the work milieu often takes the form of a hierarchic relationship (Table I. 61). Whereas French-speaking persons' use of French is in proportion to the strength of the representation of their own language group in their immediate surroundings, the use of French by English-speaking people is shown to be very considerably lower than the numerical proportion of French-speaking persons around them. This under-use, which is relative to the degree of imposition of English in functionally important work activities, is possible only to the extent to which English-speaking people dominate the labor force hierarchy. The segregation is therefore both horizontal, through juxtaposition of groups in different activity sectors, and vertical, through the placing of these groups at various levels within the hierarchy of jobs and

Diagram I. 60

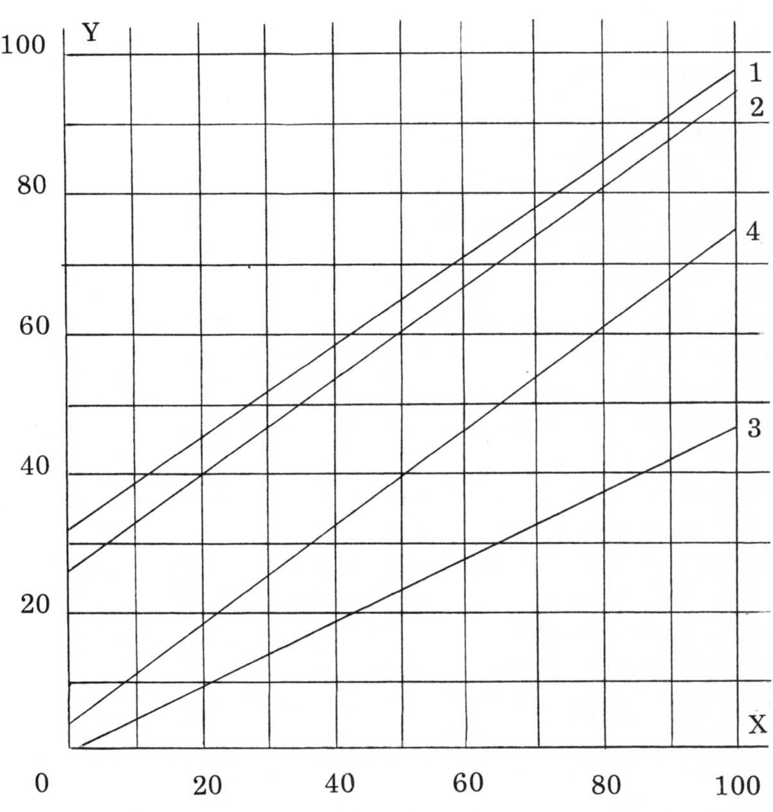

Y = Overall percentage of use of French
X = Percentage of spoken contacts with French-speaking persons

1 — French-speaking people outside Montréal
Y = 32.3 — 0.65 X

2 — French-speaking people in Montréal
Y = 26.0 — 0.70 X

3 — English-speaking people
Y = 0.4 — 0.47 X

4 — Others
Y = 3.9 — 0.71 X

functions. For each group, both types of segregation encourage a wide autonomy in the use of the mother tongue; as for the second type, vertical segregation, this often leads to language domination of one group by the other in contact situations.

TABLE I. 61

Relationship between specific percentage of use of French and percentage of French-speaking persons in conversation milieu, according to activity and language group

Activity	French-speaking persons	English-speaking persons
Spec. Int. Writ.**	0.94*	0.20*
Gen. Int. Writ.	0.90	0.30
Spec. Int. Read.	0.91	0.41
Gen. Int. Read.	1.01	0.80
Meetings	0.93	0.49
Add. Sup.	1.01	0.34
Add. Sub.	0.89	0.35
Add. Col.	0.83	0.45

*Table reads as follows: French-speaking workers writing specific internal texts use a degree of French equivalent to 94% of the number of French-speaking people among the recipients of such texts; English-speaking workers in similar circumstances use a degree of French corresponding to only 20% of the French-speaking representation among recipients.
**See Table I.18 for explanations of abbreviations.

There is no lack of concrete evidence of horizontal segregation. In Québec, this is related to an apparent specialization of work along ethno-linguistic lines (Table I. 62). While in the Québec labor force there are 5.3 French-speaking workers for every one whose language is English (344,000 against 1,820,000), the ratio rises to 19.0 in primary industry and to 15.7 in the construction industry. These are sectors where, on a horizontal level, there is a strong concentration of French-speaking people. The same applies to a lesser extent in public administration and commerce. It can be assumed that the use of French is widespread in these areas. In finance, on the other hand, there are scarcely 2.4 French-speaking workers for each English-speaking person, and in the public utility services the ratio in only 3.2. Beyond question these are fiefdoms where the English language is lord.

2. Preponderance of English and stratification

In relations between French and English-speaking people, the prime determinant in language use is the vertical grouping of workers, or their concentration in important administrative rôles.

TABLE I. 62

Number of French-speaking workers for each English-speaking worker by activity sector

Activity sector	Number of French-speaking workers for each English-speaking worker
Primary industry	19.0
Construction industry	15.7
Public administration	9.0
Commerce	8.1
Personal and social services	5.7
Manufacturing industry	4.9
Public utility services	3.2
Finance	2.4

In any sector, there ought to be as much opportunity of using French in functionally important communications as there is French-speaking personnel in its middle and upper management levels. In this respect, two sectors are dominated throughout by French-speaking people: these are public administration and commerce, where the proportion of administrators and professional people is 7.5 and 7.2 in favor of French-speaking persons, while that for office workers and sales-people is 35.5 and 6.9 (Table I. 63). A ratio less favorable to French-speaking people is seen in the personal and social services sectors (4.7) and the construction industry (4.0). For the first of these sectors there is a favorable ratio for office workers of 5.5. In all of these sectors, moreover, occupations such as services employee, transportation and communications employee, foreman and worker are strongly dominated by French-speaking persons. On the other hand, the two sectors of finance and public utilities are thoroughly English-language dominated. Two others, differently structured, are under English-speaking domination at the top and French-language domination at the lower echelons. These are primary industry and secondary industry. In the first case, there are only 2.3 French-speaking administrators and professional people for every one who is English-speaking; in the second, 1.1 French-speaking people fall into the administration and professional categories and 3.5 into that of office worker for each

English-speaking counterpart, whereas there is an intense concentration of French-speaking people at the lower occupation levels (18.0 and 11.0 for workers and foremen).

TABLE I. 63

Number of French-speaking persons for each English-speaking person by activity sector and occupation level

Activity sector	Administrators and professionals	Office workers and salesmen	Services and transportation and communications employees	Foremen and workers %
Primary industry	2.3	10.0	12.0	18.0
Construction industry	4.0	0.2	38.0	73.5
Public administration	7.5	35.5	7.0	6.8
Commerce	7.2	6.9	6.8	15.1
Personal and social services	4.7	5.5	9.3	9.8
Manufacturing industry	1.1	3.5	8.3	11.0
Public utility services	1.8	2.1	2.2	4.9
Finance	2.4	2.5	2.0	2.0

There would appear to be a direct relationship between the level of use of French in functional communications in any given sector and the over-representation of English-speaking people, especially in administrative and professional positions: the lowest rate of French use is found in the manufacturing industry, closely followed by public utility services and finance (Table I. 64); these three sectors are also at the bottom of the scale according to the French/English-speaking relationship in administrative and professional occupations (Table I. 65). Moreover, when the occupations of office worker and salesman are added to those mentioned above, these sectors still fall into the three lowest categories. This is certainly not just coincidence. On the other hand, as far as use of French is concerned, the public administration field, which is thoroughly dominated by French-speaking people, has the highest level of French use after social services. The French-dominated commerce sector presents complications: it only occupies fourth place. We will return to this.

TABLE I. 64

Rank of activity sectors according to percentage of French use in specific communication activities for French- and English-speaking people in Montréal

Secondary industry	General rank	Writing activities			Reading activities			Oral activities		
		Percentage of use		Rank according to percentage of use in type of activity	Percentage of use		Rank according to percentage of use in type of activity	Percentage of use		Rank according to percentage of use in type of activity
		French-speaking persons	English-speaking persons		French-speaking persons	English-speaking persons		French-speaking persons	English-speaking persons	
Secondary industry	1	42%	6%	1	35%	15%	1	74%	17%	1
Public utility services	2	52%	7%	2	45%	19%	2	75%	16%	2
Finance	3	57%	5%	3	52%	12%	4	80%	11%	3
Commerce	4	64%	9%	4	55%	24%	5	83%	24%	4
Construction	5	72%	15%	5	47%	19%	3	87%	23%	7
Public administration	6	75%	19%	6	72%	21%	7	85%	24%	5
Personal and social services	7	80%	6%	7	70%	14%	6	86%	15%	6

TABLE I. 65

Comparative rank of activity sectors according to level of French use and rank of these sectors according to relations between French- and English-speaking persons in four activities

Activity sectors	Rank of sectors according to percentage of use of French	Rank of sectors according to French/English-speaking relations in administrative and professional occupations	Rank of sectors according to percentage of use of French	Rank of sectors according to French/English-speaking relations in administrative, office worker and salesman occupations
Secondary industry	1	1	1	3
Public utility services	2	2	2	1
Finance	3	3	3	2
Commerce	4	6	4	6
Construction	5	4	5	4
Public administration	6	7	6	7
Personal and social services	7	5	7	6

Evidence has already been offered of this over-representation of English-speaking people at the upper levels of administrative and technical functions. This was shown as regards major manufacturing firms by the federal Bilingualism and Biculturalism Commission which related English- and French-speaking groups with salary levels: "The proportion of Francophones declined as the salary level rose in the large manufacturing corporations (Table I. 64). Francophone personnel were always an absolute minority at the higher salary levels: they constituted about 36% of the total at the levels just above $5,000 and only about 15% at the top levels."[1] Our own data confirms this stratification phenomenon, not only in the manufacturing industry to which our survey was basically directed, but also for commerce, construction, transportation and communications, finance and the various services.[2] Our sampling took in 19 economic sectors and 69 business establishments.

In the businesses covered by the survey, valid answers were received from some 2,000 persons at the managerial level. Representation within this management framework is far from proportional to the numerical importance of French-speaking people in the labor force (Table I. 66). Not including foremen, French-speaking people make up 50% of those in management earning less than $15,000, 30% of those earning between $15,000 and $20,000, and 30% of those over the $20,000 mark.[3] Not only are French-speaking people under-represented in these management structures as a whole, but this is even more pronounced as we go up the administrative and technical ladder.

TABLE I. 66

Proportion of French-speaking persons by salary level corresponding with three work organization hierarchic levels in 2,000 private enterprise management cases

Salary levels	Excluding foremen	Including foremen
Under $15,000	50%	55%
$15,000 to $20,000	30%	30%
over $20,000	30%	30%

It must be admitted that French-speaking persons are vastly under-represented in positions of control in Québec's private enterprise, and conspicuously in the manufacturing industry (in fact, of the 19 sectors covered by the survey, 13 were manufacturing operations). And, as the federal Commission has pointed out, this applies to big business in the manufacturing area. Here again, the ethno-linguistic specialization of the workers comes into full play, with English-speaking persons concentrated in the upper job levels at a rate of 69.4% (Table I. 39) and in the large enterprise at a rate of 53.4% (Table I. 40). It is not surprising, therefore, that in the French/English-speaking relationship at the upper management and executive levels, the advantage is with English-speaking persons in the manufacturing industry sector.

This over-representation of English-speaking workers appears again at an even higher level, in the very control structures of the private sector of the economy: the head offices. The Commission carried out a partial though revealing survey on the personnel of ten head offices situated in Montréal. Out of a total of 3,125 employees in these offices, 28.2% are French-speaking. Not counting the personnel recruited from outside Québec (21.3%, almost entirely English-speaking), the head offices studied hire two English-speaking persons for each French-speaking person in Québec, despite the fact that the latter constitute nearly 4/5 of the province's labor force. This under-representation of French-speaking people becomes progressively more marked higher up the salary scale (Graph I. 67). French-speaking persons earn 35% of salaries under $10,000, but

Chart I. 67

Personnel recruited for head offices

French-speaking persons: — — —
English-speaking persons: ———

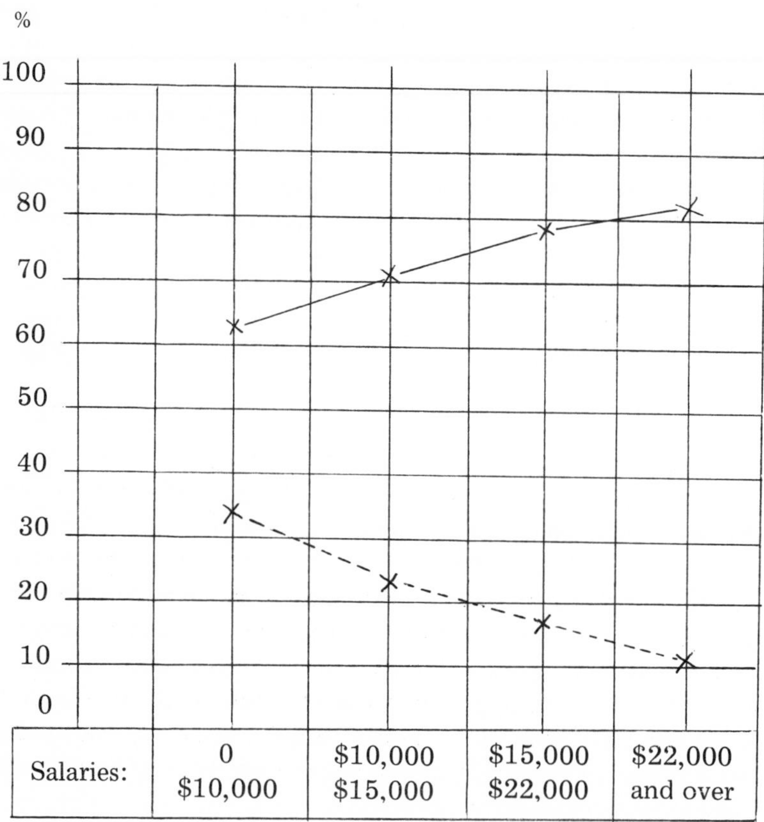

fill no more than 15% of positions where the salary is above the $22,000 mark. If, as is frequently claimed, the presence of head offices in a given region offers the advantage of allowing the local population access to decision and control positions, it must be concluded that Québec's French-speaking people derive a scant share from such benefits, and the same holds true for the minor occupations of clerk and secretary as for the upper echelons. The only equivalent situation for French-speaking persons lies in the public administration of the province.

In certain respects, use of the mother tongue has been and still is encouraged by segregation and stratification of workers. It all depends, however, on the activity sectors involved. Some of these, such as public administration and personal and social services, constitute complete communications networks, in that French-speaking people are well represented at all levels of the organization and French flows naturally upwards and downwards through the administrative hierarchy. The same working system ought to apply in commerce, but such is not the case since commerce falls into two categories, large and small. The construction industry itself is an exception, though dominated by French-speaking people. In the functional communications area of these latter two sectors, French does not flow in the way suggested by the excellent French-speaking representation at various occupation levels. Public utility services and finance are two sectors under complete English-language domination, with scant evidence of French. The manufacturing industry is the only sector offering a perfect example of ethno-linguistic stratification. As far as use of French is concerned, this turns out to be the sector where such use in functional communications is the lowest.

It is in those sectors dominated totally or partially by English-speaking people that the rôle of French is most restricted. Though this is only to be expected in our atmosphere of linguistic laisser-faire where everyone uses his own language at will, the fact must be remembered that those in control positions tend to impose their language on workers under their authority. In sectors dominated by English-speaking people, it is useless to attempt to correct the situation and increase the use of French without bringing in more French-speaking people — either at the upper echelons as in the case of the manufacturing industry, or at all occupation levels in the finance, public utility services and head office sectors. On the one hand, such a marked degree of under-representation is an aberration and, on the other, French-speaking people have a right to expect the use and spread of their language through all sectors of activity. In this respect, the prevailing ethno-linguistic stratification and specialization in the Québec work world prevent French being used to the fullest extent possible within the Province's general economic framework.

B. The Economic Framework*

The free flow of French, as we have seen, is restricted in some sectors of activity even though French-speaking people are well represented at all levels of the administrative hierarchy. This applies to both commerce and construction. We should pause at this point to examine the significance of these two cases. At first sight, the construction situation seems surprisingly anomalous. While French is used in 72% of writing activities and for 87% of oral activities, only a scant 47% of reading is done in this language (Table I. 64). How is it that the rate of use of French in reading is so low in a sector dominated by French-speaking people? One possible answer is that construction — a French sector *par excellence* — is tied in to a more open communications network to a greater extent than public administration and social and personal services, which sectors are also dominated by French-speaking people. The same doubtless applies to commerce, especially commerce on a large scale. This is seen in the percentages: 64% of French in writing and 55% in reading of documents. The same applies even more obviously in finance, public utility services and the manufacturing industry. Two sectors seem to offer a more closed communications network: personal and social services and public administration, where French is used 80% and 75% in writing and 70% and 72% in reading. It is evident that the communications networks of these two sectors are somewhat different from those of the others (Table I. 64). This is borne out by the lower rates of French used by these two sectors in the four activities involving contacts with the outside: writing texts for outside use, reading work-required documents, reading texts from outside sources, and oral communications with the outside (Table I. 68). These rates are especially low for the reading of documents (60% and 66%), many of which are known to come from English Canada or the United States.

We have offered but scant evidence to support the theory that some sectors are more closely linked than others to communications networks opening on the rest of Canada, the United States and even the world. We are aware of this, but can hardly go further on existing data. At most, we wish to draw attention to the often-reiterated observation that in written activities, French tends to give way to English (Table I. 64). The extent to which this situation derives from the fact that written activities lie in the middle and upper management area, which in certain activity sectors is characterized by a significantly greater involvement with the supraregional economic field, is a matter for speculation. Since English reigns supreme in this field, its use becomes essential in communications between those in this sector and relevant sections of the Québec labor force. This being the case, a more pronounced use of English is understandable, especially by management in the manufacturing industry, but also at the same level in the finance, commerce and communications sectors whose activities are decidedly continental in scope.

It should be stressed that there has as yet been no systematic examination of the linguistic consequences of the integration of the Québec economy into the Canadian and North American economic context and that the Commission was

*We refer here especially to the comprehensive report prepared by Mr. Pierre Laporte, the Commission's research director

TABLE I. 68

More percentage of French use in specific work activities for Montréal's French-speaking and English-speaking labor force

Activity sectors	Writing texts for outside		Writing internal texts for individuals		Writing internal texts for general use		Reading documents for outside the job		Reading internal texts from special sources		Reading general internal texts		Reading texts from outside sources		Filling out of forms		Addressing persons from outside the business		Addressing immediate superior		Addressing French-speaking subordinates		Addressing French-speaking colleagues or equals		Receiving oral communications from French-speaking colleagues		Attending meetings	
	F	E	F	E	F	E	F	E	F	E	F	E	F	E	F	E	F	E	F	E	F	E	F	E	F	E	F	E
Primary industry																												
Secondary industry	44	8	42	3	37	9	32	8	36	9	39	24	33	10	46	3	59	15	70	7	91	26	83	21	89	19	53	14
Construction	74	7	72	10	69	25	50	13	43	14	41	33	54	18	72	17	75	18	90	6	96	39	94	46	94	16	72	16
Public utility services	52	5	52	8	48	7	36	14	47	17	48	32	48	12	56	10	62	15	75	7	85	20	82	16	85	22	64	18
Commerce	61	12	57	4	76	8	46	19	60	21	59	33	54	24	64	13	71	21	80	10	93	29	89	28	91	31	76	24
Finance	60	4	57	4	54	4	46	13	59	9	53	13	50	14	57	8	70	12	78	1	88	15	86	15	87	13	72	11
Personal and social services	78	7	79	4	84	4	60	12	79	10	78	16	66	17	79	8	77	13	84	4	91	17	92	22	91	20	81	16
Administration	70	22	78	14	80	24	66	21	81	9	75	36	65	20	74	18	71	23	88	19	91	18	92	31	88	31	78	25

unable to undertake a precise study of this subject. It is a well-established fact, however, that Québec constitutes a much wider regional economic area, of national, continental and even international dimensions. Not only is Quebec business involved in financial, commercial and technical dealings on a world scale, but much more immediately, the province's industrial economy exists in complementary and dependent relationship with that of Canada and North America. On the one hand, because of its relationship with the continent's other economies, that of Québec exists as a specialized function region and therefore in a situation of interdependence; on the other hand, Québec depends on the Canadian and American economies for capital, technology and part of its highly-specialized labor force.[4] In such circumstances, there is therefore no doubt that some work communications are oriented towards the rest of Canada and the United States, and tend to be in English; thus it seems reasonable to expect, as the data shows, that certain activity sectors are more tied in than others to a continent-wide communications network where English-speaking people clearly predominate.

Thus the question arises as to the extent to which the over-use of English by French-speaking people is caused by over-representation of English-speaking persons at the upper echelons of business on the one hand, and by Québec's integration into the North American economy on the other. Unfortunately, no accurate answer, in terms of a quantitative estimate, can be given to this important question. At most, it can be deduced from what is known of language patterns at work that English-speaking over-representation at the upper levels of the administrative hierarchy explains the deferential attitude of French-speaking persons towards English, and also the custom of using this language in contact situations; by the same token, this stratification explains at least in part the habit of using English in internal written business communications. One should remember the case of workers and foremen whose functional communications activities are carried out largely in English. It seems less clear, however, that Québec's integration into the North American economy brings about a greater use of English in written communications than is found in regions less closely linked with the continental entity formed by Canada and the United States.

One of the two results of this economic integration — that of technical integration — is pointed up by the data we collected. The communications activity in which the rate of use of French is lowest for the entire Québec labor force, as well as for French-speaking people, is that of reading work-required documentation such as manuals, catalogs, specifications, files, periodicals, plans, reports and the like. This is an indication of the high degree of diffusion of English as a technical language, since Quebec's economy today, as in the past, remains in a very marked state of technological dependency in relation to the American economy. Short of any profound and unforeseeable upheaval within the Quebec economy, this dependency is likely to endure.

This diffusion of English as the language of technology constitutes at once an obstacle and a limit to the development of French. This applies at all work organization levels, but especially at that of laborers and foremen who make up the mass of the labor force. Compared with the situation in the multi-national corporations of Europe, what seems peculiar to Québec is the much more extensive use of English as the language of technology at the workshop level; in addition, English terms are much more wide-spread in the everyday vocabulary of laborers and foremen, whereas in Europe this tendency is confined more to the upper levels. From this point of view, this is hardly a normal situation. As in Europe, steps should be taken to ensure that language transfers on technical subjects take place at the upper management levels. This implies development of French-speaking management structures, or, alternatively, an advanced degree of bilingualism for English-speaking management. As we have pointed out, limits are imposed by economic integration, in that technological development takes place in English in the United States, and Québec can hardly hope to escape this restriction. Through the machinery of translation, however, the policy of business should be to situate language transfers at the upper management levels.

The second result of supra-regional economic integration is the administrative integration of the decision centres which, very often, are situated outside of Québec. The language implications of this are difficult to estimate. Certainly a parent company, especially when it is American, will tend to use English, which is its language of use; this also applies to other parent companies, however, since English has become the lingua franca of business throughout the world. Though there is an understandable need for coordination and efficiency, this nevertheless imposes a certain limit on the diffusion of French. The difficulty lies in determining the exact point at which this limit is reached, and the Commission lacks the means to do this. . .[5] A long and serious study would have to be undertaken to obtain valid answers. Consideration, however, can still be given to speeding up an emergent tendency towards decentralization through the regionalization not only of the administration of business, but also of the technological and scientific development centres. This would offer French enormous opportunities for development, since the language could become the vehicle for top management functions and for creative scientific and technological innovation. In Québec, a few Canadian banks have started this trend towards regionalization of their administrative centres; the I.B.M. company has set up a research centre in Ontario. Though these examples may be limited, they are nevertheless indicative of a trend which, in some cases, it could be to Québec's advantage to encourage.

C. The Juridical Framework

As pointed out in our report on language rights, an atmosphere of almost total juridical freedom pervades the entire language-life of the people of Québec. It should be noted that since 1867, only Article 133 of the *B.N.A. Act* has established a constitutional framework for language use, and that particular constitutional framework is very limited. Little more enterprise or initiative in the area of language-use legislation has been shown by the Québec Legislature. The general reluctance, on the part of the Québec government, to make use of the Province of Québec's considerable legislative powers in the language field is demonstrated by the inventory of language laws and regulations adopted by the Province's governments.[6] This applies as much to the labor field as to all other areas of activity. Whether at the level of the language governing the relationship between people working together within a business (language of internal communication) or that of legal and financial business administration, both the law and administrative regulations remain silent.

Québec has never had any legislation or regulations defining working language in terms of its rôle as an instrument of internal communications in business, or as a language in which workers or employees have to perform their jobs. Social and economic forces have been allowed to determine this. The federal Commission on Bilingualism and Biculturalism discovered that these forces act to the detriment of French-speaking people; though development trends have been more favorable over recent years, it is precisely this abundantly evident divorce between the worker's mother tongue and the language in which he has to work which must still be considered one of the major reasons for the present wave of language discontent in Québec. Our inventory shows that apart from Bill 64 dealing with access to the study and the practice of a profession, there are no language-competence regulations requiring that professional people have a knowledge of French; in the labor relations field, the right of employees to work in French is certainly recognized in some collective agreements between the Government and the Civil Service, but these remain exceptional cases, since this has not yet become one of the labor movement's firmly-established goals; language is dealt with only in Article 51 of the *Labor Code*, which at best grants one of the parties to a collective agreement the right to require that this be drawn up in that party's mother tongue; finally, under the *Workmen's Compensation Act*, all employers affected by this act are required to provide the Workmen's Compensation Commission with a written notice of the work accident in French or English according to the victim's language, or in whichever of these two languages he may choose. This is the only requirement in all our labor legislation which requires respect of worker's language. In short, legislation and regulations governing Québec workers' language rights are virtually non-existent.

The inventory drawn up for the Commission shows that there is no recognition in Québec legislation of the right to use any particular language as the language of work. There is no provision anywhere in Québec law enshrining the right of any group of employees to require that they may work in their own language. No one can legally force an employer to recognize either French or English as a language of work. There is a complete absence of legislative or even administrative texts on this subject. Thus the whole question is settled by the interplay of forces existing within the work world and, in the rare instances where they deal with language, by collective agreements. On the juridical level, this means that apart from a collective agreement (or a decree arising from this) no one can claim a legally-recognized right to work in his own language; in Québec, therefore, no one can appeal to any court or official authority to insist that he be allowed to work in his own language.

As a result, the powers conferred on the French Language Bureau under section 14a of the Cultural Affairs Department Act are fictitious. After hearing any employee's grievance "to the effect that his or their right to use the French language as the working language is not respected," the Bureau may well make the appropriate recommendations, but this in no way amounts to enshrining a right. Section 14a does not formulate or define any right. It merely authorizes the French Language Bureau to hear grievances and offer recommendations which do not, however, involve penalties. This is an area concerned with expression of a desire, rather than the definition of a recognized right whose infringement involves appropriate penalties. That the use of French (or English) is not a legally recognized right in the Québec work world seems therefore beyond question, in spite of any *de facto* special status conferred on either language by tradition or practice.

Nor are there any government regulations stipulating that the language of work is to be that of the legal and financial administration of a business, namely the language of its legal structures, of relationships between shareholders and management, in permits and compulsory communication with government, or of accounting and required record-keeping. Careful examination reveals that all this is left to the entire discretion of business. This means that business is free to use either French or English in all upper administrative functions. These can be formed, structured and operated in either language. Requests for authorizations and permits can be made in French or English. In addition, either language may be used for records and reports.

It is obvious that business has to deal with an enormous amount of official regulation. The language impact of all this is considerable. Language plays an important part in all administrative operations affecting business. This derives not only from the fact that business develops certain linguistic characteristics from the language used to establish its legal structures, but even more so from the fact that, depending on the size of the business, all these activities involve a certain number of people for whom the language of work or the linguistic situation at time of hiring will be largely determined by the language in which all these administrative functions are performed. In addition, since all this documentation has to be interpreted, evaluated and inspected by public officials, the language in which it must be prepared will contribute to the determination of the working language and degree of language ability required of the civil service personnel concerned. Despite this, government has not seen fit to intervene here any more than in the area of communication between employers and employees.

On the language level, Québec business operates in this atmosphere of almost total legal freedom. Both English and French enjoy equal status. Language use is determined by the interplay of existing forces. It is understandable that in functionally important activities (written activities) English should win out over French, especially in activity sectors dominated by English-speaking people, such as the manufacturing industry, finance and public utility services. In the economic area, this interplay of forces in no way encourages any French predominance. Most important among the various reasons for this are: the over-representation of English-speaking people in the upper echelons of business, the integration of Québec's economy with the North American economic whole and, as a consequence of these two factors, the predominance of English as the language of top administration and technology. In some activity sectors and types of communication, everything is weighted against the use of French in Québec — even if we discount the tendency of past influences to develop in French Canadians a deferential attitude towards English, an attitude shown by our data to be scarcely mitigated by their present position of economic inferiority.

The results of this juridical freedom and of the interplay of forces discouraging the use of French as the language of work and of the legal and financial administration of business are well known: the development by business and other work organizations of language policies which reflect much more their own interests rather than a respect for the individuals who make up the majority of Québec's workers and whose mother tongue is French.

Certainly, the picture is not entirely black and some improvements have been noted regarding the respect of French and French-speaking people.[7] But all this will never be a substitute for a valid, coherent language policy which deals with fundamentals. Superimposed on this language policy of business is a middle and upper management recruitment and promotion policy which has constantly worked against the French-speaking persons in such key economic areas as large-scale industry and commerce, finance and public utility services. Since English-speaking persons are naturally most adept at exploiting linguistic and related sensory subtleties in communications with others of their own language, these two policies become complementary. As the federal Commission on Bilingualism and Biculturalism has amply demonstrated, cultural differences[8] between French and English speaking people in business explain the extent to which a recruitment and promotion policy derives from an implicit linguistic and cultural policy. Ample evidence to support this point of view is provided by our data on this subject.[9]

The results of the language and cultural policies developed by Québec business in this climate of judicial freedom are well known. They can be summed up as follows: almost total freedom for English-speaking people to use their own language at work and, consequently, the well-nigh complete lack of a need for French on their part; the evident predominance of English within business in inter-personal relationships with French-speaking persons and inter-group (work meetings) relationships within the business; a lower degree of second language ability and bilingualism requirements for English-speaking people than for French-speaking people during career; numerical predominance of English-speaking people in key positions in vital sectors of business (large-scale industry and finance), which control economic development.

Is government intervention required to alter this state of affairs or could the situation change under the prevailing conditions of linguistic liberalism? To find out, we sought the opinions of those who constitute Québec's economic elite and thus formulate business policy.[10] Their replies are scarcely encouraging, either as regards the establishment of French in work communications or the development of French-language management structures through the promotion of persons of that language to the upper levels of responsibility and decision-making within business *(francophonisation).*

Among English-speaking people questioned, 45% do not feel that French can be implanted as the language of work at any administrative level whatsoever, while 26% believe this can be done only at certain levels (Table I. 69). The percentages related to levels are significant: 87% of those replying feel that French can be used by laborers, but not more than 67% of English-speaking subjects are of this same opinion regarding its use by office workers and 27% where intermediate management is concerned. At the upper management level, only 7% feel that French could become their working language. The opinion of French-speaking executives differs somewhat, with 78% maintaining that French can be used at all or some levels, as opposed to 55% among English-speaking persons. The French-speaking subjects are also more optimistic about the introduction of French at the intermediate management level, but by contrast they are less optimistic than their English-speaking counterparts regarding laborers and office workers. Both language groups agree that at the upper management level, there is little room for French. Though the attitude of French-speaking executives tends on the whole to be somewhat more encouraging than that of their English-speaking counterparts, the common underlying opinion detected is that while there is a place for French at the bottom of the hierarchical ladder — especially among laborers — there is much less at the intermediate levels and just about none at all at the top. Business executives can scarcely be counted upon to promote a policy of the diffusion and use of French at the higher work organization levels. Given the present state of uncertainty surrounding the problem of French as the language of work, this is something they appear to have difficulty in imagining.

TABLE I. 69

Levels at which implantation of French could be considered practicable

Level	French-speaking persons	English-speaking persons	Total
No level	22%	45%	35%
All levels	49%	29%	38%
Some levels	29%	26%	27%
Upper management	8%	7%	7%
Intermediate management	42%	27%	33%
White-collar workers	58%	67%	63%
Blue-collar workers	83%	87%	85%

What about the promotion of French-speaking people? The attitude of both French-and English-speaking business executives is strongly conditioned by their overall opinion of French Canadians and especially of the business training they receive in their educational establishments. The result more often than not is a negative opinion of the French Canadian as a business-man and large-scale business administrator. There is however, a sharp divergence of opinion between old and young informants: the former are inclined to base their opinion on the stereotyped image of French Canadians oriented towards the liberal professions and incompetent in business, whereas the latter seem to appreciate better the education received by the new generation of French Canadians. This involves the acknowledgment of a higher degree of business management ability and of the fact that the training offered today in some French-language establishments is equal or superior to that received in reputable English-language institutions. Thus the stereotyped image is changing to the benefit of French-speaking people.

The English-speaking attitude is strongly conditioned by emotional factors as regards both the promotion of French and that of French-speaking persons. This arises especially from the fact that English-speaking values and interests are quite foreign to the values and interests at the root of the current wave of language demands — the national values and interests of French-Canadians; however it is also due to the feeling that since government, as the principal instrument of change, is largely in the hands of French-speaking people, it is also somewhat remote from English-speaking people and thus not automatically inclined to be on their side. Clearly this makes very difficult their adherence to a cause so dear to French-Canadians, that of more equitable distribution of French-speaking people and more widespread use of French in all activity sectors and types of communication. Thus English-speaking people can hardly be expected joyfully to throw open the doors to French and to their French-speaking counterparts.

It seems evident, therefore, that the existing juridical framework, which has produced the results we have seen, is not designed to ensure a greater rôle in the business world — and especially in the big business world — for French and French-speaking people. From now on, government intervention will be needed to define the path and the form of change.

D. The Social Framework

Our studies of the language use of the people of Québec revealed that 84% of the Province's English-speaking population exists in a state of virtual unilingualism. Extrapolation of the 1961 data leads to the conclusion that 60% of third group members are in either a unilingual English situation or in another unilingual situation which is neither English nor French (average percentages from Table I. 9). It is clear that a good portion of Québec's population does not need to use French in the ordinary course of events. How can this be? The answer lies in the social organization which serves as a framework for the everyday life of Québecers. The Province has a double network of institutions and services which allows anyone not involved in the work routine to live his life while having to learn or use only one of the two major languages — French or English. Herein lies the explanation of this peculiar phenomenon of two communities living together side by side without having to communicate with each other. Under these circumstances, the English-speaking minority enjoys as much, if not more, freedom of action at the language level as the French-speaking majority. This double network of institutions and services is a known fact. It is so well known and such an accepted part of Québec life, that it escapes attention. It is the social autonomy enjoyed by Québec's English-speaking population which opens the door to this high degree of linguistic independence. This is seen at the legislative, judicial, educational and hospital levels; it is evident in the information media and entertainment fields (newspapers, magazines, radio, television and so forth); it applies in the area of culture and even at the administration level (since the Provincial administration customarily deals with citizens in English as well as French); and it exists in private organizations such as banks and even, to some extent, in commerce.

The English-speaking population's lack of motivation to learn and use French is consequently understandable. There is not really any powerful inducement for them to do so. This applies even to work situations which alone, in such a social system, could exert healthy pressures on this group. On the contrary, we have established that in work situations, English-speaking people enjoy a wider degree of autonomy than their French-speaking counterparts. No situation was seen where an English-speaking person had to use French as much as some members of this latter group have to use English. For a group in a distinctly minority position, this is a very unusual state of affairs, especially in a Western type society such as ours. Be that as it may, this state of affairs shelters the English-speaking community from all pressure, inducement or motivation to know and use French as a second language in everyday living and especially at work.

There is no doubt that the social framework we have described is involved here. The English-speaking community's parallel life is made possible only by this double *regime* of institutions and services. Should this then be abolished in order to terminate the minority's privileged status and facilitate integration of the two communities? Should steps be taken to ensure that French-speaking people are no longer obliged to sacrifice their language when necessary and inevitable communication between the two language groups is involved? The question arises because, whatever justification may be found in the past, it is not normal that the minority within Québec should be able to avoid the need to use French, while in inter-group relations the majority is forced to communicate in English, thereby conferring upon it the status of common language in the midst of the linguistic diversity which marks the province.

More widespread use of French within the English-speaking community can doubtless be achieved without the need to resort to such revolutionary procedures. This goal could be achieved if a single, powerfully-compelling motivation could be found. We considered this motivation in the first chapter, when we pointed to bilingualism at work as the only authentic compulsion under our present social regime. It is known that this bilingualism is currently a reality for only a minority of English-speaking people and, in addition, it has been established that this minority uses French to only a very limited extent. In future, this bilingualism at work must be extended gradually to embrace the entire English-speaking labor force. With the majority of English-speaking people having thus paid the price of breaking the language barrier which separates them from their French-speaking counterparts, the double institutions *regime* can legitimately be maintained. Should this fail to come about under the minimal conditions of change we suggest, then serious consideration would have to be given to altering existing social structures, beginning with the education system.

Within the Québec social framework, including the work world's existing ethno-linguistic structures, French is a useful and necessary language only for French-speaking people and a minority of members of the third group, but not for English-speaking people. This framework and these structures can be made favorable to the development of French and its promotion through all activity sectors only if, first of all, this language becomes a necessity in work activities; then, beyond this initial goal, if French is regarded by Québecers as a whole as their common language, meaning by that the language which everyone knows and is able to use in contacts between persons whose mother tongues are different.

E. Workers' Attitude Towards a Possible Increase in the Use of French at Work

Interesting indications of possible areas of resistance to or support for a program of change are offered by Québec workers' concepts of what is desirable and what is possible, as well as by the obstacles they envisage to an increase in the use of French at work.

1. The attitude of French-speaking workers

There is a high degree of agreement among French-speaking people on what would be desirable to improve the lot of their language (Table I. 70). They agree, for example, that everyone living in Québec should be able to speak French (Question B, 95%); that French should some day become Québec's language of business and finance (Question F, 88%); that new immigrants to the province should learn French before English (Question I, 93%); that French-speaking people in Québec should have the right to work in their own language (Question L, 97%); and, finally, since being French means above all speaking French, that French Canadians should insist on making greater use of their language (Question P, 96%). Though regional variations exist, these are minimal — with the exception of Montréal's French-speaking people, only 83% of whom feel that French should become the language of business and finance. Between 90% and 92% of others in the province, however, believe that this is a desirable goal. Thus almost the entire French-speaking population would like to see their language situation improved.

TABLE I. 70

Percentages of subjects completely or partially in agreement with statements of what is "desirable" regarding the increase in French use at work, according to language group and region

Language group and region	Statement B	F	I	L	P
Others	87	47	63	88	84
English-speaking	83	23	42	89	73
French-speaking (All)	95	88	93	97	96
French-speaking (Montréal)	94	83	91	96	95
French-speaking (Towns in proportion)	95	92	95	97	97
French-speaking (Province)	96	90	95	97	97

This degree of near unanimity in desire, however, is not maintained as regards what is considered possible (Table I. 71). A minority feels that, given Québec's situation, English must inevitably be the language of business and finance (Question A, 36%), that French is not suited to the requirements of modern technology (Question J, 39%), that it is better for immigrants to learn English instead of French (Question K, 31%), and that many Québec businesses would likely go bankrupt if they had to begin to operate in French (Question M, 35%); on the other hand, a majority believes that since Québec is part of North America, French Canadians will always have to be bilingual (Question D, 77%) and that it is unrealistic for a French Canadian to expect to work solely in French, when his employer is English (Question H, 62%).

TABLE I. 71

Percentages of subjects completely or partially in agreement with statements of what is possible regarding French use increase, by language group and region

	Statement					
Language group and region	A	D	H	J	K	M
Others	63	93	67	49	60	53
English-speaking	80	90	69	55	64	63
French-speaking (All)	36	77	62	39	31	35
French-speaking (Montréal)	42	82	65	42	38	38
French-speaking (Towns selected)	37	80	64	35	29	35
French-speaking (Province)	30	72	57	39	25	31

When the reading is reversed, however, a French-speaking majority (about two-thirds) emerges which does not believe that English must inevitably be the language of business and finance or, again, that French is not suited to the requirements of modern technology, or that it is better for immigrants to learn English instead of French, or finally, that businesses would go bankrupt if they had to begin to operate in French. There is a gap between what is desirable and what is possible, but only one third of the subjects divorce one idea from the other. Though French-speaking people show less unanimity on what is possible than on what is desirable, there still remains a clear majority which feels that what is desirable can also become possible.

The desire of French-speaking people to see a change in the situation and improvement in the lot of their language is beyond question. Experience of life induces a minority of them to draw a distinction between wishes and their realization. This divorce, however, is not accepted by the majority which unequivocally associates what is possible with what is desirable. The need for bilingualism and implicit recognition on the language level of the owner's right to conduct his own business as he sees fit, are just about the only two exceptions.

There is clearly confusion here between owner and top executive personnel, at least as far as big business is concerned. The depth of this desire for change in the minds of French-speaking people, moreover, is clearly shown in the opinions they express on certain questions (Table I. 72). There is agreement by 85% of them with the proposition that the sooner French Canadians insist on using their own language at work, the better off they will be (Question C); by the same token, 67% feel that many laws protect the interests of English Canadians to the detriment of those of French Canadians (Question G). Finally, 56% of French-speaking people disagree with the idea that French Canadians have not much to complain about and do not know how lucky they are (Question O). A considerable number of French-speaking people (44%) do not fail to associate this unquestioned desire for change with a certain general feeling of satisfaction with the situation they are in at present. All things considered, however, the attitude of French-speaking people is clearly in favor of change.

TABLE I. 72

Percentages of subjects in complete or partial agreement with "militant" language statements, by language group and region

	Statement		
Language group and region	**O***	**G**	**C**
Others	38	29	54
English-speaking	64	13	14
French-speaking (All)	56	67	85
French-speaking (Montréal)	58	67	81
French-speaking (Towns selected)	48	65	85
French-speaking (Province)	56	68	89

*The percentage of those "completely or partially in disagreement" is reported for this statement.

2. The attitude of English-speaking workers

English-speaking people display a much more ambiguous attitude than French-speaking people. Thus, though 89% of English-speaking subjects recognize the right of their French-speaking counterparts to work in their own language (L), they are, at the same time, no less strongly inclined to feel that bilingualism is a necessity for these same people (D), that English must inevitably be Québec's language of business (A) and that the right to work in French can apply to only a limited extent in businesses where the employer is French-speaking (H). Despite this, they generally agree that everyone in Quebec should know French (B), and feel it is essential that French Canadians insist on using their own language (P). It is difficult here to discern the true rôle which English-speaking people see for French in a situation where what is desirable becomes reality. They do not understand how French could become Québec's language of business and finance (F), especially when this language is hardly suited to the requirements of modern technology (J) and since many companies would likely go bankrupt if they had to begin to operate in French (M). In the same vein, many English-speaking people logically consider that it is much better for immigrants to learn English instead of French (K). All things considered, the predominant situation of English in the work world would suffer little should that which is desirable ever be translated into reality. And despite all this, French-speaking people ought to be satisfied, since there is general agreement with their language demands! The question of how to reconcile these conflicting requirements remains in abeyance.

3. The attitude of Third Group workers

Members of the third group offer another example of this ambiguity shown by the English-speaking people. Should new immigrants to Québec learn French before English? Yes, certainly! (I). But in practice, it would be much better if they were to learn English instead of French (K). Everyone in Québec ought to know French (B), French-speaking people ought to have the right to use their own language at work (L) and it is essential that they insist on doing so (P). All things considered, however, members of the third group adopt the same attitude as English-speaking people concerning the rôle French can play as the language of work and business.

While recognizing the general rights of French-speaking people, members of other language groups tend to defend the position of English in the economic world. Among French-speaking people themselves, only two-thirds believe possible the realization of what by an overwhelming majority they desire. French-speaking people thus reveal a certain inability to accept the notion of a change in the situation. And this inability is even much stronger among English-speaking people and "others." All these answers reflect a sort of fatalism on the workers' part, a feeling that though the situation should be changed to allow French to take its rightful place, they do not see how this can come about, given Québec's economic integration in the North American whole. So powerful is the weight of English in economic life that it is impossible to visualize for French a rôle any different from that which it currently occupies. This inability to visualize a viable alternative situation is largely responsible for the ambiguity revealed in the comparison between what is desirable and what is possible.

TABLE I. 73

Percentages of affirmative answers, by language group, to statements concerning obstacles to a possible increase in French use in work communications

Language group	Working in		Working in		Working in		Working in		Working in		Working in	
	English only	Both languages	English only	Both languages	English only	Both languages	English only	Both languages	English only	Both languages	Engligh only	Both languages
French-speaking	38%	11%	42%	21%	79%	50%	68%	43%	76%	37%	64%	34%
English-speaking	77%	28%	82%	60%	54%	43%	50%	36%	43%	42%	54%	50%
Other	79%	17%	63%	28%	33%	36%	34%	38%	39%	37%	39%	40%
	Practical obstacles				Economic obstacles				Social obstacles			
Obstacles to possible increase of French at work	Most people understand English very well, so there is no need to speak French at work		My work would require a great deal of time if I had to do it in French		I might harm my promotion chances if I spoke only French at work		I absolutely need English, if I used only French I would lose my job		If I insisted on using only French, relations with others at work would be strained		I would feel cut off from people if I spoke only French at work	

4. Obstacles to a possible increase in the use of French at work

Among both French-speaking and non-French-speaking workers, however, this ambiguity derives also from what are seen as real obstacles to a possible increase of French use in work communications (Table I. 73). French-speaking people are very aware of obstacles of an economic and social nature: they are almost as fearful of ostracization from their milieu as of harming their promotion chances or losing their job; English-speaking people and third group members tend rather to fear the practical results of a possible change in language use — especially loss of personal efficiency in work performance. The significant difference, however, is to be found between workers in a quasi-unilingual English position and those in a bilingual situation. When French-speaking people are able to use their mother tongue, the perception of obstacles becomes considerably blurred. In other words, they can more easily imagine French as a language more widely used at work. By the same token, English-speaking people and "others" subjected to bilingualism are much less aware of obstacles of a practical nature, especially of the fact that English ought to be the sole communications language at work; but in comparison with third group workers, English-speaking people see themselves as being much less capable of job efficiency if they had to use French (60% against 28%); this would suggest that their bilingualism is less advanced than that of the "others," most likely in written activities, as we have already established.

It is clear from all this that workers' attitudes are largely related to their language use at work and to their consequent ability to visualize that French could rank with English as a communications instrument. The obstacle is psychological. The more the worker already uses French, the easier it can be overcome; the change will have to be made very gradually for unilingual English-speaking workers and even for French-speaking workers and "others" in quasi-unilingual English situations.

French-speaking people turn without reservation to the Government both for help in their efforts to bridge the gap between what is desirable and what is possible, and in their struggle to overcome obstacles to an increase in the use of French. Only 19% of them (against 39% of English-speaking people and 35% of "others") are undecided as to the relevance of a government policy on language use at work. Not only are some 80% of French-speaking people in favor of government action, but just as many (82%) feel that such intervention would be effective, even though only 71% believe that French will become the language of work. Almost as many English-speaking people and third group members as French-speaking people (74% and 77% in each of these groups) feel that government action to increase the use of French would be effective. Only 51% and 63% respectively, however, believe that French could become the language of work. It would appear that individuals, overwhelmed by the magnitude of the problem, would welcome the intervention of a higher authority to help them resolve an equation whose solution lies beyond their powers.

NOTES

[1] Royal Commission of Inquiry on Bilingualism and Biculturalism. Volume III, b. *The Work World*, The Private Sector, page 1022.

[2] Inquiry carried out at the Commission's request by the International Institute of Quantitative Economics covering 2,000 management cases in private enterprise, especially in the manufacturing industry.

[3] Our results could legitimately be compared with those brought to light by the federal Commission only if the samples themselves and the definition of French and English-speaking persons were comparable. Whatever the case for percentages, the trend remains the same for both inquiries.

[4] The continental nature of the Québec economy has been described by the economist Albert Faucher in his article: "Le caractère continental de l'industrialisation du Québec" (The continental nature of Québec's industrialization) in *Recherches Sociographiques*, Vol. VI, No. 3, Sept/Dec., 1965.

[5] In recent months, the French Language Bureau has achieved considerable success in this area. But since the operation is long and costly, such special activities should perhaps form part of a general policy with defined objectives offering a frame of reference to allow a more active co-operation on the part of business.

[6] See, in this regard, the inventory drawn up, at the Commission's request, by Mr. Claude-Armand Sheppard. In this section of the chapter, we make special use of the breakdown report which he prepared for us.

[7] See briefs to the Commission from industrial, commercial and financial enterprises.

[8] Report of the Royal Commission on Bilingualism and Biculturalism, Book III. *The Work World*, Part 2, the Private Sector, pages 532-53.

[9] Survey conducted for the Commission by Mr. Jean-Claude de Brouwer on "Ce que pensent les élites économiques du Québec du français comme langue de travail" (What Québec's economic elite feel about French as a working language).

[10] Survey conducted by Mr. Jean-Claude de Brouwer of the firm Sondage d'opinion du Québec (International Surveys Limited). We also refer to the analytical report on the language of work prepared by Mr. Pierre Laporte, research director for the Commission.

SECTION FIVE

Legislation and Response

IN SEARCH OF A LANGUAGE POLICY: FRANCOPHONE REACTIONS TO BILLS 85 AND 63

Robert J. Macdonald

Introduction

Two autonomous and somewhat divergent school systems have traditionally been permitted to exist in Québec — the Protestant and Roman Catholic systems. For all intents and purposes, Protestant meant English, though during the 1950's a small French Protestant sector had reemerged. Even within the Roman Catholic system, the English were given considerable autonomy. As a consequence English Québecers historically had controlled their own educational system, without necessary reference to the francophones. Even though the creation of a Ministry of Education in 1964 had reduced this autonomy, and made educational policy throughout the Province a political consideration (determined by the needs and aspirations of the francophone majority), still there were no clear references in Québec law to language rights — only religious rights.

The decline of the influence of the Roman Catholic Church, to the point in Montréal where practising Catholics were but one-third of nominal members, the catastrophic drop in the birth rate to the point where it approached zero population growth, and the continuing tendency of immigrants to associate themselves with the anglophone milieu had caused many francophones to question whether survival of the culture, founded primarily on language, was assured. Despite obvious signs of cultural vitality, such as the popular prestige of poets, novelists, chansonniers and filmmakers, continued anxiety over the future of the language had caused many to seek political solutions to the crisis of culture.

Throughout the Quiet Revolution, a number of new political and cultural organisations emerged to give vent to feelings of frustration and concern. Organisations were founded such as the *Rassemblement pour l'Indépendence Nationale* (RIN), the *Mouvement Laïque de la Langue Française*, and the *Club Fleur de Lys de Québec.* Illustrative of the concern for the future of Québec's culture was the formation of the *Etats Généraux du Canada Français.* Established during the mid-sixties, it attempted to map out the direction which French Canada would take. Even older groups such as the *Sociétés Saint-Jean-Baptiste* (SSJB) were galvanised into new and rigourous action. For example, when the school elections in the Montréal suburb of Saint-Léonard were fought over the issue of abolishing bilingual (French-English) classes, that is, over the existence of language rights in education, organisations outside the municipality were quick to intervene. And because Saint-Léonard reflected tensions in the larger community, what was initially a local issue quickly jumped municipal boundaries and became not only a Montréal but a province-wide issue of major proportions.[1]

The tumultuous school elections in Saint-Léonard, and the consequent decision of the school board to phase out bilingual classes had, by September 1968, resulted in the boycott of school registration by hundreds of largely non-francophone parents. Demonstrations, and a worsening linguistic conflict in the Montréal area, compounded by the government's inability (legal or political) to intervene, meant that the Saint-Léonard crisis festered throughout the fall of 1968. Conscious of this situation and desirous to fulfill the pledges of the late Daniel Johnson, Premier Jean-Jacques Bertrand promised to an English-language open-line radio audience that he was prepared to introduce legislation to protect minority rights.[2]

Although this legislation was not brought forward until after the bye-elections of 4th, December the Premier was immediately attacked by French unilingualists who charged him with attempting to gain votes, especially in the opposition's (Liberal) stronghold of Notre-Dame-de-Grâce. Claude Ryan of *Le Devoir* suggested that the delay in introducing the legislation until after the bye-elections was a wise move: however, he was critical of the apparent decision to introduce a general law governing language rights, which he suggested could only be done in the light of constitutional talks and a royal commission of enquiry (which he proposed).[3]

Within days of the Premier's first announcement, pressure groups led by the Saint-Léonard based *Mouvement Pour l'Intégration Scolaire* (MIS), the *Fédération des Sociétés Saint-Jean-Baptiste du Québec*, and *La Ligue de l'Action Nationale* began organizing opposition to the move. On the 25th of November the Premier met with representatives of the coalition. The spokesmen argued that French not English was in danger (because English was the language of work), that it needed protection, and that since French was the language of the majority it ought to be the language of instruction. To charges that he had no mandate, the Premier replied that the late Premier Johnson had declared in June and September that the rights of anglophones would not be abrogated by the decision of the local boards. In reply, the *Union Général des Etudiants du Québec* threatened extra-parliamentary of even extra legal action.[4] Not satisfied with the Premier's response, the MIS called a general meeting on 28 November, at which Yvon Groulx of the *Fédération des SSJB* indicated "*Nous sommes sur un pied de guerre offensive. . .Pour nous, c'est une question de survie. . .Sinon, nous courons frénétiquement au suicide*". Raymond Lemieux of the MIS pointed out that the *Etats Généraux* had passed a resolution favouring French as the only official language in Québec: Lemieux indicated his view that the government was acting against the declared wishes of the people, which he interpreted as being synonymous with the views of the *Etats Généraux*[5]

The meeting of the 28th November drew up plans for a mass protest in front of the legislature. A "teach-in" was organised and plans made to distribute pamphlets. The common front drew support from a number of areas, ranging from large nationalist groups such as the SSJB to smaller nationalist groupings such as *La Ligue des Patriotes du Québec*, to groups organised for other purposes. At the Laval "teach-in" the Premier was denounced as a traitor.[6] Throughout the demonstrations and public protests, the issue of *indépendantisme* became confused with French unilingualism. Although Raymond Laliberté of the *Corporation des Enseignants du Québec* (CEQ) pointed this out, the fact seemed to be ignored. The vigourous intervention in the dispute by noted *indépendantistes* such as Pierre Bourgault and the fact that many unilingualists were also *indépendantiste* clouded the issue of language rights in education, and a strictly educational issue was viewed in the context of cultural, economic and even political liberation. Consequently, while many anglophones charged unilingualists with being separatists, many who turned up for the protests and demonstrations had done so not so much in protest over Bill 85 but in support of liberation in its many facets.

On the 5th of December a noisy demonstration took place before the legislature. Though inclement weather prevented many from attending, around 3,000 demonstrators gathered. The large numbers of secondary students drew bitter comment from both government and opposition benches, particularly on the possible role of teachers in inciting the demonstrators: even René Lévesque denounced "*L'embrigadement des écoliers*" and claimed the demonstrators had been led by hotheads.[7]

Bill 85: an unwanted child?

All this activity had taken place before the terms of the legislation were announced. In brief, the opposition of many francophone groups would be based not so much on legal technicalities (of the legislation) but on the principle of parental choice of the language of instruction, which the legislation was thought to embody. On the 9th December 1968, Premier Bertrand introduced Bill 85 designed to "*préciser le rôle de la langue française dans le domaine de l'éducation au Québec*", the bill envisage the creation of a linguistic committee within the Superior Council of Education which would establish regulations governing language of education. Although school commissions would be required to provide education in either language if the pupils so desired, all pupils were required to have a working knowledge *(connaissance d'usage)* of French. In this way the Premier sought to protect the rights of the minority at the same time as securing the position of the majority in Québec society.[8]

With the Premier ill in hospital, the government decided to send the bill to committee instead of proceeding with the legislation to second reading. The government, led by the Acting Premier and Minister of Education, Jean-Guy Cardinal, argued that a bill of this importance should not be passed quickly but that interested groups should be given an opportunity to express their views. On the other hand, the Liberal Opposition claimed that the urgency of the situation demanded a vote on principle (second reading) before the committee discussed technicalities of the bill. On the 16th of December, Bill 85 was sent to committee.

Considerable comment and public debate had already arisen within the francophone community. Editorially, Clement Brown of *Montréal-Matin* suggested that the Bertrand proposals were realistic and that Bill 85 normalised the situation by effectively making French the language of usage in the province. Claude Ryan felt that the Premier had chosen a middle way and had arrived at an honourable compromise. Renaude Lapointe echoed this view in *La Presse*, though her colleague Roger Champoux considered the solutions of Bill 85 as "*étonnantes, rigides et menaçantes*".[9]

In an article in the Jesuit periodical, *Relations*, the very respected Father Richard Arès indicated that the crisis for language survival in Québec was focussed in Montréal.[10] Concerning Bill 85 he concluded "*Le Bill 85. . .s'il était adopté sans autre garantie pour le français, ne pourrait qu'aggraver une situation déjà fort alarmante, une situation qui est en train de compromettre à jamais l'avenir même de la communauté de langue française dans la région de Montréal*"[11] *Maintenant* also commented on Bill 85 in the form of a collective editorial.[12] Sensing that Bill 85 would extend the already precarious position of French, the editors called for the government to renounce any measure favouring English, to declare French the language of work "*sans réserve*", and to develop a "*francisation radicale de l'enseignement dit français*", including integration of immigrants and anglophones.[13]

Pressure groups continued their attack. Raymond Lemieux labelled Bill 85 "*un projet de loi qui légalise le vol du français au Québec par les minorités*".[14] According to Yvon Groulx of the *Fédération des SSJB*, the legislation granted rights hitherto not recognised in law and rather than correcting the basic situation, that is, reducing the danger to the French language, it protected minorities. Moreover, he criticised the centralisation of power in the hands of the Minister of Education as well as the alleged overrepresentation of minorities on the linguistic committee.[15] For its part, the *Union Générale des Etudiants du Québec* charged that the bill demonstrated "*l'absence de politique d'ensemble du gouvernement Québécois*".[16] A measure of francophone reaction can be seen in the establishment of a common front to oppose the bill which was labelled a Trojan horse which would accelerate the trend towards making the French Canadians a minority. The bill was an affront: "*un soufflet à tous les francophones à Québec*."

Francophone groups, however, were pleased with the decision of the legislature to send the bill to the Education Committee for hearings, for they realised that in committee they could put their point of view forward more effectively to the deputies, especially those who were wavering. They also realised that until the bill was passed the situation in Saint-Léonard (the phasing out of bilingual classes) and the general language position (no legal rights for language minorities) was effectively frozen.

In examining the briefs and the testimony before the committee, one can identify a number of common themes. These include not only an outline of the reasons why certain groups felt the French language was in danger, they also discuss the importance of preserving the French language over and above any consideration of the position of minorities. This is not surprising in view of the fact that the francophone assault on Bill 85 was led by the nationalist groups, many with *independantiste* learnings. Bill 85 dealt with educational rights, and since school commissions, teachers' organisations and parent-teacher groups would have been affected most by the legislation, it would have been logical to assume that they would have opinions about the proposed legislation. As it was, very few strictly French educational bodies showed up to comment on the principles of the bill.[18]

Francophone groups first underlined the reasons why minority rights had to be made subservient to the protection of the rights of the majority. Of prime consideration was the relationship between language and the economy. The twelve-member *Le Conseil Québécois de la Légitimité Nationale* claimed that the dominant rôle which English played in the economy was due to the economic exploitation of the workers (French Canadians) by the bosses who were English: "*l'occupation linguistique se relie à l'exploitation économique*".[19] In support of its view, the *Association Québécoise des Professeurs de Français* (AQPF) cited reports from the federal Royal Commission on Bilingualism and Biculturalism to the effect that the French Canadian suffered economic and other discrimination in work.[20] English domination, according to Rosaire Morin of the *Etats Généraux*, would be solved only "*si le Québec établissait le français comme seule langue officielle, si la toponymie du Québec était refrancisée, si l'affichage était prioritairement français, si le français devient la langue du travail dans l'industrie et dans les affaires.*"[21] Because the domination of English led to the decision of the Néo-Québécois[22] to send his children to English schools, the situation could only be reversed by making French the language of work. Hence the French public school for all would not be hardship, for it would prepare children for a French working environment.[23]

Moreover, francophone opponents of Bill 85 based their position on the belief that the nation (the *franco-québécois*) had the right to impose its language on all, particularly when that *franco-québécois* nation was in danger. Consequently Rosaire Morin argued (somewhat incorrectly) that in no other country were minorities given the right to their own schools and that the Québec majority had the right to deny schools to the minority. Citing the philosopher of anti-colonialism, Albert Memni, the unilingualists maintained that as long as economic domination existed, cultural sub-ordination resulted. Hence the French language, the language of the nation had to be liberated in all areas.[24]

Although anglophones readily accepted the fact that English was the predominant language of the economy throughout North America, their conclusions and solutions differed from those of francophone unilingualists. They argued that it was precisely because English was the language of the North American economy that the right to an English-language education was necessary. Moreover, they contended that a French-only policy, which denied parental rights, was inimical to the bicultural and bilingual nature of Canadian as distinct from Québec society.[25]

Secondly, francophone spokesmen anchored their demands for a French unilingual school system on certain demographic realities. The *Mouvement pour l'Unilingualisme Français au Québec* recognised that French Canadians were surrounded by English-speakers, and suggested that for *"l'impéralisme anglosaxon, 59 états ne lui suffisent pas, lui faut-il encore s'emparer de notre seul Etat"*.[26] The Anglo-Saxon pressure led the *Société Culturelle Québécoise* to suggest that the only way the survival of French on the continent could be guaranteed was if the Quebec government took advantage of its sovereign power to guarantee French in all facets of Québec life: that is, by making Quebec unilingual.[27]

The position of French as a minority language in North America has been made all the more precarious by the recent decline in the French-Canadian birth rate. Thus, for Raymond Lemieux of the *MIS*, *"la revanche des berceaux"* was over and *"l'accroissement naturel de la population n'est plus en soi une garantie de survie"*.[28] It is important to note that the *Etats Généraux* had already debated the issue of the declining birth rate and that its deliberations and research (especially by Rosaire Morin) were used to buttress the arguments of other groups such as the *Société Culturelle Québécoise*. In their view, the "minorisation" of French could only be stopped by the introduction of a French unilingual school system attended by all.

Closely related to the decline of the birth rate were the perceived trends in immigration and the anglicisation of francophones. According to Rosaire Morin, Anglo-Celtic domination of the economy clearly drove the immigrant to the English school. Moreover, the antagonism shown towards immigrants was illustrated by the *SSJB de Montréal* view that Québec was merely a staging place for many of them. If a French unilingual Québec meant that immigrants would bypass the province, then Québec would be saved the trouble and expense of their education. Figures cited by the *SSJB de Montréal* suggested that in 1962-1963 over three-quarters of Néo-Québécois attended the English section of the *Commission des Ecoles Catholiques de Montréal* (CECM) a percentage which increased throughout the decade. Moreover, Protestant immigrants attended Protestant and therefore English schools. Consequently, few *Néo-Québécois* were attracted to the French-Canadian society. But as the *Etats Généraux* pointed out, it was not normal that a minority assimilate the immigrant. For these reasons, the French unilingualists opposed the free choice of language of instruction which Bill 85 provided.[29]

Immigration, according to the ultranationalists, had been used by the anglophone element to drown the French element. The *Mouvement Pour l'Unilinguisme Français au Québec* justified this view by citing quotations from Lord Durham and Clifford Sifton, or showing that more immigration offices were located in Britain or Germany than in France.[30]

The continued anglicisation of French-Canadians also illustrated the precariousness of the French fact. Francophone briefs suggested that outside Québec the French were rapidly being anglicised — for example, over one third of *Franco-Ontariens* were effectively anglophone.[31] In addition, many francophones had opted to send their children to English-language schools. In so doing they were working against the national interest, or so François-Albert Angers claimed. He suggested that it was "*le rôle de l'Etat. . .de voir que les parents ne travaillent pas contre l'intérêt national*".[32] As a result, to introduce Bill 85 which allowed French-Canadians to choose English schools and thus to anglicise was to betray "*nos valeureux ancêtres*" — including Papineau, Lafontaine, Riel, Delormier, Chénier, Mercier, Garneau, Bourassa, Groulx and "*les centaines de héros inconnus de notre histoire nationale qui ont défendu aux prix de lourds sacrifices. . .notre héritage culturel français.*"[33]

A corollary to this belief that attendance at English schools led to anglicisation was the belief of the *Etats Généraux* that bilingualism (or the too early introduction of English in primary school) led to a decline in French and progressive anglicisation. In testimony before the Education Committee, Rosaire Morin cited a 1962 UNESCO conference, the philosopher Etienne Gilson, and the linguist William Mackay (sic), among others, to support the contention that bilingualism led to assimilation. He was backed by the AQPF.[34]

In order to put the unilingualist view in perspective, it should be pointed out that they were not opposed to learning English as a second language. They believed, however, that it should be introduced only after a sound foundation in French had been given, that is, in the secondary school. Nor were they opposed to personal bilingualism, for they were aware the North American economy meant contacts beyond Québec would necessitate the learning of English. Rather they were opposed to official bilingualism which they claimed would undermine French. Bill 85, they contended, would consecrate Québec as an officially bilingual province.

In contrast to the French unilingualists who favoured coercion, anglophone and some francophone groups supported the principle of free choice contained in Bill 85. And, unlike the French unilingualists, anglophones were more likely to accept the compulsory learning of the second language. Finally, anglophones pointed out that the use of modern educational methods permitted the early teaching of a second language without any detrimental effect on the mother tongue.[35]

Although the Catholic tradition in French-Canadian education supported parental rights and the concept of the parents as the first educator of the child, francophone groups suggested that collective rights superseded individual rights. François-Albert Angers, for example, of *La Ligue de l'Action Nationale* claimed that while parental rights *within* family matters were important, family life including school rights were not the exclusive property of parents. He noted that the State had limited parental rights in the areas of life and death, and had required parents to send their children to school. In this way the State illustrated it had a legitimate role in determining the nature of the education of children. According to this view, language was a national and collective good. Moreover, the parental right to choose the language of instruction could not be found in "*les collectivités normales*".[36] Francophones also pointed out that French minorities in other provinces (presumably "normal collectivities") were not accorded legal equality with the anglophones. Yet in Québec Bill 85 would accord the minority equality with the majority. The *Etats Généraux* therefore claimed that the fundamental question of the debate was whether or not the Québec government should first protect the rights of the French-Canadian collectivity. The *SSJB de Jacques Cartier* claimed that Bill 85 gave anglophones privileges and contravened the rights of the francophone majority. It was argued that elsewhere minorities were normally granted only those rights which the majority conferred on them. Everywhere that is except where the English were in the minority and then they claimed equal rights.[37] The upshot of this argument by the unilingualists was that by passing Bill 85, the government would restrict French-Canadian thought and action.

In contrast to this emphasis on the rights of the collectivity, anglophone briefs stressed the related issues of individual and parental rights. Their authors argued that a unilingual Québec would result in the government being the servant of the majority rather than of all citizens. Nonetheless, they did not reject the view that French should become the priority language in the province.[38]

Francophone groups generally tended to attack the underlying principles of the bill, while anglophones and bilingualists supported them (although criticising certain technicalities of the bill including ministerial power, lack of appeal to the discretionary power, and the vagueness of the phrases "cause to be taught" (*faire instruire*) or "persons settling in the province of Quebec"). Francophones nevertheless perceived specific weaknesses in the bill. They were concerned, for example, about the composition and powers of the linguistic committee which would establish regulations and advise the Minister in matters of linguistic rights. According to the *Société Culturelle Québécoise*, granting the minorities five out of fifteen places on the committee, meant that they were overrepresented, since they were but one fifth the population.[39] On the other hand, the *Fédération des SSJB du Québec* felt that the mere existence of the committee imposed too many restrictions on the Minister.[40]

Withdrawal of Bill 85

The public debate and the hearings of the Education Committee revealed that throughout Québec, pressure groups had combined to attack both the principles and the details of Bill 85. Indeed, the hearings had permitted opponents of the bill to get maximum publicity for their position. Late in February 1969, the *Conseil Supérieur de l'Education* transmitted its view of Bill 85 to the Minister of Education. It recommended that the Bill be withdrawn on the grounds that it was a piecemeal approach to a much larger problem. The *Conseil* also suggested that to continue with the bill would be to risk causing even graver problems than existed in Saint-Léonard.[41]

In rendering this advice public, Jean-Guy Cardinal dismissed it as being simply another opinion on the matter. Vincent Prince of *Le Devoir*, however, considered the opinion wise, because it underlined the fact that it was outside the school that the linguistic problem would be solved. Nevertheless, he expressed his disappointment that there was no specific advice on how the government should act to restore the *status quo*.[42]

Given the nature of the controversy surrounding Bill 85, it was not surprising that Premier Bertrand hinted to the *Union Nationale* Council that Bill 85 might be withdrawn. In his press conference of the 17th of March, he suggested that the pressure groups had perceived it as "a bad piece of legislation" and that the committee hearings were merely sounding boards for extremists. (As we shall see, the latter position is important in understanding the controversy over Bill 63 which would break out in the fall.) Though the Premier indicated he would not impose the bill on either the caucus or the legislature, he made it clear that he would not abandon the principle of guaranteeing English-language school rights. Three days later he announced the Bill was "*un bébé que personne ne veut*", and that the problem would be submitted to the Gendron Commission.[43]

The withdrawal was generally well received, particularly within the francophone community. The *SSJB de Montréal*, secure in the knowledge that under existing law English-language rights were not guaranteed, declared itself satisfied.[44] Sylvio St. Amant in *Le Nouvelliste* remarked that the government had created a precedeng by withdrawing its own bill, though St. Amant was pleased to see a bill whose principles he opposed dropped. In *Montréal-Matin*, Lucien Langlois commented that while the intentions and inspirations of the bill were noble and generous, too many groups had raised serious objections to it. Because it failed to reconcile the partisans of "fairplay" (that is the anglophones) and "survival" (that is francophones), Bertrand had no other choice but to withdraw the bill.[45]

Ultimately the fate of the legislation had been determined by pressure groups. Because the deputies had never had a chance to debate the principles, the only public debate revolved around the positions of pressure groups, individuals and newspaper editorials. The dramatic fashion in which opposition was expressed led the Premier to withdraw the legislation. Possibly the weak and uncertain nature of his majority was a contributing factor. But the committee hearings brought out into the open the general tenor of the diverging arguments over linguistic rights. These deep-seated and fiercely held views challenged the provincial government to try and reconcile a badly divided population. Alleged splits within the governing *Union Nationale* did little to make its task easier.[46]

In the four months before Bill 85 was finally withdrawn, the linguistic issue had shifted from an issue of purely local concern to one of province-wide action. Whereas Saint-Léonard had been the first (and, except for some small rural commissions near Québec City and Granby), the only commission to declare itself in opposition to linguistic choice, events in the suburb were quickly forgotten. Their symbolic value, of course, remained. Now, however, the battle for linguistic rights was waged across the province. It was no longer sufficient to rectify the situation in Saint-Léonard, language rights for all in the province had to be clarified before agitation would cease. The fate of Bill 85 showed just how difficult the task would be.

The failure of the government to secure passage of Bill 85 left it with no immediate plans to solve the contentious Saint-Léonard situation. For the next six months the crisis went from bad to worse. Despite attempts by Cardinal to reach a compromise in June, it remained a thorn in the government's side. The worsening situation and the growing boldness of pressure groups, particularly the French unilingualists, meant that the task was immensely more difficult in November 1969 when the government introduced Bill 63.

A renewed effort: Bill 63

Throughout the summer of 1969, the open sore that was Saint-Léonard continued to fester. The Saint-Léonard dispute, moreover, was intimately linked both to the reorganisation of school administration on Montréal Island and the provincial issue of language guarantees throughout all aspects of Québec society including education.[47] The Saint-Léonard riots of 10 September 1969, in which the French unilingualists and the Italophone population clashed, underlined the seriousness of the situation. By late September and early October, there were unmistakeable signs that the Bertrand government was prepared to take action. Speaking to the Canadian Club on 29 September, the Premier linked the resolution of the Saint-Léonard dispute to the reorganisation of schools in Montréal. Even more significant in terms of language rights, he emphasized the linguistic and cultural duality of Québec and stressed the necessity of arriving at a solution whereby the English minority could achieve greater participation in the province.[48] Newspaper accounts suggested, however, that a split had developed between the Premier and the Minister of Education over the need for specific legislation recognising English as a language of instruction. In addition, there were a number of backbenchers who remained to be convinced. On the 20th and 21st of October, the *Union Nationale* caucus grappled with the issue.[49]

In the end, the Premier's views prevailed, and on the 21st of October he announced to the Assembly that a specific bill dealing with the language of education would be put before parliament.[50] On the 23rd of October, Jean-Guy Cardinal moved first reading of Bill 63, "*Loi pour promouvoir l'enseignement de la langue française*". But questions arose concerning Cardinal's commitment towards the bill, considering his very brief statement and his relative lack of participation in the subsequent debate. According to the Education Minister, the three articles of the bill had as an objective:

> d'assurer que les enfants de langue anglaise de Québec acquièrent une connaissance d'usage de la langue française et que les personnes qui s'établissent au Québec acquièrent, dès leur arrivée, la connaissance de la langue française. Il confirme, en outre, la possibilité pour les parents, de choisir entre le français et l'anglais, la langue dans laquelle les cours seront donnés à leurs enfants.[51]

The Premier, in his statement, indicated that he would avoid what he considered was the mistake of Bill 85. The Bill would not be sent to the Education Committee to allow pressure groups to present views and delay or prevent passage.[52]

A live, televised press-conference, attended by the Premier and his cabinet ministers Marcel Masse (Public Service), Mario Beaulieu (Immigration), Jean-Noël Tremblay (Cultural Affairs) and Jean-Guy Cardinal, revealed that the government considered Bill 63 to be the first step toward making French the priority language in Québec. The Premier justified the move on the basis of the 1966 *Union Nationale* platform (which promised to strengthen the French language) and on the collective needs of the Québec nation. Though the legislation provided for liberty of choice, Québec would be officially French. To illustrate that Bill 63 was just one of a series of contemplated measures, the ministers indicated what further steps would be taken to safeguard the French language. For example, the Ministry of Immigration would be given funds and powers to assist ethnic groups and encourage them to integrate with the French milieu. The status of French as the priority language used in the public service would be made official. And more funds would be allocated to the Ministry of Cultural Affairs to promote the French language and culture. These anticipated measures would presumably be reviewed after the Gendron Commission had submitted its report, and strengthened in view of its findings and recommendations. Finally, in the course of the news conference, Cardinal agreed that public hearings on the legislation were not necessary.[53]

Not unexpectedly, this move by the cabinet was attacked from several quarters. According to the Liberal leader (and former Premier), Jean Lesage, the principles which the bill outlined were acceptable. This, too, was hardly surprising considering his party had passed resolutions favouring this approach at their convention in October 1968. But Lesage chastised the government for the delay in introducing the legislation. Deputies for anglophone ridings (such as William Tetley in Notre-Dame-de-Grâce and Arthur Séguin in Robert Baldwin) appeared satisfied with the bill "under the circumstances" but felt that it was badly drafted. The major opponent of the legislation was *Parti-Québécois* leader, René Lévesque. Though he was happy to see that the anglophone would no longer be able to isolate himself in his ghetto, cut off from the majority, Lévesque felt that the bill did not go far enough. That is, it failed to *compel* future immigrants and their children to attend French schools, at least until they acquired citizenship. Moreover, like many others, he found the phraseology grossly imprecise.[54]

Editorial opinion expressed lukewarm support for the government. Claude Ryan in *Le Devoir* supported what he termed "*L'esprit foncièrement libéral et le souci de servir la langue française qui ont inspiré les rédacteurs du projet de loi 63*". He felt, however, that the government had acted with excessive haste in not consulting either with the Gendron Commission or the *Conseil Supérieur de l'Education.*[55] Moreover, Ryan viewed the brevity of the bill with alarm, for it did not state precisely how the principles (of promoting French and parental choice) would be carried out. Editorial writers in *La Presse* were somewhat divided. Although he recognised that "Democracy requires that dissidents within a society be respected", Guy Cormier suggested that democracy "also establishes the uncontested rights of the majority". In this case he questioned the uncontested rights given for parental choice. On the other hand, Renaude Lapointe merely asked that more positive steps be taken to ensure the primacy of French. Writing in the *Union Nationale* tabloid, *Montréal-Matin*, Lucien Langlois remarked "*Pour la première fois dans l'Histoire du Québec, ceux qui auront choisi l'anglais comme langue d'enseignement en toute liberté ne pourront autant faire bon marché de la langue de la majorité*". The action taken to ensure minority rights at the same time as making French the priority language, he felt to be sufficiently generous and just.[56]

For Richard Arès of *Relations*, Bill 63 was an "*entreprise prématurée et hasardeuse*". He suggested that it was far from resolving, in a complete and decisive fashion, the question of the immigrants, and thus it failed to satisfy the majority opinion. Moreover, the bill failed to solve the problem of the language of work. Arès also criticised the government for not waiting at least for the Gendron Report and thus giving the appearance of stubbornness. *Maintenant's* condemnation of Bill 63 was even more striking:

> Pour la première fois de notre histoire, un projet de loi consacre dans un texte juridique de notre législation québécoise le présumé droit des parents à choisir la langue d'enseignement au risque de sacrifier les intérêts supérieurs de la nation québécoise. . .Accepter le principe du libre choix de la langue. . .c'est. . .à accepter de "fouer" notre vie collective au risque de nous perdre.[57]

Outside Montréal, *Le Soleil* felt it an overdue but fair policy, while *La Tribune* compared it to the situation in Ontario in which the French minority had their own schools but English was the priority language. The generally cautious note sounded by the French press was illustrated by Roger Bruneau in *L'Action.* Though he praised the Premier for his courage in introducing the controversial bill, Bruneau was critical of the provisions with regard to immigrants and the imprecision of the term "working knowledge" (*connaissance d'usage*). Like others, however, he pointed out that the law was but one of several which would make up the language policy.[58]

Anglophone editorials similarily praised a Bill which they believed promoted French but also guaranteed English and the principle of free choice. In addition, *The Gazette* cautioned that to succeed, the bill had to have the support of the people.[59] Anglophones were more concerned about how Bill 63 would be implemented. More specifically, they wanted to know how school reorganisation in Montréal would guarantee that language minorities received quality education.[60]

The response of francophone pressure groups

More important than editorial opinion were the actions of the various pressure groups. French unilingualists condemned the bill's principles outright. According to Raymond Lemieux of the *Ligue pour l'Intégration Scolaire* (LIS, formerly MIS), the bill consecrated a privilege gained by military occupation because it made French and English equal. This "*acte de lâcheté posé avec cynisme*", he claimed, would only assist what he referred to as the galloping anglicisation of the province. In this way Durham's wish (expressed in 1840) that the French Canadian would disappear would be fulfilled. Predicting that the bill would not reduce tension, Lemieux demanded that a referendum be held so that the people could determine their linguistic future. He apparently felt that pressure groups, such as those which appeared at the hearings on Bill 85, reflected the will of the people and were not extremist as Jean-Noël Tremblay had suggested. The government's action was deemed hypocritical because it did nothing to ensure the survival of the French culture. Lemieux's right-hand man, Laurier Gravel, said cynically "Rejoice and be glad, for the French have yellowed". François-Albert Angers, on behalf of the *SSJB de Montréal* demounced the bill as a "fundamental capitulation". He also challenged the claim of the deputies to represent the people on this issue which had never been submitted to the electorate. Thus he called for the formation of a popular front to oppose (and subsequently defeat) the legislation. Another important group, and one which would exercise significant influence on the viability of a system aimed at improving the teaching of French and English was the *CEQ*. Through its president, Raymond Laliberté, it demanded the withdrawal of Bill 63, its replacement by legislation which proclaimed official French unilingualism, and which obliged future immigrants to Québec to send their children to French school.[61]

Some francophones defended the principle of free choice, notably Joseph Pagé, former chairman of the *CECM*, who called upon French-Canadians to create a dynamic school system which would attract immigrants without coercion, and Jean Drapeau, mayor of Montréal, who suggested the bill responded to the needs of the province.[62] These voices of moderation were drowned by the often shrill voices of those attacking the bill.

Among anglophones, whom the bill was obviously designed to satisfy, opinion was cautious. They were concerned particularly with ministerial power, the lack of precision as to how a "working knowledge of French" would be achieved and the vagueness of the phrase "persons locating in Québec". These concerns reflected a growing impatience with, and lack of confidence in the *Union Nationale* government and especially Jean-Guy Cardinal. Thus, while applauding the principles even to the point of calling it a "sane and rational approach to what was becoming an increasingly irrational debate", anglophone groups by and large adopted a wait and see attitude.[63]

Legislative filibuster

Though Bill 63 was adopted with amendments, it was not done without a lengthy debate by the "Circumstantial Opposition"[64] of René Lévesque, Antoine Flamand, Jérôme Proulx and Yves Michaud. Briefly, the group considered the legislation to be "an intellectually dishonest fabrication", which rather than promote French would lead to its decline. According to Lévesque, free choice of the language of instruction would permit the minority to become dominant, since the English economic power would continue to attract the immigrants. Flamand cited a study by *Université de Montréal* demographers to the effect that the anglicisation in the Montréal region would continue even without legislation. Proulx forecast that Bill 63 would increase the trend to anglicisation by both francophones and immigrants. To support this view, Lévesque was able to point to statistics of the *CECM* to the effect that *Néo-Québécois* made up over fifty percent of the English section while immigrants opted ninety percent for English schools.[65] In Flamand's terms Bill 63 would fulfill the aims of Durham and Confederation: that is, the gradual erosion and final disappearance of the French element in Québec. In brief, the application of the principle of free choice would only worsen the position of the French language.[66]

As a counterpoint to the principle of free choice, the "Circumstantial Opposition" turned to the principle of collective rights. This stated that the rights of the collectivity took precedence over those of the individual, and that consequently the state had the right and duty to protect the French language. Indeed, to require future immigrants to send their children to French schools infringed on no one's rights, for these immigrants were not yet in Québec. In support of this contention, Jérôme Proulx cited the position taken by the European Court of Human Rights which, in commenting on the language issue in Belgium stated, "*Il était normal qu'un Etat, sur un territoire donné n'accorde pas cette liberté de choix lorsque le bien de la collectivité et l'intérêt supérieur de la nation le demandaient*".[67]

The "Circumstantial Opposition", then, claimed that Bill 63 did nothing to ensure either the primacy of the French language or the attendence of immigrant children at French schools. Yet despite their vigorous attempt at a filibuster, which included repeated attempts at amendments limiting access to English as the language of instruction to those whose children were currently in English schools, or those whose mother tongue was English, or even to refer the bill to the constitutional committee for study (and public reaction), the bill passed.[68]

Le front du Québec français

The filibuster did permit the extra-parliamentary opposition to organise and hold protest rallies, however. In fact, even before Bill 63 had been announced, moves were afoot to oppose it. On the 17th of October the *SSJB* called for an *Assemblée d'urgence* to deal with anticipated legislation aimed at reorganising the school administration on Montréal Island, which it felt would create English as an official language there.[69] As a consequence, when Bill 63 was introduced there was already a mechanism around which anti-bill forces could coalesce.

On the 25th of October the *Assemblée* met at the Restaurant Sambo in the east-end of Montréal. Though the 600 people present claimed to represent over eighty associations, journalists present questioned whether or not the "representatives" had been delegated by their associations. Moreover, many were members of the several *SSJB* organisations. The tone of the meeting was set by François-Albert Angers of the *SSJB de Montréal.* According to him:

> La Société Saint-Jean-Baptiste de Montréal dénonce la duplicité de ce bill 63 qui entent promouvoir la langue française. Il proclame en fait l'égalité de l'anglais. Une seule chose y est établie clairement. C'est la "Primauté du français comme langue seconde! ". . .c'est une nouvelle bataille des Plaines d'Abraham qui commence. Déjà les forces vouées à la défense des anglophones sont en place: le général Wolfe s'appelle Jean-Jacques Bertrand.

Raymond Lemieux expressed the belief that the "people of Québec were behind us and not the government". He rationalised this view of popular support by implying that the *SSJB* and the *Etats Généraux*, who had passed resolutions favouring French unilingualism, were more representative of the population than the duly elected members.[70]

A declaration of the *Assemblée d'Urgence* maintained that the affirmation of parental choice in the language of instruction and the division of schooling along linguistic lines consecrated the already privileged position of the English. In place of Bill 63, the *Assemblée* demanded a global French-language policy submitted to and approved by the people. Then, and then only, should there be any consideration given to the rights of the minority. French unilingualism, the *Assemblée* declared, should be implemented at all levels of Québec society.

One result of the meeting was the establishment of *Le Front de Québec Français (FQF)* directed by leaders of the *SSJB de Montréal*, the *Fédération des SSJB du Québec*, the *LIS*, the *Confédération des Syndicats Nationaux (CSN)* and the teachers' associations. Confident that their position was supported by the people and that they could cause the government to withdraw bill 63, the Front called for a week of demonstrations. The Premier would be challenged to a televised debate, and the culmination of the Front's efforts would be a giant rally in front of the legislative building.[71]

Despite the buoyant optimism of the Front, its tactics did not draw support from all quarters. For example, Renaude Lapointe of *La Presse* criticised both the presumption that the Front, not the elected deputies, represented the people, and the insidiousness of comparing the Premier to Wolfe. Claude Ryan, while he also challenged the representativeness of the Front, stated "*aucune force ne doit être autorisée à empêcher le Parlement de se prononcer librement. . .Si la loi Bertrand est adoptée malgré les obstentions des adversaires il restera à ceux-ci. . .le recours électoral*".[72]

Front members quickly moved outside Montréal to rally support. At Rimouski, Angers criticised nationalist members of the cabinet (Masse, Tremblay and Cardinal) for betraying their duty and accepting the compromise of Bill 63. Marcel Marceau of the *SSN* also spoke of betrayal by leaders, in this case, the traditional élite.[73] Petitions were organised in an attempt to encourage dissident *Union Nationale* members to block the bill, either by resigning and destroying the government majority or by fighting in caucus. As the Front's views became known, support came from several directions. Telegrams, often by leaders or executives of organisations, were sent to the Premier protesting the bill on the grounds that it would facilitate the integration of the immigrant to the English milieu. Many of those declaring support for the Front came from the world of trade unionism. Indeed, pressure from the regional councils forced the confederal (or executive) bureau of the *CSN* to withdraw its initial conditional support of the legislation (which was given on the understanding that the legislation would be amended to contain clauses proclaiming French the language of work and sanctions for those violating this). Though Louis Laberge of the *Fédération des Travailleurs du Québec (FTQ)* attempted to remain aloof from the "clique of Angers", constituent members, notably the Steelworkers, declared opposition to the bill. Some Junior Chambers of Commerce also supported the Front. But its major support came from constituent *SSJB* or teacher bodies, notably at *CEGEP's*,[74] *social science* faculties, and the *CEQ*, as well as students in *CEGEP's* and some university faculties.[75]

It must be made clear, however, that many declarations of support were made either by executives of the bodies concerned or by prominent members of these organisations. It was by no means evident that these spokesmen had consulted their memberships in a meaningful way. For example, although the Montréal Council of the *CSN* supported the Front, it is doubtful that the large Italian membership in the construction unions supported the move. It thus becomes problematic whether the declared support accurately reflected the positions of the membership of these groups. And even then, it was entirely possible for people to belong to several of these groups. Nonetheless, René

Lévesque suggested that since the numbers represented by the Front were equal in size to the anglophone vote, the Front had a right to be heard.[76]

A number of tactical moves were planned by the Front. Petitions were reported to be circulating which called for the Bill's withdrawal. Lemieux, for example, had asked the students to begin one, to be presented at the mass rally in front of the legislature.[77] In addition, a referendum was to be held, premised on the belief that those supporting the *FQF* were supported in turn by the population at large and that such a popular consultation would be in the democratic tradition.[78] This implied, of course, that the Premier did not enjoy popular support and that his refusal to consult the people was undemocratic. Work on a number of working papers, to be used as background material for the referendum, also got under way. In a survey of 4,000 people in Montreal, completed by psychology students at the *Université de Montréal*, it was suggested that 32.8 per cent favoured the bill, 38.04 per cent opposed it, and 17.23 per cent were undecided. Few apparently changed their minds after the Premier had announced amendments. Among the young, francophones opposed the bill, while anglophones were more generally satisfied. The more one knew about the legislation, the stronger the opposition.[79] Though the survey was questioned on the grounds of sampling procedures (which incidentally were not revealed), and on the haste with which the survey was drawn up and made, Lévesque cited it to suggest that the Montréal population had reservations and consequently did not support the Premier.[80]

For the purposes of propaganda and in order to organise the referendum, the *FQF* established committees in fourteen regions. Their primary function was to act as organisational bases for the information campaign designed to sensitise the population to the dangers inherent in Bill 63. The position papers mentioned above would be used, and people would be informed about "*Projet de Loi Québec No. 1*" which would be the FQF's proposed language policy.[81] Other techniques proposed included the preparation of a tabloid to outline the *FQF*'s position.[82] The referendum, however, was indefinitely postponed, ostensibly because of the difficulties of setting up such a vast undertaking. Nonetheless, the committees did serve as bases for the propaganda campaign against Bill 63.

Student power

The most dramatic and well-publicised tactics employed against Bill 63 were the student and teacher strikes and stoppages. These began on the 28th of October when the students in the Montréal area started a series of teach-ins. The same day, secondary students from about twenty schools failed to show up for classes and instead headed for a rally in *Parc Laurier*. Shortly afterwards they marched from the park to the *Centre Sportif* at the *Université de Montréal* at which point they were joined by *CEGEP* and university students. Here an estimated 15,000 listened to speakers from the *FQF*, particularly Raymond Lemieux, Pierre Bourgault, Michel Chartrand and Jacques Larue-Langlois.

According to Bourgault, "*Nous sommes réunis ici pour dire à l'Assemblée nationale, qui prétend représenter le peuple, que l'Assemblée nationale, c'est nous*". He compared the situation of the *Québécois* to the American blacks. For Lemieux, the protesters were fighting to end English privileges which had been wrestled from the *Québécois* by force of arms: "*nous allons être en mesure de 'calisser' le bill 63 et de 'calisser' dehors le gouvernement Bertrand*". Andrée Bertrand-Ferretti (of the left wing of the old *Rassemblement pour l'Indépendance Nationale*) denounced the acquired rights of 1760 which permitted the government to betray "*la nation québécoise qui a un droit fondamental à l'autodétermination, car elle répond à tous les critères qui permettent à un peuple de conquérir la liberté et son indépendence*".[83] The speeches and slogans were inextricably tied up with *independantiste* sentiment and the political struggles of contemporary Québec and elsewhere. Indeed, it may have been this *independantiste* flavour to the protest which more than anything else attracted the demonstrators. After the speeches, the students, and professors who had cancelled their classes, marched to the *Union Nationale* Club in Montréal, the Club Renaissance, where after a few more speeches they dispersed. What was remarkable about the marches and demonstrations was the order with which they were conducted (and in which they contrasted strongly with those of December, 1968 and September, 1969).

Similar demonstrations occurred throughout the province. In Québec City, some 3,000 students left the *Université Laval* and *CEGEP Sainte-Foy* to demonstrate in front of the offices of the Ministry of Education. At *CEGEP Sainte-Foy*, where enthusiasm had turned a teach-in into a march, Raymond Laliberté of the CEQ states "*La véritable opposition était en train de naître hors les murs du Parlement, puisque l'officiel a accepté de former une espèce de gouvernement de coalition avec le parti au pouvoir*".[84] A group of demonstrators visited a local television station to protest its policy concerning public affairs, alleging that it was biased in its reporting. In Sherbrooke, Cegepiens and university students held a teach-in with Camille Laurin of the *PQ* as the featured speaker and later marched to the home of Reynauld Fréchette, chairman of the Committee of the Whole. Elsewhere in Trois-Rivières, Rimouski, Saint-Hyacinthe, Granby, Rouyn-Noranda, Sept Iles, Hull and the Lac-Saint-Jean region, students repeated the pattern of teach-ins, speeches, and marches to the homes of local deputies, in the hope that they could persuade the deputies to vote against the bill.

Students walked out of classrooms in support of local *FQF* groups. At Shawinigan, they occupied a radio station and began broadcasting their own programmes.[85] In Montréal effigies of Premier Bertrand, Justice Minister Rémi Paul and Jean Drapeau were burned. At Québec, Michel Chartrand harangued a crowd, stating "*l'incongruité c'est de voir qu'un gouvernement légifère à l'aide de cordons de police, et cela pour favoriser le français au Québec*".[86] At Trois-Rivières Yvon Groulx of the *SSJB* spoke. In Chicoutimi, home of Jean-Noël

Tremblay, a demonstrator shouted "Bertrand to the stake, Jean-Noël to the ashcan".[87] Each demonstration was widely reported in the press and brought more pledges of support. Enthusiasm among student and teaching ranks (including those in the private schools) multiplied. The organisers of the *FQF* were ecstatic.

The culmination of the week-long disturbances was a giant rally in front of the legislature on the 31st of October. Depending on one's source, 20 — 35,000 people were estimated to have attended. Leaders of the *FQF* gave their expected harangues. Chartrand said Bill 63 symbolised English-dominated capitalism and had to be removed. Angers called for Bertrand's resignation. Jacques Rivet of Laval pointed to the deputies and said "*Allez sièger au Musée du Québec. . . Vous êtes les derniers spécimens anthropologiques de la race des vaincus, en voie d'extinction*".[88] Speeches were punctuated by cries of "*Des élections, des élections*", "*PQ, PQ*", and "*Le Québec aux Québécois*", the latter illustrating the close relationship between unilingualism and independence. An air of celebration was lent by the presence of several artists such as Pauline Julien, Louise Forestier, Gaston Miron and Raymond Lévesque. The overall mood was characterized by defiance and the certainty that history was on their side. Again the demonstration was remarkable for its order; no altercations with security policy occurred until well after most of the demonstrators had dispersed.

Not unexpectedly, critics launched attacks on teachers and professional agitators who had allegedly manipulated the young into demonstrating. The Premier claimed that the teachers did not carry out their responsibilities to prepare "*véritable citoyens conscients de leur responsabilité*". Jean Lesage had similarly tough words.[89] Editorials were also condemning. Renaude Lapointe in *La Presse* suggested the rallies were "*L'école du fanaticisme*" directed by such doctors in revolutionary science as Raymond Lemieux, Michel Chartrand, Pierre Bourgault and Jacques Larue-Langlois. She argued that if the teachers were to put as much energy into teaching as they did into preaching absenteeism, narrowmindedness, separation and maoism "*notre langue respirerait beaucoup mieux et leur diplômés sauraient au moins comment faire accorder correctement les participes passés*". Cyrille Felteau commented that the claim that the government had betrayed the people was too gross for any truth to reside in it. According to Marcel Gingras of *Le Droit*, using "babes in arms" was criminal. The respected editor of *Le Devoir*, Claude Ryan, put it best:

> . . .il était attristant plus que réjouissant d'observer le spectacle de certaines ephrebres de 12 à 16 ans, gesticulant et criant à la suite d'animateurs beaucoup plus expérimentés qu'eux autour d'une cause et de slogans dont la plupart d'entre eux ne comprennent visiblement pas l'abc. Cette utilisation des adolescents pour des spectacles politiques est un chapitre honteux de l'histoire présente du Québec. . .Elle est une carricature de la démocratie. Elle fait honte aux éducateurs qui en sont, dans trop de cas, les complices. . .[90]

The demonstration of the 31th October was the climax of the movement. The disturbances, however, had illustrated the extent to which the young in

Québec had been politicised, a fact which had serious implications for the political life of the Province. A clear link had been forged between French unilingualism and economic liberation. It was now a logical step for some to believe that a declaration establishing French as the only language of instruction in the schools would mean a French-only province, and that immigrants would attend French schools under coercion and only if English lost its primacy in the economy. In short, French unilingualism in schools was symbolic of economic and political and cultural liberation.

Conclusion

In the end, extra-parliamentary action and the filibuster failed to dissaude *Union Nationale* and Liberal deputies from passing Bill 63. A number of important conclusions can be drawn from the attempt, however. First, it demonstrated the extent to which well-organised groups were able to exercise their strength against the government. And, in view of a numerically weak opposition in the legislature, this was extremely significant. Second, both the briefs to the Education Committee on Bill 85 and the demonstrations over Bill 63, underscored the fact that significant numbers of *Québécois* were both articulate and organised in their opposition to the principle of official bilingualism and the parental right to choose the language of education. Questions would, of course, be raised as to whether these positions were shared by the majority of the population. Peter Regenstrief's poll in April 1969, for example, suggested that only thirty per cent of francophones favoured a French-only policy and fewer still considered it to be a practical alternative.[91] Nevertheless, the reality of the situation was now abundantly clear. An organised and active opposition to official bilingualism existed and it was determined to make Québec a unilingual and thoroughly French province.[92]

Although Bill 63 had become law, the controversial issue of language rights and the broader problem of the relationship between the major cultural groups in Québec remained unresolved. Francophone opposition to the bill suggested that, even in the short run, the legislation had failed. Moreover, by introducing legislation at this time, the *Union Nationale* had seriously undercut the work of the Gendron Commission. For many *Québécois* its role in the shaping of an overall language policy was therefore suspect before it had even submitted its report and recommendations. Important groups continued to proclaim French unilingualism and work for the repeal of Bill 63. Any perceived discrimination against French Canadians would be seized upon and utilized to these ends. In addition, educational statistics would be regularly employed to demonstrate that the bill had accelerated the trend toward the anglicisation of immigrants and francophones alike. It was to these groups and to these concerns that the government would in future have to respond. As later events all too clearly demonstrated, Québec's search for a coherent and acceptable language policy was far from complete.

NOTES

[1] For a discussion of the rôle of pressure groups in the conflict see John Edward Parisella, Pressure Group Politics: A Case Study of the St. Léonard Crisis, unpublished M.A. thesis, McGill University, 1972.

[2] *Le Devoir*, November 23, 1968; *The Montreal Star*, November 23, 1968.

[3] *La Presse*, November 29, 1968; *The Globe and Mail*, December 4, 1968; *Le Devoir*, November 27, 1968.

[4] *Le Devoir*, November 26, 1968; *Le Devoir*, November 28, 1968.

[5] *La Presse*, November 29, 1968; *The Montreal Star*, November 29, 1968.

[6] *Le Soleil*, *L'Action*, December 5, 1968.

[7] As a result, the government conducted an enquiry into the demonstration and the rôle of the teachers, an enquiry that tended to exonerate the teachers. *Journal des Débats*, December 5, 1968, pp. 4505-7; December 6, 1968, p. 4568; *The Chronicle Telegraph*, *The Montreal Star*, December 6, 1968; *Le Devoir*, December 6, 1968.

[8] René Lévesque denounced the bill as *un chef d'oeuvre d'illusionisme* and in its stead proposed a bill in which French would become the principle language of work and economic life, in which immigrants would be required to send their children to French schools, and by which English schools would be maintained according to demographic pressures determined by a five-year census, *Montréal-Matin*, *L'Action*, *Le Devoir*, December 11, 1968; *The Montreal Star*, December 11, 1968.

[9] *Montréal-Matin*, *Le Devoir*, December 12, 1968, *La Presse*, January 15, 1969.

[10] Richard Arès, "Autour du Bill 85: langues parlées par les Néo-Québécois à Montréal", *Relations*, vol. 337, April 1969, pp. 102-5.

[11] *Ibid.*, p. 105.

[12] Jacques Poisson, "Pour Un Québec Français", *Maintenant*, no. 84, March 1969, pp. 66-71.

[13] *Ibid.*, p. 71.

[14] *Montréal-Matin*, December 10, 1968.

[15] *Le Devoir*, *Montréal-Matin*, December 11, 1968.

[16] *Le Soleil*, December 12, 1968.

[17] *Le Devoir*, *Montréal-Matin*, December 12, 1968.

[18] These principles included parental rights in education, free choice over language of instruction and a dual-language school system

[19] *Journal des Débats*, January 23, 1969, p. 184. This view was echoed by Raymond Lemieux and La Ligue de l'Action Nationale *Journal des Débats*, February 4, 1969, pp. 460, 447.

[20] *Journal des Débats*, January 15, 1969, p. 97.

[21] *Journal des Débats*, February 20, 1969, p. 699.

[22]The term *Néo-Québécois*, variously meaning immigrants or ethnic groups (regardless of length of stay in the province), has many of the nuances of the term "New Canadians" used by the dominant Anglo-Americans of the Canadian Prairies during the first decades of the twentieth century.

[23]*Journal des Débats*, February 4, 1969, p. 429.

[24]CEQ, *Mémoire sur le Bill 85*, p. 2; *Journal des Débats*, February 20, 1969, p. 699; February 4, 1969, p. 451.

[25]*Journal des Débats*, January 14, 1969, p. 29; February 20, 1969, p. 680.

[26]*Journal des Débats*, February 4, 1969, p. 449.

[27]*Journal des Débats*, February 20, 1969, p. 708.

[28]*Journal des Débats*, February 4, 1969, p. 460.

[29]*Journal des Débats*, February 20, 1969, p. 704; February 4, 1969, p. 432.; February 4, 1969, p. 427.

[30]*Journal des Débats*, February 4, 1969, p. 450. This argument neglected the fact that offices could only be opened with the permission of the host country.

[31]*Journal des Débats*, February 20, 1969, p. 701.

[32]*Journal des Débats*, February, 4, 1969, p. 447.

[33]*Journal des Débats*, February 20, 1969, p. 708.

[34]*Journal des Débats*, February 20, 1969, p. 698; January 15, 1969, p. 64.

[35]*Journal des Débats*, January 14, 1969, p. 26; February 20, 1969, p. 652; February 29, 1969, p. 653.

[36]*Journal des Débats*, February 4, 1969, pp. 438-9.

[37]*Journal des Débats*, February 20, 1969, pp. 709, 710, 699.

[38]*Journal des Débats*, February 20, 1969, p. 656.

[39]*Journal des Débats*, February 20, 1969, p. 707. Since the establishment of the *Conseil de l'Instruction Publique* in the 1850's, representatives of the minority groups had comprised one third of its membership, and thus the government's proposal was not without precedent.

[40]*Journal des Débats*, February 4, 1969, p. 477. It may be that the *Fédération* feared a coalition of anglophone members with "conservative" francophones would result in regulations favouring English to the detriment of the French. Perhaps too, they thought it would be easier to influence a minister than a committee.

[41]*La Presse, Le Devoir*, March 7, 1969.

[42]*Le Devoir*, March 8, 1969. Cardinal's view was a strange one since the *Conseil* had been established for the purpose of advising the government.

[43]*The Montreal Star*, March 17, 1969, *Le Devoir*, March 20, 1969. Jean-Noël Tremblay indicated that the fate of francophone minorities elsewhere in Canada would not be the fate of the anglophone minority.

[44]*Le Devoir, La Presse*, March 4, 1969.

[45]*Le Nouvelliste*, March 20, 1969; *Montréal-Matin*, March 21, 1969.

[46]Jérôme Proulx, *Le Panier des Crabes*, Montréal, Parti-Pris, 1972, pp. 122-3. Jean Lesage and Emilien Lafrance had commented on this split as early as

December 16, *Journal des Débats*, pp. 4946-8. *The Gazette*, December 16, 1968; *The Montreal Star*, January 30, 1969.

[47] For further information on this aspect of the language debate see Pierre Fournier, A Political Analysis of School Reorganization in Montreal, unpublished M.A., McGill University, 1971 and Robert James MacDonald, Une Question de Survivance/A Question of Survival: The Struggle for Language Rights in Education in Contemporary Quebec, unpublished Ph. D. Calgary, 1975.

[48] *La Presse*, September 29, 1969, *The Gazette*, September 29, 1969.

[49] *La Presse, October 15, 1969*, Jérôme Proulx, *Le Panier des Crabes*, pp. 157-9.

[50] *Journal des Débats*, October 21, 1969, p. 3205.

[51] *Journal des Débats*, October 23, 1969, p. 3293.

[52] *Journal des Débats*, October 23, 1969, p. 3294.

[53] *Montréal-Matin, L'Action, La Presse, Le Devoir*, October 24, 1969.

[54] *The Gazette, The Montreal Star, La Presse, Le Devoir*, October 24, 1969.

[55] The Premier had indicated in March that he would submit the issue of Saint-Léonard to the Gendron Commission.

[56] *La Presse, Montréal-Matin*, October 24, 1969, *Le Devoir, La Presse*, October 25, 1969.

[57] Richard Arès, "Le Bill 63; entreprise prématurée et hasardeuse", *Relations*, no. 344, December 1969, p. 323. He suggested that by the precipitous introduction of Bill 63, the government had acted ineptly. "L'Avenir du Français au Québec", *Maintenant*, no. 91, December 1969, p. 293.

[58] *Le Soleil, La Tribune, L'Action*, October 24, 1969.

[59] *The Gazette*, October 25, 1969.

[60] See also Robert J. MacDonald, "Education, Language Rights and Cultural Survival in Quebec, A Review Essay", *The Journal of Educational Thought*, vol. 9, no. 1, April 1975, pp. 49-64.

[61] *The Gazette, The Montreal Star, Le Devoir, La Presse*, October 24, 1969.

[62] *The Montreal Star*, October 25, October 27, 1969.

[63] *The Gazette, The Montreal Star*, October 25, 1969.

[64] The term was used by the group itself to indicate that they were the real opposition brought together by the circumstances of Bill 63 and serving only as a temporary grouping.

[65] *Journal des Débats*, October 30, 1969, pp. 3441, 3456-7; November 4, 1969, pp. 3539, 3541.

[66] *Journal des Débats*, November 4, 1969, p. 3539.

[67] *Journal des Débats*, November 4, 1969, pp. 3527, 3541.

[68] *Journal des Débats*, November 20, 1969.

[69] *Le Devoir*, October 18, 1969.

[70] *Le Devoir, La Presse*, October 27, 1969, *The Montreal Star*, October 27, 1969. It is worth nothing that though Bill 63 only dealt with the schools, and the Bertrand press conference promised other measures, the French unilingualists considered the schools to be the key to cultural survival. Moreover, they clearly

believed the promotion of the French language was only possible if English were excluded. Or, to put it another way, equality for English meant the eventual domination of French by English.

[71] *Le Devoir, La Presse, The Montreal Star*, October 27, 1969.

[72] *La Presse*, October 27, 1969, *Le Devoir*, October 28, 1969.

[73] *Le Soleil*, October 27, 1969, *L'Action*, October 28, 1969.

[74] *CEGEPs* or *Collèges d'Enseignement Général et Professionnel* are post-secondary institutions created in 1967-8. They embody both a two-year pre-university and a two or three year technical or vocational education, and are Québec's unique answer to the need to provide better educated people in an industrial society.

[75] *Le Devoir*, October 28, 29, 30, November 1, 4, 1969; *La Presse*, October 28, 30, November 4, 1969; *Montréal-Matin*, October 28, 30, November 4, 1969; *Le Soleil*, October 27, 28, 30, November 4, 1969; *The Montreal Star*, October 28, 31, November 4, 1969.

[76] *Journal des Débats*, November 6, 1969, p. 3648.

[77] *La Presse*, October 30, 1969.

[78] *Le Devoir*, November 4, 1969.

[79] *Le Devoir*, November 7, 1969.

[80] *Journal des Débats*, November 12, 1969, p. 3765.

[81] *Le Devoir*, November 8, 10, 1969.

[82] *Le Devoir*, November 20, 1969, *Le Soleil*, November 14, 1969.

[83] *Le Devoir, La Presse, Montréal-Matin*, Octobre 28, 29, 1969.

[84] *Le Soleil*, October 29, 1969.

[85] *Montréal-Matin*, October 30, 1969, *The Montreal Star*, October 30, 1969.

[86] *Le Soleil, La Presse*, October 30, 1969.

[87] *Le Soleil*, October 30, 1969.

[88] *L'Action, La Presse, Le Soleil*, November 1, 1969.

[89] *Journal des Débats*, October 29, 1969, pp. 3409-10.

[90] *La Presse*, October 29, 31, 1969, *Le Droit*, October 31, 1969, *Le Devoir*, October 29, 1969.

[91] *The Montreal Star*, April 29, 1969.

[92] This included opposition to the Duhamel report on bilingual districts for federal services. The claim was made that Bill 22 applied to federal responsibilities such as the Canadian National Railway, and illustrated the confusion between provincial and federal powers, responsibilities and policies.

BILL 22 AND THE NON-FRANCOPHONE POPULATION IN QUEBEC: A CASE STUDY OF MINORITY GROUP ATTITUDES ON LANGUAGE LEGISLATION*

Michael B. Stein

Of all the problems exacerbating conflict between majority and minority populations in multicultural societies, that of language is likely to arouse the greatest passions. This is almost self-evident, since language is often the central factor differentiating the various cultural groups, and is, of course, a crucial component of daily life. It is not surprising, therefore, that language has been a cause of much political turmoil and unrest in Belgium, Switzerland, Yugoslavia, Czechoslovakia, India and Pakistan. Quebec is no exception in this respect. Language has always been a key component of the collective consciousness of the Québécois, a people of fewer than five million Francophones surrounded by a sea of over 225 million Anglophone North Americans.

Since the Quiet Revolution of the early 1960's, which introduced numerous political, economic, and cultural reforms resulting in the modernization of Quebec society, the Québécois have become increasingly self-conscious of their identity as a nation. They have reinforced this identity in numerous ways, including efforts at increasing the autonomy of the provincial government in federal-provincial relations, establishing closer relations with Francophone minorities outside Quebec and with Francophone countries in Europe, Africa and Asia, and fostering Quebec literature, poetry, visual arts, humanities and social sciences. However, some of the reforms, including a more broadly based and secular educational system, more rapid urbanization and industrialization, and the liberation of Quebec thought and action from traditional clerically determined mores have threatened to destroy the most important linch-pin of Québécois

*Published in French in slightly revised form in *Choix, Le Nationalisme Québécois à la croisée des chemins* (Centre québécois de relations internationales, Université Laval, 1975), pp. 127-159.

survival and existence, the vitality of its French language.

The most serious threat to the survival of the French language in Quebec stems from a situation largely beyond the control of governmental authorities in a liberal democratic state: the pervasiveness of English in the electronic and print media of North America. There is also the more subtle incursion of American private enterprise, which determines the language of work. Thirdly, a more recent and more direct by-product of the Quiet Revolution is the sudden sharp decline in the birthrate of the Québécois. From the time of the conquest in 1763 until recent decades, Quebec had had the highest birthrate of all regions or provinces of Canada; this demographic pattern was associated with the strong attachment by the Québécois to the Roman Catholic Church and to the notion of survival, and was wryly referred to as "la revanche des berceaux."

Since 1961 Quebec's birthrate has dropped to the lowest of any province in Canada; moreover, the Francophone population of Quebec has a lower birthrate than the Anglophone population.[1] At the same time, the immigrant population which might be expected to fill the gap has overwhelmingly assimilated to the Anglophone sector.[2] The census figures show a slight drop in French language usage in the province (from 81.0% to 80.0%) between 1961 and 1971, and a slight increase in English language usage (from 14.2% to 14.7%).[3] The estimated transfers from French to English (19,600) were considerably higher than the estimated transfers from English to French (13,100). Although both groups gained transfers from those who used a language other than French or English in their home, the English acquired five times as many transfers from this third group (51,457) as the French (10,439).[4]

This slight advantage for the Anglophone sector is aggravated by the pattern of mobility of Francophones and the heavy concentration of Anglophones and non-Francophone immigrants in the most dynamic center of Quebec, the metropolitan region of Montreal. Thus, although the proportion of those of French ethnic origin in Quebec as a whole is 79.0% (in comparison to 10.7% of British origin and 10.4% of "other" origin), in metropolitan Montreal this proportion drops to 64.3%, as opposed to 16.0% of British origin and 19.7% of "other" ethnic origin. Nevertheless, the proportion of those of French origin residing in Montreal has increased from 31.9% to 37.0% in the last decade, reflecting patterns of mobility from rural to urban life. The most highly urbanized group is the non-French, non-English group (néo-Québécois), including Italians, Jews, Asiatics, Poles and Ukrainians. With the exception of the Italians, all of these nationality groups acquire a much greater knowledge of English than of French. And yet, in population terms, they comprise the most rapidly growing sector in the metropolitan region.[5] Moreover, according to recent projections of Statistics Canada, the most optimistic projections for Quebec envisage a decline of the Quebec population between 1971 and 2001 from 27.9% to 24.9% of the Canadian population. In consequence, the influence of the province on federal government policy will probably be correspondingly weakened.[5a]

These trends have naturally aroused widespread concern among Francophone leaders in Quebec. In the late 1960's and early 1970's the language question became the focal point of much political activity by organized and ad hoc groups and by governmental authorities. The culmination of this activity was the passage in July of 1974 of the Official Language Act, generally known as Bill 22. It declared French to be the official language of Quebec and established a language board designed to promote French usage in public administration, public utilities and professional bodies, labour, business, and education.

My concern in this essay is with the political implications of this language question in Quebec. In particular I shall focus on the reactions of the Anglophone and non-Francophone immigrant populations in order to gain some preliminary insight into minority group attitudes and behaviour in such situations.[6] To facilitate this task, I shall concentrate on the period between the tabling and the final passage of Bill 22, that is, May 22 to July 31, 1974. The discussion will be divided into three sections: the historical background to the language question in Quebec; the events surrounding Bill 22 and Anglophone and non-Francophone immigrant reaction to it; and, my interpretation and explanation of Anglophone and non-Francophone immigrant attitudes and behaviour.

The historical background to the language question in Quebec

Bill 22 is the most recent of a long series of efforts by both federal and provincial authorities to regulate language differences in the Province of Quebec. Although the British North America Act of 1867, Canada's constitution, did not treat the subject of general public jurisdiction over language, it provided in section 133 for explicit protection of the minority language of Quebec, English, in both houses of the legislature and in the courts of Quebec. Moreover, the federal government was charged under section 93 with the responsibility of protecting the right to separate denominational schools of the Protestant dissentient minority in Quebec. There was no specific guarantee of the language rights of the Anglophone minority in education; the practice of allowing the Protestants to educate their children in English, which had been followed in Quebec since the time of the British conquest of 1763, was accepted as a matter of custom and convenience.

The Quiet Revolution brought with it a heightening of French-Canadian nationalism and led to demands for a larger role for Francophones in federal governmental institutions. The Royal Commission on Bilingualism and Biculturalism was established by the federal Liberal Government in 1963 with a mandate "to inquire into and report upon the existing state of bilingualism and biculturalism in Canada and to recommend what steps should be taken to develop the Canadian Confederation on the basis of an equal partnership between the two founding races, taking into account the contribution made by the other ethnic groups to the cultural enrichment of Canada and the measures that should be taken to safeguard that contribution. . . ."[7] The Commission did not limit its recommendations to the federal political level when it issued the first volume of its Report four years later. It formulated the concept of the "bilingual district", which would provide for government services, educational institutions and courts in both official languages of Canada in areas in which the population of the minority language exceeded 10%. It also recommended that an agreement be worked out between federal and provincial governments under which the entire provinces of Quebec, Ontario and New Brunswick, and the Ottawa-Hull region (designated as a federal capital district) would be declared "bilingual districts."

The recommendations concerning "bilingual districts" were severely criticized in Quebec by many government officials and leading spokesmen of major Francophone groups. They flatly rejected the concept of official bilingualism for Quebec, the "homeland of the French-Canadians." Consequently, no serious effort was made by the federal government to negotiate arrangements with the provinces providing for "bilingual districts."[8] The Commission did manage, however, to win partial acceptance of its proposals in New Brunswick and, to a lesser extent, in Ontario.[9] Official bilingualism also became the accepted policy of the federal government, and was enshrined in the Official Languages Act passed by the Trudeau administration in 1968. The Anglophone population of Quebec warmly endorsed this stand, and many sought to have the same principles implemented at the provincial level.

The role played by the Quebec government in the sphere of language, was, as we have seen, largely a reactive one until this time (1968). However, a resolution passed by a local Catholic school board in the expanding eastern Montreal municipality of St. Léonard in November of 1967 sparked the language conflict known as the St. Léonard Schools Crisis. The reverberations of the conflict were finally to prod the provincial authorities into legislative action.

The resolution in question proposed that the bilingual classes which had been in operation in the district since September, 1963 for grades 1 to 3 be eliminated and replaced by a unilingual French programme. It was argued that the bilingual classes, which were originally intended to help integrate the children of the large immigrant population of St. Léonard into the Francophone community, were actually encouraging their assimilation into the Anglophone sector.[10] The resolution also called for the teaching of English as a second language in the new programme beginning in Grade One.[11]

The successful passage of the resolution provoked an immediate and strong response from the local Italian population, which organized itself into the Association of Parents of St. Léonard in order to contest the approaching school board elections. Their response was met in turn by a Francophone decision to organize their own association, called *Le Mouvement pour l'Intégration Scolaire* (M.I.S.). The two groups fought an unusually heated campaign, which ended in complete victory for the better organized, more cohesive and more effectively led Francophone group.

Following the school board election in June, 1968 the non-Francophone association reorganized itself, chose an Anglo-Catholic, Robert Beale, as its leader, and changed its tactics to appeal beyond the local community. It enlisted the support of important notables in the Montreal Anglophone community, particularly in education and business, obtained widespread backing in the English press, radio and television, won pledges of assistance from some influential provincial legislators, and appealed directly to the provincial cabinet for its intervention.[12] The Association also organized a demonstration on Parliament Hill in Ottawa in protest against the alleged violation of Anglophone human rights.[13]

In the fall of 1968, the situation in St. Léonard became increasingly tense. Largely in response to it, Prime Minister Bertrand tabled Bill 85 on December 9, 1968. The bill followed the recommendations of the Pagé Commission, which had advocated the establishment of separate linguistic school boards and the adoption of the principle of parental choice of the language of education. At the same time, the Quebec Prime Minister announced the establishment of the Gendron Commission*, which was charged with recommending ways to promote the French language in Quebec.

Bill 85 immediately triggered strong opposition from wide segments of the Francophone community, including all the major French-language newspapers, radio and television stations, many educational leaders and most of the principal nationalist organizations. Even the Anglophone community, led by the Association, condemned the bill as too ambiguous on the question of language rights. The M.I.S. leaders, who had reconstituted themselves into a province-wide movement including many nationalist and separatist groups, organized protests, mass demonstrations and a march on the National Assembly of Quebec. Their efforts proved successful, and the bill was sent to the Education Committee before the debate on principle. Here, after two months of briefs and strong criticism of the bill, the government decided to allow it to die.

But the language question did not remain dormant for long. Following the national leadership convention in June, 1969, a compromise was struck between moderate and nationalist wings of the governing party, leading to the introduction of Bills 63 and 62 in October and November that year.[14] Bill 63 explicitly guaranteed the right of choice of parents of the language of instruction of their children, and at the same time contained a number of measures designed to promote the teaching of the French language in Quebec. Bill 62 reverted to a recommendation of the Parent Commission and envisaged the creation of unified school boards for the island of Montreal.

*So-called after Jean-Denis Gendron, Chairman, Commission of Inquiry on the Position of the French Language and on Language Rights in Quebec.

The opposition to Bill 63 from nationalist elements in the Francophone community was even stronger and more sustained than in the case of Bill 85; there were pressure tactics, protests and demonstrations from a large variety of groups. Prime Minister Bertrand, however, was determined to push the bill through and agreed to a number of amendments advanced by the opposition Liberals, guaranteeing the priority of the French language. Moreover, the government seemed to succumb to direct pressure from some Anglophone businessmen who argued that the bill's passage would give a considerable boost to the province's economic position.[15]

Opposition to Bill 62, on the other hand, came largely from the Anglophones. They feared that the establishment of unified regional school boards would effectively subvert the guarantees provided in Bill 63. They also protested against the allegedly undemocratic nature of the appointment procedures for the new regional boards, which centralized control in the Ministry of Education. The opposition was led by the Protestant School Board of Greater Montreal and the Montreal English-language dailies. The bill did not proceed further than the Education Committee of the National Assembly before a general provincial election was called for April, 1970. With the defeat of the *Union Nationale*, the bill lapsed.

The Liberal Government of Robert Bourassa, which assumed power in 1970, proceeded slowly on the language question, in order to avoid the mistakes of its predecessor. It promised to consider changes in Bill 63 after receiving the recommendations of the Gendron Commission. It also agreed to review the problem of school reorganization in Montreal. In June, 1971 it introduced Bill 28, which maintained the principle of unified non-denominational school boards envisaged by Bill 62, but democratized the administrative structure to allow for parallel linguistic administrators at the school board level. Like Bill 62, it met with determined opposition by elite groups in the Anglophone community, and the government succumbed to their pressure for withdrawal. Guy St. Pierre, the Education Minister who had sponsored the bill, was replaced in the portfolio by Dr. François Cloutier. He reverted to the status quo and introduced administrative reforms within the existing confessional structure.[16]

By 1972 pressure had begun to mount on the Gendron Commission to present its long-awaited report. The Commission, as previously indicated, was established at the end of 1968 "to inquire into the position of the French language in Quebec, and measures to be taken to ensure its full expansion, and to inquire into the linguistic rights of Quebec citizens."[17] It was established as a five-man commission headed by Jean-Denis Gendron, vice-dean of Laval University's *Faculté des Lettres*; two of its members, Edward McWhinney of McGill University and Nicholas Mateesco-Matte of the University of Montreal were chosen in part to represent Anglophone and non-Francophone immigrant viewpoints. The Commission placed priority on four areas of investigation: (1) linguistic rights, (2) language of work, (3) language in the schools, and (4) immigrant and ethnic groups.

The Commission was initially given a mandate of one year and a budget of $1 million to conduct its investigation; however, in the fall of 1969, it decided to hold public hearings in which briefs would be received from organizations and private individuals. Over the next 8 months 174 organizations presented briefs.[18] Extensive field research into problem areas was also conducted. As a result, although the first volume of its report was originally projected for the summer of 1970, it was not until December 31, 1972, four years later and after expenditures of over $2.3 million, that the entire report of three books was deposited with the government.[19] Books 1 and 2 on the language of communications of work and consumption and linguistic rights contained 92 recommendations in all, but highlighted the following: (1) French should be the official language of the province, but English and French should be recognized as national languages, (2) only persuasive measures should be applied to increase the use of French in the work world, although coercive measures might be held in reserve for later application if necessary, (3) in education, there should be a delay of 3-5 years before Bill 63 would be considered for repeal, in order to allow it to be evaluated against longer-term experience. Priority was given to the work world over education, since this was the area in which the danger of anglicization was thought to be greatest. Book 3, on immigrant and ethnic groups, also recommended the use of persuasion rather than force to integrate immigrants into the Francophone sector through such measures as nurseries in French for immigrant children of pre-school age, special language courses for mothers, and summer camps in French for immigrant children of school age. The Commission suggested that a state board be established to help implement these measures and that a commissioner of languages be appointed to perform the function of watchdog over infractions of linguistic rights.

The reaction of the Anglophone and non-Francophone immigrant community to the Report was generally positive. The press and most leading spokesmen expressed relief that the Commission had recommended persuasive rather than coercive measures in the spheres of work and integration of immigrants and had advocated temporary retention of Bill 63. They also endorsed positive inducements to promote increasing use of French in the work world and in education. The Francophone community was far less pleased. Nationalist groups and advocates of unilingualism condemned the Report as a "Trojan horse" for anglicization of the province, a "farce", or a "camouflage" of the status quo".[20] More moderate analysts criticized it for being excessively timid, too legalistic in approach, not sufficiently tied to data presented in research reports or to the real world of experience, lacking in a global perspective, uneven in quality and reflecting too obviously the differing perspectives of its various authors.[21] The initial reaction of the provincial government appeared, however, to be more favourable. Education Minister Cloutier announced that the recommendations of the Commission would be studied carefully by his ministry, but that no legislation based on them would be introduced until the end of 1979, and not before the next provincial election.

The Bourassa government did not remain completely idle in the language field in the interim period. In the area of work it urged Anglophone businesses to implement the norms laid down by its French Language Bureau (*Office de la Langue Française*), an agency established by the *Union Nationale* government under Daniel Johnson to promote francization of private corporations with dealings in the province. In the field of immigration it entered into negotiations with the federal government to acquire greater control over the flow of French-speaking immigrants to the province. In the election of October, 1973, it won an overwhelming mandate by gaining 102 of the province's 110 seats in the National Assembly. All segments of the population, both Francophone and Anglophone, gave it a plurality.[22] It hesitated, nevertheless, to introduce its long-promised legislation, and waited for an opportune moment. It feared another divisive reaction similar to that which plagued the *Union Nationale* government over Bills 85 and 63.

Bill 22 and the Anglophone and non-Francophone immigrant response

The opportune moment arrived in the late spring of 1974, after classes had been recessed in universities and CEGEPs, and preparations were being made for summer vacation. On May 22, 1974 Bill No. 22, entitled the Official Language Act, was tabled and given first reading in the National Assembly of Quebec. The preamble of the bill outlined the purposes and principles of the legislation. It declared that "the French language is a national heritage which the body politic is in duty bound to preserve (so that) it is incumbent upon the government of the province of Quebec to employ every means in its power to ensure the preeminence of that language and to promote its vigour and quality."[23] Toward this end, it proclaimed French to be the official language of the province of Quebec (section I) and prescribed ways to promote its use in the public administration (sections 6 to 17), the public utilities and the professions (sections 18 to 23), labour (sections 24 to 35), business (sections 36 to 47), and education (sections 48 to 52). It established a nine member French Language Board (*Régie de la langue française*), to oversee the implementation of these provisions. It also provided for the repeal of Bill 63.

Among the major specific features of the bill were 1) the requirement that French would be the official language of the public service and no one would be admitted to an administrative office in this service unless his knowledge of that language was appropriate to the employment sought; 2) all contracts with the government and para-governmental bodies would have to be written in French if contracted totally in Quebec, and in French and another language if contracted elsewhere; 3) governmental contracts would be awarded under a preferential system to companies favoring the use of French; 4) the government would provide grants and teaching assistance to businesses wishing to comply with its guidelines on the use of French; 5) tests would be administered by school boards to determine whether a child is to be placed in the English-language or French-language schools.[24]

The government diverged from the recommendations of the Gendron Commission in a number of important ways. In the first place, it dropped the idea of declaring English and French to be national languages, presumably because the terminology was confusing. Secondly, it went beyond mere persuasion, as advocated in the Gendron Report. Coercive, as well as monetary incentive measures, were to be applied to businesses to ensure their compliance with the government guidelines, including fines, revocation of licenses and permits, and refusal of government contracts. Thirdly, it acted contrary to the Commission's recommendation that Bill 63 be tested for a further period of three to five years, and that only persuasive measures be applied in efforts to integrate immigrants. Bill 22 removed the absolute right of choice of parents of the language of instruction of their children, and substituted for it a conditional right, one qualified by compulsory language tests. In short, the government had decided to adopt a tougher stance toward the Anglophone and immigrant communities on the francization issue.

The bill was also vague in a number of areas, reflecting the government's preference for leaving precise details of definition and application to executive and administrative discretion. This was particularly the case in the sphere of business, where the cabinet would have the power to provide by regulation for the issuance of certificates to business firms attesting to their proper adoption and application of a francization programme.[25] It also applied to the educational sector, in which provision of English schools was made dependent on local school boards and the discretionary power of the Minister of Education. Moreover, the Minister was permitted to set tests in accordance with cabinet regulations to ascertain whether pupils have sufficient knowledge of the language of instruction in order to qualify for admission.[26]

The reaction to Bill 22 from the Anglophone and non-Francophone immigrant populations was immediate and strongly adverse. Three Anglophone Liberals, John Ciaccia (Mount Royal), Kenneth Fraser (Huntingdon), and George Springate (Ste. Anne) abstained on First Reading. Two others, Harry Blank (St. Louis) and Glendon Brown (Brome-Missisquoi) declared that they would vote against it in later readings if it was not changed substantially. Some Francophone MNAs with large Anglophone populations in their ridings, such as Art Séguin (Pointe-Claire), Lucien Caron (Verdun) and Guy Fortier (Gaspé) threatened to do likewise. One member, Fraser, went so far as to compare the bill to the early education acts of the Nazis against the Jews.[27] The renegade members of caucus, twelve in all, made plans to meet the following week to discuss their opposition to the bill. The three Anglophone cabinet members, Kevin Drummond (Westmount), Victor Goldbloom (D'Arcy McGee) and William Tetley (Notre Dame de Grâce) made only half-hearted attempts to defend the measure.[28]

The reaction outside the Quebec legislature was equally vocal. Both major English-language dailies, *The Gazette* and *The Montreal Star*, strongly condemned the bill for being ambiguous, poorly drafted, vague and discriminatory. *The*

Gazette ran a series of editorials dealing with each major section of the bill. It complained that English would become the language of exception in Quebec and more exceptional for some than for others; that it would lose its status as a language of justice under the Constitution; that the language of management would become the language of officials involving "a massive dose of regulating, officiating, investigating, and discriminating under cabinet or ministerial direction"; that the bill would discriminate against Anglophone Catholics by failing to guarantee their right to English education; and that it would undermine the cause of bilingualism and biculturalism on the national level, as well as the advance of French in other provinces.[29] The *Star* laid particular stress on the vagueness of the provisions and the administrative abuse which it invited.[30]

The first Anglophone groups to attack the bill were in the field of education. The Montreal Protestant School Board Chairman Rev. John Simms and the President of the Protestant Teachers Association Donald Peacock both strongly condemned the legislation. Similarly spokesmen for the Quebec Association of Protestant School Boards and the Provincial Association of Protestant Teachers expressed their fear that the bill would encourage the formation of "language ghettos". Anglophone Catholic representatives such as the President of the Federation of English-speaking Catholic Teachers likewise deplored the lack of English-language guarantees, but Anglophone Catholics were outvoted by Francophones on the Montreal Catholic School Commission, which called for tougher measures for integrating immigrants into the French educational sector. The Anglophone business groups at first seemed unconcerned by the bill, but later associations such as the Montreal Chamber of Commerce, the Montreal Board of Trade, and the Canadian Federation of Independent Businesses expressed concern on behalf of small and medium-sized firms most likely to be disrupted by the francization measures. Influential spokesmen such as F.R. Scott, the former dean of the McGill University Law School, and Dale Thomson, Vice-Principal in charge of Planning at McGill University, expressed their objections in their unofficial capacities. Scott pointed out that several of the articles of the bill, including that giving pre-eminence to French translations in legal texts and that dealing with education, might be unconstitutional. Thomson expressed his agreement with the fundamental objectives of the legislation, but criticized the ambiguities and "shoddy draftsmanship" of the bill.[31]

Even federal politicians, then contesting an election campaign, were drawn into the controversy. The leaders of all four major parties objected to the arbitrary nature of the delegation provisions and the encroachment on the principle of parental freedom of choice in education. But all preferred to keep the matter out of the federal election campaign. Several of the Quebec candidates, however, disregarded these directives and injected the issue into their campaigns.[32]

Ironically, the opposition in the Francophone community from both nationalist and moderate groups was equally acerbic. This was contrary to past patterns of group response to language and educational legislation. The major attacks on bills 85 and 63 had come from the Francophone community, while the Anglophones had remained relatively quiescent. The reverse was true for bills 62 and 28.

Both opposition parties represented in the National Assembly, the *Parti Québécois* and the *Ralliement Créditiste du Québec*, objected strenously to the bill's halfway measures; they sought much more sweeping francization efforts in all spheres. Most of the leading French-language associations, such as *La Société Saint-Jean-Baptiste*, *La Ligue Des Droits de l'Homme*, the Quebec Bar Association (BQ), the Quebec Federation of Labour (FTQ), the Quebec Teacher's Corporation (CEQ), the Confederation of National Trade Unions (CSN), and the Montreal Catholic School Commission (CECM) demanded more radical steps ranging from compulsory integration of non-Francophone immigrants into the French sector to complete unilingualism in all sectors of society. The major French-language dailies in Montreal and Quebec generally agreed with this line of argument. Thus *Le Devoir*'s influential editor Claude Ryan wrote that although the legislation offered interesting solutions in the sphere of public administration, it was too timid in regulating the language of labour and business, and failed lamentably in the field of education.[33]

Prime Minister Bourassa had initially hoped to win support from the broad center of public opinion in Quebec in both Anglophone and Francophone communities. He therefore defended his measure as a "middle way" between the extremes of the Anglophone "Orangemen" and separatist *Parti Québécois.*[34] He also promised to consider amendments in cabinet, a move designed to assuage both the nationalists and the renegade caucus of backbenchers within his own party. However, it became more and more apparent as the committee hearings progressed that the legislation had fallen between two poles of public opinion representing two conflicting principles. The Anglophones and non-Francophone immigrants were committed for the most part to the principle of bilingualism and to the absolute right of parents to choose the language of instruction of their children. The Francophones were devoted to what they regarded as their collective right to exist as a nation and to making French at least the priority language and therefore the primary vehicle of integration of immigrants.

This divergence in viewpoint was reflected in a province-wide public opinion survey conducted jointly by *The Gazette*, *Le Devoir*, and *Le Soleil*, in conjunction with the Quebec Institute of Public Opinion. With respect to the status of languages, 18.9% of Francophones preferred to see French as the only official language of Quebec and 47.6% supported French as the official language and English as the second language, constituting a total of 66.5% in favour of at least priority status for French. Only 32.3% favoured establishing both French and English as the official languages of the province (i.e. official bilingualism). However, no less than 79.2% of the Anglophones and 65.6% of "Others" (non-francophone immigrants) advocated official bilingualism. Similarly, with respect to the language of instruction, 59.4% of Francophones thought that the law should oblige future immigrants whose mother tongue is English to send their children to a French school and 71.6% of Francophones thought that this should apply in the case of future immigrants whose mother tongue is not English. On the other hand only 15.2% of Anglophones and 25.2% of "Others" supported the compulsory integration of English-speaking immigrants into the French educational sector, and only 25.8% of Anglophones and 34.4% of "Others" supported such integration for non-English-speaking immigrants. On most other issues, however, including whether or not French-speaking parents should retain their right to send their children to English schools, the language of communication within business firms, the promotion of French-Canadians to management positions, the necessity to know the English language in order to succeed in Quebec, and the publication of laws and regulations in both languages, differences of opinion between Francophones, Anglophones and "Others" were not very significant.[35]

A similar divergence in public opinion was reflected in the month-long hearings held in the Standing Committee on Education, Cultural Affairs and Communications of the National Assembly beginning on June 11. A total of 157 briefs had been submitted to the Committee, of which 76 were received orally; and 23 of the 27 Anglophone briefs were heard, of which the vast majority (19) were by educational organizations. They stressed principally the need to provide clear guarantees for the English schools and the absolute right of choice by parents. The business groups emphasized the adverse economic effects of the francization program. There were only slight differences in emphasis by British origin and ethnic groups; the former pressed for guarantees of the educational status quo, whereas the latter stressed freedom of choice and lack of good faith on the part of the government. The Francophone groups, more diverse in nature, dealt more widely with the whole range of provisions of the bill, and most called for much more stringent francization measures and a tougher stance toward immigrants. They were also much better prepared than the Anglophones, who wilted under the gruelling cross-examination of the *Péquiste* constitutional expert and former law professor, J.-Y. Morin. All associations, no matter what their linguistic group affiliation, vociferously attacked the lack of clarity of the bill and its susceptibility to administrative abuses.[36]

On July 12th, the government terminated committee discussion of the bill by using its guillotine and brought the bill to the floor of the Assembly for Second Reading. Before initiating debate, Education Minister Cloutier introduced several important amendments, including: 1) a guarantee for the continuation of English-language schools, but also restriction on their expansion; 2) compulsory francization certificates for firms in order to be eligible for provincial grants and loans, by changing the wording from "may" to "will"; 3) establishment of a language ombudsman and a commission to which parents might appeal the results of language tests.[37] These changes satisfied several of the rebellious Liberal backbenchers. Two of the Francophone ministers, L'Allier and Choquette, expressed reservations about the bill's failure to go far enough in the direction of francization, but agreed to support it as a first step. The final bill was thus a compromise between the nationalist Francophone and the Anglophone critics within the Liberal caucus. In the vote on Second Reading, the count was 80-10 in favour; Ciaccia and Springate broke ranks and voted with the opposition *Péquistes* and *Créditistes.*[38]

Following Second Reading, the bill went to committee, where it was supposed to be subjected to clause-by-clause discussion and amendment. However, the *Parti Québécois* were determined to filibuster and refused to permit debate to proceed beyond article 1. Attacks on the bill by both Francophone nationalists and Anglophones intensified and the debate was interrupted at one stage by a small group of women protesters in chains. The Prime Minister, determined to pass the bill before the end of July, finally invoked closure. On July 30, the bill won final approval in a Third Reading vote of 92-10, and the following day received the lieutenant governor's assent. Once again, Ciaccia and Springate voted with the opposition. The Liberals retaliated by voting to suspend them from the caucus.

Passage of the bill into law did not silence its critics. Just before Third Reading, a group of McGill law professors, led by former dean F.R. Scott, released a long public statement challenging the constitutionality of the legislation. They argued, *inter alia*, that the articles dealing with the pre-eminence of French in legal texts contravened section 133 of the BNA Act, and those dealing with education violated section 93.[39] The federal government announced as well that it had submitted the bill for study by its own constitutional experts, in order to determine its constitutionality and its own future course of action with respect to the legislation. Under Canadian law, the federal government had the right to disallow the bill or to submit a reference to the Supreme Court asking them to rule on its constitutionality. A third possibility, which was to permit the bill to be challenged by private individuals or groups in the lower courts, seemed politically the most pallatable procedure. The provincial government remained unmoved, however, and pointed out that its own legal experts, including Prof. McWhinney, had declared the bill to be constitutional.

Anglophone and non-Francophone immigrant attitudes and behaviour: some explanatory hypotheses

Analysis of the pattern of Anglophone and non-Francophone immigrant response to the evolving language conflict sheds some light on the problems of minority group behaviour. Prior to the Quiet Revolution of the 1960's, the Anglophone community of Quebec had always maintained a privileged status in key sectors such as business and education. The Third Book of the Report of the Royal Commission on Bilingualism and Biculturalism had shown that Anglophones have predominated in industry ownership and top management positions in Quebec, particularly in the technologically advanced and highly productive industries.[40] They had made little effort to provide adequate French instruction for themselves or their children in their schools, or to use the French language along with English as a vehicle of communication in the upper echelons of business. They remained satisfied with the limited guarantees provided them in the courts and legislature of the province by section 133 of the BNA Act, and assumed that the separate English school system had been established as a matter or right rather than custom. They made little effort to participate in the Quebec public service, where French had become virtually the only language of communication, and their involvement in provincial political party and legislative institutions became increasingly halfhearted. On most issues their response was a quiescent and passive one; they relied on direct access to provincial political powerholders by business elites and community leaders. Very little effort was made to organize effective pressure groups which could act both as opinion leaders and community representatives on major public issues.

The neo-nationalism in Quebec of the early 1960's first made the Anglophone community aware that its privileged position was in danger. The Francophone population strove not only to modernize their own society through reforms in their educational, clerical, cultural and public administrative institutions; they sought a larger share of political and economic power. This could only come at the expense of the Anglophone community.

The initial efforts of the Francophone population were concentrated at the federal level. The Royal Commission on Bilingualism and Biculturalism was formed largely at the behest of *Le Devoir* editor André Laurendeau, and the insistence of Quebec Francophone Liberal MPs. Its call for "equal partnership" at both the federal and provincial levels received a most receptive hearing by Anglophone Quebeckers, since it ensured a retention of their privileges and so-called "acquired rights" in the province. They therefore applauded the Commission's recommendations for extension of French in the federal public service and strongly supported the concept of "bilingual districts". They lauded Prime Minister Trudeau, elected from one of the Quebec constituencies (Mount Royal) in which they were numerically preponderant, for fostering and ultimately passing the Official Languages Act.

However, when the Quebec Francophone population, through their elected representatives at the school board and provincial government level, began to press their educational and language reforms and political and economic modernization, the Anglophone and immigrant populations reacted defensively with deep emotion, anxiety, even a degree of paranoia. The St. Léonard Affair first triggered a reaction of fear among non-Francophone immigrants, particularly Italians, but the Anglophone Catholic and Protestant communities were quick to come to their defence. They organized effectively both at the local level (the Association of Parents of St. Léonard) and at the provincial level (elite pressure) to assert their "acquired rights" and prevail upon the divided *Union Nationale* government to write the principle of parental choice in education into law.

The St. Léonard Affair and the ensuing conflict with nationalist Francophones over Bills 85 and 63 marked the beginnings of Anglophone Quebec self-awareness as a minority community. It also led to the first real efforts on its part to adapt to its changing environment and status. In the educational sector, French immersion courses were instituted in a number of elementary and secondary schools for the first time. In business and professional spheres there was renewed vigour in programmes of recruitment of Francophone personnel and promotion of French-speaking employees to positions of authority and responsibility. In West Island local associations and municipal structures, bilingualism became much more widespread.

However, these initiatives were not expanded, and after the passage of Bill 63, much of the pressure for change was dissipated. The successful opposition waged by Anglophones against the reorganization schemes of Bills 62 and 28 through timely application of direct pressure at the elite level further encouraged a relapse into feelings of security and self-satisfaction.

The Anglophone and non-Francophone immigrant community had always disproportionately supported the Quebec Liberal Party. When that party was swept back into power in 1970 with an overwhelming majority of 72 seats, the non-Francophone community, which had given the Liberals over 90% of their votes, heaved a collective sigh of relief. The sober appearance and pragmatic emphasis on economic federalism of the Bourassa government also acted as a soporific. The moderate recommendations of the Gendron Commission Report confirmed most Anglophones in the belief that the Quebec situation had returned to the pre-St. Léonard "normalcy". And the overwhelming re-election of the Bourassa government in late 1973 with 102 of the 110 provincial seats was seen as effectively securing the matter for the foreseeable future.

The contents of Bill 22 came, therefore, as something of a shock. The non-Francophone population reacted swiftly and with emotion, but without any clear plan. They could not exert much influence through their elected representatives in caucus and in the cabinet, their public statements and media interventions fell on deaf ears and their organizational briefs, which were poorly prepared, had little effect. Direct pressures exerted by influential corporate heads likewise were of no avail.[41]

The measures to promote the French language actually envisaged in Bill 22 were not, as one acute observer pointed out,[42] very far-reaching in their scope. Much depended, of course, on the precise applications of the rather general and vague provisions of the legislation through administrative and ministerial regulation. However, the guidelines for regulations released by the government indicated that a moderate *ad hoc* approach would be adopted. The Anglophone response was therefore clearly an over-reaction, reflecting once again the minority community's deep sense of anxiety about its position in the province.

It is notable that non-Francophone immigrant groups, whose status is much more vulnerable, did not exhibit a pattern of response to the legislation very different from the Anglophones. There were relatively small numbers of briefs emanating from specifically ethnic associations presented to the Education Committee of the National Assembly. The failure by the non-Francophone immigrant groups seems to reflect their continuing and serious organizational weakness.[43]

What accounts for this erratic pattern of response by non-Francophones in conflicts over language? In my view, Anglophone and non-Francophone immigrant behaviour reflects the contradictions and shortcomings of a community which operates with a majority group psychology in a political situation in which it clearly exists and must act as a minority group. The dissonance between its misguided self-image and its actual political status, power and role in Quebec gives rise to strain and anxiety which reflects itself in emotive and defensive behaviour. Often such behaviour is totally out of proportion to the actual threat it confronts.

The majority group psychology of the Anglophone community is manifested in a number of ways. In the first place, Quebec Anglophones perceive themselves as part of the large Canadian and North-American English-speaking majority culture. They read the same newspapers, periodicals and books, are exposed to the same radio and television programmes, share many of the same political, cultural and artistic symbols, and enjoy many of the same sporting and recreational events. Secondly, Quebec Anglophones conceive of themselves as part of the Anglo-Canadian political majority. They regard the federal government as their protector as well as their instrument, and they look to the rest of English-speaking Canada for sympathy and support when their "rights" are threatened. Thirdly, Quebec Anglophones take pride in their superior economic status and technical know-how in comparison to Francophones, which they associate with what they regard as better and more dynamic English-speaking educational institutions and culture.

As a political community, however, Quebec Anglophones are clearly a minority, and increasingly a weaker and more isolated one. *De jure* minority political status has been with Quebec Anglophones since the Quebec Act of 1774 and the Constitutional Act of 1791 guaranteed to the Québécois the preservation of their language and their law, and provided them with the right to elect a legislative assembly. It was not, however, until responsible government had been established in the United Canadas and *de facto* federalism was in operation in Canada East that effective political power devolved to the Francophone majority. Since Confederation, this power has been enshrined in the Constitution, but exercised within a limited sphere, consistent with the prevailing French-Canadian and Roman Catholic philosophy of the negative, laissez faire state. In the post-Confederation period Anglophones continued to play a large and active role in Quebec political and administrative institutions, out of proportion to their numbers. They were also permitted to operate separate educational, social, cultural and municipal institutions.

The Quiet Revolution of the 1960's changed the *de facto* political position of the Anglophones in two major ways. First, the Francophones transformed their defensive concept of a nation to an affirmative one, and thereby began to exercise the provincial powers accorded them by the BNA Act to the fullest degree. This meant that they would legislate in social, cultural and economic spheres hitherto considered beyond the sphere of interest of provincial authorities, including reorganization and standardization of educational structures, regulation of professional and charitable associations, regrouping of municipalities and the creation of regional and metropolitan governments, and intervention and state participation in large and risky economic ventures such as a steel complex or a hydro-electric power project. Intervention on this scale was bound to encroach upon the hitherto autonomous operation of Anglo-Quebec local institutions. The Anglophones were no longer to be a self-governing community, but a minority group subject to the will and political aspirations of the governing Francophone majority. Secondly, a strong separatist movement emerged in the province and offered Quebeckers the very real option of establishing their own independent nation-state. In such a situation Quebec Anglophones could no longer call upon English-speaking people from other provinces or the federal government to protect their rights. They would have to subject themselves entirely to the will of the Francophone majority or leave the territory and jurisdiction of Quebec. Any provincial authority, including one faithful to the federal system in Canada, had to bear this in mind when dealing with the Anglophone community.

Quebec Anglophones manifest this combination of a majority group psychology and an inability to reconcile themselves to the reality of their new political position as a minority group in a number of distinct attitudinal and behavioural ways. First, whereas the Francophones emphasize their collective rights as a community and the priority of these rights over all others, Quebec Anglophones continue to stress individual rights and the centrality of these rights in any liberal democratic state. Individual rights are an integral part of the Anglo-Saxon legal culture, and reflect the emphasis which this culture places on the pre-eminence of the individual over the state. Quebec Anglophones, perhaps in part due to their Anglo-Saxon cultural heritage, continue to cast their political and legal arguments in the language of the enlightened majority rather than in that of the threatened minority. Thus alleged abuses of Bill 22 were generally attacked by Anglophones as violations of the rights of the individual, rather than of the Anglophone collectivity. There was little understanding of, or openness to, Francophone invocations of their collective rights.

Secondly, Quebec Anglophones incorrectly speak of their language and educational institutions as "rights" rather than "privileges". Throughout the period of the language dispute, reference was made to protections accorded by the Universal Declaration of Human Rights, the BNA Act, the Official Languages Act of Canada, and Bill 63. Yet nowhere in Canada is there a clear constitutional legislative guarantee of minority language rights. In fact, in most societies, the language of the majority is automatically enforced as the primary language of education and communication of all citizens, including those of minority linguistic and cultural groups. At best, Anglophones can claim that protection of their language is recognized in Quebec law as a convention. Only in that sense can one speak of "acquired language rights".

Thirdly, Quebec Anglophones have not relied primarily on normal institutional channels to advance their political cause, such as action within political parties, organized pressure groups, elections, public protests, or support by legislative and cabinet members. Their success in persuading the government to pass Bill 63 and in blocking school reorganization in Bills 62 and 28, as we have seen, came largely through covert pressure applied by strategic economic elites on key decision-makers. Similarly, at times of defeat or temporary frustration, as occurred just after the St. Léonard school board election in June, 1968, and after the tabling of Bill 22 in May, 1974, they have appealed to federal institutions such as the Prime Minister and cabinet, the higher courts, and sitting federal members, or to leaders in other provinces to intervene on their behalf. These modes of action suggest that the Anglophone community is aware of its own political weakness in Quebec. However, to date there has been little effort by Anglophones to overcome this weakness by strengthening their representation within existing political institutions and devising new modes of collective political action at the mass level. The weakness of the ethnic and immigrant communities in this respect is even more apparent. It is interesting to recall that the one major success that non-Francophone immigrants achieved in the language conflict came when they organized The Association of Parents of St. Léonard under the leadership of Robert Beale in the summer of 1968 and enlisted the support of influential Anglophones for their cause.[44]

Fourthly, despite frequent warnings that further francisation of the province would cause wholesale emigration of non-Francophones from Quebec, there is little evidence that the minority community is prepared or able to do so under normal conditions. Many of those who are most mobile have already left in the wake of the first wave of neo-nationalism; the rate of emigration from Quebec has levelled off at about 35,000 people annually, of whom over 75% are Anglophones, and they are quickly replaced by new immigrants. A large proportion of the non-Francophone community is tied to the province through occupations or professions which are not readily transferable, local businesses, property, etc. Those who are of average or below average income, which comprise by far the largest proportion of the community, are the least likely to leave, and have indicated that they would not do so even if unilingualism were to come to Quebec.[45] The threat of emigration, then, is not a very credible one, and moreover, would not deter the most determined nationalist elements from pursuing their objectives. Indeed, many such Francophones would welcome this opportunity to increase their numerical proportion and relative power within

Quebec.

The most sensible approach for the Anglophone and non-Francophone population then, in my opinion, is to accept the fact of their minority group status in Quebec and attempt to maximize their political potential within these limits. This commitment to Quebec would be a conditional one, which would be contingent on the willingness of the majority community to provide the non-Francophone community with the normal safeguards extended to minority groups and populations in liberal democracies. Such safeguards might include the drafting of a bill of rights which would be entrenched in the Quebec constitution and which would contain provisions for use of the English language in courts, in the legislature, in municipal institutions, and in English-language schools. The Anglophone school system would have to be explicitly protected, in accordance with pledges made by all major Quebec political parties, including the *Parti Québécois.*[46] If such assurances were not kept in practice, then the minority community could exercise its ultimate option of emigration.

Accepting minority group status does not mean surrendering to feelings of impotence and defeatism, or naively trusting the good will of the majority. Linguistic, ethnic and racial groups in many other societies have demonstrated that it is possible for minority groups to organize themselves politically and exercise great influence within democratic institutions. The Blacks in the United States, the French in the Jura district of Switzerland, the Christians in Lebanon, and the Swedes in Finland have all succeeded in winning important concessions from the majority community and ensuring a large role for themselves in their country's or region's political institutions. Devices have been instituted which symbolically or actually reflect the partnership of majority and minority communities, including the institution of a Deputy Premiership filled by a member of the minority group, reservation of seats or provision of electoral system guarantees for minorities, and granting of veto power in certain spheres. The minority community, rather than operating primarily in a covert fashion through the intermediary of economic elites and influential spokesmen, or seeking support from the federal government, should organize itself into effective pressure groups in all major social and economic spheres; should devise strategies for instituting mass demonstrations and public protests when necessary (perhaps under the umbrella of a common action front); should coordinate a strategy for nominating candidates for public office of higher caliber and greater prestige (including potential cabinet ministers); and should form cohesive blocs within existing political parties, or help initiate the establishment of new and more open political parties. Most important, the Anglophone and non-Francophone immigrant communities should demonstrate that they have finally divested themselves of their majority group attitude by embracing wholeheartedly programmes designed to increase their capacity to use French as a medium of communication in all spheres, and to enhance their understanding of and contacts with the French-speaking community of Quebec.[47]

NOTES

[1] Jacques Henripin, "Quebec and the Demographic Dilemma of French Canadian Society" in Dale Thomson (ed.), *Quebec Society & Politics: Views from the Inside* (Toronto: McClelland and Stewart, 1973), p. 161. See also *Le Devoir*, le 21 juin, 1974, p. 5.

[2] This pattern began with the earliest immigrants but has intensified since that time. Thus in the period 1931-37, 52.3% of immigrant children in the Montreal Catholic School system were in French-language schools and 47.7% were in English schools. By 1962-63 the percentage of immigrants in French schools had dropped to only 25.3%, whereas that in English schools had risen to 74.7%. See John Parisella, "Pressure Group Politics: St. Léonard Schools Crisis", unpublished M.A. thesis, McGill University, 1971, p. 41, note 2.

[3] André Lespérance, "Les transferts linguistiques au Québec de 1961 à 1971", *Le Devoir*, le 30 juillet, 1974, p. 5.

[4] *Ibid.* According to the author one can obtain a transfers balance by calculating the difference between language of use and mother tongue. This is only an approximate estimate which would be useless to refine by sophisticated methods of calculation. For a very different and far more optimistic view of the 1971 census results, see Richard J. Joy, "Les groupes linguistiques et le recensement de 1971", *Le Devoir*, le 19 juillet, 1973, p. 5, and "Comment on peut tirer du recensement des conclusions qui n'y sont point", *Le Devoir*, 6 septembre, 1974, p. 5. See also Yvon Allaire, "De l'utilisation abusive des statistiques", *Le Devoir*, le 31 juillet, 1974.

[5] Richard Ares, s.j., "Les langues parlées chez les groupes ethniques de Montréal", *Le Devoir*, le 16-18 juillet, 1974.

[5a] See Rejean Lachapelle, "Quand le Québec tombe de 28% à 22% de la population." *Le Devoir*, le 20 août, 1974, p. 5.

[6] This paper is intended to be preliminary to a projected investigation of Anglophone Political Culture in Quebec. The author wishes to thank the Social Science Committee on Research, McGill University, for its support of this project.

[7] Royal Commission on Bilingualism and Biculturalism, *Report*, Book 1, Appendix I, (Ottawa: Queen's Printer, 1967), p. 173.

[8] Some soundings on the question were made by the federal government at the 1968 Federal-Provincial Constitutional Conference in Ottawa, but there was little enthusiasm for it by the provincial representatives, and so the idea was dropped.

[9] See Arthur Blakeley, "Language policy: Pulling apart instead of together", *The Gazette*, Montreal, June 7, 1974, p. 9. New Brunswick passed an Official Language Act declaring the province to be officially bilingual, but it has yet to implement that policy in the educational sphere. Ontario has introduced certain changes largely in non-legislative policy areas to facilitate communication in

French by Franco-Ontarians.

[10]St. Léonard was in many respects a microcosm of the larger Montreal community in 1968. It had a Francophone population of 53.1% and the balance was composed overwhelmingly of new immigrants (*néo-Québécois*), of whom the largest group (27.6% of the local population) were Italians. The Francophone population included a large number of middle-class people concerned about French-Canadian cultural survival. Parisella, *op. cit.* p. 49.

[11]*Ibid.*, pp. 49-50. The analysis below closely follows that of this study.

[12]Their efforts, however, received a cold shoulder from Education Minister Jean-Guy Cardinal, who seemed sympathetic to the M.I.S. demands for local school board autonomy. The other *Union Nationale* cabinet ministers were divided on the question.

[13]The delegation met with Prime Minister Trudeau, who gave them assurances of his moral support, but nothing more, since the question was considered by federal authorities to lie within provincial jurisdiction.

[14]The drafting of these bills was in large part a cabinet response to the tense atmosphere brought about by an outbreak of violence in St. Léonard between Italians and French, which resulted in a reading of the Riot Act by the local mayor.

[15]For example, Senator Hartland Molson. See Parisella, *op. cit.*, p. 173.

[16]The reorganization under Cloutier was embodied in Bill 71.

[17]*The Montreal Star*, May 16, 1970.

[18]Some of the nationalist groups, however, boycotted its meetings.

[19]*The Montreal Star*, May 16, 1970 and *Le Devoir*, 13 février, 1973. The contents of this report were leaked by *Le Devoir* in February 1973, prior to the government's intended publication data, and were published in three instalments.

[20]*Le Devoir*, le 14, 16 and 17 février, 1973. The spokesmen were *Parti Québécois* leader René Lévesque, independent federal M.P. Roch Lasalle, and Fernand Daoust, secretary-general of the Quebec Federation of Labour (FTQ).

[21]*Le Devoir*, le 16, 27 et 28 février, 1973. Analyses were by Laurent Laplante and Claude Ryan of *Le Devoir's* editorial board, and Prof. Léon Dion of Laval University. Particular disapproval was expressed about the ambiguity in the Commission's use of the concepts "official" and "national" languages, and concerning its failure to propose immediate action to repeal Bill 63.

[22]The Anglophones voted much more disproportionately in favour of the Liberals, however. In fact over 90% of Anglophones in all socio-economic categories, except young blue-collar workers, supported the Liberals. See Serge Carlos, Edouard Cloutier et Daniel Latouche, "L'autopsie des élections", *La Presse*, le 19 novembre, 1973.

[23]Bill No. 22 (Official Language Act), Québec Official Publisher, 1974, p. 1.

[24]*The Gazette*, May 22, 1974, p. 1.

[25]Bill No. 22, article 33.

[26]*Ibid.*, articles 48, 51.

[27] *The Gazette*, May 22, 1974.

[28] *Ibid.*, May 24, 1974.

[29] *Ibid.*, May 22-26, 1974.

[30] *The Montreal Star*, May 22-23, 1974.

[31] See *The Gazette*, May 23-25, 1974 and *The Montreal Star*, May 23-26, 1974.

[32] For example, Michael Meighen, Progressive Conservative candidate in Westmount, ran advertisements in Montreal English-language papers strongly attacking the bill.

[33] *Le Devoir*, le 23 mai, 1974.

[34] *The Gazette* May 24, 1974. See also *Le Devoir*, le 24 mai, 1974.

[35] *Ibid.*, June 8, 1974.

[36] For a more detailed analysis of these briefs see *La Ligue Des Droits de l'Homme*, "Analyse des Mémoires à la Commission Parlementaire sur le projet de loi 22", juillet, 1974, miméo.

[37] There were at least three other significant amendments. They were: 1) a requirement that English-language instruction be upgraded in the French schools, 2) elimination of the proposed subsidy for companies which implement government policy with respect to francization of businesses, 3) removal of clauses dealing with labour contracts and ancillary writings by placing them in the Quebec Labour Code.

[38] Kenneth Fraser explained his affirmative vote on Second Reading as a "political" one, necessitated by the requirements of governmental largesse for his (largely francophone) Huntingdon constituency. He was absent for the vote on Third Reading.

[39] *The Montreal Star*, July 19, 1974. See also *The Gazette*, July 20, 1974.

[40] The Royal Commission on Bilingualism and Biculturalism, *Report*, Book 3 (Ottawa: Queen's Printer, 1969) Chapter 4. See also André Raynault, "The Quebec Economy: A General Assessment" in Dale Thomson (ed.), *op. cit.*, p. 149.

[41] For example, the President of the Bank of Montreal, Mr. G. Arnold Hart, wrote confidentially to Prime Minister Bourassa on June 19, 1974, expressing his strong reservations about Bill 22, particularly in the economic sphere. The letter was published in *Le Devoir*, le 20 juillet, 1974, p. 5 and incorrectly attributed to Mr. Fred M. McNeil.

[42] See Dominique Clift, "Bill 22: An Elusive Target", *The Montreal Star*, July 23, 1974.

[43] The federal government, in attempting to implement the recommendations of the fourth book of the Royal Commission on Bilingualism and Biculturalism, established a programme of multiculturalism in 1971. It was designed to help ethnic and immigrant groups adapt and acquire feelings of self-consciousness, and to establish the institutional structures to buttress them. The

"emergent" groups of more recent arrivals (e.g. Greeks, Portuguese, West Indians) required considerable external direction and prodding to develop their programmes, particularly in the early stages of implementation of the federal legislation. See. Richard Stock, "Multiculturalism as a Community Development Program", unpublished M.A. thesis, McGill University, 1973.

[44] Parisella, *op. cit.*, p. 177 makes a similar point.

[45] See *The Gazette*, Nov. 29, 1973.

[46] To be acceptable to Francophones, perhaps this guarantee would have to be accompanied by an engagement by the Anglophones to increase the content of French in their curricula.

[47] One possible concrete proposal is the establishment of truly bilingual schools, attended by the children of immigrants, francophones and anglophones. Unfortunately, as the St.-Léonard Affair has demonstrated so clearly, this plan is perceived as a threat to the survival of the francophone community. A project of this type might nevertheless be established if the courses taught in these schools were sufficiently based on, or offered a predominant position to, the French language. This might be a compromise formula acceptable to the francophone community. I would like to thank Mr. Alfred Hero for this argument.

APPENDICES

BILL 85

Loi modifiant la Loi du ministère de l'éducation, la Loi du Conseil supérieur de l'éducation et la Loi de l'instruction publique.

SA MAJESTE, de l'avis et du consentement du Conseil législatif et de l'Assemblée législative de Québec, décrète ce qui suit:

1. L'article 2 de la Loi du ministère de l'éducation (Statuts refondus, 1964, chapitre 233) est modifié en ajoutant, à la fin de l'article 2, l'alinéa suivant:

"Le ministre a aussi la responsabilité de prendre, de concert avec le ministre de l'immigration, les dispositions nécessaires pour que les personnes qui s'établissent au Québec puissent acquérir, dès leur arrivée, une connaissance d'usage de la langue française et faire instruire leurs enfants dans des écoles reconnues par le ministre comme étant de langue française".

2. La Loi du Conseil supérieur de l'éducation (Status refondus, 1964, chapitre 234) est modifiée en insérant, dans la sixième ligne du quatrième alinéa du préambule, après les mots "un comité protestant", ce qui suit: ", un comité linguistique".

3. L'article 6 de ladite loi est modifié en remplaçant, dans la première ligne, le mot "deux" par le mot "trois".

4. L'article 15 de ladite loi est remplacé par le suivant:

"**15.** Un comité catholique, un comité protestant et un comité linguistique du Conseil, composés chacun de quinze membres, sont institués".

BILL 85

An Act to amend the Education Department Act, the Superior Council of Education Act and the Education Act.

HER MAJESTY, with the advice and consent of the Legislative Council and of the Legislative Assembly of Québec, enacts as follows:

1. Section 2 of the Education Department Act (Revised Statutes, 1964, chapter 233) is amended by adding at the end of section 2 the following paragraph:

"The Minister shall also be responsible for taking, in co-operation with the Minister of Immigration, the measures necessary to ensure that persons settling in the Province of Québec may acquire, upon arrival, a working knowledge of the French language and cause their children to be taught in schools recognized by the Minister as being French language schools".

2. The Superior Council of Education Act (Revised Statutes, 1964, chapter 234) is amended by inserting, after the words "a Protestant committee" in the sixth line of the fourth paragraph of the preamble, the words ", a Linguistic Committee".

3. Section 6 of the said act is amended by replacing the word "two" in the first line by the word "three".

4. Section 15 of the said act is replaced by the following:

"**15.** A Catholic committee, a Protestant committee and a Linguistic Committee of the Council, each consisting of fifteen members, are established".

5. Ladite loi est modifiée en insérant, après l'article 17, le suivant.

"17*a.* Le comité linguistique est composé de dix représentants francophones et de cinq représentants anglophones.

Ces représentants sont nommés par le lieutenant-gouverneur en conseil sur la recommandation du Conseil qui consulte au préalable les associations ou organisations les plus représentatives des éducateurs et des parents des groupes linguistiques francophones et anglophones du Québec".

6. L'article 19 de ladite loi est modifié en ajoutant, à la fin du premier alinéa, ce qui suit: "Il est d'office membre adjoint du comité linguistique."

7. L'article 22 de ladite loi est modifié en remplaçant, dans la première ligne, les mots "Ces comités" par les suivants: "Le comité catholique et le comité protestant".

8. Ladite loi est modifiée en insérant, après l'article 22, le suivant:

"22*a.* Le comité linguistique est chargé:

(a) de faire des règlements suivant lesquels le ministre reconnaît comme étant de langue française ou de langue anglaise les institutions d'enseignement soumises aux règlements visés au paragraphe *b* de l'article 28;

(b) de faire des règlements régissant les programmes d'études et les examens pour tous les enseignements, sauf les enseignements qui conduisent à un grade universitaire et les enseignements privés qui ne conduisent pas à un diplôme décerné sous l'autorité du ministre, de façon à assurer une connaissance d'usage de la langue française à toute personne qui fréquente une institution visée au paragraphe *a* et reconnue comme étant de langue anglaise;

5. The said act is amended by inserting after section 17 the following:

"17*a.* The Linguistic Committee shall consist of ten French-speaking representatives and five English-speaking representatives.

Such representatives shall be appointed by the Lieutenant-Governor in Council on the recommendation of the Council which shall first consult the associations or organizations most representative of the educators and of the parents of the French and English linguistic groups of the Province of Québec".

6. Section 19 of the said act is amended by adding at the end of the first paragraph the following: "He shall be *ex officio* an associate member of the linguistic committee".

7. Section 22 of the said act is amended by replacing the words "such committees" in the first and second lines by the words "the Catholic committee and the Protestant committee".

8. The said act is amended by inserting after section 22 the following:

"22*a.* It shall be the duty of the Linguistic Committee:

(a) to make regulations under which the Minister shall recognize as being French-language or English-language institutions the educational institutions subject to the regulations contemplated in sub-paragraph *b* of section 28;

(b) to make regulations governing the curricula and examinations for all subjects except subjects leading to a university degree and private education not leading to a diploma conferred under the authority of the Minister, in such a manner as to ensure a working knowledge of the French language to every person who attends an institution contemplated in sub-paragraph *a* and recognized as being an English-language institution;

(c) de faire au Conseil ou au ministre des recommandations sur toute question de sa compétence, et en particulier sur la qualification, au point de vue linguistique, du personnel dirigeant et du personnel enseignant dans les institutions visées au paragraphe *a* et reconnues comme étant de langue française ou de langue anglaise.

Les règlements faits en vertu du présent article entrent en vigueur après leur approbation par le lieutenant-gouverneur en conseil; ils sont déposés sans délai à l'Assemblée législative et publiés dans la *Gazette officielle de Québec*".

9. L'article 28 de ladite loi est modifié en remplaçant, dans la deuxième ligne du paragraphe *b*, les mots "à l'article 22" par les mots "aux articles 22 et 22*a*".

10. L'article 203 de la Loi de l'instruction publique (Statuts refondus, 1964, chapitre 235), modifié par l'article 1 de la loi 15-16 Elizabeth II, chapitre 62, est de nouveau modifié:

(a) en remplaçant le paragraphe 3° par le suivant:

"3° De prendre les mesures nécessaires pour que les cours d'études du niveau de la première année à celui de la onzième année inclusivement, adoptés ou reconnus pour les écoles publiques catholiques ou protestantes, de langue française ou de langue anglaise, selon le cas, soient dispensés à tous les enfants domiciliés dans le territoire soumis à leur juridiction s'ils sont jugés aptes à suivre ces cours et si leurs parents ou les personnes qui en tiennent lieu sont désireux de les y inscrire. A ces fins, les commissaires ou les syndics d'écoles doivent, soit organiser ces cours dans leurs écoles, soit se prévaloir des dispositions des articles 469 à 495, soit se prévaloir des dispositions de l'article 496, soit prendre à la fois plusieurs de ces mesures":

(c) to make recommendations to the Council or to the Minister respecting any matter within its competence, and particularly as to the qualifications, from a linguistic point of view, of the administrative staff and the teaching staff in the institutions contemplated in sub-paragraph *a* and recognized as being English-language or French-language institutions.

The regulations made under this section shall come into force after approval by the Lieutenant-Governor in Council; they shall be laid before the Legislative Assembly forthwith and published in the *Québec Official Gazette.*"

9. Section 28 of the said act is amended by replacing the words "in section 22" in the second line of sub-paragraph *b* by the words "in sections 22 and 22*a*".

10. Section 203 of the Education Act (Revised Statutes, 1964, chapter 235), amended by section 1 of the act 15-16 Elizabeth II, chapter 62, is again amended:

(a) by replacing sub-paragraph 3 by the following:

"(3) To take the measures necessary to have the courses of study from the first year level to the eleventh year level inclusive, adopted or recognized for Catholic or Protestant, English-language or French-language public schools, as the case may be, given to all the children domiciled in the territory under their jurisdiction if they are deemed capable of following such courses and if their parents or the persons acting in their stead are desirous of enrolling them therein. For such purposes, the school commissioners or trustees must either establish such courses in their schools or avail themselves of the provisions of sections 469 to 495, or of those of section 496, or take two or more of such steps at the same time":

(b) en insérant, dans la cinquième ligne du paragraphe 4°, après le mot "protestantes", ce qui suit: ", de langue française ou de langue anglaise";

(c) en ajoutant, après le paragraphe 17°, l'alinéa suivant:

"À la requête de tout intéressé, une résolution qui déroge au paragraphe 3° ou au paragraphe 4° du présent article doit être soumise au ministre. Ce dernier peut l'approuver, la modifier ou l'annuler quatre-vingt-dix jours après avoir demandé l'avis du comité linguistique du Conseil supérieur de l'éducation ou plus tôt, s'il a déjà reçu cet avis. La décision du ministre doit être transmise sans délai à l'intéressé et elle est homologuée par la Cour provinciale à la demande du ministre ou de l'intéressée".

11. La présente loi entrera en vigueur à la date qui sera fixée par proclamation du lieutenant-gouverneur en conseil à l'exception de l'article 1 qui entre en vigueur le jour de sa sanction.

(b) by inserting after the word "Protestant" in the fourth line of sub-paragraph 4 the following: ", English-language or French-language";

(c) by adding after sub-paragraph 17 the following paragraph:

"At the request of any interested party, a resolution which derogates from sub-paragraph 3 or 4 of this section shall be submitted to the Minister. He may approve, amend or annul it ninety days after he has taken the advice of the Linguistic Committee of the Superior Council of Education, or sooner if he has already received such advice. The decision of the Minister shall be communicated forthwith to the interested party and shall be homologated by the Provincial Court upon the application of the Minister or of the interested party".

11. This act shall come into force on a date to be fixed by proclamation of the Lieutenant-Governor in Council, except section 1 which shall come into force on the day of its sanction.

NOTES EXPLICATIVES

Ce projet a pour objet de préciser le rôle de la langue française dans le domaine de l'éducation au Québec. Il confie au ministre de l'éducation des responsabilités nouvelles relativement aux mesures à prendre pour assurer une connaissance d'usage de la langue française aux personnes qui s'établissent au Québec et à leurs enfants ainsi qu'aux personnes qui y fréquentent des institutions d'enseignement publiques de langue anglaise. Il vise aussi à faire établir par un comité du Conseil supérieur de l'éducation, qui est institué par le projet sous le nom de "Comité linguistique", des règlements suivant lesquels le ministre reconnaîtra les institutions d'enseignement publiques comme étant de langue française ou de langue anglaise.

L'article 1 donne au ministre de l'éducation la responsabilité de prendre, de concert avec le ministre de l'immigration, les dispositions nécessaires pour que les personnes qui s'établissent au Québec puissent acquérir, dès leur arrivée, une connaissance d'usage de la langue française et faire instruire leurs enfants dans des écoles reconnues par le ministre comme étant de langue française.

Les articles 2 à 7 instituent le comité linguistique du Conseil supérieur de l'éducation. Ce comité sera composé, comme les autres comités du Conseil, de 15 membres; dix d'entre eux seront francophones et cinq seront anglopho-

EXPLANATORY NOTES

The object of this bill is to specify the role of the French language in the field of education in the Province of Québec. It entrusts the Minister of Education with new responsibilities respecting the steps to be taken to ensure that persons who settle in Québec and their children, and also persons who attend English-language public educational institutions there, may have a working knowledge of the French language. It also provides for the establishment, by a committee of the Superior Council of Education constituted by the bill under the name of the "Linguistic Committee", of regulations whereby the Minister will recognize public educational institutions as being English-language or French-language institutions.

Section 1 makes the Minister of Education responsible for taking, in cooperation with the Minister of Immigration, the measures necessary to ensure that persons settling in the Province of Québec may acquire, upon arrival, a working knowledge of the French language and cause their children to be taught in schools recognized by the Minister as being French-language institutions.

Sections 2 to 7 establish the Linguistic Committee of the Superior Council of Education. This committee, like the other committees of the Council, will be composed of 15 members, ten of them French-speaking and five English-

nes. Les membres seront nommés par le gouvernement sur la recommandation du Conseil, qui aura au préalable consulté les associations ou organisations les plus représentatives des éducateurs et des parents des groupes linguistiques francophones du Québec.

L'article 8 définit les pouvoirs du comité linguistique; il sera chargé:

(a) *de faire des règlements suivant lesquels le ministre de l'éducation reconnaîtra comme étant de langue française ou de langue anglaise les institutions d'enseignement publiques;*

(b) *de faire des règlements régissant les programmes d'études et les examens pour tous les enseignements dans les institutions reconnues comme étant de langue anglaise, de façon à assurer une connaissance d'usage de la langue française aux personnes qui fréquentent ces institutions;*

(c) *de faire au Conseil ou au ministre des recommandations, notamment sur la qualification, au point de vue linguistique, du personnel dirigeant et du personnel enseignant de toutes les institutions d'enseignement publiques.*

Les règlements du comité devront être approuvés par le gouvernement, déposés sans délai auprès de la Législature et publiés dans la Gazette officielle de Québec.

L'article 9 est de concordance.

L'article 10 ajoute aux devoirs imposés par la Loi de l'instruction publique aux commissaires et aux syndics d'écoles, ceux de prendre les mesures nécessaires pour que les cours qu'ils sont tenus de donner de la première à la onzième année soient non plus seulement ceux qui sont adoptés ou reconnus pour les écoles publiques catholiques ou protestantes, mais aussi ceux qui sont adoptés ou reconnus pour les écoles qui sont de langue française ou de langue anglaise. Ces cours seront donnés à tous les enfants domiciliés dans le territoire soumis à leur juridiction s'ils

speaking. The members will be appointed by the Government on the recommendation of the Council, which will first have consulted the associations or organizations most representative of the educators and of the parents of the French and English linguistic groups of the Province of Québec.

Section 8 defines the powers of the Linguistic Committee; its functions will be:

(a) *to make regulations under which the Minister of Education will recognize the public educational institutions as being French-language or English-language institutions;*

(b) *to make regulations governing the curricula and examinations for all subjects in the institutions recognized as being English-language institutions, in such a manner as to ensure a working knowledge of the French-language to persons who attend such institutions;*

(c) *to make to the Council or the Minister recommendations, particularly as to the qualifications, from a linguistic point of view, of the administrative staff and the teaching staff of all public educational institutions.*

The regulations of the Committee must be approved by the Government, laid before the Legislature forthwith and published in the Québec Official Gazette.

Section 9 is a concordance provision.

Section 10 adds to the duties of school commissioners and trustees under the Education Act those of taking the measures necessary to ensure that the courses of study that they are required to give from the first to the eleventh year are no longer merely those adopted or recognized for Catholic or Protestant public schools, but also those adopted or recognized for English-language or French-language schools. Such courses will be given to all children domiciled in the territory under their jurisdiction if they are deemed capable of following such

sont jugés aptes à suivre ces cours et si leurs parents ou les personnes qui en tiennent lieu sont désireux de les y inscrire.

Les commissaires devront aussi s'assurer que les cours donnés dans leurs écoles seront conformes aux règlements édictés ou approuvés non seulement pour les écoles publiques catholiques ou protestantes, mais aussi pour les écoles de langue française ou de langue anglaise.

Toute résolution qui dérogera aux devoirs ainsi imposés aux commissaires ou syndics pourra être annulée par le ministre à la demande de tout intéressé, après consultation du comité linguistique du Conseil supérieur de l'éducation qui aura 90 jours pour donner son avis.

courses and if their parents or the persons acting in their stead are desirous of enrolling them therein.

The commissioners must also ensure that the courses given in their schools comply with the regulations made or approved not only for Catholic or Protestant, but also for French-language or English-language schools.

Any resolution which derogates from the duties so imposed on the commissioners or trustees may be annulled by the Minister at the request of any interested party, after consulting the Linguistic Committee of the Superior Council of Education which will have 90 days to give its advice.

CHAPITRE 9

Loi pour promouvoir la langue française au Québec

[*Sanctionnée le 28 novembre 1969*]

SA MAJESTÉ, de l'avis et du consentement de l'Assemblée nationale du Québec, décrète ce qui suit:

S.R., c. 233, a. 2, mod.

1. L'article 2 de la Loi du ministère de l'éducation (Statuts refondus, 1964, chapitre 233) est modifié en ajoutant, à la fin, l'alinéa suivant:

Devoirs du ministre.

« Le ministre doit prendre les dispositions nécessaires pour que les programmes d'études édictés ou approuvés pour ces institutions d'enseignement et les examens qui les sanctionnent assurent une connaissance d'usage de la langue française aux enfants à qui l'enseignement est donné en langue anglaise. ».

S.R., c. 235, a. 203, mod.

2. L'article 203 de la Loi de l'instruction publique (Statuts refondus, 1964, chapitre 235), modifié par l'article 1 du chapitre 62 des lois de 1966/1967, est de nouveau modifié en remplaçant les paragraphes 3° et 4° par les suivants:

Cours d'études.

« 3° De prendre les mesures nécessaires pour que les cours d'études du niveau de la première année à celui de la onzième inclusivement, adoptés ou reconnus pour les écoles publiques catholiques, protestantes ou autres, selon le cas, soient dispensés à tous les enfants domiciliés dans le territoire soumis à leur juridiction s'ils sont jugés aptes à suivre ces cours et désireux de s'y inscrire.

Cours en français.

Ces cours doivent être donnés en langue française.

CHAPTER 9

An Act to promote the French language in Québec

[*Assented to 28th November 1969*]

HER MAJESTY, with the advice and consent of the National Assembly of Québec, enacts as follows:

1. Section 2 of the Education Department Act (Revised Statutes, 1964, chapter 233) is amended by adding at the end the following paragraph:

R.S., c. 233, s. 2, am.

"The Minister shall take the measures necessary to have the curricula, made or approved for such educational institutions, and the examinations which confirm them, ensure a working knowledge of the French language to children to whom instruction is given in the English language.".

Duties of Minister.

2. Section 203 of the Education Act (Revised Statutes, 1964, chapter 235), amended by section 1 of chapter 62 of the statutes of 1966/1967, is again amended by replacing sub-paragraphs 3 and 4 by the following:

R.S., c. 235, s. 203, am.

"(3) To take the measures necessary to have the courses of study from the first year level to the eleventh year level inclusive, adopted or recognized for Catholic, Protestant or other public schools, as the case may be, given to all the children domiciled in the territory under their jurisdiction if they are deemed capable of following such courses and desirous of enrolling for them.

Courses of study.

Such courses must be given in the French language.

Courses in French.

Choix de l'anglais et connaissance d'usage du français.

Ils sont donnés en langue anglaise à chaque enfant dont les parents ou les personnes qui en tiennent lieu en font la demande lors de son inscription; les programmes d'études et les examens doivent assurer une connaissance d'usage de la langue française à ces enfants et le ministre doit prendre les mesures nécessaires à cette fin.

Devoirs des commissaires d'écoles;

Les commissaires ou les syndics d'écoles doivent, soit organiser ces cours dans leurs écoles, soit se prévaloir des dispositions des articles 469 à 495, soit se prévaloir des dispositions de l'article 496, soit prendre à la fois plusieurs de ces mesures;

Cours d'études;

« 4° De s'assurer que les cours d'études dispensés dans leurs écoles sont conformes aux programmes d'études et aux règlements édictés ou approuvés pour les écoles publiques catholiques, protestantes ou autres, selon le cas; ».

1968, c. 68, a. 3, mod.

3. L'article 3 de la Loi du ministère de l'immigration (1968, chapitre 68) est modifié en ajoutant, à la fin, le paragraphe suivant:

« *e*) prendre, de concert avec le ministre de l'éducation, les dispositions nécessaires pour que les personnes qui s'établissent au Québec acquièrent dès leur arrivée ou même avant qu'elles quittent leur pays d'origine la connaissance de la langue française et qu'elles fassent instruire leurs enfants dans des institutions d'enseignement où les cours sont donnés en langue française. ».

S.R., c. 57, a. 14, remp.

4. L'article 14 de la Loi du ministère des affaires culturelles (Statuts refondus, 1964, chapitre 57) est remplacé par les suivants:

Devoirs.

« **14.** L'Office de la Langue française doit, sous la direction du ministre:

a) veiller à la correction et l'enrichissement de la langue parlée et écrite;

b) conseiller le gouvernement sur toute mesure législative ou administrative qui pourrait être adoptée pour faire en sorte que la langue française soit la langue d'usage dans les entreprises publiques et privées au Québec;

c) élaborer, de concert avec ces entreprises, des programmes pour faire en sorte que la langue française y soit la langue

They shall be given in the English language to any child for whom his parents or the persons acting in their stead so request at his enrolment; the curricula and examinations must ensure a working knowledge of the French language to such children and the Minister shall take the measures necessary for such purpose.

Option of English and working knowledge of French.

The school commissioners or trustees must either establish such courses in their schools or avail themselves of the provisions of sections 469 to 495, or of those of section 496, or take two or more of such steps at the same time;

Duties of school boards;

"(4) To ensure that the courses of study given in their schools comply with the curricula and regulations made or approved for Catholic, Protestant or other public schools, as the case may be;".

Courses of study;

3. Section 3 of the Immigration Department Act (1968, chapter 68) is amended by adding at the end the following paragraph:

1968, c. 68, s. 3, am.

"(*e*) in co-operation with the Minister of Education, take the measures necessary so that the persons who settle in Québec may acquire the knowledge of the French language upon arrival or even before they leave their country of origin, and may have their children instructed in educational institutions where courses are given in the French language.".

4. Section 14 of the Cultural Affairs Department Act (Revised Statutes, 1964, chapter 57) is replaced by the following:

R.S., c. 57, s. 14, replaced.

"**14.** Under the Minister's direction, the French Language Bureau shall:

Duties.

(*a*) foster the correction and enrichment of the spoken and written language;

(*b*) advise the government on any legislative or administrative measures which might be passed to see to it that French is the working language in public and private undertakings in Québec;

(*c*) in co-operation with such undertakings, prepare programs to see to it that the French language is the working

d'usage et pour assurer à leurs dirigeants et à leurs employés une connaissance d'usage de cette langue;

d) conseiller le gouvernement sur toute mesure législative ou administrative qui pourrait être adoptée en matière d'affichage public pour faire en sorte que la langue française y soit prioritaire;

e) créer un centre de recherches linguistiques et coordonner dans le Québec toute activité de recherches en ce domaine.

Audition de plaintes.

« **14*a*.** L'Office de la Langue française peut entendre toute plainte de tout employé ou tout groupe d'employés à l'effet que son droit à l'usage de la langue française comme langue de travail n'est pas respecté.

Recommandations.

Après avoir entendu les parties, considéré la langue de la majorité dans l'entreprise ou dans la division de l'entreprise dont il s'agit, la nature du travail, et toutes les autres circonstances, l'Office fait les recommandations qui s'imposent, lesquelles sont publiques.

Pouvoirs d'enquête.

L'Office, dans l'exercice de l'autorité conférée par le présent article, possède tous les pouvoirs d'un commissaire nommé en vertu de la Loi des commissions d'enquête (chap. 11). ».

Entrée en vigueur.

5. La présente loi entre en vigueur le jour de sa sanction sauf les articles 1 et 2 qui entreront en vigueur le 1er juillet 1970 ou à toute autre date antérieure qui sera fixée par proclamation du lieutenant-gouverneur en conseil.

language there, and to ensure a working knowledge of such language to their administrators and employees;

(*d*) advise the government on any legislative or administrative measures which might be passed in regard to public posting to ensure the priority of the French language therein;

(*e*) establish a linguistic research centre and co-ordinate all research activities in such field in Québec.

Hearing of complaints.

"**14*a*.** The French Language Bureau may hear any complaint by any employee or group of employees to the effect that his or their right to use the French language as the working language is not respected.

Recommendations.

After having heard the parties, taken into consideration the language of the majority in the undertaking or department of the undertaking in question, the nature of the work and all the other circumstances, the Bureau shall make the necessary recommendations, which shall be public.

Powers of investigation.

The Bureau, in the exercise of the authority assigned to it by this section, shall have all the powers of a commissioner appointed under the Public Inquiry Commission Act (Chap. 11).".

Coming into force.

5. This act shall come into force on the day of its sanction except for sections 1 and 2 which shall come into force on the 1st of July 1970 or on any prior date to be fixed by proclamation of the Lieutenant-Governor in Council.

NOTES EXPLICATIVES

Ce projet a pour but d'assurer que les enfants de langue anglaise du Québec acquièrent une connaissance d'usage de la langue française et que les personnes qui s'établissent au Québec acquièrent la connaissance de la langue française et fassent instruire leurs enfants dans cette langue. Il confirme en outre la possibilité pour les parents de choisir, entre le français et l'anglais, la langue dans laquelle les cours seront donnés à leurs enfants. Il confie aussi à l'Office de la Langue française des devoirs particuliers relativement à l'utilisation de la langue française au Québec.

A ces fins, l'article 1 prévoit que le ministre de l'éducation doit prendre les dispositions nécessaires pour que les programmes d'études et les examens qui les sanctionnent assurent, tant au niveau élémentaire et secondaire qu'au niveau collégial, une connaissance d'usage de la langue française aux enfants à qui l'enseignement est donné en langue anglaise.

L'article 2 prévoit que les cours organisés par les commissions scolaires doivent être donnés en langue française. Ils sont donnés en langue anglaise lorsque les parents ou les personnes qui en tiennent lieu en font la demande; ces cours doivent assurer aux enfants une connaissance d'usage de la langue française.

L'article 2 prévoit aussi que les commissions scolaires doivent offrir les cours adoptés ou reconnus pour les écoles publiques catholiques, protestantes ou autres, selon le cas.

EXPLANATORY NOTES

The object of this bill is to ensure that the English-speaking children of Québec acquire a working knowledge of the French language and that persons who settle in Québec may acquire the knowledge of the French language and have their children instructed in such language. It also confirms the parents' option to choose either French or English as the language in which courses will be given to their children. It also entrusts the French Language Bureau with special duties respecting the use of the French language in Québec.

For such purposes, section 1 provides that the Minister of Education must take the measures necessary to have the curricula, and the examinations which confirm them, at the elementary, secondary and college levels, ensure a working knowledge of the French language to children to whom instruction is given in the English language.

Section 2 provides that the courses established by school boards must be given in French. They shall be given in English when the parents or the persons acting in their stead so request; such courses must ensure a working knowledge of the French language to the children.

Section 2 also prescribes that school boards must provide the courses adopted or recognized for Catholic, Protestant or other public schools, as the case may be.

L'article 3 prévoit que le ministre de l'immigration doit, de concert avec le ministre de l'éducation, prendre les dispositions nécessaires pour que les personnes qui s'établissent au Québec acquièrent dès leur arrivée ou même avant qu'elles quittent leur pays d'origine, la connaissance de la langue française et qu'elles fassent instruire leurs enfants en langue française.

L'article 4 charge l'Office de la Langue française de conseiller le gouvernement sur toute mesure pouvant être adoptée pour faire en sorte que la langue française soit la langue d'usage dans les entreprises publiques et privées au Québec et qu'elle soit prioritaire en matière d'affichage public; il lui confie aussi la tâche d'élaborer des programmes à ces fins avec ces entreprises et de coordonner la recherche linguistique au Québec au sein d'un centre de recherches qu'il a mission de créer. Cet article autorise aussi l'Office à entendre toute plainte d'employés sur le respect du droit à l'usage de la langue française comme langue de travail, à faire enquête et à faire les recommandations qui s'imposent; ces recommandations seront publiques.

Section 3 provides that, in co-operation with the Minister of Education, the Minister of Immigration must take the measures necessary so that the persons who settle in Québec may acquire the knowledge of the French language upon arrival or even before they leave their country of origin, and may have their children instructed in the French language.

Section 4 entrusts the French Language Bureau with advising the government on any measures which might be passed to see to it that French be the working language in public and private undertakings in Québec and that it have priority in matters of public posting; it also entrusts such Bureau with preparing programs for such purposes with such undertakings, and with coordinating language research in Québec within the research centre which it is authorized to create. This section also authorizes the Bureau to hear any complaint by employees regarding the respect of the right to use the French language as the working language, and to conduct inquiries and to make the necessary recommendations; these recommendations will be public.

CHAPITRE 6

Loi sur la langue officielle

[*Sanctionnée le 31 juillet 1974*]

Préambule. ATTENDU que la langue française constitue un patrimoine national que l'état a le devoir de préserver, et qu'il incombe au gouvernement du Québec de tout mettre en oeuvre pour en assurer la prééminence et pour en favoriser l'épanouissement et la qualité;

Attendu que la langue française doit être la langue de communication courante de l'administration publique;

Attendu que les entreprises d'utilité publique et les professions doivent l'employer pour communiquer avec la population et avec l'administration publique;

Attendu que les membres du personnel des entreprises doivent pouvoir, dans leur travail, communiquer en français entre eux et avec leurs supérieurs;

Attendu que la langue française doit être omniprésente dans le monde des affaires, particulièrement en ce qui concerne la direction des entreprises, les raisons sociales, l'affichage public, les contrats d'adhésion et les contrats conclus par les consommateurs;

Attendu qu'il importe de déterminer le statut de la langue française dans l'enseignement;

À ces causes, Sa Majesté, de l'avis et du consentement de l'Assemblée nationale du Québec, décrète ce qui suit:

TITRE I

LA LANGUE OFFICIELLE DU QUÉBEC

Langue officielle. **1.** Le français est la langue officielle du Québec.

CHAPTER 6

Official Language Act

[*Assented to 31st July 1974*]

WHEREAS the French language is a national heritage which the body politic is in duty bound to preserve, and it is incumbent upon the government of the province of Québec to employ every means in its power to ensure the pre-eminence of that language and to promote its vigour and quality; Preamble.

Whereas the French language must be the ordinary language of communication in the public administration;

Whereas the public utilities and the professional bodies must use it in communicating with the public and with the public administration;

Whereas the members of the personnel of business firms must, in their work, be able to communicate in French among themselves and with their superior officers;

Whereas the French language must be in use at every level of business activity, especially in corporate management and in firm names, on public signs, in contracts pre-determined by one party and in consumer contracts;

Whereas it is relevant to determine the status of the French language in instruction;

Therefore, Her Majesty, with the advice and consent of the National Assembly of Québec, enacts as follows:

TITLE I

THE OFFICIAL LANGUAGE OF QUÉBEC

1. French is the official language of the province of Québec. Official language.

TITRE II

DISPOSITIONS D'ORDRE GÉNÉRAL

Divergence d'interprétation.

2. En cas de divergence que les règles ordinaires d'interprétation ne permettent pas de résoudre convenablement, le texte français des lois du Québec prévaut sur le texte anglais.

Interprétation: « ministre »;

3. Dans la présente loi, on entend par:

a) « ministre », le ministre désigné par le lieutenant-gouverneur en conseil;

« Régie »;

b) « Régie », la Régie de la langue française;

« règlement ».

c) « règlement », tout règlement adopté en vertu de la présente loi par le lieutenant-gouverneur en conseil.

Services, etc., visés.

4. Sont énumérés en annexe les divers services de l'administration publique, les entreprises d'utilité publique et les corporations professionnelles visés par la présente loi.

TITRE III

STATUT DE LA LANGUE OFFICIELLE

But du titre III.

5. Le présent titre règle les effets juridiques de l'article 1.

CHAPITRE I

LA LANGUE DE L'ADMINISTRATION PUBLIQUE

Langue des textes officiels.

6. Doivent être rédigés en français les textes et documents officiels émanant de l'administration publique.

Textes, etc., réputés officiels.

7. Sont réputés officiels:

a) les textes et documents qui émanent de l'administration publique et que la loi déclare authentiques en raison de leur caractère public, notamment les écrits visés à l'article 1207 du Code civil;

b) les autorisations, les avis et les autres documents de même nature émanant de l'administration publique.

Version anglaise.

8. Les textes et documents officiels peuvent être accompagnés d'une version

TITLE II

GENERAL PROVISIONS

2. Where any discrepancy cannot be satisfactorily resolved by the ordinary rules of interpretation, the French text of the statutes of Québec prevails over the English text.

Discrepancy in interpretation.

3. In this act,

Interpretation: "Minister";

(*a*) "Minister" means the Minister designated by the Lieutenant-Governor in Council;

"Régie";

(*b*) "Régie" means the *Régie de la langue française*;

"regulation".

(*c*) "regulation" means any regulation made in virtue of this act by the Lieutenant-Governor in Council.

4. The various services of the public administration, the public utilities and the professional corporations contemplated by this act are listed in the Schedule.

Services, etc., contemplated.

TITLE III

STATUS OF THE OFFICIAL LANGUAGE

5. This title governs the juridical effects of section 1.

Scope of title III.

CHAPTER I

THE LANGUAGE OF THE PUBLIC ADMINISTRATION

6. Official texts and documents emanating from the public administration must be drawn up in French.

Official texts in French.

7. The following are deemed official:

Texts, etc., deemed official.

(*a*) texts and documents emanating from the public administration and declared authentic by law because of their public nature, particularly the writings contemplated in article 1207 of the Civil Code;

(*b*) authorizations, notices and other documents of the same kind emanating from the public administration.

8. Official texts and documents may be accompanied with an English version; in

English version.

anglaise; en pareil cas et sauf les exceptions prévues par la présente loi, seule la version française est authentique.

such a case, only the French version is authentic, subject to the exceptions provided in this act.

Textes officiels des organismes municipaux et scolaires.

9. Les organismes municipaux et scolaires dont au moins dix pour cent des administrés sont de langue anglaise et qui rédigent déjà leurs textes et documents officiels en anglais, doivent les rédiger à la fois en français et en anglais.

Détermination.

Le titre IV précise la façon dont sont déterminés les organismes municipaux et scolaires susvisés.

Réduction de pourcentage par fusion.

Au cas de fusion réduisant à moins de dix pour cent le pourcentage prévu au premier alinéa,le présent article continue à régir l'organisme issu de la fusion, si l'acte constatant la fusion y pourvoit, pour la période fixée par le lieutenant-gouverneur en conseil.

Official texts of municipal or school body.

9. If at least ten per cent of the persons administered by a municipal or school body are English-speaking and it has been its practice to draw up its official texts and documents in English, it must draw them up in both French and English.

How determined.

Title IV specifies the manner in which the municipal and school bodies contemplated above are determined.

Reduction of percentage through amalgamation.

Where an amalgamation or union reduces the percentage contemplated in the first paragraph to less than ten per cent, this section continues to govern the body resulting from the amalgamation or union, if the deed establishing it so provides, for the period determined by the Lieutenant-Governor in Council.

Communications avec autres gouvernements, etc.

10. L'administration publique doit utiliser la langue officielle pour communiquer avec les autres gouvernements du Canada et, au Québec, avec les personnes morales.

Choix.

Toute personne a le droit de s'adresser à l'administration publique en français ou en anglais, à son choix.

Communication with other governments, etc.

10. The public administration must use the official language to communicate with the other governments of Canada and, within the province of Québec, with moral persons.

Option.

Every person may address the public administration in French or in English, as he may choose.

Désignation d'organismes.

11. Les organismes gouvernementaux sont désignés par leur seule dénomination française.

Government agencies.

11. Government agencies shall be designated by their French names alone.

Communication interne.

12. La langue officielle est la langue de communication interne de l'administration publique.

Internal communication.

12. The official language is the language of internal communication in the public administration.

Organismes municipaux et scolaires.

13. Le français et l'anglais sont les langues de communication interne des organismes municipaux et scolaires dont les administrés sont en majorité de langue anglaise.

Choix.

Ces organismes communiquent en français ou en anglais avec les autres gouvernements et avec les personnes morales.

Détermination.

Le titre IV précise la façon dont sont déterminés les organismes municipaux susvisés.

Languages in municipal and school bodies.

13. French and English are the languages of internal communication in municipal and school bodies in which the majority of the persons administered are English-speaking.

Option.

Such bodies shall communicate in French or in English with other governments and with moral persons.

How determined.

Title IV specifies the manner in which the municipal and school bodies contemplated above are determined.

Nomination à une fonction administrative.

14. Nul ne peut être nommé, muté ou promu à une fonction administrative dans l'administration publique s'il n'a de la

Knowledge for appointment, etc.

14. No one shall be appointed, transferred or promoted to an administrative office in the public administration unless langue officielle une connaissance appropriée à l'emploi qu'il postule.

Normes. Cette connaissance doit être prouvée suivant les normes fixées par les règlements adoptés à cet égard par le lieutenant-gouverneur en conseil.

Détermination de fonctions. Les fonctions susdites sont déterminées par les règlements visés au deuxième alinéa; ceux-ci peuvent cependant exclure de l'application du présent article les fonctions n'entraînant pas de contacts directs avec le public.

Exception. Le présent article ne s'applique pas aux organismes visés à l'article 13.

Intervention dans débats officiels. **15.** En assemblée délibérante dans l'administration publique, les interventions dans les débats officiels peuvent être faites en langue française ou en langue anglaise, au choix de ceux qui interviennent.

Traduction des jugements. **16.** Le ministre de la justice doit faire en sorte que les jugements prononcés en anglais par les tribunaux soient traduits dans la langue officielle.

Langue des contrats. **17.** Les contrats conclus au Québec par l'administration publique ainsi que les sous-contrats qui s'y rattachent doivent être rédigés dans la langue officielle; ils peuvent aussi être rédigés à la fois en français et en anglais ou, lorsque l'administration publique contracte avec l'étranger, à la fois en français et dans la langue du pays intéressé.

CHAPITRE II

LA LANGUE DES ENTREPRISES D'UTILITÉ PUBLIQUE ET DES PROFESSIONS

Services offerts en français **18.** Les entreprises d'utilité publique et les corporations professionnelles doivent faire en sorte que leurs services soient offerts au public dans la langue officielle.

Langue de communication avec administration publique. **19.** Les entreprises d'utilité publique et les corporations professionnelles doivent utiliser la langue officielle pour s'adresser à l'administration publique.

Langue des avis, etc. **20.** Les entreprises d'utilité publique et les corporations professionnelles doivent

his knowledge of the official language is appropriate to the employment sought.

Such knowledge must be proved by application of the standards established by the regulations made to that effect by the Lieutenant-Governor in Council. Standards.

The offices mentioned above shall be determined by the regulations contemplated in the second paragraph; those regulations may, however, exclude from the application of this section offices which do not entail direct contact with the public. Offices determined by regulations.

This section does not apply to bodies contemplated in section 13. Exception.

15. Remarks addressed to the chair at formal discussions held within the public administration may be made in the French language or in the English language, at the option of the persons addressing the remarks. Option for remarks to chair.

16. The Minister of Justice must see to it that judgments pronounced by the courts in English are translated into the official language. Translation of judgments.

17. Contracts formed in the province of Québec by the public administration, and the related sub-contracts, must be drawn up in the official language; they may also be drawn up in both French and English, or, when the public administration contracts with a foreign party, in both French and the language of the interested country. Language of contracts.

CHAPTER II

THE LANGUAGE OF PUBLIC UTILITIES AND PROFESSIONAL BODIES

18. Public utilities and professional corporations must see to it that their services are offered to the public in the official language. Services offered in French.

19. Public utilities and professional corporations must use the official language when addressing the public administration. Addressing public administration.

20. Notices, communications, forms and printed matter issued by public Notices, etc., in French.

émettre dans la langue officielle les avis, communications, formulaires et imprimés qu'elles destinent au public; le présent article s'applique également aux titres de transport.

Version anglaise. Les textes et documents susdits peuvent néanmoins être accompagnés d'une version anglaise.

Connaissance d'usage du français pour permis. **21.** Nulle corporation professionnelle ne peut délivrer un permis à une personne qui n'a pas une connaissance d'usage de la langue française déterminée suivant les normes établies à cette fin par règlement du lieutenant-gouverneur en conseil.

Permis temporaire. **22.** Une corporation professionelle peut toutefois délivrer un permis temporaire valable pour une période d'un an à une personne qui n'a pas la connaissance d'usage de la langue française requise suivant l'article 21. Elle ne peut renouveler un tel permis qu'avec l'autorisation du lieutenant-gouverneur en conseil, lorsque l'intérêt public le requiert.

Permis restrictif. **23.** Une corporation professionelle peut délivrer à un citoyen canadien qui est membre d'une semblable corporation d'une autre province et qui n'a pas la connaissance d'usage de la langue française requise suivant l'article 21 un permis restrictif, qui autorise son détenteur à exercer sa profession exclusivement pour le compte d'un seul employeur dans une fonction ne l'amenant pas à traiter directement avec le public.

CHAPITRE III

LA LANGUE DU TRAVAIL

Avis, etc., en français. **24.** Les employeurs doivent rédiger en français les avis, communications et directives qu'ils adressent à leur personnel.

Version anglaise. Les textes et documents susdits peuvent cependant être accompagnés d'une version anglaise lorsque le personnel est en partie de langue anglaise.

Langue des relations du travail. **25.** Le français est la langue des relations du travail, dans la mesure et suivant les modalités prévues au Code du travail.

utilities and professional corporations and intended for the public must be in the official language; this section also applies to passenger tickets and bills of lading.

The texts and documents mentioned above may nevertheless be accompanied with an English version. English version.

21. No professional corporation shall issue a permit to a person who does not have a working-knowledge of the French language determined in accordance with the standards established for that purpose by regulation of the Lieutenant-Governor in Council. Working-knowledge prior to issue of permit.

22. A professional corporation may however issue a temporary permit valid for one year to a person who does not have the working-knowledge of the French language required in accordance with section 21. It shall not renew such a permit except with the authorization of the Lieutenant-Governor in Council, when the public interest requires it. Temporary permit.

23. A professional corporation may issue, to a Canadian citizen who is a member of a similar corporation of another province and who does not have the working-knowledge of the French language required in accordance with section 21, a restrictive permit which authorizes its holder to practise his profession for the exclusive account of one employer in a function which does not lead him to deal directly with the public. Restrictive permit.

CHAPTER III

THE LANGUAGE OF THE LABOUR FIELD

24. Employers must draw up in French the notices, communications and directions addressed to their personnel. Notices, etc., in French.

The texts and documents mentioned above may however be accompanied with an English version when the personnel are partly English speaking. English version.

25. French is the language of labour relations, to the extent and in accordance with the terms and conditions provided in the Labour Code. French in labour relations.

Certificats attestant programmes de francisation.

26. Le lieutenant-gouverneur en conseil pourvoit, par règlement, à l'émission de certificats en faveur des entreprises, attestant qu'elles ont adopté et qu'elles appliquent un programme de francisation conformément aux articles 29 et 39 ou que la langue française y possède déjà le statut que ces programmes ont pour objet d'assurer.

Catégories d'entreprises.

Ces règlements établissent des catégories d'entreprises suivant leur genre d'activités, l'importance de leur personnel, l'ampleur des programmes à adopter et les autres éléments pertinents; ils déterminent aussi, pour chacune des catégories ainsi établies, la date à laquelle le certificat susdit devient exigible pour l'application de l'article 28.

Demande d'élaboration de programme.

27. La Régie peut demander à toute entreprise qui ne possède pas le certificat visé à l'article 26 de procéder à l'élaboration et à l'implantation d'un programme de francisation.

Rapport au ministre.

La Régie doit faire chaque année au ministre un rapport des demandes qu'elle a ainsi faites et des mesures prises par les entreprises à la suite de ses demandes.

Certificat requis pour obtenir primes, etc.

28. Outre les exigences de toute autre loi, les entreprises doivent posséder le certificat visé à l'article 26 pour avoir le droit de recevoir de l'administration publique, à compter de la date fixée conformément audit article, les primes, subventions, concessions ou avantages déterminés par les règlements, ou pour conclure avec le gouvernement les contrats d'achat, de service, de location ou de travaux publics aussi déterminés par les règlements.

Certificats provisoires.

Ces règlements peuvent prévoir l'émission de certificats provisoires tenant lieu du certificat prévu au premier alinéa, en faveur d'entreprises qui se proposent d'adopter le programme de francisation susvisé, si elles démontrent qu'elles ont pris les dispositions voulues à cet effet.

Portée du programme de francisation.

29. Les programmes de francisation que doivent adopter et appliquer les entreprises désireuses d'obtenir le certificat susdit doivent, compte tenu de la situation et de la structure de chaque entreprise, de son siège social et de ses filiales et succursales, porter notamment sur:

Certificates attesting francization program.

26. The Lieutenant-Governor in Council shall, by regulation, provide for the issue of certificates to business firms attesting that they have adopted and are applying a francization program in accordance with sections 29 and 39 or that the status of the French language within their firms is already that envisaged by such programs.

Class of business firms.

Such regulations shall establish classes of business firms on the basis of their kinds of activities, the size of their personnel, the breadth of the programs to be adopted and other relevant particulars; they shall also determine, for each class so established, the date on which the certificates mentioned above become exigible for the application of section 28.

Request to take up program.

27. The Régie may request any business firm which does not have the certificate contemplated in section 26 to take up the elaboration and implementation of a francization program.

Report to Minister.

The Régie must each year make a report to the Minister of the requests it has so made and of the steps taken by the business firms pursuant to such requests.

Certificates prior requisite for premiums, etc.

28. In addition to the requirements of any other act, business firms must have the certificates contemplated in section 26 in order to be entitled to receive the premiums, subsidies, concessions or benefits from the public administration determined by regulation, or to make with the government the contracts of purchase, service, lease or public works also determined by regulation, from the date fixed in accordance with that section.

Provisional certificates.

Such regulations may provide for the issue of provisional certificates in lieu of the certificates provided for in the first paragraph to business firms which plan to adopt the francization program contemplated above if they show that they have made the required provisions to that effect.

Scope of francization programs.

29. The francization programs which must be adopted and applied by business firms wishing to obtain the certificates mentioned above, must, while taking account of the situation and structure of each firm, of its head office and of its subsidiaries and branches, relate especially to:

a) la connaissance de la langue officielle que doivent posséder les dirigeants et le personnel;

b) la présence francophone dans l'administration;

c) la langue des manuels, des catalogues, des instructions écrites et des autres documents distribués au personnel;

d) les dispositions que doivent prendre les entreprises pour que les membres de leur personnel puissent, dans leur travail, communiquer en français entre eux et avec leurs supérieurs;

e) la terminologie employée.

Objectifs. Les programmes susdits doivent aussi rechercher les objectifs visés à l'article 39.

CHAPITRE IV

LA LANGUE DES AFFAIRES

Langue des raisons sociales. **30.** La personnalité juridique ne peut être conférée à moins que la raison sociale adoptée ne soit en langue française. Les raisons sociales peuvent néanmoins être accompagnées d'une version anglaise.

Modifications. La modification des raisons sociales est soumise aux mêmes règles. Il en est de même de l'enregistrement des raisons sociales effectué en vertu de la Loi des déclarations des compagnies et sociétés (Statuts refondus, 1964, chapitre 272).

Noms propres, etc. **31.** Peuvent figurer dans les raisons sociales, conformément aux autres lois, les noms propres ou les expressions formées de la combinaison artificielle de lettres, de syllabes ou de chiffres.

Raisons sociales françaises. **32.** Les raisons sociales françaises doivent ressortir, ou à tout le moins figurer dans les textes et documents d'une manière aussi avantageuse que les versions anglaises.

Langue des contrats d'adhésion, etc. **33.** Doivent être rédigés en français les contrats d'adhésion, les contrats où figurent des clauses-types imprimées ainsi que les bons de commande, les factures et les reçus imprimés.

En anglais sur demande. Ces documents doivent cependant être rédigés en anglais lorsque le client ou la

(*a*) the knowledge that the management and the personel must have of the official language;

(*b*) the francophone presence in management;

(*c*) the language in which the manuals, catalogues, written instructions and other documents distributed to the personnel must be drawn up;

(*d*) the provisions that the business firms must make for communication in French by the members of their personnel, in their work, among themselves and with their superior officers;

(*e*) the terminology employed.

The programs mentioned above must also pursue the objectives contemplated in section 39. Objectives.

CHAPTER IV

THE LANGUAGE OF BUSINESS

30. Juridical personality shall not be conferred unless the adopted firm name is in the French language. Firm names may nevertheless be accompanied with an English version. French obligatory for firm name.

Changes of firm names are subject to the sames rules. The same applies to the registration of firm names effected in virtue of the Companies and Partnerships Declaration Act (Revised Statutes, 1964, chapter 272). Changes of firm names.

31. Proper names or expressions formed by the artificial combination of letters, syllables or figures may appear in firm names, in conformity with the law. Proper names, etc.

32. The French firm names must stand out or at least figure no less prominently in the texts and documents than their English versions. French firm names.

33. Contracts pre-determined by one party, contracts containing printed standard clauses, and printed order forms, invoices and receipts must be drawn up in French. Contracts pre-determined by one party, etc.

Such documents must however be drawn up in English when the customer or the English upon request.

personne qui adhère au contrat l'exige.

Inter-prétation. Tout contrat rédigé en français et en anglais est conforme au présent article. Au cas de contradiction entre les deux textes, l'interprétation la plus favorable au client ou à la personne qui adhère au contrat prévaut.

Étiquetage des produits, etc. **34.** L'étiquetage des produits doit se faire en français, sauf dans la mesure prévue par les règlements; il en est de même des certificats de garantie et des notices qui accompagnent les produits, ainsi que des menus et cartes de vins.

Infraction et peine. Quiconque contrevient au présent article est passible, sur poursuite sommaire intentée par le procureur général ou par une personne qu'il autorise, en outre des frais,

a) pour une première infraction, d'une amende d'au moins $25 et d'au plus $500, dans le cas d'un individu, et d'au moins $50 et d'au plus $1,000 dans le cas d'une corporation;

b) pour toute récidive dans les deux ans, d'une amende de $3,000 dans le cas d'un individu, et de $5,000, dans le cas d'une corporation.

Poursuites sommaires. La deuxième partie de la Loi des poursuites sommaires s'applique à ces poursuites.

Affichage public, etc. **35.** L'affichage public doit se faire en français, ou à la fois en français et dans une autre langue, sauf dans la mesure prévue par les règlements. Le présent article s'applique également aux annonces publicitaires écrites, notamment aux panneaux-réclame et aux enseignes lumineuses.

Disposition non applicable. **36.** L'article 35 ne s'applique pas aux annonces publicitaires paraissant dans des journaux ou périodiques publiés dans une autre langue que le français.

Délai pour se conformer. **37.** Les propriétaires de panneaux-réclame ou d'enseignes lumineuses installés avant le 31 juillet 1974 disposent, à compter de ladite date, d'un délai de cinq ans pour se conformer à l'article 35.

Enlèvement d'annonces. **38.** Tout tribunal de juridiction civile peut, à la demande du procureur général

person who accedes to the contract so requires.

Every contract drawn up in French and English conforms to this section. In the case of contradiction between the two texts, the interpretation more favourable to the client or the person who accepts the contract prevails. Interpretation of contract.

34. Products must be labelled in French, except within certain limits provided by regulation; the same applies to the warranty certificates and directions supplied with products, and to menus and wine lists. Products, etc., to be labelled in French.

Every person who contravenes this section is liable, on summary proceedings instituted by the Attorney-General or by the person authorized by him, in addition to the costs, Offence and penalty.

(*a*) for the first offence, to a fine of not less than $25 nor more than $500, in the case of an individual, and of not less than $50 nor more than $1,000 in the case of a corporation;

(*b*) for any subsequent offence within two years, to a fine of $3,000 in the case of an individual, and of $5,000 in the case of a corporation.

Part II of the Summary Convictions Act applies to such proceedings. Procedure.

35. Public signs must be drawn up in French or in both French and another language, except within certain limits provided by regulation. This section also applies to advertisements in writing, in particular to bill-boards and electric signs. Public signs, etc.

36. Section 35 does not apply to advertisements appearing in newspapers or periodicals published in a language other than French. Provision not to apply.

37. Owners of bill-boards or electric signs erected before 31 July 1974 shall have a delay of five years from that date to comply with section 35. Delay for owners to comply.

38. Any court of civil jurisdiction may on a demand brought by the Attorney- Order for removal, etc.

formulée par voie de requête, ordonner que soient enlevés ou détruits dans un délai de huit jours à compter du jugement, les annonces, notamment les panneaux-réclame et les enseignes lumineuses, contrevenant aux dispositions de la présente loi, et ce, aux frais des intimés.

Personne visée. La requête peut être dirigée contre l'annonceur ou contre quiconque a placé ou fait placer l'annonce.

Portée du programme de francisation. **39.** Le programme de francisation adopté par toute entreprise désireuse d'obtenir le certificat visé aux articles 26 et 28 doit, compte tenu de la situation et de la structure de chaque entreprise, de son siège social et de ses filiales et succursales, porter en outre sur:

a) la raison sociale de l'entreprise;

b) la langue dans laquelle l'entreprise doit, dans le cours normal de ses affaires, répondre à ses clients et aux personnes qui s'adressent à elle;

c) la langue dans laquelle doivent être rédigés les avis, communications, certificats et formulaires destinés au public ou aux actionnaires ou membres de l'entreprise qui résident au Québec.

CHAPITRE V

LA LANGUE DE L'ENSEIGNEMENT

Enseignement en français. **40.** L'enseignement se donne en langue française dans les écoles régies par les commissions scolaires, les commissions scolaires régionales et les corporations de syndics.

Enseignement continueé en anglais. Les commissions scolaires, les commissions scolaires régionales et les corporations de syndics continuent de donner l'enseignement en langue anglaise.

Autorisation pour commencer, etc., l'enseignement en anglais. Une commission scolaire, une commission scolaire régionale ou une corporation de syndics actuelle ou future ne peut valablement prendre la décision de commencer, de cesser, d'accroître ou de réduire l'enseignement en langue anglaise à moins d'avoir obtenu l'autorisation préalable du ministre de l'éducation, lequel ne la donne que s'il est d'avis que le nombre d'élèves de langue maternelle anglaise relevant de la compétence de l'organisme le justifie; lorsqu'il s'agit de cesser ou de réduire cet ensei-

General by way of a motion, order the removal or destruction within eight days of the judgment, of any advertisement, particularly a bill-board or electric sign, which contravenes this act, at the expense of the respondent.

The motion may be directed against the advertiser or against whoever placed the advertisement or had it placed. Person affected.

39. The francization program adopted by any business firm wishing to obtain the certificate contemplated in sections 26 and 28 must, while taking account of the situation and structure of each firm, of its head office and of its subsidiaries and branches, also relate to: Scope of francization program.

(*a*) the firm name of the business;

(*b*) the language in which the firm must carry on its day-to-day dealings with its customers and other persons;

(*c*) the language in which notices, communications, certificates and forms intended for the public, or for the shareholders or members of the firm resident in the province of Québec, must de drawn up.

CHAPTER V

THE LANGUAGE OF INSTRUCTION

40. The language of instruction shall be French in the schools governed by the school boards, the regional school boards and the corporations of trustees. Language of instruction.

The school boards, regional school boards and corporations of trustees shall continue to provide instruction in English. English to be continued.

An existing or future school board, regional school board or corporation of trustees cannot validly decide to commence, cease, increase or reduce instruction in English unless it has received prior authorization from the Minister of Education, who shall not give it unless he considers that the number of pupils whose mother tongue is English and who are under the jurisdiction of such body warrants it; in the case of cessation or reduction of such instruction, the Minister shall Authorization to commence, etc., English instruction.

gnement, le ministre tient aussi compte, en donnant son autorisation, du nombre d'élèves autrement admissibles.

Indiens et Inuits.

Néanmoins, la Commission scolaire du Nouveau-Québec peut donner l'enseignement, dans leurs langues, aux Indiens et aux Inuits.

Connaissance de la langue.

41. Les élèves doivent connaître suffisamment la langue d'enseignenent pour recevoir l'enseignement dans cette langue.

Français à défaut de connaissance suffisante.

Les élèves qui ne connaissent suffisamment aucune des langues d'enseignement reçoivent l'enseignement en langue française.

Classe, etc., d'intégration.

42. Il appartient à chaque commission scolaire, commission scolaire régionale et corporation de syndics de déterminer la classe, le groupe ou le cours auquel un élève peut être intégré, eu égard à ses aptitudes dans la langue d'enseignement.

Tests pour vérifier connaissance suffisante.

43. Le ministre de l'éducation peut cependant, conformément aux règlements, imposer des tests pour s'assurer que les élèves ont une connaissance suffisante de la langue d'enseignement pour recevoir l'enseignement dans cette langue. Il peut, le cas échéant, exiger qu'une commission scolaire, une commission scolaire régionale ou une corporation de syndics révise l'intégration des élèves conformément aux résultats de ces tests.

Portée des tests.

Ces tests doivent tenir compte des niveaux d'enseignement, y compris la maternelle, pour lesquels les demandes d'inscription sont faites, ainsi que de l'âge et du niveau de formation des candidats.

Appel au ministre.

Les règlements doivent prévoir un appel au ministre qui doit, avant d'en disposer, prendre l'avis d'une commission de surveillance de la langue d'enseignement instituée à cette fin. La décision du ministre est sans appel.

Connaissance du français assurée par programmes.

44. Les programmes d'études doivent assurer la connaissance de la langue française, parlée et écrite, aux élèves qui reçoivent l'enseignement en langue anglaise, et le ministre de l'éducation doit prendre les mesures nécessaires à cet effet.

Anglais langue seconde.

Le ministre de l'éducation doit également prendre les mesures nécessaires pour

also take into account, when giving his authorization, the number of pupils otherwise qualified.

Indians and Inuits.

Nevertheless, the School Board of New Québec may provide instruction to the Indians and Inuits in their own languages.

Sufficient knowledge.

41. Pupils must have a sufficient knowledge of the language of instruction to receive their instruction in that language.

French when knowledge. insufficient.

Pupils who do not have a sufficient knowledge of any of the languages of instruction must receive their instruction in French.

School board, etc., to determine class, etc.

42. It is the function of each school board, regional school board and corporation of trustees to determine to what class, group or course any pupil may be assigned, having regard to his aptitudes in the language of instruction.

Tests to ascertain sufficient knowledge.

43. The Minister of Education may however, in accordance with the regulations, set tests to ascertain that the pupils have sufficient knowledge of the language of instruction to receive their instruction in that language. He may, if need be, require a school board, regional school board or corporation of trustees to reassign the pupils on the basis of the results of those tests.

Scope of tests.

Such tests must take account of the levels of instruction, including kindergarten, for which the applications for enrolment are made, and of the age and previous education of the examinees.

Appeal to Minister.

The regulations must provide for an appeal to the Minister, who, before deciding the matter, must obtain the advice of a supervisory committee on the language of instruction established for that purpose. His decision is final.

Curricula to ensure knowledge of French.

44. The curricula must ensure that pupils receiving their instruction in English acquire a knowledge of spoken and written French, and the Minister of Education shall adopt the necessary measures to that effect.

English as second language.

The Minister of Education must also take the necessary measures to ensure

assurer l'enseignement de la langue anglaise, langue seconde, aux élèves qui reçoivent l'enseignement en langue française.

CHAPITRE VI

DISPOSITIONS DIVERSES

Avis seulement en français.

45. Les avis émanant de l'administration publique et dont une loi prescrit la publication en français et en anglais peuvent néanmoins être publiés uniquement en français.

Publication dans journal français.

De même, les avis émanant de l'administration publique et dont une loi prescrit la publication dans un journal français et dans un journal anglais peuvent être publiés uniquement dans un journal français.

Règles non applicables.

Toutefois, ces règles ne s'appliquent pas aux organismes municipaux et scolaires visés à l'article 9. Au cas de fusion, le troisième alinéa dudit article 9 s'applique également au présent article.

Portée du titre IV.

Le titre IV précise la façon dont sont déterminés les organismes municipaux et scolaires susvisés.

Qualité de la version française.

46. La version française des textes et documents visés par la présente loi doit ressortir, ou à tout le moins figurer d'une manière au moins aussi avantageuse que toute version dans une autre langue.

Cas où la version française prévaut.

47. Sous réserve de l'article 33, lorsque des textes peuvent ou doivent, en vertu de la loi, être rédigés à la fois en français et dans une autre langue, alors que la version française n'est pas la seule authentique, et qu'il y a divergence entre les deux versions sans qu'il soit possible de la résoudre au moyen des règles ordinaires d'interprétation, la version française prévaut sur l'autre.

Emprunts de prêteurs étrangers.

48. Les articles 6, 8, 17 et 47 ne s'appliquent pas aux emprunts contractés par l'administration publique auprès de prêteurs dont le domicile ou le siège social est situé hors du Canada, ni aux documents qui les autorisent, les constatent ou s'y rattachent, sans égard au lieu de la passation, de la signature ou de l'émission de ces contrats et documents.

instruction in English as a second language to pupils whose language of instruction is French.

CHAPTER VI

MISCELLANEOUS

Notices in French only.

45. Notices emanating from the public administration and required by law to be published in French and English may nevertheless be published only in French.

Notices in French newspaper.

Similarly, notices emanating from the public administration and required by law to be published in a French newspaper and an English newspaper may be published only in a French newspaper.

Rules not to apply.

These rules do not apply, however, to municipal and school bodies contemplated in section 9. In the case of an amalgamation or union, the third paragraph of such section 9 also applies to this section.

Scope of Title IV.

Title IV specifies the manner in which the municipal and school bodies contemplated above are determined.

French version to stand out.

46. The French version of the texts and documents contemplated by this act must stand out, or at least figure no less prominently than any version in another language.

French version to prevail.

47. Subject to section 33, where texts may or must by law be drawn up in both French and another language, the French version not being the only authentic one, and any discrepancy between the two versions cannot be satisfactorily resolved by the ordinary rules of interpretation, the French version prevails over the other.

Provisions not to apply to loans with foreign lenders.

48. Sections 6, 8, 17 and 47 do not apply to loans contracted by the public administration with a lender whose domicile or head office is situated outside Canada, nor to the documents authorizing or authenticating them or attached thereto, regardless of where such contracts and documents are entered into, signed or issued.

Usage d'une autre langue. Rien n'empêche l'emploi d'une langue en dérogation avec la présente loi afin de se conformer aux usages internationaux.

Use of other language. Nothing shall prevent the use of a language in derogation of this act where international usage requires it.

TITRE IV

LES MÉCANISMES DE CONTRÔLE ET D'EXÉCUTION

TITLE IV

MACHINERY FOR SUPERVISION AND ENFORCEMENT

CHAPITRE I

LA RECHERCHE EN MATIÈRE LINGUISTIQUE — LES COMMISSIONS DE TERMINOLOGIE

CHAPTER I

LINGUISTICS RESEARCH — TERMINOLOGY COMMITTEES

Responsabilité du ministre. **49.** Le ministre a pour responsabilité de développer la recherche en matière linguistique et de coordonner les activités de recherche en cette matière au Québec.

Responsibility of Minister. **49.** It shall be the responsibility of the Minister to develop research in linguistics and to coordinate linguistics research in the province of Québec.

Commission de terminologie. **50.** Le lieutenant-gouverneur en conseil peut, par règlement, instituer des commissions de terminologie, dont il détermine la composition et les modalités de fonctionnement, et les déléguer auprès des divers ministères et organismes de l'administration publique.

Terminology committees. **50.** The Lieutenant-Governor in Council may by regulation establish terminology committees, determine their composition and their terms and conditions of operation, and attach them to the various departments and agencies of the public administration.

Mission. **51.** Les commissions de terminologie ont pour mission de faire l'inventaire des mots techniques employés dans le secteur qui leur est assigné, d'indiquer les lacunes qu'elles trouvent et de dresser la liste des termes qu'elles préconisent, notamment en matière de néologismes et d'emprunts.

Mandate. **51.** The mandate of the terminology committees shall be to make an inventory of the technical expressions in use in the sector assigned to them, to indicate any lacunae that become apparent, and to prepare a list of the terms they recommend, particularly in the field of neologisms and borrowings.

Conclusion à la Régie. **52.** Dès leurs travaux terminés, les commissions de terminologie soumettent leurs conclusions à l'approbation de la Régie, qui doit veiller à la normalisation des termes employés.

Listes des expressions normalisées. Les expressions et les termes normalisés sont adressés aux ministres ou aux directions des organismes intéressés qui peuvent les entériner et en dresser la liste.

Approval of conclusions, etc. **52.** Once their work has been completed, the terminology committees shall submit their conclusions to the Board for approval, and it must see to the standardizing of the usage of the terms.

List of standardized expressions, etc. The standardized expressions and terms shall be forwarded to the ministers or to the managing officers of the interested agencies, and they may confirm them and prepare a list of them.

Emploi obligatoire sur publication. **53.** Sur publication de la liste visée à l'article 52 dans la *Gazette officielle du Québec*, l'emploi des expressions et termes y figurant devient obligatoire dans les textes et documents émanant de l'administration publique, dans les contrats dont l'administration publique est partie ainsi

Use of list obligatory upon publication. **53.** Upon publication in the *Québec Official Gazette* of the list contemplated in section 52, the use of the expressions and terms appearing in it shall become obligatory in texts and documents emanating from the public administration, in contracts to which the public adminis-

que dans les ouvrages d'enseignement, de formation ou de recherche publiés en français au Québec et approuvés par le ministre de l'éducation.

tration is a party and in teaching manuals and educational and research works published in French in the province of Québec and approved by the Minister of Education.

CHAPITRE II

LA RÉGIE DE LA LANGUE FRANÇAISE

SECTION I

CRÉATION ET FONCTIONS DE LA RÉGIE

Institution.

54. Il est institué une Régie de la langue française.

Rôle.

55. La Régie a pour rôle:

a) de donner son avis au ministre sur les règlements prévus par la présente loi, à l'exception des règlements visés à l'article 43 qui doivent être soumis à l'examen du Conseil supérieur de l'éducation;

b) de veiller à la correction et à l'enrichissement de la langue parlée et écrite;

c) de donner son avis au gouvernement sur les questions que celui-ci lui soumet;

d) de reconnaître, pour l'application des articles 9, 13 et 45, les organismes municipaux et scolaires visés à l'article 9 ou à l'article 13;

e) de mener les enquêtes prévues par la présente loi afin de vérifier si les lois et les règlements relatifs à la langue française sont observés;

f) de donner son avis au ministre sur l'attribution, par le ministre, des crédits destinés à la recherche en linguistique et à la diffusion de la langue française;

g) de collaborer avec les entreprises à l'élaboration et la mise en oeuvre de programmes de francisation;

h) de délivrer les certificats visés aux articles 26 et 28;

i) de normaliser le vocabulaire utilisé au Québec et d'approuver les expressions et les termes recommandés par les commissions de terminologie.

Pouvoirs.

56. La Régie peut:

a) solliciter des avis, recevoir et entendre les requêtes et suggestions du public concernant le statut de la langue française;

CHAPTER II

THE "RÉGIE DE LA LANGUE FRANÇAISE"

DIVISION I

ESTABLISHMENT AND FUNCTIONS

54. A *Régie de la langue française* is established.

Régie established.

55. The functions of the Régie are:

Functions.

(*a*) to give its opinion to the Minister on the regulations provided for by this act, except those contemplated in section 43 which must be submitted for study to the Superior Council of Education;

(*b*) to see to the correction and enrichment of the spoken and written language;

(*c*) to advise the government on questions submitted by it to the Régie;

(*d*) to recognize, for the purposes of sections 9, 13 and 45, the municipal and school bodies contemplated in section 9 or in section 13;

(*e*) to conduct the inquiries contemplated by this act in order to ascertain whether the statutes and regulations regarding the French language are observed;

(*f*) to advise the Minister on the allocation by him of appropriations to linguistics research and to the dissemination of the French language;

(*g*) to cooperate with business firms in elaborating and implementing francization programs;

(*h*) to issue the certificates contemplated in sections 26 and 28;

(*i*) to standardize the usage of vocabulary in the province of Québec and to approve the expressions and terms recommended by the terminology committees.

56. The Régie may:

Powers.

(*a*) solicit opinions and receive and hear petitions and suggestions from the public regarding the status of the French language;

b) soumettre au ministre des recommandations sur toute question concernant la langue française;

c) faire effectuer les études et recherches qu'elle juge utiles ou nécessaires à l'accomplissement de sa tâche;

d) moyennant l'approbation du lieutenant-gouverneur en conseil, se donner des règlements internes;

e) établir par règlement les services et les comités nécessaires à l'accomplissement de sa tâche;

f) avec l'approbation du lieutenant-gouverneur en conseil, conclure des ententes avec tout autre organisme ou tout gouvernement afin de faciliter l'application de la présente loi.

(*b*) submit recommendations to the Minister on any matter regarding the French language;

(*c*) have any study or research done which it considers expedient or necessary for the attainment of its purposes;

(*d*) subject to approval by the Lieutenant-Governor in Council, adopt internal by-laws;

(*e*) establish by by-law the services and committees necessary for the attainment of its purposes;

(*f*) with the approval of the Lieutenant-Governor in Council, make agreements with any other agency or government to facilitate the application of this act.

Concours des services.

57. Le lieutenant-gouverneur en conseil peut, par règlement, prescrire les mesures que les services de l'administration publique doivent prendre pour apporter leur concours à la Régie.

Assistance by services.

57. The Lieutenant-Governor in Council may prescribe, by regulation, the measures by which the services of the public administration must lend their assistance to the Régie.

Soumission à la Régie.

58. Les entreprises qui adoptent un programme visé aux articles 29 et 39 le soumettent à la Régie.

Approbation de la demande.

Si la Régie est d'avis que le programme est suffisant pour la réalisation des objectifs recherchés et que l'entreprise l'applique efficacement, elle transmet la demande au ministre pour son approbation.

Recommandations.

Si elle est d'avis que le programme n'est pas suffisant ou que l'entreprise ne l'applique pas efficacement, elle doit faire des recommandations au ministre sur les améliorations qu'elle juge nécessaires.

Submission of program.

58. Business firms which adopt a program contemplated in sections 29 and 39 shall submit it to the Régie.

Approval of application.

If the Régie considers that the program is adequate to the desired objectives and that it is being effectively applied by the firm, it shall forward the application to the Minister for his approval.

Recommendations.

If it considers that the program is inadequate or that it is not being effectively applied by the firm, it must make recommendations to the Minister on the improvements it believes necessary.

Certificat.

59. La Régie délivre le certificat susvisé après approbation du ministre.

Retrait.

La Régie peut, avec l'accord du ministre et pour des raisons valables, retirer le certificat.

Certificate.

59. The Régie shall issue the certificate contemplated above after approval by the Minister.

Revocation.

With the approval of the Minister and for valid cause, the Régie may revoke the certificate.

Nombre d'administrés de langue anglaise.

60. La Régie établit tous les trois ans, pour chaque organisme municipal et scolaire, le nombre d'administrés de langue anglaise. Elle utilise, pour ce faire, les statistiques disponibles, les archives et documents des organismes en question et les autres renseignements qu'elle peut obtenir.

Publication.

Elle publie alors dans la *Gazette officielle du Québec*, en se basant sur les renseigne-

Number of English-speaking to be ascertained.

60. Every three years, the Régie shall ascertain the number of English-speaking persons administered in each municipal and school body. For that purpose, it shall consult the available statistics, the records and documents of the bodies in question and any other information it may obtain.

Publication.

On the basis of the information so acquired, it shall then publish, in the

ments ainsi obtenus, une liste des corps municipaux et scolaires visés à l'article 9 et une liste de ceux visés à l'article 13.

Critère d'application. Ces listes, qui sont incontestables, servent d'unique critère pour l'application des articles 9, 13 et 45.

Révision de décision. La Régie peut, pour cause, réviser toute décision qu'elle a rendue en vertu du présent article, à la demande de toute personne intéressée.

Québec Official Gazette, a list of the municipal and school bodies contemplated in section 9 and a list of those contemplated in section 13.

These lists shall be incontestable and shall be the sole criterion for the application of sections 9, 13 and 45. Lists incontestable.

The Régie, for cause, upon the application of any interested person, may review any decision it has rendered under this section. Review of decision.

SECTION II

COMPOSITION ET ACTIVITÉS DE LA RÉGIE

Membres. **61.** La Régie est composée de neuf membres, dont le président et deux vice-présidents, nommés par le lieutenant-gouverneur en conseil.

Mandat. Le président et les vice-présidents sont nommés pour au plus dix ans et les autres membres pour au plus cinq ans.

Honoraires, etc. **62.** Le lieutenant-gouverneur en conseil fixe les honoraires, les allocations ou le traitement du président et des vice-présidents de la Régie ou, le cas échéant, leur traitement supplémentaire.

Indemnisation. Les autres membres ne sont pas rémunérés. Toutefois, ils ont droit au remboursement des frais justifiables engagés par eux dans l'exercice de leurs fonctions et ils reçoivent une allocation de présence fixée par le lieutenant-gouverneur en conseil.

Serments. **63.** Les membres de la Régie doivent, avant de commencer à exercer leurs fonctions, prêter les serments prévus aux annexes A et B de la Loi de la fonction publique.

Incompatibilité. **64.** La qualité de président ou de vice-président de la Régie est incompatible avec l'exercice de toute autre fonction.

Remplacement du président. **65.** Au cas d'incapacité d'agir du président, ses pouvoirs sont exercés par le vice-président qu'il désigne ou, si le président est incapable de faire cette désignation, par le vice-président désigné par le lieutenant-gouverneur en conseil.

DIVISION II

COMPOSITION AND OPERATIONS OF THE RÉGIE

61. The Régie is composed of nine members, including the president and two vice-presidents, appointed by the Lieutenant-Governor in Council. Composition.

The president and the vice-presidents shall be appointed for not more than ten years and the other members for not more than five years. Terms.

62. The Lieutenant-Governor in Council shall determine the fees, allowances or salaries of the president and the vice-presidents of the Régie, or, as the case may be, their additional salaries. Fees, allowances, etc.

The other members shall not be remunerated. They are entitled however to reimbursement of their justifiable expenses in the exercise of their functions and they shall receive an attendance allowance fixed by the Lieutenant-Governor in Council. No remuneration for other members.

63. Before entering on their functions, the members of the Régie shall take the oaths provided in Schedules A and B to the Civil Service Act. Oaths.

64. The office of president or vice-president of the Régie is incompatible with any other office. Incompatible office.

65. If the president is unable to act, his powers shall be exercised by the vice-president designated by him, or, if he is unable to make such designation, by the vice-president designated by the Lieutenant-Governor in Council. Replacement of president.

Fonctions continuées.

66. Nonobstant l'expiration de leur mandat, les membres de la Régie restent en fonction jusqu'à ce qu'ils soient nommés de nouveau ou remplacés.

Term continued.

66. Notwithstanding the expiry of their term, the members of the Régie shall remain in office until they are reappointed or replaced.

Intérêt personnel.

67. Les membres de la Régie ne peuvent prendre part aux délibérations sur une question dans laquelle ils ont un intérêt personnel.

Décision de la Régie.

La Régie décide s'ils ont un intérêt personnel dans la question; les membres en cause ne peuvent participer à pareille décision.

Personal interest.

67. The members of the Régie shall not participate in the discussion of matters in which they have a personal interest.

Discretion of Régie.

The Régie shall decide whether they have any personal interest in the matter; the members in question shall have no part in such decision.

Quorum.

68. Le quorum de la Régie est constitué de trois membres, dont le président ou l'un des vice-présidents.

Voix prépondérante.

La voix du président est prépondérante.

Quorum.

68. Three members of the Régie, including the president or one of the vice-presidents, are a quorum.

Casting vote.

The president has a casting vote.

Séances simultanées.

69. La Régie peut siéger simultanément en plusieurs divisions composées chacune d'au moins trois membres, lesquels sont désignés par le président.

Voix prépondérante.

La voix du président de toute division est prépondérante.

Simultaneous sittings.

69. The Régie may sit simultaneously in several sections each composed of at least three members designated by the president.

Casting vote.

The president of each section has a casting vote.

Siège.

70. La Régie a son siège dans la Ville de Québec ou dans celle de Montréal selon que le décide le lieutenant-gouverneur en conseil par un arrêté qui entre en vigueur sur publication dans la *Gazette officielle du Québec*.

Bureau.

La Régie a aussi un bureau dans l'une des villes susvisées dans laquelle elle n'a pas son siège.

Head office.

70. The head office of the Régie is in the City of Québec or in the City of Montreal, as the Lieutenant-Governor in Council may decide by an order which shall come into force on publication in the *Québec Official Gazette*.

Other office.

The Régie shall also have an office in that city of the two mentioned above in which it does not have its head office.

Lieu des séances.

71. La Régie peut tenir ses séances à tout endroit du Québec.

Fréquence.

Elle doit se réunir au moins une fois par mois.

Place of sittings.

71. The Régie may hold sittings anywhere in the province of Québec.

Time.

It must meet at least once each month.

Authenticité des procès-verbaux, etc.

72. Sont authentiques les procès-verbaux des séances approuvés par la Régie et certifiés par le président ou le secrétaire. Il en est de même des documents ou des copies émanant de la Régie ou faisant partie de ses archives, lorsqu'ils sont signés par le président de la Régie ou le directeur général.

Minutes, etc., authentic.

72. The minutes of sittings approved by the Régie and certified by the president or the secretary are authentic. The same applies to documents or copies emanating from the Régie or forming part of its records, if they are signed by the president of the Régie or the director general.

Directeur général.

73. L'administration courante de la Régie relève d'un directeur général, qui est nommé par celle-ci.

Director general.

73. The Régie shall appoint a director general, who shall have the day to day administration thereof.

Exercice de fonctions. Le directeur général exerce ses fonctions conformément aux règlements adoptés par la Régie.

Nomination du directeur général, etc. **74.** Le directeur général et les autres membres du personnel de la Régie sont nommés et rémunérés suivant la Loi de la fonction publique (1965, 1re session, chapitre 14).

Pouvoirs d'un sous-chef. Le président de la Régie exerce à cet égard les pouvoirs que ladite loi attribue aux sous-chefs de ministère.

Immunité. **75.** Les membres de la Régie et de son personnel ne peuvent être poursuivis en justice en raison d'actes officiels accomplis par eux de bonne foi dans l'exercice de leurs fonctions.

Recours prohibés. **76.** Aucun des recours extraordinaires prévus aux articles 834 à 850 du Code de procédure civile ne peut être exercé ni aucune injonction accordée contre la Régie ou les membres de la Régie, lorsque ceux-ci agissent en leur qualité officielle.

Annulation de bref, etc. **77.** Deux juges de la Cour d'appel peuvent, sur requête, annuler sommairement tout bref et toute ordonnance ou injonction allant à l'encontre de l'article 76.

CHAPITRE III

ENQUÊTES

Commissaires-enquêteurs. **78.** Un commissaire-enquêteur en chef et des commissaires-enquêteurs sont nommés à la Régie. Ces personnes ainsi que le personnel qui les seconde sont nommés et rémunérés suivant la Loi de la fonction publique.

Fonctions. Outre les attributions qui lui sont conférées ci-dessous, le commissaire-enquêteur en chef dirige, coordonne et répartit, sous l'autorité de la Régie, le travail des commissaires-enquêteurs.

Dispositions applicables. **79.** Les articles 75 et 76 s'appliquent au commissaire-enquêteur en chef, aux commissaires-enquêteurs et à leur personnel.

The director general shall exercise his functions in conformity with the by-laws adopted by the Régie. Exercise of functions.

74. The director general and the other staff members of the Régie shall be appointed and remunerated in accordance with the Civil Service Act (1965, 1st session, chapter 14). Appointment of director general, etc.

The president of the Régie shall exercise in this regard the powers granted by the said act to the deputy-heads of departments. President's powers.

75. The members and the staff of the Régie shall not be prosecuted for official acts performed in good faith in the exercise of their functions. Immunity.

76. No extraordinary recourse provided in articles 834 to 850 of the Code of Civil Procedure shall be exercised nor shall any injunction be granted against the Régie or the members of the Régie when they act in their official capacity. Recourses denied.

77. Two judges of the Court of Appeal may, upon motion, summarily annul any writ, order or injunction inconsistent with section 76. Annulment of writ, etc.

CHAPTER III

INQUIRIES

78. A chief investigation-commissioner and investigation commissioners shall be appointed to the Régie. These persons and their support staff shall be appointed and remunerated in accordance with the Civil Service Act. Investigation commissioners.

In addition to his attributions under the sections following, the chief investigation-commissioner shall, under the authority of the Régie, direct, coordinate and assign the work of the investigation commissioners. Powers.

79. Sections 75 and 76 apply to the chief investigation-commissioner, to the investigation commissioners and to their staff. Provisions to apply.

Enquêtes. **80.** Les commissaires-enquêteurs procèdent à des enquêtes chaque fois qu'ils ont raison de croire que la présente loi n'a pas été observée ou qu'une entreprise ne se conforme pas aux exigences d'un programme visé aux articles 29 et 39.

Idem. Doivent également, à la demande du ministre, faire l'objet d'enquêtes de la part des enquêteurs, les demandes de certificat faisant l'objet de l'article 59.

Demande d'enquête. **81.** Toute personne ou tout groupe de personnes peut demander une enquête.

Motifs de refus d'enquêter. **82.** Les commissaires-enquêteurs doivent refuser d'enquêter dans les cas où:

a) ils n'ont pas la compétence voulue aux termes de la présente loi;

b) les requérants disposent d'un appel ou d'un recours suffisant;

c) les requérants auraient pu présenter leur demande plus d'un an auparavant;

d) la question en est une qui relève du Protecteur du citoyen.

Dossier au Protecteur du citoyen. Dans le cas prévu au paragraphe *d*, les commissaires-enquêteurs font parvenir le dossier au Protecteur du citoyen.

Motifs de refus d'enquêter. **83.** Les commissaires-enquêteurs peuvent refuser d'enquêter lorsqu'ils estiment que:

a) les requérants n'ont pas un intérêt personnel suffisant;

b) la demande est frivole, vexatoire ou de mauvaise foi;

c) les circonstances ne le justifient pas.

Avis aux requérants. **84.** En cas de refus, les commissaires-enquêteurs doivent en informer les requérants, leur en donner les motifs et leur indiquer les éventuels droits de recours dont ils disposent.

Contenu des demandes. **85.** Les demandes d'enquêtes doivent être faites par écrit et être accompagnées de renseignements établissant les motifs des requérants ainsi que leur identité.

Assistance des commissaires. **86.** Les requérants ont droit à l'assistance des commissaires-enquêteurs et de leur personnel pour la rédaction de leurs demandes.

80. The investigation commissioners shall make an inquiry whenever they have reason to believe that this act has not been observed or that a business firm fails to comply with the requirements of a program contemplated in sections 29 and 39. Inquiries.

Applications for certificates provided for in section 59 must also be inquired into by the commissioners, at the request of the Minister. Idem.

81. Any person or group of persons may petition for an inquiry. Petition for inquiry.

82. The investigation commissioners must refuse to make an inquiry: Refusing inquiry.

(*a*) if they do not have the required competence under the terms of this act;

(*b*) if the petitioners have a right of appeal or other sufficient recourse;

(*c*) if the petitioners could have brought their petition more than one year previously;

(*d*) if the question is a matter within the jurisdiction of the Public Protector.

In the case contemplated in subparagraph *d*, the investigation-commissioners shall forward the record to the Public Protector. Record to Public Protector.

83. The investigation commissioners may refuse to make an inquiry if, in their opinion, Refusing inquiry.

(*a*) the petitioners do not have a sufficient personal interest;

(*b*) the petition is frivolous, vexatious or in bad faith;

(*c*) the circumstances do not justify it.

84. If they refuse the petition, the investigation commissioners must notify the petitioners, give them the reasons for their refusal, and advise them of their other recourses, if any. Notice in case of refusal.

85. Petitions for inquiry must be in writing and be accompanied with indications of the grounds on which they are based and identification of the petitioners. Petitions in writing.

86. The petitioners are entitled to the assistance of the investigation commissioners and their staff to draw up their petitions. Assistance.

Pouvoirs de commissaires.

87. Pour leurs enquêtes, les commissaires-enquêteurs et les membres de leur personnel qu'ils désignent sont investis des pouvoirs et de l'immunité accordés aux commissaires nommés en vertu de la Loi des commissions d'enquête (Statuts refondus, 1964, chapitre 11).

Dispositions applicables.

88. Les articles 307, 308 et 309 du Code de procédure civile s'appliquent aux témoins entendus par les commissaires-enquêteurs.

Invitation aux parties de se faire entendre.

89. Lorsque les commissaires-enquêteurs chargés d'une enquête estiment qu'il y a manquement à un programme visé aux articles 29 et 39 ou que la présente loi n'a pas été observée, ils doivent, en terminant leur enquête, inviter les parties en cause à se faire entendre devant la Régie.

Audition par la Régie.

90. La Régie entend les parties en cause. Elle peut se faire communiquer tous les documents et renseignements qu'elle estime indispensables pour l'instruction de l'affaire et entendre toutes les personnes intéressées.

Dispositions applicables.

Les articles 87 et 88 s'appliquent à la Régie et à ses membres ainsi qu'aux témoins qu'ils entendent.

Avis au chef du ministère.

91. Si la Régie conclut que la présente loi n'a pas été observée, elle en avise le chef du ministère ou de l'organisme intéressé.

Recommandations.

Elle peut joindre à l'avis qu'elle donne ainsi les recommandations qu'elle juge utiles et requérir d'être informée des mesures d'une part envisagées et d'autre part prises pour leur mise en application.

Avis aux intéressés.

Lorsque la Régie est d'avis que justice a été rendue, elle doit également en aviser les personnes intéressées.

Avis au lt-gouv. en conseil, etc.

92. La Régie peut, si elle juge qu'il n'est pas donné suite à ses recommandations assez rapidement, en aviser le lieutenant-gouverneur en conseil ou, si elle le juge à propos, soumettre un rapport spécial au ministre, qui le dépose sans délai à l'Assemblée nationale; elle peut

Powers of investigation.

87. For the purposes of their inquiries, the investigation commissioners and any members of their staff they may designate are vested with the powers and immunity granted commissioners appointed under the Public Inquiry Commission Act (Revised Statutes, 1964, chapter 11).

Provisions to apply.

88. Articles 307, 308 and 309 of the Code of Civil Procedure apply to witnesses heard by the investigation commissioners.

Inviting parties to be heard.

89. When the investigation commissioners entrusted with an inquiry consider that a program contemplated in sections 29 and 39 is not being properly applied or that this act has not been observed, they must, at the conclusion of their inquiry, invite the parties concerned to appear before the Régie.

Hearing parties.

90. The Régie shall hear the parties concerned. It may have all the documents and information it considers essential to the hearing communicated to it and hear all the interested persons.

Provisions to apply.

Sections 87 and 88 apply to the Régie and its members and to the witnesses appearing before it.

Notice to head of department.

91. If the Régie concludes that this act has not been observed, it shall give notice of that fact to the head of the interested department or agency.

Recommendations.

It may add to the notice so given the recommendations it considers expedient and it may require that it be kept informed of the measures envisaged, on the one hand, and, on the other hand, of those adopted, to implement such recommendations.

Notice.

When, in the opinion of the Régie, justice has been done, it must also notify the interested persons of that fact.

Notice when recommendations not followed.

92. If the Régie considers that its recommendations have not been followed with sufficient haste, it may notify the Lieutenant-Governor in Council, or, if it sees fit, submit a special report to the Minister, who shall immediately lay it before the National Assembly; it may also,

aussi choisir d'exposer la situation dans son rapport annuel.

if it so chooses, set forth the situation in its annual report.

Modifications au cas d'injustice, etc.

93. Si la Régie est d'avis qu'une personne a subi une injustice en raison de la teneur d'une loi ou d'un règlement, elle peut suggérer des modifications au lieutenant-gouverneur en conseil et, si elle le juge à propos, soumettre un rapport spécial au ministre, qui le dépose sans délai à l'Assemblée nationale; elle peut aussi choisir d'exposer la situation dans son rapport annuel.

Amendments suggested and special report.

93. If, in the opinion of the Régie, a person has suffered an injustice by the effect of any act or regulation, it may suggest amendments to the Lieutenant-Governor in Council and, if it sees fit, submit a special report to the Minister, who shall immediately lay it before the National Assembly; it may also, if it so chooses, set forth the situation in its annual report.

Compétence du Protecteur du citoyen.

94. Le Protecteur du citoyen peut être saisi directement d'une question découlant de la présente loi et relevant de sa compétence.

Public Protector.

94. The Public Protector may be seized directly with any matter arising under this act within his jurisdiction.

Information aux requérants.

95. Les commissaires-enquêteurs doivent, après avoir fait enquête sans que la Régie soit par la suite saisie de l'affaire, informer les requérants du résultat de l'enquête dans un délai raisonnable.

Results of inquiry.

95. The investigation commissioners, after making an inquiry which does not entail referral of the matter to the Régie, must inform the petitioners of the results of the inquiry within a reasonable period of time.

Rapport annuel.

96. La Régie doit, au plus tard le 31 mars de chaque année, remettre au ministre un rapport de ses activités de l'année civile précédente, sur l'état de la langue française au Québec et sur les enquêtes effectuées.

Dépôt.

Le ministre dépose ce rapport devant l'Assemblée nationale s'il le reçoit en cours de session; sinon dans les trente jours de l'ouverture de la session suivante.

Annual report.

96. Not later than 31 March each year, the Régie must submit to the Minister a report of its activities of the preceding calendar year, on the state of the French language in the province of Québec and on the inquiries made.

Deposit.

The Minister shall lay such report before the National Assembly if he receives it during a session, or, if between sessions, within thirty days of the opening of the next session.

Infraction et peine.

97. Tout membre de la Régie ou de son personnel qui se rend coupable d'indiscrétion sur des questions reliées à l'exercice de ses fonctions, commet une infraction et est passible de poursuites sommaires pouvant entraîner, outre toutes autres peines éventuellement encourues, une amende de $100 à $1,000 et le paiement des frais.

Offence and penalty.

97. Every member of the Régie or its staff who is guilty of an indiscretion regarding any question in connection with the exercise of his functions commits an offence and is liable to summary prosecution which may entail, in addition to any other penalties possibly incurred, a fine of $100 to $1,000 and payment of the costs.

Exemption de témoigner, etc.

98. Nonobstant toute autre loi, ni les membres de la Régie ni son personnel ne peuvent être contraints de témoigner ou déposer des documents, relativement aux questions reliées à l'exercice de leurs fonctions.

No compulsion to testify, etc.

98. Notwithstanding any other provision of law, neither the members of the Régie nor its staff shall be compelled to testify or to file documents in relation to any question in connection with the exercise of their functions.

Immunité découlant de publication de rapports.

99. Aucune action civile ne peut être intentée en raison ou en conséquence de la publication de tout ou partie des rapports faits par la Régie en vertu de la présente loi, ou de la publication, de bonne foi, de résumés desdits rapports.

Immunity from action.

99. No civil action may be instituted by reason or in consequence of the publication of the whole or part of the reports made by the Régie in virtue of this act, or of the publication in good faith of summaries of such reports.

TITRE V

DISPOSITIONS FINALES

Préavis des projets de règlement.

100. Les projets de règlement ayant trait à la présente loi ne peuvent être adoptés que moyennant préavis de quatre-vingt-dix jours publié dans la *Gazette officielle du Québec* et en reproduisant le texte.

Entrée en vigueur.

Les règlements susdits entrent en vigueur le jour de la publication dans la *Gazette officielle du Québec* soit d'un avis signalant qu'ils ont reçu l'approbation du lieutenant-gouverneur en conseil, soit, en cas de modification par ce dernier, de leur texte définitif.

Application de la loi.

101. Le ministre désigné par le lieutenant-gouverneur en conseil est chargé de l'application de la présente loi.

Rapport à l'Assemblée.

102. Dans les quinze jours de l'ouverture de chaque session, le ministre soumet à l'Assemblée nationale un rapport détaillé sur les activités de son ministère dans le domaine de la diffusion de la langue française au cours de l'année financière précédente.

C.c., aa. 1682*c*, 1682*d*, ab.

103. Les articles 1682*c* et 1682*d* du Code civil, édictés par l'article 1 du chapitre 40 des lois de 1910, sont abrogés.

S.R., c. 57, a. 3, mod.

104. L'article 3 de la Loi du ministère des affaires culturelles (Statuts refondus, 1964, chapitre 57), modifié par l'article 17 du chapitre 26 des lois de 1969, est de nouveau modifié en retranchant le paragraphe *a*.

Id., a. 13, ab.

105. L'article 13 de ladite loi est abrogé.

Id., a. 14, ab.

106. L'article 14 de ladite loi, remplacé par l'article 4 du chapitre 9 des lois de 1969, est abrogé.

TITLE V

FINAL PROVISIONS

Prior notice of draft regulations.

100. Draft regulations related to this act shall be adopted only on prior notice of ninety days published in the *Québec Official Gazette* together with the text of the draft.

Coming into force.

The regulations mentioned above shall come into force on the day of publication in the *Québec Official Gazette* of a notice of their approval by the Lieutenant-Governor in Council or, if amended by him, approval of the final text.

Minister to apply act.

101. The Minister designated by the Lieutenant-Governor in Council is entrusted with the application of this act.

Report of activities.

102. Within fifteen days of the opening of each session, the Minister shall submit a detailed report to the National Assembly of the activities of his department devoted to dissemination of the French language during the preceding fiscal year.

C.C., aa. 1682*c*, 1682*d*, repealed.

103. Articles 1682*c* and 1682*d* of the Civil Code, enacted by section 1 of chapter 40 of the statutes of 1910, are repealed.

R.S., c. 57, s. 3, am.

104. Section 3 of the Cultural Affairs Department Act (Revised Statutes, 1964, chapter 57), amended by section 17 of chapter 26 of the statutes of 1969, is amended by striking out paragraph *a*.

Id., s. 13, repealed.

105. Section 13 of the said act is repealed.

Id., s. 14, repealed.

106. Section 14 of the said act, replaced by section 4 of chapter 9 of the statutes of 1969, is repealed.

S.R., c. 57, a. 14*a*, ab.

107. L'article 14*a* de ladite loi, édicté par l'article 4 du chapitre 9 des lois de 1969, est abrogé.

Id., a. 15, ab.

108. L'article 15 de ladite loi est abrogé.

S.R., c. 235, a. 203, mod.

109. L'article 203 de la Loi de l'instruction publique (Statuts refondus, 1964, chapitre 235), modifié par l'article 1 du chapitre 62 des lois de 1966/1967, l'article 2 du chapitre 67 et l'article 2 du chapitre 9 des lois de 1969 et l'article 43 du chapitre 67 des lois de 1971, est de nouveau modifié en remplaçant les paragraphes 3° et 4° par les suivants:

Cours d'étude;

« 3° De prendre les mesures nécessaires pour que les cours du niveau de la première année à celui de la onzième inclusivement, adoptés ou reconnus pour les écoles publiques catholiques ou protestantes, selon le cas, soient dispensés à tous les enfants domiciliés dans le territoire soumis à leur juridiction s'il sont jugés aptes à suivre ces cours et désireux de s'y inscrire. À cette fin, les commissaires ou les syndics d'écoles doivent prendre l'une ou plusieurs des mesures suivantes, à savoir, organiser ces cours dans leurs écoles ou se prévaloir des dispositions des articles 469 à 495 ou de l'article 496;

Idem.

« 4° De s'assurer que les cours d'études dispensés dans leurs écoles sont conformes aux programmes d'études et aux règlements édictés ou approuvés pour les écoles publiques catholiques, protestantes ou autres, selon le cas; ».

S.R., c. 233, a. 2, mod.

110. L'article 2 de la Loi du ministère de l'éducation (Statuts refondus, 1964, chapitre 233), modifié par l'article 1 du chapitre 9 des lois de 1969, est de nouveau modifié en retranchant le deuxième alinéa.

1968, c. 68, a. 3, mod.

111. L'article 3 de la Loi du ministère de l'immigration (1968, chapitre 68), modifié par l'artcle 3 du chapitre 9 des lois de 1969, est de nouveau modifié en retranchant le paragraphe *e*.

1969, c. 9, ab.

112. La Loi pour promouvoir la langue française au Québec (1969, chapitre 9) est abrogée.

107. Section 14*a* of the said act, enacted by section 4 of chapter 9 of the statutes of 1969, is repealed.

R.S., c. 57, s. 14*a*, repealed.

108. Section 15 of the said act is repealed.

Id., s. 15, repealed.

109. Section 203 of the Education Act (Revised Statutes, 1964, chapter 235), amended by section 1 of chapter 62 of the statutes of 1966/1967, section 2 of chapter 67 and section 2 of chapter 9 of the statutes of 1969 and section 43 of chapter 67 of the statutes of 1971, is again amended by replacing paragraphs 3 and 4 by the following:

R.S., c. 235, s. 203, am.

"(3) To take the measures necessary to have the courses from the first year level to the eleventh year level inclusively, adopted or recognized for Catholic or Protestant public schools, as the case may be, given to all the children domiciled in the territory under their jurisdiction if they are deemed capable of following such courses and desirous of enrolling for them. For that purpose, the school commissioners or trustees must adopt one or more of the following measures, namely, provide such courses in their schools or avail themselves of the provisions of sections 469 to 495 or of section 496;

Courses of study;

"(4) To ensure that the courses of study given in their schools comply with the curricula and regulations prescribed or approved for Catholic, Protestant or other public schools, as the case may be;".

Idem.

110. Section 2 of the Education Department Act (Revised Statutes, 1964, chapter 233), amended by section 1 of chapter 9 of the statutes of 1969, is again amended by striking out the second paragraph.

R.S., c. 233, s. 2, am.

111. Section 3 of the Immigration Department Act (1968, chapter 68), amended by section 3 of chapter 9 of the statutes of 1969, is again amended by striking out subparagraph *e*.

1968, c. 68, s. 3, am.

112. The Act to promote the French language in Québec (1969, chapter 9) is repealed.

1969, c. 9, repealed.

1973, c. 43, aa. 45-48, 197, ab. et a. 41, mod.

113. Les articles 45 à 48 et 197 du Code des professions (1973, chapitre 43) sont abrogés et l'article 41 dudit Code est modifié en remplaçant, dans la première ligne, le chiffre « 47 » par ce qui suit: « 22 de la Loi sur la langue officielle ».

Personnel de l'Office de la langue française.

114. Les membres du personnel du ministère de l'éducation affectés à l'Office de la langue française demeurent en fonction au ministère de l'éducation jusqu'à ce que le lieutenant-gouverneur en conseil décide de les muter.

Interprétation.

115. Dans les lois ou proclamations ainsi que dans les arrêtés en conseil, contrats ou documents:

a) les renvois aux dispositions abrogées par la présente loi sont réputés renvoyer à la présente loi;

b) l'expression « Office de la langue française » s'entend de la Régie de la langue française.

Paiement des dépenses.

116. Les sommes mises à la disposition du ministère de l'éducation au poste de l'Office de la langue française sont affectées au paiement des dépenses engagées pour l'application de la présente loi; les dépenses supplémentaires engagées pour l'application de la présente loi sont payées, pour les exercices financiers 1974/1975 et 1975/1976, à même le fonds consolidé du revenu.

Date d'application.

117. Les articles 6 à 9, le premier alinéa de l'article 10 et l'article 13 s'appliquent à compter du 1er janvier 1976 dans le cas des organismes municipaux et à compter du 1er juillet 1976 dans le cas des organismes scolaires.

Idem.

118. L'article 19 s'aplique à compter du 1er janvier 1976.

Idem.

119. L'article 21 s'applique à la délivrance d'un permis à un citoyen canadien à compter du 1er juillet 1976.

Idem.

120. Les articles 33, 35 et 36 s'appliquent à compter du 31 juillet 1974.

Idem.

121. Les articles 40 à 44 s'appliquent à compter du 1er septembre 1974, mais les règlements prévus à ces articles peuvent

113. Sections 46 to 48 and 197 of the Professional Code (1973, chapter 43) are repealed and section 41 of the said Code is amended by replacing the figure "47" in the first line by the following: "22 of the Official Language Act".

1973, c. 43, ss. 46-48, 197, repealed and s. 41, am.

114. The staff members of the Department of Education assigned to the French Language Bureau shall continue to be employed at the Department of Education until the Lieutenant-Governor in Council decides to transfer them.

Staff members of French Language Bureau.

115. In any act, proclamation, order in council, contract or document:

Interpretation.

(*a*) references to provisions repealed by this act are presumed to refer to this act;

(*b*) the expression "French Language Bureau" is to be construed as *Régie de la langue française.*

116. The sums made available to the Department of Education under the entry of the French Language Bureau shall be affected to the payment of the expenditures incurred toward the application of this act; the supplementary expenditures incurred toward the application of this act shall be paid for the 1974/1975 and 1975/1976 fiscal years out of the consolidated revenue fund.

Payment of expenses.

117. Sections 6 to 9, the first paragraph of section 10 and section 13 apply from 1 January 1976 in the case of municipal bodies and from 1 July 1976 in the case of school bodies.

Date of application.

118. Section 19 applies from 1 January 1976.

Idem.

119. Section 21 applies to the issue of a permit to a Canadian citizen from 1 July 1976.

Idem.

120. Sections 33, 35 and 36 apply from 31 July 1974.

Idem.

121. Sections 40 to 44 apply from 1 September 1974 but the regulations provided for in such sections may be adopted

Idem.

être adoptés et publiés avant cette date, pour prendre effet à cette date.

Dispositions non applicables. Les articles 40 à 44 ne s'appliquent pas à l'égard des inscriptions faites pour l'année scolaire 1974/1975.

Entrée en vigueur. **122.** Les articles 26 à 29, 34, 39, 78 à 99 et 111 entreront en vigueur à la date qui sera fixée par proclamation du lieutenant-gouverneur en conseil.

Entrée en vigueur. **123.** Sous réserve de l'article 122, la présente loi entre en vigueur le jour de sa sanction.

ANNEXE

A. *Administration publique*

1. Le gouvernement et ses ministères;

2. Les organismes gouvernementaux:

Les organismes dont le lieutenant-gouverneur en conseil ou un ministre nomme la majorité des membres, dont la loi ordonne que les fonctionnaires ou employés soient nommés ou rémunérés suivant la Loi de la fonction publique, ou dont les ressources proviennent, pour la moitié ou plus, du fonds consolidé du revenu;

3. Les organismes municipaux et scolaires:

a) les communautés urbaines:

La Communauté urbaine de Québec, la Communauté urbaine de Montréal et la Communauté régionale de l'Outaouais, la Commission de transport de la Communauté urbaine de Québec, le Bureau d'assainissement des eaux du Québec métropolitain, la Commission de transport de la Communauté urbaine de Montréal, la Commission de transport de la Communauté régionale de l'Outaouais, la Société d'aménagement de l'Outaouais, la Commission de transport de la Ville de Laval et la Commission de transport de la Rive Sud de Montréal;

b) les municipalités:

Les corporations de cité, de ville, de village, de campagne ou de comté, qu'elles soient constituées en corporation en vertu d'une loi générale ou d'une loi spéciale, ainsi que les autres organismes relevant de l'autorité de ces corporations et participant à l'administration de leur territoire;

and published before that date, to become effective on that date.

Sections 40 to 44 do not apply in respect of registrations for the school year 1974/1975. Provisions not to apply.

122. Sections 26 to 29, 34, 39, 78 to 99 and 111 shall come into force on the date to be fixed by proclamation of the Lieutenant-Governor in Council. Coming into force.

123. Subject to section 122, this act shall come into force on the day of its sanction. Coming into force.

SCHEDULE

A. *Public administration*

1. The government and the government departments;

2. The government agencies:

Agencies to which the Lieutenant-Governor in Council or a minister appoints the majority of the members, to which, by law, the officers or employees are appointed or remunerated in accordance with the Civil Service Act, or at least half of whose resources are derived from the Consolidated Revenue Fund;

3. The municipal and school bodies:

(*a*) the urban communities:

The Québec Urban Community, the Montreal Urban Community and the Outaouais Regional Community, the Québec Urban Community Transit Commission, the Greater Québec Water Purification Board, the Montreal Urban Community Transit Commission, the Outaouais Regional Community Transit Commission, the Outaouais Development Corporation, the City of Laval Transit Commission and the Montreal South Shore Transit Commission;

(*b*) the municipalities:

The city, town, village, country and county corporations, whether incorporated under a general law or a special act, and the agencies under the jurisdiction of such corporations which participate in the administration of their territory;

c) les organismes scolaires:

Les commissions scolaires régionales, les commissions scolaires et les corporations de syndics régies par la Loi de l'instruction publique (Statuts refondus, 1964, chapitre 235), le Conseil scolaire de l'Île de Montréal, les collèges d'enseignement général et professionnel et les universités;

B. *Entreprises d'utilité publique*

Les établissements au sens de la Loi sur les services de santé et les services sociaux, les entreprises de téléphone, de télégraphe, de transport par avion, bateau, autobus ou chemin de fer, les entreprises de production, transport, distribution ou vente de gaz, d'eau ou d'électricité, ainsi que les entreprises titulaires d'une autorisation de la Commission des transports;

C. *Corporations professionnelles*

Les corporations professionnelles dont la liste apparaît à l'annexe I du Code des professions (1973, chapitre 43) sous la désignation de: « corporations professionnelles », ou qui sont constituées conformément audit Code.

(*c*) the school bodies:

The regional school boards, the school boards and the corporations of school trustees governed by the Education Act (Revised Statutes, 1964, chapter 235), the School Council of the island of Montreal, the general and vocational colleges and the universities;

B. *Public utilities*

Establishments within the meaning of the Act respecting health services and social services, the telephone and telegraph companies, the air, ship, autobus and rail transport companies, the companies which produce, transport, distribute or sell gas, water or electricity, and those enterprises which hold authorization from the Transport Commission;

C. *Professional corporations*

The professional corporations listed in Schedule I to the Professional Code (1973, chapter 43) under the designation "professional corporations", or established in accordance with that Code.

LOIS ET RÈGLEMENTS
PARTIE 2
LAWS AND
REGULATIONS

107e ANNÉE
5 AVRIL 1975
No 12

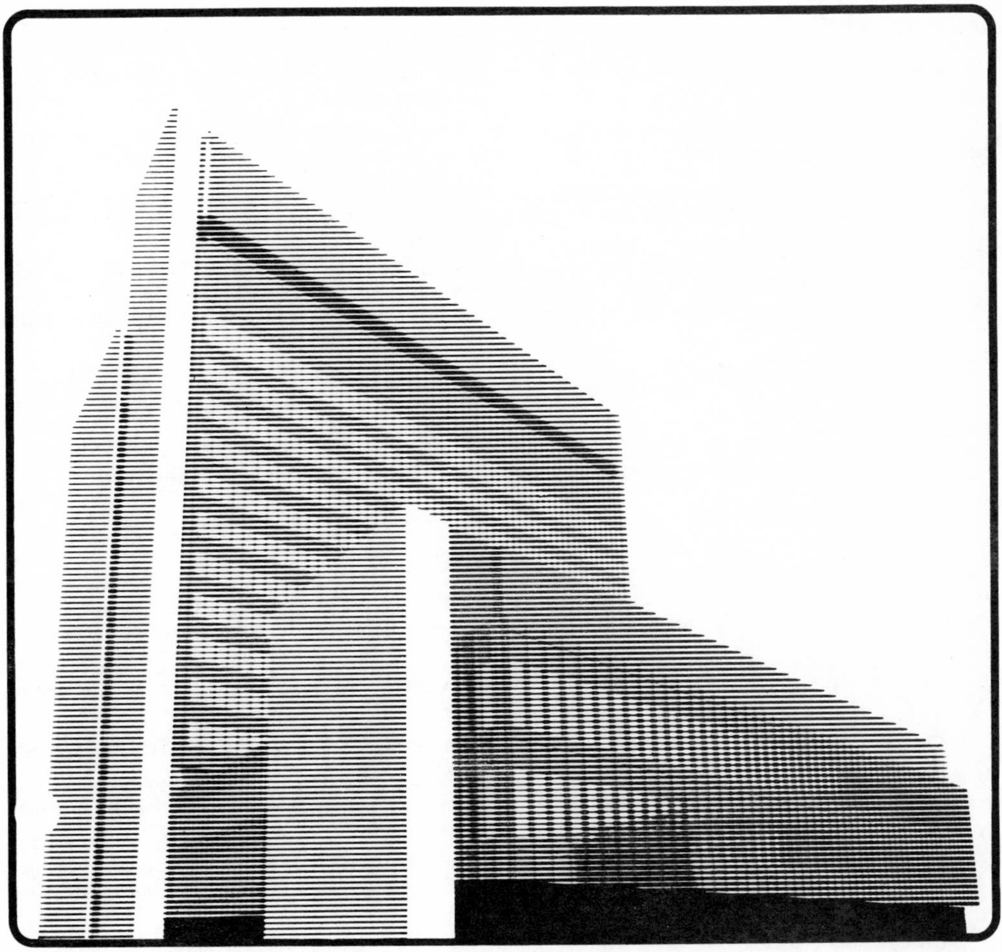

LOIS ET RÈGLEMENTS

Texte réglementaire

A.C. 1347-75 du 2 avril 1975
Règ. 75-129 du 2 avril 1975

LOI SUR LA LANGUE OFFICIELLE
(L.Q., 1974, ch. 6)

Connaissance de la langue d'enseignement

Présent: Le lieutenant-gouverneur en conseil.

CONCERNANT le règlement relatif à la connaissance de la langue d'enseignement.

IL EST ORDONNÉ sur la proposition du ministre de l'éducation:

QUE le règlement concernant la connaissance de la langue d'enseignement, annexé au présent arrêté en conseil, soit approuvé;

QUE cet arrêté en conseil, ainsi que le règlement qui y est annexé, soient publiés dans la *Gazette officielle du Québec* conformément au deuxième paragraphe de l'article 100 de la Loi sur la langue officielle (L.Q., 1974, ch. 6).

Le greffier du conseil exécutif,
JULIEN CHOUINARD.

Règlement relatif à la connaissance de la langue d'enseignement

DÉFINITIONS

1. Dans ce règlement:

a) les mots «Commission de surveillance» désignent la Commission de surveillance de la langue d'enseignement;

b) le mot «ministre» désigne le ministre de l'Éducation;

c) le mot «loi» désigne la Loi sur la langue officielle;

d) le mot «tests» réfère aux instruments de mesure préparés et administrés sous l'autorité du ministre;

e) les mots «commission scolaire» désignent une commission scolaire, une commission scolaire régionale ou une corporation de syndics régies en totalité ou en partie par la Loi de l'instruction publique;

f) le mot «parents» désigne le père, la mère ou une personne qui en tient lieu;

LAWS AND REGULATIONS

Statutory instrument

O.C. 1347-75, 2 April 1975
Reg. 75-129, 2 April 1975

OFFICIAL LANGUAGE ACT
(1974, ch. 6)

Knowledge of the language of instruction

Present: The Lieutenant-Governor in Council.

CONCERNING the Regulation respecting knowledge of the language of instruction.

IT IS ORDERED upon the recommendation of the Minister of Education:

THAT the Regulation respecting knowledge of the language of instruction, annexed to this Order in Council, be approved;

THAT this Order in Council, as well as the Regulation annexed hereto, be published in the *Québec Official Gazette* in accordance with the second paragraph of section 100 of the Official Language Act (1974, ch. 6).

JULIEN CHOUINARD,
Clerk of the Executive Council.

Regulation respecting knowledge of the language of instruction

DEFINITIONS

1. In this Regulation:

(a) the words "Supervisory Committee" mean the Supervisory Committee on the language of instruction;

(b) the word "Minister" means the Minister of Education;

(c) the word "Act" means the Official Language Act;

(d) the word "tests" refers to evaluation criteria prepared and administered under the authority of the Minister;

(e) the words "school board" mean a school board, a regional school board or a corporation of trustees governed in whole or in part by the Education Act;

(f) the word "parents" means the father, mother or a person acting in lieu thereof;

g) le mot «élève» désigne tout enfant de la classe maternelle et tout élève des niveaux élémentaire et secondaire à l'exception de celui qui a dépassé de plus d'un an l'âge de la fréquentation scolaire obligatoire et qui n'a pas fréquenté l'école depuis au moins un an;

h) les mots «fiche d'inscription» désignent la fiche d'inscription prévue par le règlement relatif à l'inscription obligatoire des élèves.

COMMISSION DE SURVEILLANCE

2. La Commission de surveillance assiste le ministre dans l'accomplissement des tâches qui lui sont confiées en vertu des articles 40 et 43 de la Loi.

3. La Commission de surveillance peut également donner un avis au ministre sur toute question relative à l'application des articles 40 à 44 de la Loi.

4. La Commission de surveillance est composée de six (6) membres de langue française, de deux (2) membres de langue anglaise et d'un (1) membre d'origine ethnique autre qu'anglaise ou française, nommés chaque année par le ministre.

Le ministre nomme le président parmi les membres.

La Commission est maître de sa procédure.

DÉTERMINATION DE LA CONNAISSANCE SUFFISANTE DE LA LANGUE D'ENSEIGNEMENT

5. Chaque commission scolaire prend les moyens pour s'assurer que les élèves ont une connaissance suffisante de la langue d'enseignement pour recevoir l'enseignement dans cette langue.

6. Chaque commission scolaire peut, pour les fins de l'application de l'article 5, recourir aux tests préparés et administrés sous l'autorité du ministre.

Le ministre met alors à la disposition des commissions scolaires les services techniques nécessaires à l'application des tests, à la correction des feuilles de réponses et à la production des résultats.

7. Chaque commission scolaire peut exiger qu'un élève subisse les tests, si elle a des raisons de croire que sa connaissance de la langue d'enseignement n'est pas suffisante.

Le ministre peut également exiger que tout élève subisse les tests.

8. Eu égard aux niveaux d'enseignement, à l'âge ou au niveau de formation des candidats, ces tests mesurent l'une

(g) the word "pupil" means every child in kindergarten and every pupil of the elementary or secondary level, with the exception of pupils who are one year older than the prescribed age for compulsory school attendance and who have not attended school for at least one year;

(h) the words "enrolement card" means the enrolment card referred to in the Regulation respecting the compulsory enrolment of pupils.

SUPERVISORY COMMITTEE

2. The Supervisory Committee assists the Minister in the performance of the tasks entrusted to him under sections 40 and 43 of the Act.

3. The Supervisory Committe may also advise the minister on any matter relating to the application of sections 40 to 44 of the Act.

4. The Supervisory Committee is composed of six (6) French-speaking members, two (2) English-speaking members and one (1) member of an ethnic origin other than English or French, appointed each year by the Minister.

The Minister shall appoint the Chairman from among the members.

The Committee has full authority over its procedure.

DETERMINATION OF SUFFICIENT KNOWLEDGE OF THE LANGUAGE OF INSTRUCTION

5. Each school board shall take measures to ensure that pupils have a sufficient knowledge of the language of instruction to receive their instruction in that language.

6. Each school board may, for the purposes of application of section 5, have recourse to the tests prepared and administered under the authority of the Minister.

The Minister shall thereupon provide the school boards with the necessary technical services for the administering of tests, the correction of answer sheets and the furnishing of the results.

7. Each school board may require that a pupil take the tests if it has reason to believe that he does not have a sufficient knowledge of the language of instruction.

The Minister may also require that any pupil take the tests.

8. Taking into consideration the educational levels, age or previous education ot the examinees, the tests shall de-

ou plusieurs des aptitudes suivantes: la compréhension et l'usage de la langue écrite, la compréhension et la discrimination auditives, et l'expression verbale.

9. Un élève subit les tests correspondant à l'année d'études qu'il entreprendrait normalement.

INTÉGRATION

10. Il appartient à chaque commission scolaire de déterminer la classe, le groupe ou le cours auquel un élève peut être intégré, eu égard à ses aptitudes dans la langue d'enseignement.

11. Un élève doit connaître suffisamment la langue d'enseignement pour recevoir l'enseignement dans cette langue.

12. Un élève qui ne connaît suffisamment que l'anglais peut cependant recevoir un enseignement spécial, si la commission scolaire dispense un tel enseignement, en vue de le rendre apte à recevoir l'enseignement en langue française.

13. Un élève qui ne connaît suffisamment aucune des langues d'enseignement reçoit l'enseignement en langue française. Le ministre prend les mesures nécessaires pour que les commissions scolaires dispensent un enseignement spécial à ces élèves en vue de les rendre aptes à recevoir l'enseignement en langue française.

14. Un élève qui connaît suffisamment le français et l'anglais reçoit l'enseignement en langue française ou, sous réserve de l'article 40 de la Loi, en langue anglaise.

15. Chaque commission scolaire doit dans le plus bref délai communiquer par écrit aux parents sa décision au sujet de l'intégration des élèves sauf lorsque la fiche d'inscription d'un élève indique qu'il demande à recevoir l'enseignement dans sa langue maternelle ou dans la langue habituellement parlée à la maison.

16. Le ministre peut exiger qu'une commission scolaire révise l'intégration des élèves à qui il a imposé des tests en vertu de l'article 7.

APPEL

17. Les parents insatisfaits de l'intégration faite par la commission scolaire peuvent, au plus tard trente (30) jours après la communication de la décision de la commission scolaire, en appeler au ministre de cette décision. Avant de disposer de l'appel, le ministre prend l'avis de la Commission de surveillance.

termine one or several of the following aptitudes: written language—understanding and ability to use; aural comprehension and perception; oral expression.

9. A pupil shall take the tests corresponding to the year of studies in which he would normally enrol.

ASSIGMENT

10. It is the function of the school board to determine to what class, group or course a pupil may be assigned, taking his aptitudes in the language of instruction into consideration.

11. A pupil must have a sufficient knowledge of the language of instruction to receive his instruction in that language.

12. A pupil who has a sufficient knowledge of English only may however receive special instruction, if the school board provides such instruction, in order to enable him to receive his instruction in French.

13. A pupil who does not have a sufficient knowledge of either of the languages of instruction shall receive his instruction in French. The Minister shall take the necessary measures to ensure that the school boards provide special instruction to such pupils in order to enable them to receive their instruction in French.

14. A pupil who has a sufficient knowledge of both French and English shall receive his instruction in French, or, subject to section 40 of the Act, in English.

15. Each school board must make its decision know to the parents in writing without delay respecting the assignment of pupils except where the enrolment card of a pupil indicates that he wishes to receive his instruction in his mother tongue or in the language normally spoken at home.

16. The Minister may require that a school board revise the assignment of pupils to whom he administers tests pursuant to section 7.

APPEAL

17. Parents who are not satisfied with the assignment made by the school board may, not latter than thirty (30) days after the school board's decision is made known, appeal to the Minister from such decision. Before deciding the appeal, the Minister shall obtain the advice of the Supervisory Committee.

18. Le ministre donne droit au requérant, ou maintient la décision de la commission scolaire, ou exige l'intégration selon une modalité autre que celles qui ont donné lieu à l'appel.

19. Chaque commission scolaire doit fournir au ministre, à sa demande, les renseignements requis pour l'application du présent règlement.

687-o

18. The Minister shall render a decision in favour of the applicant, or abide by the decision of the school board, or require an assignment in conformity with a situation other than that which gave rise to the appeal.

19. Every school board must provide the Minister, upon his request, with the information required for the application of this Regulation.

687-o

Achevé d'imprimer par les travailleurs
des ateliers Marquis Ltée de Montmagny
en avril 1977